DINERS,

Bowling Alleys

and

TRAILER PARKS

Also by Andrew Hurley

Environmental Inequalities: Class, Race, and Industrial Pollution in Gary, Indiana, 1945–1980

Common Fields: An Environmental History of St. Louis

DINERS,
Bowling Alleys
and
Trailer Parks

*Chasing the American Dream
in the Postwar Consumer Culture*

Andrew Hurley

BASIC BOOKS A Member of the Perseus Books Group

Published by Basic Books,
A Member of the Perseus Books Group

"Portions of Chapter 1 initially appeared in Andrew Hurley, "From Hash House to Family Restaurant: The Transformation of the Diner and Post–World War II Consumer Culture," *The Journal of American History* 83 (March 1997), 1282–1308.

Designed by Elizabeth Lahey
Text Set in 10.5 point Weiss

FIRST EDITION

Library of Congress Cataloging-in-Publication Data
Hurley, Andrew, 1961–
Diners, bowling alleys and trailer parks : chasing the American dream
    in the postwar consumer culture / Andrew Hurley.
        p.   cm
    Includes index.
    ISBN 0-465-03186-2 (alk. paper)
        1. Consumption (Economics)—United States—History—20th century.
2. Diners—United States—History—20th century.   3. Bowling alleys—United States—
History—20th century.   4. Trailers—United States—History—20th century.
5. Middle class—United States—History—20th century.   6. United States—
Economic conditions—1945–.   I. Title.
HC110.C6 H87 2001
306.3'0973'09045—dc21

00 01 02 03 / 10 9 8 7 6 5 4 3 2 1

*For Patty, without whom
I never would have discovered the
Rosebud Diner*

CONTENTS

ILLUSTRATIONS

Bowling Alleys

Trailer Parks

Conclusion: Giving Chase

Epilogue

Credits

The author gratefully acknowledges the following institutions for permission to publish photographs and illustrations: The Heritage Society of Essex and Middle River, Essex, Maryland: p. 3; The Maryland Historical Society, Baltimore, Maryland: pp. 4, 18; The Daimler-Chrysler Corporation: p. 8; Western Historical Manuscripts Collection, St. Louis: pp. 11, 311, 312; Penton Publishing: pp. 22, 23; American Diner Museum, Providence, Rhode Island: pp. 27, 32, 34, 37, 53; Diner Archives of Richard J. S. Gutman: p. 41; Kullman Industries, Lebanon, New Jersey: pp. 57, 102; General Research Division, The New York Public Library, Astor, Lenox, and Tilden Foundations: p. 62(2); International Bowling Museum and Hall of Fame, St. Louis: pp. 112, 113, 114, 121, 128, 132, 137, 141, 154, 158, 171, 175, 179, 183, 192; RV/MH Heritage Foundation, Elkhardt, Indiana: pp. 198, 199, 207, 217, 220, 226, 232, 234, 235, 249, 265, 269; Dr Pepper/Seven Up: p. 279 (SQUIRT is a registered trademark under license © 2000 Dr Pepper/Seven Up, Inc.); Hammond Suzuki USA: p. 280; Coca-Cola Company, 292; Photo Collection/Los Angeles Public Library: p. 321.

PREFACE

       I have been fascinated with diners since I was a child. Growing up on the outskirts of New York City during the 1960s, in Bayside, Queens, I regularly pleaded with my mother to take me inside the Bell Diner, a request she just as regularly denied. Once a month she took my brother and me out for lunch, and along the way we passed the tiny metallic diner wedged tightly between two other buildings. The diner, with its trolley-like appearance, looked fun and exciting to me. But my mother refused to enter, intimating that it was not an appropriate place for us. This puzzled me. I knew that the male clerks from the shoe store across the street ate lunch there, and they seemed like nice enough people. My pestering notwithstanding, I never found out what went on inside the Bell Diner. But clearly something unsavory must have been going on behind that deceptively enticing stainless-steel façade. Invariably we ended up at Woolworth's lunch counter, where I was consoled with a hot dog and malted milk.

As I grew older, I found ample opportunity to satisfy my curiosity about diners. In my college and graduate school days I ate at more than my share, many of them virtual replicas of the one I remembered from my childhood (which by that time had been covered in brick and converted into a Chinese restaurant.) In more recent years, my curiosity has moved beyond the diners themselves to my mother's negative reaction to them. Her aversion struck me

as particularly ironic when I learned that she had occasionally
eaten at such establishments as a younger woman growing up in a
Jewish, blue-collar district of the Bronx. Yet, in her effort to provide her children with what she thought was a proper middle-class
suburban upbringing, she shunned the diner. It occurred to me that
the history of the diner, its rising popularity in the 1950s and its
decline thereafter, would make an excellent vehicle for exploring
the ways that upwardly mobile Americans reconstructed their lives
through their consumer choices in the two decades following
World War II.

I might have written an entire book about diners, but I feared
their history might be idiosyncratic, that the evolution of postwar
diners might not fully reflect the broader changes taking place in
the consumer economy. Moreover, I knew that although the prefabricated diners in which I was interested could be found in all
parts of the country, they were concentrated in the Northeast. I
wanted to do a national study that had broad rather than merely
local or regional significance. So I searched for other consumer institutions that might shed light on how the adoption of new
spending habits transformed American society in an age of widespread affluence.

Ted Steinberg, a friend and colleague at Case Western University, suggested that I take a look at bowling alleys. I was very familiar
with bowling alleys, having attended many a bowling party in my
youth with friends and classmates. Like the diner industry, the bowling industry tried to shed its working-class reputation after World
War II and deliver a product that was more in tune with middle-class
sensibilities. Indeed, bowling proprietors were more successful in
this regard than diner owners, as evidenced by my mother's lack of
concern about my visits to the local bowling center.

Trailer parks were a complete mystery to me. I did not know
anybody who lived in one. I had never been inside of a trailer park,
save for the time in graduate school I accidentally stumbled
through one on my way back from a rock concert in search of my

parked car. Yet trailer parks seemed a promising avenue of inquiry for a number of reasons. They proliferated in areas of the country where diners were scarce, like the Sun Belt. They would also give me the opportunity to write about housing, undoubtedly the most important consumer expenditure for postwar Americans. Most important, trailer parks were definitely not middle class. I knew that not all families from working-class backgrounds were as successful as mine in climbing the rungs of the social ladder. My father, the son of a skilled carpenter, was fortunate enough to establish a white-collar career. The people who lived in trailer parks, most of whom remained in blue-collar jobs, rarely had the means to construct lives that met the prevailing standards of success. Trailer parks might enable me to delineate the lower boundary of an expanding middle-class consumer culture.

For people coming of age today, diners, bowling alleys, and trailer parks have taken on very different meanings than the one they had in the 1950s. After a period of decline in the 1970s and 1980s, these institutions have recently muscled their way back to the front lines of consumer culture by becoming cool. Vintage Spartan and Airstream trailers are bought up by movie stars so they can show off their eclectic sense of style on remote movie sets. On the Embarcadero in San Francisco, young businessmen and women dine on crab cakes with sherry-cayenne mayonnaise at the Fog City Diner, a restaurant with the look and feel, but not the menu, of an authentic 1950s diner. When the clock strikes midnight, teen hipsters from Torrance, California, to Yonkers, New York, head for the bowling alley where glow-in-the-dark pins, laser lights, pounding music, and hanging disco balls provide the right ambience for late-night carousing, dancing, and maybe even a little bit of bowling. Cosmic bowling, as the phenomenon is often called, has become all the rage.

The recent comeback of house trailers, diners, and bowling alleys is largely based on the careful manipulation of nostalgic imagery. At Ed Debevic's, a chain of faux diners based in Chicago, the required costume for waitresses includes bobby sox, sneakers, and hair ribbons. A Harley Davidson motorcycle mounted behind the counter infuses a refurbished diner in Ohio with the spirit of James Dean. The marketing of nostalgia is taken to extremes in Bisbee, Arizona, where Ed Smith and Rita Personett recently converted an older trailer court into a 1950s-theme motel. At the Shady Dell Trailer Court, visitors can spend the night in one of eight vintage trailers and immerse themselves in the sights and sounds of the Sputnik era. The trailers come equipped with chenille bedspreads, Melmac dishware, aluminum coffee pots, and plastic radios. Visitors who spend the night in these echoes of a halcyon past can while away the evening hours reading Mickey Spillane novels or listening to Billie Holiday cassette tapes. When they awake in the morning, hungry for breakfast and more nostalgia, they need only stumble a few feet to Dot's, an authentic 1950s diner that Smith and Personett imported to the premises to complete the time-travel fantasy.

Nostalgia may be marketable, but it is a poor substitute for history. One of the aims of this book is to dispel the popular myth of the 1950s as a period of perpetual happy days, a time when consumer abundance underwrote social harmony and familial bliss. Certainly, the widespread availability of consumer conveniences and amenities made life easier and more comfortable for those who had known only grueling poverty in the past. Yet by focusing exclusively on the frivolity associated with cultural icons like Elvis, hula hoops, and 3-D movies, we run the risk of extracting the 1950s from the flow of history. The 1950s was not simply a fun but sterile interlude between the trauma of World War II and the turbulence of the 1960s. Rather, as I hope to show in this book, postwar abundance inspired Americans to rearticulate their aspirations and frustrations in the language of consumption, a language that ultimately gave shape to the protest movements of the 1960s.

The image of the 1950s that has since been commodified by savvy entrepreneurs, and simultaneously held up by politicians, as a golden age of happy families preceding the social breakdown of the 1960s, is a severe distortion of the historical record. Those who would employ the 1950s as a cultural benchmark against which to measure the subsequent decline of American civilization should do so with caution. An honest look at the era of consumer abundance brings us face to face with the roots of many of today's most debilitating social problems. Rising levels of personal debt, rampant hedonism, spiraling consumer ambitions, and the fracturing of familial bonds can be traced, at least in part, to the contradictory messages broadcast by manufacturers, retailers, and advertisers in their effort to expand the mass market for goods and services in the 1950s.

This book is by no means meant as a jeremiad against consumer capitalism. I have tried to approach my subject matter with a sense of balance, both respecting the excitement and promise that attended people's engagement in the world of consumer commodities and acknowledging some of the steep social costs associated with the stalking of consumer desires. Chasing the American Dream in diners, bowling alleys, and trailer parks widened the horizons of millions of middle-income families but it always remained a precarious endeavor with unseen risks.

▲ ▼ ▲

The most common reaction I get from people when they learn about the project that has absorbed my attention for the past six years is "Oh, that sounds like fun!" They are right, it has been fun. Criss-crossing the country in search of information about diners, bowling alleys, and trailer parks has been quite an adventure. Along the way, I have had the pleasure of eating dozens of hearty diner meals, knocking down more than a few bowling pins, visiting dozens of trailer parks, and in the process, meeting some wonderful people, all of whom deserve a great deal of thanks for their assistance.

To compensate for the paucity of written records dealing with my subject matter, I sought out more than one hundred individuals who had firsthand knowledge about what it was like to eat in diners, live in trailer parks, and knock down pins in bowling alleys. I am grateful to all the men and women who were kind enough to share their memories with me. I can only hope that this book does justice to their recollections and stories. I also owe a debt of gratitude to the archivists, librarians, and local historians who helped me navigate through the written records that were available. Several deserve special mention: Carl Ehry and Al Hesslebart at the Recreational Vehicle/Mobile Home Hall of Fame in Elkhart, Indiana; John Dalzell and Travis Boley at the International Bowling Museum and Hall of Fame in St. Louis, Missouri; and Daniel Zilka at the American Diner Museum in Providence, Rhode Island. Brian Butko, Marc Wagner, and Joe Manzo helped me track down material on the history of diners, while Richard Gutman granted me access to his private archival collection. Paul Blitz, Jean Flanagan, and Jackie Nickel helped me locate materials about Eastern Avenue in Baltimore. Over the years of conducting research on this project, many colleagues have provided me with valuable leads and materials. Larry Glickman brought the "Orangeburg Massacre" to my attention. Michael Ebner generously photocopied his collection of press clippings on trailer parks for my use. Chuck Korr provided me with invaluable assistance in mapping the location of Philadelphia diners.

Writing can be a lonely enterprise, but good friends and colleagues have made the process more bearable. Their criticism and advice have also made the book much better than it otherwise would have been. Jim Fisher, David Roediger, Monica McCormick, and Patricia Cleary critiqued the entire manuscript. Lizabeth Cohen, David Thelen, Roland Marchand, and Melissa Saucedo gave me valuable feedback on particular chapters. Leslie

Brown, Eric Sandweiss, Mark Tebeau, Gary Cross, and Jennifer Price provided a sounding board for my ideas and kindly offered some of their own. Good coffee also helps, and I am much indebted to Hugo and Michelle, owners of the Grind Coffeehouse in St. Louis, for keeping my blood supply saturated with caffeine. Money comes in handy as well. Financial support from the University of Missouri Research Board was instrumental to the timely completion of this undertaking.

It has been a pleasure to work with the staff at Basic Books, particularly Don Fehr and John Kemmerer. Don has shown confidence in the project from the start; John's careful editing of the manuscript improved the clarity of the prose immeasurably.

Finally, I must express my gratitude to all those friends who have indulged my research passions over the years by joining me on miscellaneous detours to visit various roadside establishments. No one has been more gracious and supportive in this regard than my dear friend and colleague Patricia Cleary. Not only has she read and critiqued more drafts of this manuscript than anyone else, but she has been a dedicated companion in my search for vintage bowling alleys, hidden trailer parks, and out-of-the-way diners. It is to her that I dedicate this book.

INTRODUCTION

Remaking the American Dream

THE AMERICAN DREAM was remade on Baltimore's Eastern Avenue. In the years following World War II, this busy thoroughfare became a glittering spectacle of consumer enticements. As they drove through the working-class suburbs just beyond the Baltimore city limit, motorists gazed at billboards, blinking neon signs, and storefront displays that beckoned to them with promises of fulfilling that dream. The enthusiastic shoppers included men and women who had migrated from Appalachia during World War II to work in nearby defense plants and GIs who had returned from overseas after the war to start new families away

1

from the oppressive congestion and constricting ethnic traditions of the inner city. The war was over, America had triumphed, and these men and women expected to be rewarded for services rendered, whether their contribution came on the battlefield or the home front. Holding union jobs and earning steady wages, they celebrated by going on a consumer binge.

Satisfying New Consumer Desires

First and foremost on the consumers' wish list was a private home. For generations, home ownership had stood as a symbol of achieving middle-class status in the United States. Due to the ready availability of federally insured mortgages, that benchmark of social success was now within the reach of many blue-collar workers. For most people who settled in the recently developed suburbs just outside Baltimore, a new home meant a modest single-family dwelling surrounded by a small front lawn and backyard. To satisfy the explosion in demand for new shelter following the war, developers laid out sprawling subdivisions of brick bungalows and small frame houses.

Not all families, however, were able to acquire the standard suburban package. Immediately after the war, developers simply could not build homes fast enough to meet the brisk demand. Moreover, many younger couples were still not in a strong enough financial position to afford a new home, despite the available government incentives. For these people, the house trailer emerged as a popular alternative to the fixed single-family dwelling. If the trailer did not quite fit the prevailing domestic ideal of the aspiring middle-class consumer, it was nonetheless seen as an improvement over an inner-city apartment or a house shared with intrusive parents or in-laws. Along Eastern Avenue, no fewer than five trailer courts invited tenants to park their mobile homes atop concrete pads, each of these courts attempting to re-create the feel of a suburban neighborhood.

Eastern Avenue, Essex, Md., circa 1939, just before the postwar boom

As people who inhabited conventional homes and trailers filled these burgeoning suburban blue-collar communities, a wide variety of commercial establishments opened for business along Eastern Avenue to serve their needs. There were no high-fashion clothing boutiques or esoteric bookshops to be found among them. Nor were there any fancy restaurants or exclusive country clubs. Instead, consumer passions were gratified in humbler establishments like bowling alleys and diners. For a modest sum, bowling alleys, equipped with the latest mechanical pinsetting devices, gave families an opportunity to spend a fun afternoon or evening together. Mothers who sought relief from their household chores could join their husbands for a "home-cooked meal" in the clean and convivial Essex Diner. These trailer parks, bowling alleys, and diners may not have been glamorous, but they provided customers with confirmation of their rising social status. Indeed, over the course of the 1950s, the owners of these businesses worked diligently to upgrade their establishments, both to improve their reputations and to keep in line with the expectations of their upwardly mobile customers.

Unidentified trailer park, 1962, one of several that did business along Eastern Avenue in Essex, Md., and Eastern Boulevard in Middle River, Md., during the postwar years

In an age of unparalleled prosperity, a prosperity that reached far beyond Eastern Avenue to hundreds of similar communities on the fringes of urban America, people of modest means struggled to attain the good life. That they would have defined the good life in terms of such mundane pleasures and modest accommodations might have struck previous generations of Americans as odd. In the quest for a better life, they reached not for the top but for the solid, stable middle. In their effort to secure a place in the American mainstream, they charted new frontiers, not in the wilderness but in the former wilderness: the sprawling suburban subdivisions and flashy commercial strips that displaced farms and fields all across America. Rather than seeking honor solely through productive work like their Puritan forebears, they pursued comfort and happiness, even a kind of luxury, through the consumption of goods and services. In places like Eastern Avenue, the American Dream was made over, given a good shine, and put up for sale.

If the two decades after World War II bring to mind tail-finned cars, suburban ranch houses, and families gathered around living room television sets, it is because this image of consumer abundance contains a fair measure of accuracy. In just the four years following the end of the war, Americans purchased 21.4 million cars, 20 million refrigerators, 5.5 million stoves, and 11.6 million television sets. During the late 1940s and 1950s, annual expenditures on jewelry, toys, and kitchen appliances were twice what they had been in the immediate prewar era. By the late 1950s, Americans were spending close to $300 billion a year on consumer purchases. The significance of these figures can be better appreciated when we consider that, before World War II, most households lacked refrigerators, automatic washing machines, and electric vacuum cleaners. Television had only just been invented and was not yet available for home use. Despite the dramatic drop in car prices made possible by Henry Ford's assembly line, only about half of all urban families owned automobiles at the outbreak of World War II. By 1960, however, ownership of at least one car had become the norm, and, in the case of television sets and refrigerators, their diffusion across the consuming public was nearly universal. Of all changes in consumer behavior, the most dramatic lay in the area of housing. Before World War II, most Americans rented rather than owned their homes. By 1956, three out of five city dwellers were homeowners.

Shiny stainless-steel diners, clean, mechanized bowling alleys, and boxlike trailer coaches arranged in neat, orderly rows were products of a new culture of abundance that crystallized in the late 1940s and 1950s. These three quintessentially American institutions, each possessing a long, colorful prewar history, underwent profound transformations in the postwar years as working-class families sought to insert themselves in the mainstream of American life. They were physical manifestations of the world that Americans created as they wrestled with the social implications of widespread prosperity, not only blue-collar workers earning white-collar incomes but women and children acquiring greater purchasing power, the sons and daughters of immigrants trading their ethnic identities for consumer identities, and racial minorities seeking opportunity and justice in the nation's rapidly growing metropolises. They were places where ordinary women and men redefined what it meant to be successful in America, and indeed what it meant to be American in an age of consumer abundance. They were places where people redrew social boundaries, places where proprietors and customers determined who would have access to the American Dream and who would not. The story of these three institutions is the story of the expansion of a mass consumer market and by extension, the remaking of American society.

Moving on Up: From the Good War to the Good Life

Prior to World War II, most Americans would have found it unthinkable to express their aspirations through the purchase of consumer commodities for the simple reason that they lacked sufficient income. Living from hand to mouth and from day to day, the working-class families who formed the bulk of the urban population devoted their energies and efforts to procuring the basic necessities of food, clothing, and shelter. In an industrial economy where unskilled work paid poorly and employment was erratic, survival required that families organize themselves as units of production, with the tasks of wage earning, cooking, canning, cleaning, sewing, and parenting divided among all able-bodied members. For men, women, and children alike, daily life revolved around work. This is not to deny that even the poorest of families enjoyed the occasional day at the ballpark, evening at the vaudeville show, or excursion to a nearby seaside resort. Recreational activities of these sorts were cheap and required little more than the cost of carfare and the price of admission. Small pleasures and cheap diversions, however, could hardly operate as lasting symbols of their consumers' social aspirations. And whereas urban wage-earners certainly entered into commercial transactions to procure items of food and clothing, their participation in the consumer economy remained limited by a narrow range of choices: the inexpensive goods sold at the five-and-dime as opposed to the fashionable wares displayed at downtown department stores, the loose foodstuffs at the neighborhood grocer rather than the prepackaged brand-name products found at the uptown market.

World War II changed all of that by giving workers something they had rarely known in the past, discretionary income. The booming defense industry generated an insatiable demand for labor, and unions used their muscle to secure generous contracts for their members. As unemployment vanished, wages soared. After enduring grueling poverty during the Depression, American workers rejoiced in their unprecedented gains. Some laborers watched their incomes double within a matter of months; overall, average weekly earnings in manufacturing rose 65 percent.

Increased spending power did not translate into increased consumption, at least not immediately. Although manufacturers and retailers drooled at the potential profits from all the farm girls who had never worn a Daisy Mae girdle, immigrant homemakers ignorant of the distinction between Lux liquid detergent and Palmolive, and factory workers who had yet to experience the wonders of Lifebuoy soap, commodity shortages, rationing, and the diversion of wages into war bonds prevented workers from fully gratifying their consumer desires. So corporations stoked consumer appetites with carefully crafted advertising campaigns that pointed Americans toward a postwar consumer cornucopia.

Indeed, the manufacturers of consumer goods persuaded Americans to brave the country's painful and costly involvement in the war by holding out the promise of the material possessions that would await them when peace arrived. As the fighting drew to a close, advertisers bombarded the public with idyllic domestic scenes of postwar abundance in which the latest model cars graced suburban driveways, brand-name appliances filled kitchens, and stylish outfits hung in bedroom wardrobes. Corporations sweetened the bait by insisting that the technological innovations that

Nash-Kelvinator advertisement, 1944

produced better planes, tanks, and bombs in wartime would enhance life in peacetime by enabling them to produce better cars, radios, homes, and appliances.

Wartime advertisements promised much more than just comfort and convenience, however. They also promised social mobility. Consider the advertisement that the Nash-Kelvinator corporation ran in mass-circulation magazines in 1944. In it, a soldier is stranded somewhere at sea in an inflatable lifeboat. Undergirding his will to survive is a vision of the future he articulates in terms of a steady job, a faithful wife, and "a chance to move *up*." What exactly did "moving up" mean? The answer appeared at the bottom of the page where the company displayed the automobiles, refrigerators, and cooking ranges it planned to manufacture as soon it could convert its factories to civilian production.

Advertisements like these tapped the hopeful spirit that engulfed the nation as Allied troops advanced toward Berlin and Tokyo in 1945. The war was a unifying experience, and it helped Americans clarify a vision of the world they hoped to inherit in peacetime. The celebration of social diversity in official wartime propaganda and the popular media assured previously marginalized groups, particularly immigrants and their children, that they were as American as anyone else. Through the visual cliché of the multiethnic and multiclass combat unit—the Italian street kid from Brooklyn fighting valiantly alongside the farm boy from Iowa and the rich WASP from New England—wartime posters and films promoted ethnic and class diversity as a source of strength. In contrast to its totalitarian enemies, America would not let internal social divisions stand in the way of victory. A pluralistic ideology, thus, invited Americans from diverse backgrounds to join a society that many had been excluded from in the past. Having sacrificed and struggled for nearly four years, they yearned, not just for security, but for a better life than the one they had known before the war. Like the soldier in the lifeboat, they expected to be going someplace. Wartime advertisers provided a roadmap.

If Americans emerged from the war with a clear sense of what they wanted from the postwar world, they were less confident of their ability to get it. A vague sense of apprehension wafted across the nation as political leaders and ordinary citizens alike pondered an unknown future. Memories of the recent depression and the violent clashes of the 1930s hung like a dark cloud over the nation's psyche—unemployed veterans tear-gassed by federal troops just miles from the White House; labor organizers brutally beaten by

Ford Motor Company security guards at the Battle of the Overpass in Dearborn, Michigan; three dead and 115 hospitalized on the San Francisco waterfront where longshoremen clashed with police; ten striking steelworkers shot to death at the Memorial Day Massacre in Chicago. The question on everyone's mind was whether the American economy could perform at the same high level in peacetime as it did in wartime, whether it could provide jobs for the six million veterans streaming home, whether it could satisfy the demand for goods and services that had accrued over the previous fifteen years of depression, austerity, and sacrifice. At the very least, economists predicted a bumpy road ahead as aircraft plants, tank factories, and shipyards closed down and laid off workers. These home-front laborers would then compete with millions of returning servicemen for available jobs. Could a domestic war soon replace the world war about to be won?

The very stability of American society hung in the balance. The detonation of two atomic bombs over Japan in August 1945, settled the question of how to save the world from the specter of totalitarianism only to open a new set of concerns about how to preserve democracy and social tranquility at home. The initial outlook was grim. Only two weeks after V-J Day, 200,000 workers were out on strike against their employers. Los Angeles, Harlem, and Detroit were still reeling from violent race riots that had erupted several years earlier. Marriage rates were up but so were divorce rates. Veterans returned to a world turned topsy-turvy, a world where women had worked on assembly lines, millions of families had moved from farms to cities, and juvenile delinquency had emerged as a national problem. Society had been thoroughly transformed in nearly four war years, and now it appeared to be coming apart at the seams. Without the patriotic imperative of war to bind people together, any downturn in the economy threatened to throw society into utter chaos.

Americans breathed a huge sigh of collective relief when their worst fears about the nation's economic performance proved unfounded. Unexpectedly high levels of consumer spending provided the necessary impetus for sustained economic growth. In the

Downtown St. Louis, 1950. Downtown shopping districts such as this one thrived immediately after World War II.

immediate wake of victory celebrations, Americans cashed their war bonds, drew money from their savings accounts, and went shopping. Women stood in line for new hosiery, men traded in their old jalopies for the latest-model Chryslers and Fords, and youngsters begged their parents for model railroad sets, dollhouses, and red wagons. Department stores reported a doubling of sales volume over the previous decade. Factories that had only recently produced uniforms, parachutes, and bombs scrambled to fill orders for men's hats, table radios, and eggbeaters. *Fortune* magazine was right on target when it declared in the summer of 1946, "the Great American Boom is on." With only sporadic interruptions, Detroit's auto plants, Chicago's steel mills, Milwaukee's breweries, Akron's rubber plants, and Seattle's aircraft factories hummed at full throttle for two decades, keeping workers employed in round-the-clock shifts, sending them home with ever fatter pay envelopes and enabling them to satisfy their consumer aspirations while stoking the fire of the postwar economy.

What was particularly encouraging about the postwar economic boom was the way it distributed its bounty across the population. World War II had the effect of redistributing income downward. Between 1939 and 1945 the share of the nation's income held by the nation's richest 5 percent declined from about 24 percent to 17 percent, while the number of families with incomes under $2,000 fell by half. Simply put, the poor got richer faster than the rich got richer. In and of itself, this was not so remarkable; previous war economies also redistributed income. What set World War II apart from earlier wars was its enduring effect. A postwar economy operating at full employment, the solidification of organized labor's wartime gains, and the steady shift from low-paid unskilled jobs to better paying semi-skilled jobs in the industrial sector worked in concert to prevent workers from slipping back to their prewar status. If the prewar socio-economic hierarchy conformed to the shape of a pyramid, with only a small percentage of the population capturing the vast amount of wealth, the postwar economy approached the configuration of a diamond with a large bulge in the middle-income range. For the first time, many workers, especially those with skills, made as much or nearly as much as many white-collar workers, allowing them to indulge in the consumer conveniences and amenities that had once been the exclusive purview of the wealthy. As much as anything else it was this widespread distribution of prosperity that gave people confidence that social rifts and strains emerging from the war could be healed and the bitter class warfare that characterized the 1930s could be avoided.

Searching for the Middle Majority

The convergence of working-class and middle-class financial capabilities was not lost on retailers and manufacturers. Business executives, admen, and shop owners recognized the bulging cohort of middle-income families as an unprecedented opportunity for enlarging the market for mass-produced goods and services. During the late 1940s and 1950s, all sorts of consumer products and services were developed and redeveloped to capture the purse strings of what contemporary marketing experts termed "the middle majority." According to marketing experts, the 18 million households earning between $4,000 and $7,500 during the early 1950s constituted the most lucrative consumer market in the country; 43 percent of urban families had incomes that fell within this range. The $4,000 floor was justified on the grounds that it marked the point at which a family would likely purchase a new car rather than a used one and a frozen chicken pie rather than a fresh one. Occupationally, this group was diverse. About 40 percent worked in white-collar occupations such as bookkeeping, sales, and clerical work. The remainder was divided among skilled craftsmen, machine operatives, and unskilled laborers and service workers such as miners, truck drivers, and delivery men. If there was a typical breadwinner in this group, it might be a machinist in Detroit or a file clerk in Sheboygan. Thus, the middle majority market was located along the border of working class and middle class.

Locating a commercial business on the borderland of class held forth the potential for big profits, but it was also a precarious endeavor. As the nation emerged from World War II, the "middle majority" was no more than a statistical abstraction in the minds of marketing mavens. In the real world, economic homogeneity masked a volatile mosaic of social agendas and historical experiences. Appealing to the vast middle majority meant appealing to different audiences—not just people of different classes, but different ethnic backgrounds, ages, and genders. Because consumption was a profoundly social act, any attempt to enlarge the mass market had enormous consequences for the way people interacted with one another. For all the advantages that material affluence conferred upon upwardly mobile blue-collar families, in terms of both practical benefits and social positioning, it generated a great deal of anxiety, which could easily translate into outright resistance. If mass consumer culture was a source of liberation and a conduit for upward social mobility for some groups, for others, it constituted a threat to cherished social hierarchies and networks.

The 1955 movie *Marty* documents the struggle of a young Italian American to reconcile the pressures of assimilation with the affection and obligation he feels toward his ethnic roots. The story takes Marty Piletti, the film's protagonist, through a series of dilemmas that test his loyalty to family, peers, and traditions. He adores his mother, but she obstructs his pursuit of a better life. She objects to his new girlfriend who "doesn't look Italian" and is devastated by his suggestion that they relocate from the old neighborhood to "a nicer part of town." On the other hand, the inexorable onslaught of mass consumer culture prevents him from finding success within the framework of traditional community networks. There is a revealing scene where Marty tells his cousin about his dream of buying a butcher shop that specializes in Italian meat. His cousin promptly slaps Marty with a hard dose of reality. "Who buys Italian meat, anyway?" he chides Marty. "You think my wife buys Italian meat? She goes down to the A&P, picks up a lamb chop wrapped in cellophane, opens a can of peas, and that's dinner, boy."

For ethnic working-class families like the Pilettis, participation in the new world of brand-name products and national retail chains could be a dangerous, if not a tragic, proposition. Understandably, those who clung to Old World ways felt as though they were under siege from a mass market that could not possibly accommodate the myriad customs and traditions that sustained communities in the older immigrant neighborhoods. The potential costs were articulated every time grandparents, parents, and children argued over the proper way to prepare foods, celebrate holidays, and decorate home interiors. Husbands feared losing control over their wives as much as parents feared losing control over their children. While homemakers may have appreciated the convenience of canned peas and shrink-wrapped lamb chops, their husbands, like Marty's cousin, were just as likely to interpret modern conveniences as an excuse for women to shirk their marital obligations. Engagement in the mass market raised serious questions about what it meant to be a dutiful husband and wife, a responsible son and daughter.

From the perspective of manufacturers, retailers, and advertisers, selling the good life required more than just offering customers snazzy products and convenient services. It involved coaxing people into new social relationships, or at the very least assuring customers that their new consumer habits would not unduly threaten traditional social hierarchies. Addressing the social implications of mass consumerism required considerable finesse and ingenuity. Behind thousands and thousands of individual commercial transactions loomed the question of how the expansion of consumer culture would reorder American society. If manufacturers and retailers were intent on enlarging a mass market, where would they locate its center? How would they resolve the differences and independent yearnings of the various groups that composed a middle majority? What values would bind them together? How could they push novel forms of behavior and social interaction without tearing the social fabric too brutally and thus engendering a backlash? In the end, which groups would be included and which excluded?

Diners, bowling alleys, and trailer parks were consumer institutions that underwent profound transformations in the postwar years as consumers and producers wrestled with these questions. All three had deep roots in a prewar working-class culture. Diners owed their origin to horse-drawn lunch wagons that roamed the factory districts of New England in the late nineteenth century. Bowling alleys originated as adjuncts to taverns in immigrant neighborhoods. By World War II, urban trailer parks had become synonymous with down-on-their-luck itinerants who roamed from city to city looking for work. Yet as working-class families made the transition to something approaching middle class after the war, the proprietors of these businesses refurbished their establishments to conform to a revised set of consumer expectations. Indeed, they believed that by satisfying the newly acquired needs and tastes of an upwardly mobile working-class clientele they could position themselves in the mainstream of American society and create spaces that would appeal to people from a wide variety of back-grounds.

All three industries took advantage of mass-production tech-nologies in gearing their product to a mass audience. Diners and trailers were prefabricated; bowling was revolutionized by auto-mated pinsetters that standardized operations across the country. Moreover, in each case, standardization was directed toward the goal of domesticating the consumer experience. Diner, bowling al-ley, and trailer park owners alike tried to eliminate their associa-tions with the world of industrial work by reconstructing their op-erations around the aesthetic and social norms of the middle-class household. In this endeavor, they encountered two formidable ob-stacles. First, customers disagreed as to what constituted proper domestic social relations. Second, even where customers found agreement, they often lacked the financial resources to realize pre-vailing domestic norms.

Diners, bowling alleys, and trailer parks may not have been al-together unique in soliciting a broad audience through mass-pro-duction technologies and the projection of domestic ideals, but they played a particularly important role as transitional institutions for working-class Americans being absorbed into a mass consumer market for the first time. They were among the first places where upwardly mobile Americans were introduced to standardized forms of commerce. As such, they were stepping stones to more alien forms of mass consumer culture: suburban ranch homes, fast-food restaurants, shopping malls, and even posh country clubs. The process of cultural integration was anything but smooth. A close inspection of what went on inside diners, bowling alleys, and trailer parks reveals the tensions that attended the making of a middle majority consumer market, tensions that were often aggravated by attempts to circumvent them. Indeed, by the 1960s, as women, young adults, and African Americans exposed the contradictions between American ideals and consumer practices, all three became sites of violent confrontation.

Although diners, bowling alleys, and trailer parks performed a comparable historical function and evolved in response to a similar marketing logic, they experienced widely divergent fates. As a result, each of the subsequent chapters in this book highlights different aspects of the making of a middle majority consumer culture and the remaking of the American Dream.

Diner builders and owners proved especially adept at fusing a variety of ethnic and class traditions in their attempt to develop a national standard for commercial dining. Through a series of negotiations with their patrons, they expanded the parameters of American cuisine and pioneered a more casual style of food service. By reorienting their businesses around the needs and aspirations of suburban families, they found a way to address customers on the basis of something other than class background. At the same time, the industry's erratic performance underscored the limitations of forcing social behavior into a uniform standard. Through the 1950s, class and racial tensions hampered the ability of diner owners to expand their customer base too far beyond their core constituency. By the 1960s, even that constituency was being chiseled away by national chain restaurants that further refined the concept of domesticated commercial dining.

The chapter on bowling alleys clarifies the relationship between automation and domestication. The introduction of the mechanical pinsetter transformed the bowling alley from a place where men, women, and children maintained their identities as workers to one where they were accommodated as members of families. The bowling alley fared better than the diner, in part because it did

Eastern Avenue in Essex, Md., 1962, at the height of the postwar boom

not encounter the same level of competition from rival forms of commercial recreation. Yet the enormous popularity that bowling enjoyed can also be attributed to proprietors who perfected the charade of family togetherness. While industry boosters presented the suburban bowling center as an agent of family cohesion, market expansion was based primarily on independent appeals to men, women, and children. Thus, the chapter on bowling alleys also demonstrates how the domestic ideal, as translated into a marketing strategy, ultimately deflected loyalties away from the family circle.

Of the three institutions examined in this book, the trailer park proved the least conducive to the attainment of middle-class domestic ideals. Proximity to industrial sites, congested living arrangements, and the perception of impermanence all undermined the notion that trailer parks were appropriate places to raise families. Although trailer parks remained viable businesses throughout the postwar years, they became increasingly marginalized places on the periphery of the middle majority mainstream. Thus, the story of the postwar trailer park departs dramatically from the story of the diner and the bowling alley by highlighting the elusive nature of the American Dream for many families living on modest incomes. Trailer parks were among the consumer institutions that set the lower boundaries of the new middle majority market.

Taken together, these three histories enable us to interpret the consumer landscapes that arose on the outskirts of American cities. America's postwar consumer binge permanently altered the arrangement of metropolitan space by heightening the disparity between a production-oriented downtown and a residential periphery organized according to the logic of consumption. The postwar landscape of consumption came in for a considerable amount of condemnation. Critics assailed both the monotony of sprawling cookie-cutter subdivisions and the visual cacophony of the commercial strip with its colorful neon signs beckoning motorists to "Eat Here," "Buy Cheap," "Save 50 Percent," and "Stop Here for Gas." Newly minted suburban housing developments may have been uniform and commercial strips may have been exuberant, but together they said a great deal about how Americans decided to organize their lives and relate to one another. It was a landscape that was comfortable and familiar enough to millions of Americans that the motorist traveling along Eastern Avenue on the outskirts of Baltimore on a snowy night in 1955 would have known what lay in store when he or she turned off the road drawn by the flashing neon sign spelling out the letters "D-I-N-E-R."

DINERS

GEORGE YONKO was having trouble thinking up a name for the prefabricated diner he had just purchased. The son of a Romanian immigrant, Yonko had no previous experience in the restaurant business. During the war years, however, he regularly patronized a small lunch car that stood across the street from the Continental Foundry and Machine factory in East Chicago, Indiana, where he worked. Every evening, when his shift ended at eleven, Yonko and some of his co-workers from the machine tool shop met

Chuck Wagon Diner at its new location, Gary, Ind., 1955

at the diner for a quick hamburger before catching the bus back to their homes. After the war, as Yonko pondered his future, he noticed an abandoned dining car situated along Route 6 in the neighboring town of Gary. Fully aware that this thoroughfare carried hundreds of workers to and from the city's steel mills each day, Yonko purchased the structure and prepared to develop a business that would replicate his old haunt in East Chicago. All he needed was a catchy name.

Driving past the home of a friend who made a hobby of sketching covered wagons, Yonko was struck with an inspiration. He would call his new diner the Chuck Wagon. The term evoked an image of hardy pioneers trekking across the continent in pursuit of a better life. Perhaps a Western motif would resonate with the region's many European immigrants who had made their own journeys across vast distances to make a better life for themselves and their families. Yonko was tickled by the idea that "chuck wagon" was the only truly American designation for an eatery. It was, he thought, a perfect fit for a place that would bring together people from diverse ethnic backgrounds, people who had put their lives on the line for a nation that now promised to reward them with the full benefits of citizenship.

When the Chuck Wagon opened for business in 1945, it fit the stereotype of the working man's diner. With a limited menu that

Interior of Chuck Wagon Diner at new location, 1955

featured only chili, hamburgers, french fries, soup, pie, coffee, and milk shakes, it quickly developed a regular following among shift workers from the steel mills along with some locals. Years later, Yonko recalled that during peak hours, he often had twelve people sitting at the counter, twelve people standing against a ledge by the back wall, and another twelve waiting to get inside. The overwhelming majority of these customers were men.

Over the next several years, Yonko took aggressive steps to expand upon his client base of male factory workers. First, he traded in his tiny prewar lunch car for a larger model and placed it on a plot of land that could accommodate automobile parking. Next, he posted billboards along the major highways within a 75-mile radius of his diner, hoping to entice hungry families traveling through Gary on their way to summer vacation destinations. Yonko expanded his offerings to accommodate women and children, introducing special kiddie menus and adding lighter fare, including salads. Upon discovering that his new patrons tended to shun the counter in favor of the more comfortable booths and tables, Yonko embarked on an extensive remodeling program. Within several years, the ambitious entrepreneur had dismantled the original counter and added several dining room annexes that featured table service. In making these changes, Yonko created a new consumer space that not only reflected the shifting market for commercial dining but that promoted novel forms of consumer behavior and social interaction.

The metamorphosis of the Chuck Wagon exemplified the postwar transformation of the diner from a male, working-class eatery to a middle-income family restaurant. The people who built and owned diners in the years following World War II adapted their trade in response to dramatic changes in American society—changes that influenced the way people spent their money and, more specifically, the way they ate their meals. Widespread prosperity widened the horizons of working-class families and allowed them to imagine a life that was more secure, comfortable, and rewarding than the one they had known before the war. After years of privation and restricted opportunities, they discovered an exciting outlet for their ambitions in the world of consumer goods. Joining the middle class in the stampede to the suburbs, they spent their money on both big-ticket items and small luxuries such as an occasional meal away from home. But these newly affluent families were not content eating at just any greasy spoon. So, simple and scruffy diners had to evolve to suit the new tastes and needs of their expanding and upwardly mobile clientele.

The renovated Chuck Wagon resembled thousands of prefabricated diners that were shipped to roadside locations across the country in the two decades after World War II. To accommodate a constituency that was becoming increasingly suburban, increasingly affluent, and increasingly preoccupied with displaying its status aspirations through consumer expenditures, the diner industry created a new kind of experience. In order to provide a clean and wholesome environment for men, women, and children, operators instructed diner builders to lay out spacious interiors and comfortable seating arrangements. If the prewar diner had functioned as a scrappy adjunct to the factory, the postwar variant would cultivate its identity as a tidy and inviting extension of the happy suburban home, at the same time obscuring its blue-collar roots. The postwar diner promised to transform America's poor, tired, and hungry into its affluent, relaxed, and stuffed.

Blending a wide variety of class and ethnic traditions, the postwar diner established new aesthetic and social norms for commercial dining, and in so doing, it prepared the way for the fast-food empires of the 1970s. In the case of the Chuck Wagon Diner, the link was unusually direct. While attending a restaurant convention in 1952, Yonko met a dapper Southern gentleman by the name of Sanders who was peddling a secret chicken recipe. Yonko liked the product and decided to add it to his menu. The Chuck Wagon Diner thus became the sixth Kentucky Fried Chicken franchise in the United States.

Although diners were eventually eclipsed by the national restaurant chains, for two decades they served as an important vehicle for integrating an upwardly mobile working class with immigrant origins into a more inclusive mass culture. Moreover, in making decisions about where to locate, what foods to serve, and whom to grant access, builders, proprietors, and customers negotiated the boundaries of the middle majority market and determined how inclusive it would be. The postwar diner became a testing ground for the nation's democratic ideals. If for thousands of hardworking Americans in the 1940s and 1950s, a diner meal delivered on the promise of abundance, it also exposed the strains and conflicts that attended the construction of a more pluralistic mass culture.

The Workingman's Lunch Car

The roots of the shiny new postwar diner, like those of the bowl-ing alley and the trailer park, extended deep into the hard-scrabble working-class culture of the late nineteenth century. Diners owed their origins to the horse-drawn lunch wagons that prowled New England's manufacturing districts late at night. The chain of evolution that led from the portable lunch car to the stationary diner originated in Providence, Rhode Island.

In the years just before the Civil War, restaurants in Providence closed at eight in the evening, leaving late-shift workers with no place to purchase a simple meal. Walter Scott was well aware of this inconvenience; he worked in a print shop where presses ran through the early hours of the morning. Scott thought that per-haps he could earn some extra income by filling the stomachs of those hungry late-night workers. Before long, Scott could be found each evening after the end of his day shift, hawking sand-wiches and coffee at each of the city's three major newspaper of-fices. As he hauled his victuals from one print shop to another, Scott was surprised by the number of ordinary pedestrians who stopped him, offering to buy food from his cart. Recognizing an opportunity to serve an even larger group of customers, he pur-chased a horse in 1872, harnessed it to a freight wagon, quit his job, and went into business full time selling chicken, ham sand-wiches, eggs, and pie on the streets of Providence. Scott had in-vented the lunch wagon.

Scott did not maintain a monopoly on the lunch-wagon busi-ness in Providence for long. By the 1880s, there were at least nine horse-drawn lunch carts plying their trade on the streets of the city. Soon the burgeoning lunch-wagon business began to spread beyond Providence and throughout the cities of the Northeast. In 1884, Samuel Jones, a cousin of one of the Providence peddlers took the concept to Worcester, Massachusetts. There, Jones was responsible for a major innovation in lunch wagon design: the first

Iroquois Diner, 1919. An early example of a portable diner manufactured by Jerry O'Mahony.

wagon large enough to accommodate customers who wished to stand inside while they shoveled down their grub. From Worcester, the concept spread to dozens of New England mill towns, and in 1893, the lunch wagon made its first appearance in New York City. Walter Scott's invention had become such a success that two companies were able to devote themselves entirely to manufacturing and selling fleets of enclosed wooden lunch carts.

The next step in the evolution of the diner involved removing the wheels and liberating the horse. After the turn of the century, most lunch wagons were transported to a fixed site and left there, if not for good, then for at least several months or even years. Some communities hastened this trend by enacting local ordinances that restricted the business hours of roaming food vendors on the grounds that they were public nuisances. According to the lunch wagon's detractors, they were eyesores and they clogged busy streets during the daylight hours. In all likelihood, lunch wagons would have become immobile regardless of legislation. Operators were expanding their menus as well as their business; they required more room for elaborate cooking facilities and customer seating, usually in the form of stools. The lightweight movable units were no longer viable and rapidly gave way to larger, sturdier wagons that offered counter service.

The Workingman's Diner

These evolutionary changes in lunch-wagon design did not alter its basic social function. Operators continued to place wagons in locations where industrial laborers predominated. As factories became a ubiquitous feature of America's urban landscape, so too did lunch wagons, or dining cars, as some were called in reference to the Pullman dining cars to which they bore some resemblance. Diner builders and owners were quite cognizant of the visual connection. A diner builder who entered the business in 1913 deliberately set out to manufacture what he called a "Pullman"-type lunch car. A New York City proprietor made the link explicit by christening his establishment the Pullman Diner. In some cases, the resemblance was so close that patrons thought they were eating in a real railroad car. In fact, few railroad cars were ever converted into stationary eating establishments. Discarded trolley cars, however, were often made into diner-type establishments in the 1920s, further confusing the issue.

Whether fashioned from abandoned streetcars or expressly designed for food service, dining cars flourished throughout Prohibition, when their primary source of competition—the neighborhood saloon—had been eliminated. For years, saloons had offered one of the best deals around, the "free lunch." While it wasn't truly free, it was extraordinarily cheap. For the price of a glass of beer, any customer could graze on the victuals laid out on platters at the bar counter. When saloons were forced out of business after the enactment of Prohibition in 1919, the "free lunch" became a historical artifact. Diners were the most inexpensive of the remaining alternatives. They continued to fare well during the Depression and well after the repeal of Prohibition on account of their continued emphasis on low prices; some establishments even began to sell beer to dissuade patrons from returning to their saloon lunches. By the 1940s, the diner had carved out a successful niche and become a familiar sight, not only in factory precincts but also along high-volume highways, where truckers hauled industrial goods from one city to another, and in downtown retail districts that supported a high density of mechanics, craftsmen, and construction workers. According to one estimate, there were nearly 7,000 diners in operation on the eve of World War II.

Just before World War II began, Samuel Kullman, one of the nation's leading diner manufacturers, estimated that 90 percent of all diners were located within 100 miles of New York City. Perhaps this statement was something of an exaggeration. Although the heavily industrialized Northeast did indeed contain most of the nation's diners, major manufacturing centers of the Midwest such as Cleveland, Detroit, and Pittsburgh also boasted their fair share. Cleveland, for instance, contained two dozen diners on the eve of World War II, many of them manufactured in plants that had recently opened nearby. By contrast however, Worcester, Massachusetts, with a much smaller population, had twenty-two, or almost as many as Cleveland.

The immediate postwar years saw no sharp break from earlier trends and patterns. As diner builders resumed operations after a wartime hiatus, they continued to ship most of their stock to New York, Philadelphia, and Boston. Once again, manufacturers guided operators to sites that guaranteed a high volume of either factory workers or long-distance truck drivers. It was not uncommon, for example, for operators to set down their lunch cars across from the entrance to a major manufacturing plant. When Mary Townsend of Akron, Ohio, decided to trade her hamburger stand for a diner in 1948, she picked a spot just immediately adjacent to the Goodyear Tire plant, which employed several thousand workers. As late as 1949, an article in an industry trade journal recommended factory sites as "a good bet for stable business," although it warned operators to steer clear of slaughterhouses, fish markets, paper mills, and other noxious establishments. The ideal site was one that assured what people in the trade referred to as "double action," the regular patronage of both truckers and factory workers. The DiLorenzo brothers knew they had found such a location when they purchased a diner at the crossroads of routes 17 and 46 in northern New Jersey, just a block away from the massive Bendix aircraft plant. The location proved so profitable that within three years they traded their tiny, trolley-like diner for a much larger unit to accommodate the overflow crowds.

In addition to being carefully situated to capture a high-volume flow of trade, the diners purchased by Townsend and the DiLorenzo brothers were specially designed with the needs of factory hands and truckers in mind. About twelve companies manufactured and sold prefabricated diners during the late 1940s. While each company advertised its own distinct model, the diners produced in these years exhibited a remarkable degree of similarity. Even where independent proprietors built their establishments on-site or in some cases, fashioned diners from abandoned trolley cars, style and design usually mimicked the prefabricated variety. Diner architecture sacrificed aesthetics and comfort for durability, frugality, and speed. Because owners counted on rapid turnover from customers anxious to return quickly to the road or factory floor, and because the necessity of keeping menu prices low precluded any sort of operation that entailed high overhead costs, dining cars were small. The standard diner measured forty feet by sixteen feet, and many were even tinier. Invariably, the interior layout featured a long counter accompanied by a row of densely packed stools, although most models also included several booths or tables lined against the front wall or packed tightly on one end. To expedite service, manufacturers placed cooking facilities directly behind the counter, thereby eliminating any need for waiters or waitresses to carry food from cook to customer. As far as building materials were concerned, manufacturers favored stainless steel for both interiors and exteriors because it was sturdy and required little maintenance. Moreover, because the metallic compound did not tarnish easily under the assault of chemical emissions, it was an ideal construction material for buildings that were likely to end up in industrial districts.

To adequately serve the nation's burgeoning industrial labor force, most diners remained true to their origins and stayed open around the clock. Arthur Holst was so confident in the merits of twenty-four-hour service that immediately upon receiving shipment of a stainless steel diner in 1947, he flung the front door key into the Harlem River. While Holst's flair for the dramatic was a bit unusual, his underlying logic was not. Holst knew that inner-city diners did a brisk business long after the sun went down. Whether a diner was located in a New England mill town, a mid-Atlantic seaport, or a midwestern manufacturing city, a typical 2 A.M. counter scene might include an assembly of inebriated souls trying to sober up over coffee and pie, a solitary straggler taking refuge from the winter cold, and perhaps a young couple winding down after an evening of dancing at the local ballroom. Most of the night trade, however, consisted of laborers. Diners counted on third-shift factory hands, bakers, dairy workers, printers, and truckers to supply a reliable flow of customers until the breakfast trade resumed at sunrise.

In catering to the culinary needs of industrial laborers, diners conformed to a consumer market that was divided along class lines. Although the introduction of mass-production technologies in the early twentieth century made consumer products and services available to large numbers of Americans, wide income differ-

The Bendix Diner, built in 1950, continues to occupy the intersection of Routes 17 and 46 in Hasbrouck Heights, N.J.

entials separated the consumer experiences of working-class and middle-class families. In this regard it is useful to remember that the automobile, often touted as the quintessential manifestation of consumer democracy in the early twentieth century, remained beyond the reach of many urban industrial laborers who continued to rely on streetcar systems for their basic transportation needs through World War II. Moreover, those on the upper end of the income hierarchy sought to distance themselves from those of lower social standing by purchasing fancy versions or expensive brands of consumer products.

Into the 1940s, diners distinguished themselves from upscale restaurants catering to a leisure trade. In contrast to their middle-class counterparts, working-class families rarely took meals away from home except for purely utilitarian purposes. For most of the first half of the twentieth century there was little middle ground

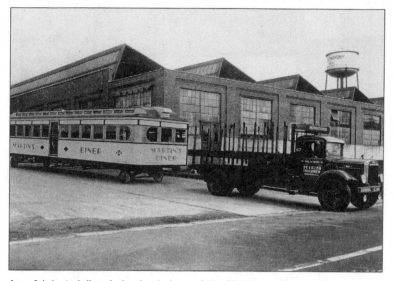

A prefabricated diner being hauled out of the O'Mahony plant in Elizabeth, N.J., circa mid-1930s

between the elegant restaurants and fancy tearooms that catered to a leisure class and the "greasy spoons" that slung hash for the poorer masses. Even the nondescript coffee shops wedged beneath skyscrapers were filled primarily with men in business suits who worked in offices above and fashionably attired women who shopped at nearby stores. On the other end of the dining spectrum were the saloons, hamburger stands such as White Castle and White Tower, and other "hash houses," which sold simple fare at low prices. While utilitarian diners might occasionally attract a slumming motorist or clerk, they were firmly grounded in the "hash house" category and studiously avoided by middle-class customers.

In an era when "middle class" was synonymous with native birth, northern European heritage, Protestant religion, and white-collar work, there was nothing middle class about diners.

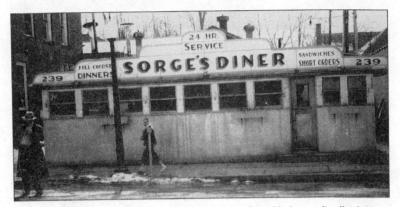

Sorge's Diner in Dunkirk, N.Y., typified the diners found in inner-city districts during the 1940s.

The majority of diner builders, operators, and customers were either immigrants or second-generation Americans. German, Irish, Italian, and Jewish families dominated the manufacturing end of the business; these same groups were well represented among the many thousand independent operators. Patrick Tierney, the son of an Irish immigrant, began building diners in a small garage behind his house in New Rochelle, New York, in 1905. After his death in 1917 (he died a millionaire), his sons took over the outfit. Bragging of its ability to churn out "a diner a day," P. J. Tierney Sons, Inc., was easily the most prolific of the prewar dining car manufacturers as well as a seedbed for other firms. Indeed, many of the company's employees went on to found their own manufacturing firms elsewhere in the region. Among them were two Italian immigrants, Joseph Fodero and Angelo DeRaffele. Fodero, who founded the Fodero Dining Car Company in Bloomfield, New Jersey, in 1933, had been employed by Tierney as a metalworker. DeRaffele was a carpenter at Tierney who went on to establish DeRaffele Diners in New Rochelle, New York, in 1947. Tierney's accountant, Samuel Kullman, was a Russian immigrant and a Jew. In 1927, he formed the Kullman Dining Car Company, which operated out of

Newark, New Jersey. Kullman, Fodero, and DeRaffele were among the leading diner manufacturers in the postwar era.

The Consolidation of the Working Class

The diner industry was by no means a generic product of and for a homogeneous working class. Like the working-class communities that sustained it, the industry still bore the imprint of ethnic fragmentation. When immigrants first arrived in the teeming industrial cities of America, they clustered in neighborhoods populated by their compatriots. Germans, Irish, Poles, Jews, Lithuanians, and Italians might have mingled in the workplace, but when they went home, they organized their lives around separate cultural and economic institutions. They read different newspapers, prayed at different churches, and borrowed money from different lenders. As the flow of immigration slowed in the 1920s and American-born children began to distance themselves from their parents' customs and social networks, ethnic attachments waned. They did not disappear entirely, however. As late as the 1940s, ethnicity proved a meaningful agent of identity for most working-class families. Sensing this, diner builders and operators attempted to manipulate ethnic loyalties to their advantage. Some manufacturers, for instance, tried to undercut their rivals by playing up ethnic animosities. One Irish manufacturer in particular developed a reputation for trying to steer northern European clients away from the Italian companies. The Kullman Dining Car Company, on the other hand, may have emphasized ethnic allegiances to its advantage; a disproportionate share of its business came from Jewish customers. For the most part, however, manufacturers were eager to sell their diners to operators regardless of ethnic background.

Certainly, diner operators attempted to secure the devotion of their foreign-stock customers by offering a generous selection of Old World dishes. Because many customers at the Club Car Diner in McKeesport, Pennsylvania, were eastern European immigrants who worked across the street at the U.S. Steel National Tube Works, owner Fred Jamison filled his menu with pierogies, goulash, stuffed cabbage, and halushki, a dish prepared with fried cabbage, onions, and noodles. The Slovak, Italian, and Hungarian patrons at Tony's Diner in Cleveland could choose from a selection of goulash, Italian sausage, oxtail soup, and several varieties of Slovakian stews. The Iannone brothers, who operated a small diner in Providence, Rhode Island, kept corned beef and cabbage on their menu for their Irish customers as well as a special snail salad for their Italian customers. Abe Kullman, who catered to a predominantly Jewish clientele in Newark, was famous for his potato pancakes, while William Ramundo and Florian Walchak featured Hungarian-style stuffed cabbage at the State Diner in Bloomfield, New Jersey.

While ethnic affiliations bound diner builders, operators, and patrons in webs of loyalty to a certain extent, class remained the fundamental social category around which the diner oriented its appeal. The American working class entered the postwar era more unified than at any previous time. Participation in labor unions, the armed forces, and public school systems provided blue-collar families with a common set of experiences, institutions, and aspirations. Diners contributed to this homogenizing trend. Because diners cultivated a constituency composed from a wide variety of ethnic backgrounds, they were sites of cultural amalgamation (even establishments that drew largely from one particular ethnic group invariably served customers from other backgrounds as well.) Indeed, early postwar diners fostered a distinctively male-oriented, working-class culture. Patronized by regular customers, they were gathering places where men could banter—often in salty language—in a common parlance of sports, politics, and work. George Yonko recalled that while his clientele comprised a mix of Serbian, Croatian, and Polish immigrants, English was the only language spoken inside the Chuck Wagon Diner. And if some diner cooks prepared exotic European fare for particular immigrant groups, they also dished out hefty por-

Interior, Lackawanna Diner, Stroudsburg, Pa. Through the 1940s, all-male scenes such as these were common in urban diners.

tions of standard American items that were popular among a much wider spectrum of working-class men. It was an unusual diner that did not feature beef stew, franks and beans, roast turkey, chipped beef on toast, pie, and coffee.

While informality, coarse language, and heavy food accounted for the diner's popularity among male wage earners, even serving to unify them despite the very real ethnic gulf that separated them, these same qualities repelled those who upheld the standards of middle-class etiquette and respectability. Popular magazines and radio programs often portrayed diners as hovels, gambling dens, and magnets for the criminal element. Many people tended to associate all diners with establishments such as Steffie's Diner, a truck driver's rest stop in Gary, Indiana, which was regularly subjected to vice squad raids and was ultimately shut down by the local health commissioner in 1949. The fact that some older dining cars lacked toilet facilities and some newer ones suffered from indifference on

the part of management regarding hygiene and cleanliness only reinforced the prevailing stereotype that diners were seedy joints
where the poor and shiftless gathered and got up to no good.

This combination of heavy food, rough talk, and questionable
hygiene also kept women away, regardless of their class background.
Although a few daring flappers were known to frequent after-hours
lunch wagons during the 1920s, few women in the subsequent
decades wished to subject themselves, let alone their children, to
what they believed was the characteristic diner experience. When
one puzzled lunch-car aficionado asked several of his female friends
to explain their disdain for diners, he was told that the buildings
looked dingy, the stools were uncomfortable, and the countermen
were rude. Even when proprietors made special efforts to refine their
establishments in order to attract a "better" crowd, the unsavory reputation of diners endured and continued to limit the extent to which
diners could move beyond their male, working-class base.

Revising the American Dream

Among operators, however, diner ownership was seen as a means
of mobility out of the working class and into the middle class. As
early as 1927, the promotional literature published by one diner
manufacturer, P. J. Tierney Sons, asserted that by purchasing a
diner, the man with no business experience and minimal capital
could climb the ladder of success and obtain "a comfortable
home—a good car—education for the children—the good things
of life for his family." Several years later, a brochure issued by the
Kullman Dining Car Company suggested that, for the wage
earner, diner ownership represented an opportunity, "to cast aside
a hum-drum existence" and "become [one's] own boss in a pleasant,
profitable business."

Through the 1950s, manufacturers would hold out this promise
of social mobility to lure individuals of modest means into the

business. Liberal financing enabled people to purchase dining cars with down payments as low as $1,000. With GI loans from the federal government, the returning veteran had little trouble obtaining the necessary start-up capital. In fact, many postwar operators came to the diner business after running mess halls in the army during the war. It was not a terribly dramatic transition from military mass feeding operations to the get-'em-in, turn-'em-out style of service one came to expect in a diner. The lack of prior training, however, was no handicap in the diner business. Inexperienced proprietors could learn the business from scratch by availing themselves of the technical expertise offered by the various manufacturing companies. Not only did manufacturing firms help prospective owners find suitable locations for their diners, but they provided valuable advice about installation, equipment purchases, exterior landscaping, and even accounting procedures. Thus, with a limited amount of start-up capital and a heavy investment of time and effort, diner ownership enabled blue-collar individuals to scrape their way up the social ladder. As one diner manufacturer put it, "the dining car companies sold the American dream."

The version of the American dream to which he referred, however, had already become anachronistic by the late 1940s. The rugged individualism that promised economic advancement in an era of small farms and small businesses had limited applicability in an age of large corporations and bureaucratic organizations. The entrepreneurial class was shrinking, and over the course of the twentieth century it became increasingly difficult for workers to amass the necessary capital to go into business for themselves. The diner business was unusual for its time in the entrepreneurial opportunities it afforded for people of limited experience and modest means. Moreover, entry into the diner business did not guarantee success. Even in the best of times, the diner business rarely, if ever, made patricians out of plebeians. Diners were marginal operations. Scratching out a decent living from the diner trade was not impossible, but it required a commitment of long hours behind the counter and the reliance on family members as workers to defray labor costs.

A Changing Strategy for a Changing Clientele

If the diner industry found it harder to deliver on the older version of the American dream, it would stake its future on its ability to satisfy the requirements of the newer version, one that promised prestige and happiness through the purchase of goods and services. At the time of his retirement in the late 1950s, Joseph Hughes had logged nearly sixty years in Worcester's lunch-car business. He had watched the trade mature since the days of roaming "night owl" wagons to a point where diners had become full-service restaurants operating twenty-four hours a day. Yet, in his mind, the formula for a successful operation had not changed all that drastically. "Give a workingman enough to eat, don't charge him too much, add a little personality—that's the recipe," he opined to a newspaper reporter. Yet by this time, many people in the industry were questioning the wisdom of the conventional marketing strategy. Widespread prosperity and mass migration to the suburbs provided an entirely new context for consumer behavior and presented the diner industry with an opportunity to re-evaluate its position in the commercial dining field. Low prices and hefty portions might have served the workingman adequately enough, but they were not sufficient for attracting the more affluent and diversified suburban clientele that operators now desperately sought. Moreover, the old-time diner "personality" clashed with the expectations of customers who measured the quality of their consumer experiences against new standards of civility. As the diner industry tried to shed its old image and adopt a new one, it found itself embroiled within a much larger struggle, a struggle to redefine the meaning of success in America. The challenge it

One of the many units manufactured by the Fodero Dining Car Company in the late 1940s

confronted was to convince Americans that an act as simple and humble as eating in a diner could embody the very essence of the good life.

Already by the late 1940s operators discovered that the traditional diner market was in deep trouble. Establishments located in inner-city industrial districts suffered from a declining customer base as manufacturers relocated to suburban regions where land was cheap and abundant. What was worse, many of these newer manufacturing plants housed their own cafeterias. A market analysis conducted by *American Restaurant Magazine* in 1952 reported that industrial dining was the fastest-growing sector of the food service trade. Thus, many diners found their traditional customer base pulled from underneath them, and more than a few went out of business as a result.

In some cases, entire cities were abandoned by the diner industry. Pat Fodero recalled that when he began working with his father at the Fodero Dining Car Company just after World War II,
much of their business came from small northeastern cities with
heavy blue-collar populations. Yet, by the 1950s, industrial flight
from towns such as Trenton, New Jersey, and Gloucester, Massachusetts, devastated the market for traditional workingmen's diners. Even in older industrial districts that continued to thrive, few
opportunities presented themselves for prospective operators as
these areas were already saturated with diners. Hence, manufacturers and aspiring operators began searching for alternative locations
and customers beyond the industrial core.

By no means were they discouraged. As they surveyed the market for commercial dining and observed changes in their own
clientele, they found reason to be optimistic. If they read the trade
journals, they learned that Americans were eating out more than
ever before. Restaurant patronage had grown sharply during the
war, not only because people had more money to spend, but because busy work schedules and food shortages made domestic dining difficult. Many of the new restaurant customers were women,
especially those who entered the full-time labor force as machine
operators, office workers, and retail clerks. Initially, postwar market analysts expected that the resumption of peace and the exodus
of women from the workforce would resuscitate prewar dining patterns. The experts were wrong; Americans continued eating out in
record numbers. If some diners suffered declining patronage, there
were plenty of others, especially those located outside industrial
districts, that had more business than they could handle.

Not only were some diners enjoying a boom in business, but
they were also attracting a more diversified clientele than they
were accustomed to in the prewar years. In addition to ladling
goulash for hungry laborers and pouring coffee for tired truckers,
countermen found themselves scrambling eggs for busy executives
on their way to work, preparing sandwiches for female clerical

workers on lunch breaks, and slicing pie for couples streaming out of nightclubs and movie theaters late at night. Diner operators saw the market changing before their very eyes. Industry leaders were confident that if they took appropriate steps, they could continue to broaden their constituency and make further inroads into a largely untapped market that consisted of businessmen, high school kids, young couples, and middle-income families. As one diner manufacturer described the situation to prospective clients in a sales brochure, a $12 billion market awaited the shrewd operator who was willing to play "host to everyone."

Location, Location, Location: The Importance of Place

The most immediate dilemma confronting owners who wanted a slice of this $12 billion market was where to do business. Because diners were built to be portable and because the vast majority of diners sat on leased land, all existing proprietors enjoyed the luxury of considering alternative locations. The field was even more wide open for individuals who purchased newly minted diners. Through the 1950s, most diner manufacturers maintained a production pace of about twenty-five units each year, accounting for an annual total of between 200 and 250 new diners for the industry as a whole.

If the diner were to "play host to everyone," it stood to reason that it could be marketed successfully to virtually any neighborhood in any region of the country. Increasingly, new units found their way to unconventional locations: suburban shopping centers, well-heeled residential neighborhoods, seaside resorts, and small college towns. In addition, several manufacturers concluded that the time was right to adopt a national strategy and invade the last great untapped market for diners, the West.

The attempt to introduce an East Coast institution to the entire nation occurred as economic analysts were reporting on the crystallization of a national consumer market for mass-produced goods and services. Tremendous population shifts during the war set the stage for this phenomenon. The general direction of movement was from the north and east to the west and south as people followed defense jobs and military assignments. This was precisely the direction in which the diner industry set its sights. Visions of a unified national consumer market were sharpened by the observation that Americans were still moving around a lot after the war: Corporate workers were transferred frequently from one location to another, and the widespread habit of taking annual summer vacations filled the nation's highways with tourists from all regions of the country. This demographic mixing may have alarmed defenders of distinctive regional culture, but it excited the imagination of manufacturers and retailers who dreamed of a homogeneous buying public. Mass production would have its required mass audience. If geographic mobility was collapsing regional differences into a national standard of consumer preference, the eastern diner manufacturers were poised to set the standard for the restaurant industry.

At the time, the field for western diners was wide open. Prior to the 1950s, it was quite unusual to find a prefabricated diner anywhere between the Mississippi River and the Pacific Ocean. Among the major postwar builders, only one, the Valentine Manufacturing Company, made any serious attempt to penetrate the commercial dining market in the western third of the country. Founded in 1938 in Wichita, Kansas, the Valentine Company sold small sandwich shops along major western truck routes, including the famed Route 66. From the inside, a Valentine unit looked like the typical workingman's diner with a grill behind the counter and a row of stools on the other side. The exterior design, however, bore little resemblance to the railroad dining car on which the eastern diners were modeled. Instead, it gave the appearance of a boxy and squat suburban home. Although the Valentine sandwich shops were beginning to make their mark on the western landscape by 1952, a great many westerners had never seen a diner, let alone an eastern-style one.

That was the year that the nation's largest diner builder, the Jerry O'Mahony Company, opened a plant in St. Louis, Missouri. Louis Camardella, its president, estimated that by establishing a presence outside the East Coast, it could quadruple its output of diners. By 1956, another East Coast manufacturer, Mountain View Diners, boasted that its agents covered the entire territory from the Atlantic Ocean to the Mississippi River and that it was contemplating sending sales representatives to Texas and California. Already, the company had shipped units to Louisiana, Washington, Arizona, Iowa, and Wisconsin. Led by these two firms, the diner industry entertained grand visions of establishing the diner as the archetypical American restaurant, from coast to coast.

But these grand visions foundered on the rocks of practical experience. Overly adventurous operators and builders ran into trouble when they tried to place diners in unfamiliar territory. In the nation's interior, many communities frowned on what they considered an intrusion from the East Coast, thereby making the diner the latest target of a long-standing hostility toward eastern culture and institutions among westerners and midwesterners. Lester Bammesburger got a taste of this attitude when he placed a diner in Bryan, Ohio. From the outset, the diner was the target of an informal but systematic campaign to drive him out of business. First, local banks refused him loans. Then, shortly after he managed to open the diner, a local candy manufacturer placed a soda fountain across the street to lure away his customers. Bammesburger persisted and, in the end, built a successful business, but this sort of frosty reception deterred the less resolute.

Perhaps the diner would have been embraced more enthusiastically out west had it not been for the popularity of another type of eatery, the drive-in. Dallas, Texas, enjoys the distinction of being the birthplace of the drive-in. In 1921, J. G. Kirby, a candy and to-bacco wholesaler, set up his first Pig Stand on the Dallas–Fort Worth Highway. There was nothing novel about the building it-self, which resembled the walk-up refreshment stands commonly found in amusement parks. The idea of curb service for automo-biles, however, marked a new stage in the evolution of commercial dining. It was wildly successful, prompting Kirby to build about sixty more. Although Texas proved fertile ground for the prolifera-tion of drive-ins, it was in California, the state with the highest rates of car ownership, where the concept really took off. By the mid-1950s, California boasted more than 2,000 drive-in outlets, most of them in the southern part of the state.

Drive-ins capitalized on America's love affair with the automo-bile, a consumer commodity widely associated with affluent subur-ban living. Eating in one's car was as close as one could get to go-ing out for a meal while remaining in the comfort and privacy of one's own domestic setting. Apparently, many customers consid-ered automobile dining more convenient and comfortable than the traditional alternatives. One journalist explained that by relying on carhops to tote trays of food from kitchen to car seat, families could eliminate "irritating waits in restaurants and uncomfortable stools at a lunch counter," while at the same time allowing families to "enjoy a good meal without the bother of dressing to 'eat out.'" Others took a more cynical view. According to one operator, "stopping in for a bite at a drive-in is following the path of least re-sistance. We cater to lazy people."

The early appearance of drive-ins on the West Coast effectively sealed off diner proprietors from the market for middle-income customers and prevented their establishments from ever gaining a foothold. The diner industry went head to head with drive-ins in the South and Midwest, but it was a losing battle. By the late 1950s, large corporations were selling franchises for chain opera-tions that enabled inexperienced operators to cash in on the drive-in craze with very little risk. In return for some sort of licensing fee, the operator acquired access to a proven formula for food preparation and service and, above all, an establishment with name recognition. Budding capitalists, who might have otherwise invested in diners, went straight for the drive-in, seeing it as a more sure-fire bet. Already by 1957, there were 1,400 A&W Root Beer stands on the road, mostly in the Midwest. An Indiana company, Carrol's Drive-In Restaurants, confidently predicted that it would blanket the country with another 1,000 drive-ins within ten years. Diner sales, on the other hand, were disappointing. Beyond the East Coast, sales by the Jerry O'Mahony and Mountain View companies never lived up to expectations; indeed, the Jerry O'Mahony company went bankrupt shortly after inaugurating its western strategy.

East of the Mississippi River, the situation was considerably brighter. Here, the diner industry attempted to capitalize on an equally impressive demographic shift, the mass migration of the population from city to suburb. Indeed, from the perspective of retailers, suburbanization was far more significant to consumer trends than the redistribution of population across regions. While people from all walks of life relocated from the eastern third of the country to the Sun Belt, suburban migration was primarily a movement of middle-income families, that is, people with money to spend. In the rush to capture these dollars, retailers who had previously relied on downtown commerce now opened branch outlets in suburban shopping centers. By riding the wave of residential migration to the suburbs, the diner industry once again attempted to position itself in the thick of the action.

Contrary to popular myth, America's postwar suburbs did not constitute an undifferentiated mass populated by like-minded people within the same income bracket. If you drove the curvy, tree-lined streets from one brand-new subdivision to the next it was easy to identify sharp differences in wealth and social class; some housing developments, including those along Philadelphia's Main Line, for example, catered almost exclusively to white-collar families while others, like the famous Levittown developments of post-war vintage, were predominantly working-class in character. Older suburban communities, including nineteenth-century residential neighborhoods built near the city limits, or industrial "satellite cities" absorbed into the expanding postwar metropolis, were equally diverse in their social composition.

As with its attempted western strategy, the industry's highest hopes were dashed by an uneven public reception that ranged from eager acceptance on the one hand to outright rejection on the other. Upper-income suburban districts accounted for the most vicious opposition to diners. The industry had encountered its fair share of hostility from such communities in the past. In the 1930s, exclusive suburbs and vacation resorts had fought the intrusion of diners in their communities with varying degrees of success. In April 1934, the *New York Times* reported that the Drake Road Neighborhood Association in Scarsdale, New York, was enraged over a bright yellow lunch wagon that had recently appeared in the center of town. The diner, situated next to a service station, enjoyed a healthy business from auto mechanics and clerks who worked in nearby shops. It did not sit well, however, with the well-heeled residents who populated the surrounding neighborhood. Condemning the diner as a blight that detracted from their quaint country-village architecture, angry homeowners insisted on its immediate removal. Elsewhere, town councils passed prohibitive legislation to prevent such unsightly intrusions on the landscape. Beginning in the 1920s, Los Angeles employed zoning codes to keep diners far away from exclusive residential districts. Throughout the 1940s, the seaside resort of Atlantic City, New Jersey, maintained a law on its books that expressly forbade diners.

Into the 1950s and 1960s, communities continued to wage war against the humble stainless-steel eatery. Harold Kullman, a New Jersey diner builder, recalled several bitter battles in the 1950s with suburban residents who felt that the diner smacked of lowbrow tastes. In Princeton, New Jersey, Kullman was only able to secure the approval of local authorities by agreeing to cover his diner exterior in brick rather than the standard stainless steel. The Fodero Dining Car Company encountered stiff resistance from wealthy residents in the New Jersey communities of Millburn and Livingston during the 1950s on the grounds that all-night diners would disrupt their tranquil suburban communities by attracting traffic and drunks at all hours of the day. These towns employed both prohibitive legislation and zoning codes to keep the Foderos away. Eventually Joe Fodero and his sons concluded that it simply was not worth the effort to try to install diners in posh neighborhoods. Hence, novices in the business were steered to safer locations, places where diners were not yet in abundance but where people were already acquainted with the institution.

If trial and error taught diner builders and operators to proceed cautiously in the western hinterlands and wealthy enclaves, it also validated a more conservative strategy of expansion that targeted East Coast suburban communities with large blue-collar populations. A 1949 advice column published in an industry trade journal counseled would-be proprietors to stick with rapidly growing, blue-collar communities that contained a high proportion of high-income wage earners. Jerry Manno remembered that when his manufacturing company scouted sites for potential customers during the early 1950s, it looked for suburban neighborhoods populated by second-generation Jewish Americans and Italian Americans.

The culmination of such advice was a pronounced shift in diner geography as new diners gravitated to what we might think of as a zone of transition between inner-city neighborhoods and mass-produced suburbs: residential communities on the fringe of cities that were experiencing an influx of upwardly mobile, middle-income families of recent European extraction. Postwar suburbanization typically involved a series of residential moves. Immediately after marriage, if they were lucky, a young couple might move from a parent's home to a modest apartment close by. The arrival of a child might trigger another move to a small house or perhaps a low-rise apartment located further from the old neighborhood. Some years down the road, a job transfer, a lucrative promotion, or perhaps the addition of more young ones might prompt relocation yet again, this time to a larger house at some distance from the urban core, perhaps in another city altogether. As the cycle repeated, populations within neighborhoods came and went. Each exchange marked the successive ascent of families up the ladder of social success. By guiding new operators to these transitional neighborhoods, trade journal columnists and builders like Jerry Manno expressed their confidence that their working-class patrons would retain their allegiance to the diner even as they blazed a trail from city to suburb.

The spatial distribution of Philadelphia diners suggests that proprietors heeded the advice of industry analysts. Few diners opened in the central part of the city during the 1950s. Further from the downtown area, diners clustered in two areas, both in north Philadelphia. When Harry Muchnik opened the Godfrey Diner along the northern reaches of Broad Street in 1955, he was undeterred by the presence of four other nearby diners. He knew this was prime diner territory: a residential community of first- and second-generation Jewish-Americans with incomes well above the city's average. The neighborhood's occupational mix was diverse, although the proportion of working-class families was rising. Only a few miles to the northeast, another string of new diners sprouted along the Frankford Avenue corridor. Heavily blue-collar in its employment profile, the neighborhood consisted largely of Italian Americans transplanted from the area just south of downtown Philadelphia.

Phil DeRaffele, who joined his father in the diner-manufacturing business just after World War II, recalled a similar shift in the spatial distribution of diners in New York City. The earliest diners in New York City were located on the far West Side of Manhattan, where light manufacturing, harbor activity, and wholesale food markets provided a reliable flow of patrons. At the end of World War II, no less than two dozen diners dotted the western flank of the island below 42nd Street. Although the DeRaffeles continued to sell diners in Manhattan in the late 1940s, an increasing percentage of their business came from the Bronx, a borough that supported much of the city's light industry and numerous residential neighborhoods populated by Italian and Jewish immigrants. Within a few years, the Bronx was glutted with diners. "That's when things went wacky on Long Island," DeRaffele remembered. In particular, the diner industry gravitated to the outlying borough of Queens, which housed the city's fastest-growing residential population, boasted home ownership rates well above the city's average, and ranked first among the five boroughs in median income. Between 1950 and 1959, roughly two-thirds of all diner sales in New York City went to locations in Queens.

An analysis of the social characteristics of neighborhoods in which diners proliferated within the Bronx and Queens during the 1950s strongly suggests that in moving from inner-city to suburban locations (although located within the city limits of New York City, many sections of these outer boroughs were still considered suburban), diners were tracing the migratory paths carved out by their traditional constituents. Of the twenty-six diners that opened in Queens during the 1950s for which precise locations can be identified, eighteen were found in neighborhoods where first- and second-generation Americans constituted at least 50 percent of the residential population. According to data from the 1960 census, over 80 percent of the inhabitants in these neighborhoods had arrived after 1939, a good many having migrated from Manhattan, Brooklyn, and the Bronx.

In other East Coast cities, the picture was much the same; diners flourished in rapidly growing residential areas with a solid base of affluent blue-collar workers. The appearance of at least four new diners along Pulaski Highway in eastern Baltimore coincided with the arrival of several thousand homeowners who made their living in the nearby steel mills. The predominantly working-class and Jewish residents who lived just across the western border of Newark, New Jersey, in Irvington, provided a buoyant market for six new diners.

Outside the major cities, the diner industry discovered a new market in blue-collar resort communities. The success of organized labor in the postwar years meant not only generous earnings for factory workers, but paid vacations as well. Hence, during summer months, it became common for blue-collar families to hop in their automobiles and drive to the nearest seaside or country resort. As they did when they migrated to the suburbs, these newly flush laborers took their cultural institutions with them on vacation, thereby explaining the proliferation of diners in locales such as the Jersey Shore, the Eastern Shore of Maryland, and the Catskill Mountains.

The spread of diners to areas recently populated by upwardly mobile blue-collar families did not deter operators from placing units in certain white-collar areas. It was not at all uncommon to find new diners in upper-income areas where second- and third-generation Americans had recently made the leap across the collar line. After spending several years scouting locations, the owners of the Claremont Diner selected a busy intersection in Verona, New Jersey, where they developed a following from the largely, white-collar Jewish clientele from the surrounding neighborhoods. The Rainbow Diner in Great Neck, New York, and the Hilltop Diner on Reisterstown Road in Baltimore also built profitable businesses in communities with a high proportion of Jewish Americans employed in professional and managerial positions.

Outside the Northeast, the area that experienced the most pronounced diner boom was, predictably, the state that witnessed the largest influx of northeasterners, Florida. Retirement sent flocks of senior citizens to the Sunshine State, some of whom stayed only for the winter months, and some of whom relocated on a perma-

Florida emerged as one of the more popular locations for new diners in the 1950s.

nent basis. Vacation trips, on the other hand, flooded the state with hordes of families with young children. Beach communities that had once been the exclusive province of white Anglo-Saxon Protestants opened up to Catholics and Jews, although only rarely to African Americans. As Florida was transformed into a paradise for the masses, it filled with modest bungalows, budget motels, dog tracks, and at least two dozen new diners. Most clustered around the fastest-rowing population centers, Miami on the east coast, and Tampa-St. Petersburg on the west coast. Although diner operators reported stiff competition from the numerous drive-ins that had already established a presence in the state, they held one important advantage. Diners could be equipped with air-conditioning, thus affording customers a pleasurable alternative to sweating in their cars.

Within these transitional suburban neighborhoods and middle-income resort towns, proprietors sought to maximize their access to a diverse range of customers by placing their units along busy commercial thoroughfares, expecting to attract business from the residents who lived, worked, and shopped nearby. In preparation for the grand opening of the Godfrey Diner in north Philadelphia, Harry Muchnik mailed 5,000 invitations to surrounding households, signaling that he wanted and anticipated their patronage. Roland Michel, who operated a diner across from an A&P supermarket in Gloucester, Massachusetts, advertised that a "delicious meal or tempting snack" at the Cape Ann Diner was a perfect way to take a break from shopping chores, thereby directing his appeal to local homemakers on their daily rounds.

The real virtue of the commercial strip, however, was that in addition to providing access to nearby residents, it enabled proprietors to tap into a virtually limitless metropolitan transient trade. A diner with a spacious parking lot and an eye-catching neon sign situated next to a highway entrance ramp, sports arena, regional airport, or string of budget motels was well-positioned to complement its local business with miscellaneous vacationers, truckers, and motorists traveling to and from work. Joe Swingle probably knew as much about opportune locations as anyone in the business, having worked as a sales agent for the Fodero Dining Car Company for many years. When he purchased his own diner in 1953, he placed it on Route 22 in the rapidly growing suburb of Springfield, New Jersey. There, he anticipated patronage not only from local residents but from nearby factory and office workers, as well as from the motorists who plied the busy highway on their way to and from New York City.

Operators such as Swingle, who hoped to cultivate a diversified clientele, faced the daunting task of striking the right balance among widely divergent audiences. The mere assumption that a working-class institution could be remolded to suit the needs of a more diversified clientele assumed a cultural elasticity that people in the industry could not be sure existed. Moreover, establishing a presence in transitional suburban neighborhoods bound owners and builders to a core constituency that was crossing all sorts of social boundaries and reevaluating its cultural expectations. Decisions about which features of the diner to retain and which to discard would test their capacity to gauge how far consumers could be pushed across unfamiliar cultural borders as well as their ability to identify those points around which divergent cultures might converge. Should diner owners expand their menus? Should they still offer counter service? Did manufacturers need to reconfigure the design of their buildings? All of these questions came under careful scrutiny as men and women in the diner business groped for new formulas. The diner industry did not tread into these murky waters alone, as we shall see in the subsequent chapters on bowling alleys and trailer parks. Indeed, the search for novel marketing formulas captured the energy of all retailers who took aim at the vast American "middle majority," that broad statistical category of middle-income consumers composed of working-class wage earners, middle-class professionals, and people trying to leap from one category to the other. Thus, in following middle-majority merchandising formulas, the diner also risked losing those features that accounted for its distinctive appeal among blue-collar workers.

As a practical matter, diners that did business along busy thoroughfares had to make adjustments to accommodate patrons who traveled by automobile, necessitating at the very least the provision of parking space. Through the 1940s, a great many diner owners placed their units flush against the sidewalk, anticipating that most customers would arrive by foot. By the 1950s, diners often resembled islands amid vast seas of concrete. Some of the larger establishments occupied more than an acre of land.

Casting a net in transient traffic to catch passing motorists made on-site advertising a necessity. The hand-painted signs that traditionally graced diner exteriors were supplemented or replaced with huge signs that could be seen from afar and read at high speed. Raised on pylons and illuminated in brightly colored neon, these signs invariably spelled out the name of the diner. Sometimes they included an attention-grabbing icon or a catchy slogan as well. The owners of the Trio Diner in Miami manipulated neon tubing to inform potential customers that they were open twenty-four hours a day, that all baking was done on the premises, and that parking was free. The sign above the Tick Tock diner in Clifton, New Jersey, simply directed passing motorists along Route 3 to "Eat Heavy."

During the 1950s, the buildings themselves became advertisements for a new kind of experience: Space Age dining. The new diners exuded modernity. Exterior floodlights illuminated brilliant stainless-steel siding, angled metallic canopies, and large plate-glass windows, giving passing motorists a glimpse of something that was more akin to a space module than an old railroad boxcar. By the time the Kullman Dining Car company unveiled its "new space age design" at the end of the decade, the connection between prefabricated diners and space travel had become explicit. Proprietors echoed this architectural trend in the names they chose for their businesses: Rocket Diner, the Comet Diner, the Flying Saucer Diner. By employing motifs of the Space Age, diner builders and operators positioned themselves at the forefront of technological progress. By inference, the buildings assured upwardly mobile customers that they were as up-to-date as anyone, that they had arrived. At the very least, futuristic imagery created a vast psychic distance between the suburban diners built in the 1950s and the typical workingman's lunch car of a previous generation.

Diner owners knew that it was not enough to advertise novelty through flashing signs and glitzy architecture. These cosmetic modifications would be self-defeating if passing motorists peered through the plate-glass windows only to have to their worst preconceptions confirmed. For a diner to replicate the scene from Edward Hopper's painting *Nighthawks*, complete with a haggard counterman disdainfully serving coffee to a grizzled trucker while a shady character at the end of the counter gazes shiftily from un-

Brochure advertising
Kullman's Space Age
Diner, circa 1962

der the brim of his hat, would certainly offset any favorable impression created by a razzle-dazzle Space Age façade. To sell the diner to a more diversified constituency, owners had to convince prospective customers that the diner had been revolutionized from the inside out.

Domesticating the Diner

The overriding broad strategy to which the industry adhered as a means of expanding its market across divisive social and cultural borders was to repackage the diner as a middle-income family restaurant. In the lexicon of the trade, "family" replaced "working-man" as the basic social unit to which the diner yoked its reputation and fortunes. Over the course of the 1950s, diner proprietors, like their bowling alley peers, went to elaborate lengths to secure the loyalty of families by making their establishments more pleasant, more comfortable, and above all, more respectable. Indeed, efforts to transform the diner into a family institution were related to, and often indistinguishable from, efforts to upgrade the social cachet of eating in a diner. In an era when middle-class status was synonymous with a set of consumption rituals organized around the nuclear household, domesticating the diner became the key to attaining social respectability. Transforming the diner from an extension of the factory floor to an extension of the happy suburban home would make the diner acceptable, if not hospitable, to a wide range of potential clients.

For diner operators who wanted to reach the widest possible audience, catering to the needs of parents and their children made a good deal of practical sense. Nuclear families were the norm in the transitional suburban neighborhoods, and household arrangements in these mixed areas were remarkably homogeneous across class divisions. Family size did not differ dramatically across the spectrum of incomes and occupation. Few suburban households contained the boarders and extended kinfolk that often populated inner-city tenements. Neither did they contain live-in servants; in the suburbs, women performed most of the housework in both middle- and working-class homes. If blue-collar and white-collar breadwinners toiled in very different settings, they nonetheless commuted to and from work along the same highways. Even the proportion of women employed in the paid labor force was roughly equivalent in working-class and middle-class households. Hence, diner proprietors could issue the same appeal to working-class and middle-class families.

More importantly, integrating women and children into the world of commercial dining through the vehicle of the nuclear family was the path of least resistance. World War II had raised troubling questions about the future of the American family. On the one hand, government propaganda told Americans they were fighting to protect the integrity of the family, which was said to represent all that was good and wholesome about America. As the locus of moral and social authority, the family also stood as a bulwark against the sort of totalitarianism that defined the nation's enemies. On the other hand, the profound dislocations of war strained domestic relations to the breaking point. The estrangement of wives from husbands, the separation of parents from children, and the movement of women into the workforce seemed to portend disaster. What would be the fate of children raised with only minimal parental supervision? Would soldiers adjust to normal domestic routines after enduring the wrenching experience of combat? Would women willingly resume their roles of faithful wives and dutiful mothers after having tasted so much independence? Postwar films, especially those of the "noir" variety like *The Blue Dahlia*, were filled with depictions of women who had "turned bad" during the war. The purveyors of consumer commodities could hardly afford to be seen as contributing to these destructive trends. Especially in courting upwardly mobile working-class Americans who were striving to fit into the cultural mainstream, the safest strategy was to absorb women and children into the world of consumption by appealing to their sense of familial responsibility.

If they were to remake the diner as a family institution, proprietors would first have to lure families out of their homes at dinnertime. Many middle-income families were not accustomed to dining together in public; they would require some coaxing to overcome any reservations they had about the propriety of the sacred family dinner occurring in a crowded diner. Diner owners were confident, however, that their product offered both practical and psychological benefits for the men, women, and children who lived in transitional suburban neighborhoods. The idea of dining out for recreational, rather than purely utilitarian, purposes may have seemed radical and probably decadent to a working class that had only recently been mired in poverty and the imposed thrift of wartime, but the diner industry was convinced that it was consistent with the novel circumstances that characterized the new life of their upwardly mobile patrons and the unconventional ways in which families were demonstrating and enjoying their newfound affluence.

Because dining out was traditionally associated with the leisure class, it carried certain status connotations. At the very least, an outing to the local diner demonstrated that a family could afford small luxuries. In catering to a population that was neither wealthy nor given to outward displays of extravagance, however, proprietors were careful not to push the luxury theme too far. Indeed, they were far more likely to market the diner experience as a sensible alternative to eating at home. Diners enabled families to feast on foods that were rarely prepared at home. Roast turkey, a dish that was simply too large to be consumed in a timely manner in most suburban households, was a staple of the 1950s diner menu precisely for this reason. A diner meal also enabled individuals to order dishes that were unpopular with the rest of the family. If father and junior wrinkled their noses at the mere suggestion of liver and onions, mother could order it with impunity at the diner. Most important, diner meals were relatively inexpensive. Promotions for family meals invariably stressed the cost for families on a budget—97-cent dinners and complete meal specials were advertised aggressively to assuage families worried about the impact of commercial dining on their budgets.

Diner proprietors learned that one of the major reasons families preferred to dine at home was the fear that their young children would create a public nuisance. The transitional suburbs were filled with young children, as middle-income couples of all class backgrounds procreated with unprecedented vigor after the war. Babysitters were hard to come by; moreover they were expensive if used on a regular basis. In most cases, grandma and grandpa still lived in the old neighborhood, making them unlikely recruits on the spur of a moment. If the choice was between dining at home on the one hand and risking the contempt and frayed nerves of waitresses and other customers in a diner on the other, most parents chose to keep their squealing babies and rambunctious children at home.

Eager to pack families into their establishments, proprietors went to great lengths to counteract the impression that the diner was no place for youngsters. Bill Noller, who ran a diner in the resort community of Beach Haven, New Jersey, during the 1950s, assured parents that children were more than welcome in his establishment. "We had kiddie menus, adequate high chairs. No girls with a sour look on their face when kids came in. We'd give kids a lollipop and a bib and make them feel at home." Other operators resorted to similar gimmicks to get their family-friendly message across. In Butler, Pennsylvania, Herman Dight printed nursery rhyme characters on his plates to encourage children to eat all of their food in order to see the drawings. From the very beginning, William Martindale targeted children by naming his Delaware establishment the Peter Pan Diner and by erecting a ten-foot cutout of the J. M. Barrie character on his roof. Martindale also gave all children a colorful Peter Pan mask, the back of which had a special children's menu featuring meals named "Tinker Bell," "Never Never Land," and "Captain Hook."

Diner owners also had to contend with customer fears that moving the dinner ritual out of the home would result in a loss of family intimacy. Proprietors were determined to make the opposite case, that a meal in a diner would strengthen family bonds. The diner meal was marketed as a ceremonial testament to core family relationships. By way of advertisements in the local press, signs draped over their windows, or in some cases, radio spots, they pushed family dining as a special event, an activity entirely appropriate for the celebration of birthdays, anniversaries, and holidays. "Enjoy Life—Eat Out More Often" was a slogan developed by the National Restaurant Association and employed liberally by diner owners in their promotional campaigns. Invariably, advertisements juxtaposed the phrase with the image of a happy family gathered around a diner booth.

Exterior of the Peter Pan Diner, New Castle, Del., 1957. Note that the Peter Pan cutout bears a remarkable resemblance to the depiction of the character in Walt Disney's *Peter Pan* film released several years earlier.

Interior of Peter Pan Diner, New Castle, Del., 1957. Diners catering to the family trade frequently employed women to wait on customers seated at booths.

While recreational dining was intended to strengthen the family as a unit, proprietors shrewdly cast women as the primary beneficiaries of the diner experience. In addition to portraying commercial dining as a catalyst for family cohesion, they explicitly promoted the activity as an antidote to domestic drudgery. When the owners of the Little Chef Diner promised that their 98-cent steak dinner would keep "evenings free and uncluttered with cooking chores and dirty dishes," they spoke directly to the frustrations of suburban wives, especially to the growing number who held part-time or full-time jobs during the 1950s as a means of financing families' expanding consumer budgets. Roughly 30 to 40 percent of women who lived in transitional suburban neighborhoods worked outside the home. Participation in the paid labor force in no way released women from their obligations in the unpaid domestic labor force. When they returned from their jobs, they faced still more work: floors to mop, furniture to polish, clothes to launder, and children to mind. For women overburdened with the double duties of housework and a paid job, a diner meal saved valuable time.

It was not only workingwomen, however, who saw dining away from home as a welcome respite from cooking and cleaning. As Betty Friedan would broadcast to the other half of the world in the early 1960s, few women found enjoyment, let alone fulfillment, in the endless routine of household chores. Housework was tedious. Moreover, because of its association with blue-collar labor, it was degrading. Historically, middle-class women did not perform household chores; they hired help to cook their meals, dust their furniture, and nurse their children. Advertisers went to absurd lengths to demonstrate that the modern tools of homemaking took the work out of housework. By depicting women mopping the kitchen floor or vacuuming the rug in pearls and heels, they suggested that housework was glamorous or, at the very least, was not incongruous with white-collar status. Few women found the advertisements convincing. Housework was menial labor, no matter what the wardrobe or the new miracle appliance. By delegating the tedious tasks of washing, chopping, and cooking to paid laborers, a restaurant meal conferred not only relief but a small measure of unaccustomed social rank on the woman who was chef and dishwasher in her own home.

Perhaps this is why a 1959 survey revealed that wives were twice as likely as their husbands to suggest that the family eat a meal away from home. For Kathy Corbett, who lived in the suburban community of Westfield, New Jersey, the nearby Clark Diner was a godsend because when she didn't have dinner waiting on the table for her husband when he arrived home from his office job in New York City at 6:20 in the evening, she had to have an alternative. Invariably, it was the Clark Diner, and on her instigation the two of them dined there with their young son on a weekly basis.

Women like Kathy Corbett may have been the primary beneficiaries of ritualistic family dining, but proprietors made sure to provide their husbands with an incentive as well: a diner meal was a gift that husbands could give to their wives to express their love and appreciation. In Fort Wayne, Indiana, the Kintz Diner pushed its "special Sunday dinners" with the slogan "Sure mother is a wonderful cook. But what a treat it is for her to dine out at least once a week with the family." Place mats at the Gwyn-Dale Diner reminded husbands that "Wives who cook and do the dishes should be granted these three wishes: a grateful mate, a well kissed cheek, and a restaurant dinner every week," at where else but the Gwyn-Dale Diner. By treating their wives to a night off from household duties, men were assured that they were fulfilling their duty as enlightened husbands.

Overburdened wives and enlightened husbands were precisely the type of customers that Charles Taxin wanted in his north Philadelphia diner. In 1957, Taxin took over what he called a "straight line type of diner operation," by which he meant a no-frills atmosphere along with a hurried style of service. Yet Taxin aimed for something different, something more in line with what people in the surrounding residential neighborhood expected in a leisurely dining experience. For an establishment that was trying to pass itself off as a dignified family restaurant, the cold industrial look that may have been appropriate for an eatery functioning as an extension of the workplace would not suffice. So Taxin upgraded the "appearance and atmosphere" of the diner, "so that customers would feel they were eating in a better quality restaurant." A canopy raised above the front entrance "added new prestige," while the addition of Chinese lanterns and window drapes created "a more distinguished effect." Taxin complemented his ornamental improvements with "more distinctive service." Large, soft napkins replaced small, coarse ones, customers drank water out of monogrammed glasses, and waitresses spoke in hushed tones.

Elsewhere, diner proprietors who did business in transitional suburban neighborhoods were coming to the same conclusion as Taxin: Atmosphere and ambience mattered as much to middle-income families as convenience. Like Taxin, they retrofitted their establishments to bring them into line with what they perceived to be the sensibilities of upwardly mobile middle-income families. The emphasis was on leisurely dining in a setting that was informal and comfortable, yet respectable. Especially in warmer climates, air-conditioning became de rigueur. Proprietors modified their streamlined interiors to give their diners a more individualized character. The owners of the Mari-Nay Diner in the Main Line suburb of Rosemont, Pennsylvania, projected an air of sophistication by decorating their walls with murals of nearby college campuses like Bryn Mawr, Haverford, and Villanova. An aquarium stocked with tropical fish created an oasis of tranquility and exoticism amid the clatter of dishes at the Lido Diner in Springfield, New Jersey. Taxin probably spoke for other owners when, in defense of his enhancements, he proclaimed, "we're not going highhat." Without question, however, these changes produced a classier diner, one that began to look more and more like a formal middle-class restaurant.

Over the course of the 1950s, proprietors relayed shifting consumer tastes to builders, thereby propelling a rapid evolution in diner design. When Adam Yaskell approached the Kullman Dining Car Company about a replacement for his diner in East Orange, New Jersey, he was skeptical about the company's ability to fulfill his vision of an informal dining venue for suburban families. East Orange epitomized the transitional postwar suburb; in the ten years since Yaskell had entered the diner business, its population had swelled with an influx of young families migrating from Newark and New York City. Yaskell was certain that the traditional diner would not bring him the expanded business he coveted. After poring over 200 issues of architecture and restaurant trade journals with his two brothers, Yaskell came up with a concept that satisfied him: a large, beautiful restaurant that would integrate a bakery, a delicatessen, a counter service operation, and a "luxuriously appointed dining room." The Kullman Dining Car Company had never built anything resembling this concoction, but it accepted the challenge nonetheless. "I don't think anything we have undertaken in 27 years of building diners gave us more headaches," Harold Kullman remarked at the time. The resulting product was truly revolutionary. The small counter service area was clearly subordinated to the spacious dining room, as Yaskell demanded. And separated from the dining area by a glass wall, Kullman installed the delicatessen-bakeshop Yaskell had commissioned.

When Yaskell's Suburban Diner opened in the summer of 1952, it was heralded by an industry trade journal as a "new concept in diner operation." Over the next several years, many of the innovations that made the Suburban Diner unique were incorporated into the standard models churned out by Kullman. With nearly 4,000 square feet of interior floor space, the Suburban Diner was unusually large for its time. By 1960, however, Kullman had built several diners of comparable size. Shipping large diners was a nightmare for the manufacturing companies. The Suburban Diner was constructed and transported in six separate sections. With the trend toward larger diners, the practice of shipping a diner in sections and assembling them on site became the convention throughout the industry.

The priority given to table and booth service over the counter and stool arrangement also established an industry-wide trend. Indeed, one reason that diners grew larger was to accommodate more tables and booths. Large upholstered booths offered advantages over the counter-and-stool arrangement for operators intent on catering to families because they could accommodate four, five, and even six patrons at a time, and they offered a modicum of privacy. The booths also appealed to patrons who treated diners as gathering places to meet friends. Aldom's Diner in Salem, Ohio, was a regular hangout for Earle Hersman and friends. On their frequent visits, the teenagers invariably commandeered the diner's rear booth, finding it an ideal space for long evenings of socializing. Because a group of aluminum-siding salesmen with a rather shady reputation monopolized the rear booths at the Hilltop Diner in Baltimore, Chip Silverman and his friends took an almost proprietary control over the booths on either side of the cash register at the front entrance for late-night joke and gossip sessions.

The "luxuriously appointed dining room" that was so important to Yaskell also became a standard option for those who purchased Kullman diners during the 1950s. Designed exclusively for table service, the Kullman dining room extension was perfect for family dinners, private parties, and customers who simply wanted the atmosphere of a fine restaurant as opposed to a diner. Indeed, by 1960, Kullman was marketing its product not as a diner, but as a diner-restaurant.

The hybrid aesthetic projected by the Kullman diner-restaurant represented a decade of incremental departures from the bare-bones, utilitarian look of the traditional workingman's lunch car. In unveiling its 1950 model, Harold Kullman explained how the introduction of large picture-frame windows brightened the diner interiors during daylight hours while the use of indirect fluorescent lighting eliminated the harsh glare of incandescent bulbs at night. Over the remainder of the decade, Kullman continued to adjust its interior design to give its product a softer and more relaxed feel. Harsh overhead lighting gave way to indirect fluorescent illumination and then to hanging brass lamps. Stainless-steel molding gave way to walnut plastic laminated ceiling beams. By 1960, Kullman Diners had jazzed up its diner-restaurant with bamboo curtains, patterned terrazzo floors, and an array of exotic wall treatments ranging from "beach pebble marble" to "genuine Italian mosaic."

Another innovator in the industry was the Jerry O'Mahony Company, based in Elizabeth, New Jersey. Having built its first lunch car in 1913, it was one of the nation's oldest manufacturers and enjoyed such rapid success in the early part of the century that it adopted the slogan "In our line, we lead the world." Certainly, it was among the leaders in transforming the appearance and function of the diner after World War II. Keeping abreast of customer needs and embarking on a careful research program, the company experimented with a variety of new materials and designs. In 1950, the Jerry O'Mahony Company announced that henceforth it would appoint its diners with mirrored ceilings to create a more spacious and luxurious atmosphere. And instead of the usual red or blue interior color scheme, it would offer a variety of pastel colors for "brightness and richer appearance, as well as for their psychological effects." Other companies followed suit, splashing their upholstery, tables, walls, and ceilings with various combinations of such quintessentially 50s colors as pink, turquoise, aqua, rose, pumpkin, and coral.

What is remarkable about all these changes in diner design is how closely they paralleled architectural trends within middle and upper income suburban homes. The same materials that diner builders turned to in the 1950s—formica, vinyl, and terrazzo— were also making an appearance in middle-class kitchens, foyers, and basements. Some patrons may have been reminded of the wallpaper in their family room or children's bedroom as they took in

the pastel color schemes and boomerang patterns on diner upholstery. The expansive picture windows that provided visual continu-
ity between the diner interior and the front parking lot corre-
sponded to the expansive glass walls so characteristic of popular
split-level ranch-style homes. Although air-conditioning remained
a rarity in working-class homes, climate-controlled interiors were
available to upper-income suburbanites. By constructing diners
with the latest materials, decorating them in the most up-to-date
styles, and fitting them with the most modern equipment, proprietors established an aesthetic and even a technological link between public consumption and private home life, thereby assuring
mothers and fathers that in visiting the diner they would not be
shirking their familial responsibilities. Above all, they were inviting
their customers into a cozy, familiar space that reassuringly reminded them of home yet still provided a modest sense of glamour.

Perhaps the most striking modification made by diner builders
and owners was the removal of the grill from behind the counter
and the installation of separate housing for cooking facilities behind the diner. As one veteran New York City operator recalled,
"When the war ended, the desire to see food prepared in front of
you decreased. . . . People didn't want greasy spoons. The griddleman was greasy." By banishing all cooking facilities to a rear
kitchen annex, the griddleman and his greasy operation could be
effectively removed from the customer's sight. By rendering invisible the labor involved in food preparation, the modern diner no
longer conveyed the atmosphere of a workplace. Rather, it was
more like a middle-class home, where meals were cooked in a
kitchen and then served in an adjacent dining area.

The appearance of waitresses in diners completed the association of the diner with home in customer's minds. After the turn of
the century, restaurateurs increasingly relied on female labor to deliver food to patrons. Diners, however, were slow to make the transition. In compact units, where all the action occurred at or near
the counter, it was simple enough for the grillman to combine

cooking and serving functions. Even if women were deemed acceptable as food servers, the grill was a man's domain. The relocation of cooking facilities and the addition of booth and table service dramatically revised the labor requirements for running a diner. Invariably, operators turned to women to wait on tables, a move that not only solved a practical problem but went a long way toward domesticating the diner experience.

In many respects, James Mears was ahead of his time when he opened his Deluxe Diner in Union Center, New Jersey, in 1946. Not only did Mears anticipate the magnitude of the postwar consumer binge by unveiling what he claimed was the largest diner in the world, but he pioneered the use of female employees. As he explained shortly after his grand opening, "Women belong in restaurants as waitresses, hostesses and cashiers. They give an atmosphere to your place which encourages the family trade." They were also cheap labor, a benefit that was not lost on Mears. Employers operated on the premise that women entering the paid labor force did so to supplement family income rather than to support an independent existence. In making this assumption, they were often off the mark. Eunice Ramsey worked both day and night shifts at the Tastee Diner in order to earn enough money to support herself as a young woman. Other waitresses, through divorce or abandonment, were struggling to raise children on their own. These harsh realities did not make much of an impression on diner owners, many of whom cavalierly justified low pay scales on the grounds that "their girls" also earned tips. If the hiring of women dispelled the notion that diners were all-male establishments, it was accomplished at a minimal cost to diner owners.

Women's presence as waitresses could make all the difference in the world with respect to the pattern of social interaction in the diner. Female servers acted as surrogate mothers and wives. Parents felt secure sending their children off to the diner after school for soda and ice cream, knowing that a familiar maternal figure was keeping an eye out for them. Waitresses further contributed to the

creation of a homey atmosphere by referring to customers in familiar terms, calling them "Hon" and kidding with them as if they
were close family members. Lonely men looking for female companionship found all they desired by sitting at the counter of a
diner staffed with female help. In fact, one of the perils of the trade
was unwanted attention from men when terms of endearment and
friendly service were mistaken for authentic romantic interest.
Thus, diner waitresses had to devise techniques to discourage male
customers from exceeding the bounds of appropriate social intimacy. Jenny Bryant, who served customers on roller skates at a
diner in Winchester, Virginia, prided herself on her ability to handle unruly male customers. When harsh words did not suffice, she
resorted to more drastic measures. On one occasion, Bryant became so annoyed with a solitary customer at the counter who continued to throw lewd glances in her direction that she felt compelled to cool his ardor by dumping a plate of ham and eggs over
his head.

Domesticating architecture and service may have added an element of sexual tension to the diner, but most people in the business were convinced that the strategy was essential for expanding
trade. Certainly diner manufacturers tried to impress upon their
clients that only by trading in their old-fashioned dining cars for
the most up-to-date models could they hope to diversify their customer base and boost their profits. Sales brochures made the case
using testimonials from owners who had enjoyed dramatic changes
in patronage after replacing their old-fashioned lunch wagons with
modern diner-restaurants: "More women have been coming in because of the booths and we are doing a bigger Sunday dinner business as well"; "My customers are now treating the whole family to
dinners"; "More than 25 percent of my noon business now comes
from women as against the fact that we didn't get any of the fair
sex at all before." One manufacturer insisted that the improved appearance of its new diner guaranteed not only more customers but
a "better class of trade." Given the number of operators who pur-

chased modern diner-restaurants and turned to female help to serve food, it appears that they were equally convinced of the virtues of domesticating the diner.

Americanizing the Diner

When it functioned as intended, the domesticated diner affirmed the American identity of its customers, many of whom had not been considered fully American before World War II. By circumscribing family boundaries around the nuclear unit, the suburban diner of the 1950s liberated customers from the encumbrances of an older immigrant generation and redirected their allegiances to community and nation. Diner builders and owners blatantly appropriated the nation's founding myths of colonial settlement and westward expansion in the names they chose for their establishments and the motifs they employed to enrich the dining experience. In crafting polyglot menus that were not overly threatening, they attempted something even more ambitious, a standardized national cuisine that would make items like spaghetti and kosher pickles as American as apple pie. Ever so gently, the postwar suburban diner nudged the nation toward a more pluralistic concept of citizenship, one that tolerated ethnic diversity and enabled the sons and daughters of European immigrants to assert their status as real Americans.

When George Charbulak entered the diner business in the 1930s, he followed the customary practice of inscribing his name on the front of his lunch wagon. "George's Diner" was a perfectly appropriate designation for a place where most patrons sat at the counter, knew George personally, and enjoyed both his company and food. Through the 1950s, tiny boxcars named after their owners—Pete's Grill, Al's Lunch, Marzocchi's Diner, Tooley's Diner, Kless's Diner—still littered the older industrial area of urban America. Miles away, however, in the residential neighborhoods of suburbia, it was much less common for owners to draw attention to themselves and their ethnic origins (as they invariably did when they attached surnames to their businesses.) Instead, flashing neon spelled out a different sort of relationship between consumer and the wider world. The Woburn Diner outside of Boston, the Strongsville Diner outside of Cleveland, and the Roslyn Diner outside of New York City were three among hundreds of diners that adopted the name of their suburban locales during the 1950s. By the end of the decade, the number of diners named after the towns in which they were located approached the number named after their owners.

At the same time, diner owners and manufacturers reached deep into the nation's historical treasury for meaningful motifs. George Yonko was not the only proprietor taken with the concept of the American West. The decade of the 1950s saw the grand opening of two additional Chuck Wagon Diners, one in Champaign, Illinois, and another in Denver, Colorado. Meanwhile, the Stage Coach Diner brought a slice of the old West to Fall River, Massachusetts, and the Log Cabin Diner added a rustic flavor to the landscape of Queens. The Mayflower Diner in Quincy, Massachusetts, the William Penn Diner in Philadelphia, and the Pilgrim Diner in Cedar Grove, New Jersey (which did not open until the 1960s), evoked another historical moment altogether, but one equally resonant with customers' experience of migration and mobility. It was not long before diner builders formalized the deployment of patriotic imagery by incorporating both western and colonial themes in their designs. Several dining car companies accessorized their interiors with an assortment of colonial fixtures, most notably wooden beams in the ceiling and hanging lanterns. The Summit Diner, built by the Swingle Dining Car Company in 1960, had it both ways, juxtaposing these colonial embellishments with artifacts from the Old West: saddles, harnesses, and wagon wheels.

Deciding what foods to serve in the all-American diner presented diner owners with one of their biggest challenges. For the suburban proprietor who aimed for the widest possible audience, it made little sense to specialize in a particular ethnic cuisine. Moreover, the hearty ragouts and stews that sated the appetites of hungry truckers and factory laborers did not necessarily suit the palates of men, women, and children eager to validate both their middle-class status and their growing sense of identity as Americans. Hence, owners struggled to devise menus that balanced traditional diner favorites with offerings that were more sophisticated and at the same time, more American.

Ernest Weber, a European-trained chef employed at the Village Diner in Tuckahoe, New York, spoke for many others in the diner industry when he explained, "we have a fight on our hands to correct this impression [that diners] are hash houses where most people grab a cup of coffee and gulp down a hamburger." Weber may have been schooled abroad, but his solution to the problem did not involve the importation of fancy European cooking. From Tuckahoe to Tampa, cooks like Weber upgraded their repertoires by borrowing from the traditions of the American middle class. At the very least, diner menus featured salads and fountain drinks to attract more women, children, and teenagers. As early as 1946, a column in an industry trade journal urged operators to secure the female market by featuring "attractive salads and luncheon meats." Several years later, another article suggested that a good salad selection would appeal to all sorts of customers, especially during the hot summer months. Although the salad may have boasted a European lineage, the species that evolved in diners during the 1950s—various combinations of raw vegetables and Jell-O—evinced no foreign ancestry whatsoever.

For patrons who wanted something a little more substantial but equally classy, operators featured steaks and seafood, both of which were found routinely on the menus of more formal American restaurants. Although the New Ideal Diner sat along a major trucking corridor, Route 40 in Maryland, the owners geared their business toward the tourists, salesmen, and foreign diplomats who also traveled the busy thoroughfare and had more finicky tastes. Planning their menu accordingly, Peter Mikes and Steve Karas emphasized fresh seafood, including stuffed flounder, deep sea scallops, Chesapeake oysters, and Maryland-style crab cakes. Lobster, rarely found on diner menus in the 1940s, emerged as a standard top-of-the-line item. At the Mary-O Grill on Long Island, patrons were invited to pick their own live crustacean from the large tank that stood next to the counter. Roland Michel announced in the local newspaper that in conjunction with the grand opening of his diner, which would replace an older one that had occupied the same spot, lobster would make a debut on his menu. Not to be outdone, the Claremont Diner enticed patrons with a dish consisting of Norfolk shrimp and lobster cured in champagne sauce.

At the same time that owners added more sophisticated American items to their menus, they systematically eliminated the most exotic ethnic foods. Although individuals of recent European extraction, particularly Greeks, continued to dominate the proprietary end of the business, they purposefully underplayed their particular ethnic roots. Hence, when the owners of the working-class Club Car Diner in McKeesport, Pennsylvania, opened several outlets in suburban Pittsburgh, they dropped items such as halushki and pierogies from their menu. Angelo and Fanny Blentsen made a similar decision after emigrating from Greece and opening several diners in Virginia in the late 1950s and early 1960s. Although one of their establishments, the Blue Star Diner, might have catered to the sizable Greek community in Newport News, the Blentsens decided not to emphasize their native cuisine except to offer a Greek salad. Fanny Blentsen recalled that if friends or relatives stopped by and requested a special Greek dish she was happy to oblige. Otherwise, she served what she considered to be standard American fare: steaks, hamburgers, chicken, and seafood.

Blentsen's decision to serve hamburger, and more importantly her decision to retain the Greek salad, rested on the assumption that customers from all walks of life were now prepared to tolerate certain foods that were once considered strange or even disreputable. Hamburgers and frankfurters fell into the latter category. Only a few decades earlier, dishes prepared with chopped or processed meat suffered from a dubious reputation. In the popular mind, cooks used ground beef to camouflage either spoiled or inferior-quality meat. The hamburger, in particular, was associated with low-income diets; middle-class families avoided it when dining out. By the 1950s, however, improvements in refrigeration and more stringent sanitary codes convinced diner owners that the lowly hamburger sandwich might find a wider following. For much the same reasons, frankfurters enjoyed a similar reversal of fortune in the postwar era. Commonly sold at carnivals and sporting events around the turn of the century, the red-hot wiener or "hot dog" was not the sort of item respectable people ordered in a sit-down restaurant. Although owners avoided the term "hot dog," "frankfurter on a roll" and "franks and beans" were mainstays on diner menus and remained so through the 1950s and 1960s.

The widespread popularity of hamburgers and frankfurters, both with Germanic roots, signaled a growing tolerance for certain foods that had once been associated with particular immigrant populations. In the workingman's diner of the 1940s, menu items were targeted to particular ethnic constituencies. Yet, patrons were certainly free to sample a wide variety of foods that their mothers had never prepared at home. If the workingman's diner of the 1940s diffused immigrant traditions across the working class, the suburban family diner of the 1950s furthered the process of cultural amalgamation by introducing certain working-class foods to the middle class. Over time, owners learned which dishes enjoyed a broader constituency, and more important, they learned how to prepare them in ways that extended their appeal across ethnic and class borders. Through the elimination of offensive spices and sauces, Italian cuisine became Italian-American and other foreign foods fell under the vaguely defined heading of "home-style cooking." While steaks, seafood, fruit pies, and milk shakes increasingly anchored a uniform selection of foods, it was not unusual to find kosher pickles, spaghetti, chili con carne, shish-ka-bob, and Greek salads listed alongside these standbys, even in areas where there were few Jewish, Italian, Mexican, or Greek customers.

By serving spaghetti, kosher-style deli sandwiches, and Greek salad, diners pushed the definition of what it meant to be American, expanding the boundaries to ensure the inclusion of the second- and third-generation Americans who constituted the vast majority of their customers. This was nothing less than revolutionary, considering that only a few decades earlier the terms of assimilation were nonnegotiable. Through the 1920s, when anti-immigrant sentiment was at its most vicious, foreign-stock men and women who held any hope of receiving the status of full-fledged Americans were forced to adopt the habits and customs of the dominant white, Anglo-Saxon Protestant group. In revising the recipe for citizenship, diner operators were no doubt assisted by the political rhetoric of World War II and the Cold War, which made a virtue out of ethnic diversity for the first time. Yet, it was down at the level of the diner where abstract rhetoric was tested against the prejudices and parochiality of the real world.

Narrowing the Gap

The postwar diner, with its domesticated environment, its pluralistic cuisine, and its patriotic motifs, marked the cultural distance that upwardly mobile middle-income families had traveled in the postwar years. The diner had come a long way and so had its customers. As a consequence of dramatic changes in diner geography, design, and operation, millions of American families adopted the routine of dining away from home for the first time in their lives. Although the restaurant meal had long been a staple of consumer expenditures among businessmen and upper-income families, it was a new concept for those with modest incomes, especially among those who hailed from immigrant families. Upper-income families continued to spend greater sums on restaurant meals than middle and lower income families. Even at similar income levels, households headed by white-collar breadwinners—managers, professionals, and clerical workers—spent more money on out-of-home food consumption than did wage earners in the 1950s. Yet, the gap was narrowing. Perhaps even more telling were the results of a 1959 survey on American dining habits showing that unlike families at both the higher and lower ends of the socioeconomic spectrum, those in the middle-income brackets wanted to dine out even more often than they customarily did. Middle-income families, it seemed, had developed an insatiable appetite for commercial dining. And at least in the eastern part of the country, the diner was partly responsible for creating this demand.

By domesticating and Americanizing the diner, operators and owners narrowed the chasm in cultural experiences that had once separated blue-collar families from their white-collar counterparts. From the perspective of the diner industry, the collapse of cultural distinctions among people of different class and ethnic backgrounds made it possible to entertain visions of establishing the domesticated diner, with its modernized architecture and pluralistic cuisine, as the quintessential American restaurant, one that was sufficiently flexible to meet the needs of a wide variety of customers. Proprietors correctly anticipated that the changes in layout they had made to attract families also drew a wide range of middle-income patrons who did not dine in family units: women who came in for lunch, teenage boys who brought their dates, and even church choirs that adjourned to the diner after practice. Moreover, there were indications that the domesticated diner supported a certain amount of class mixing. While modern diner-restaurants may have flourished in affluent blue-collar neighborhoods, it was becoming more common to find them in white-collar areas as well, even where there were few families with recent immigrant backgrounds. At the same time, diners located in predominantly working-class suburbs began to enjoy a fair amount of white-collar patronage. According to George Yonko, the revamped Chuck Wagon Diner may have received most of its business from affluent steelworker families, but it also drew customers from the exclusive Morningside district of Gary, which housed many corporate executives. Tony Zappone recalled that in his Cleveland diner, "You could have a fur coat on one hook and a factory worker's cap on another." In the parking lot of the New Ideal Diner, chauffeured limousines supposedly sat side by side with jeeps, hot rods, and station wagons.

Even in factory districts, proprietors who spruced up their appearance and modernized their operation could count on patronage from the swelling ranks of managers, accountants, clerks, and secretaries who worked in manufacturing establishments. In an effort to secure a diverse clientele for his new diner located in an industrial section of Queens, New York, Lenny Danza placed a premium on cleanliness and hired waitresses to serve customers seated at booths. Danza estimated that during the late 1950s, at least 15 percent of his customers consisted of white-collar employees who worked in nearby factories. In a country that celebrated the erosion of class distinctions as a fulfillment of its democratic destiny, the diner's ability to accommodate both blue-collar and white-collar patrons would be no small accomplishment.

A Precarious Balancing Act: Class, Generation, and Racial Segregation in the Diner

Yet class divisions did not entirely dissolve in the diner. Although owners and builders alike may have touted the diner as the epitome of democratic social interaction, they knew that their efforts to "play host to everyone" could easily backfire if they pushed the idea of cultural amalgamation too far. Indeed, they risked the prospect of playing host to no one if they departed too rapidly from the familiar diner concept or if they failed to acknowledge the wide variety of appetites and expectations that customers brought to the diner. As much as owners wanted to reorient their trade toward middle-income families, they were not prepared to abandon the truckers and factory hands who continued to provide a steady stream of revenue in many locations. Nor were they prepared to abandon those customers who felt a certain affinity for the flavor of the old-time workingman's diner.

A small cartoon buried in the back pages of a 1955 trade journal betrayed one of the diner industry's deep, dark secrets. In it, a male customer seated at a counter remarks to the grillman, "I miss my wife's cooking—whenever I can." The men and women who owned and operated diners in the 1950s knew quite well that many of their customers were not looking for the quintessential family experience, but rather, were seeking refuge. Not all customers wanted a wholesome family atmosphere. Blake Ehrlich had eaten at many a run-down hash house with his father in the 1920s, and he admired the new sleek and spacious stainless-steel diners that were popping up across the country in the late 1940s. Yet he was uncomfortable with diners that went too far in trying to appear classy. Upon entering one establishment, he was relieved to find a counterman tossing clean bowls through the air to a coworker for stacking, yelling "touchdown" after every pass. That was the sort of behavior he expected to find in a diner, and that was the sort of behavior that kept him coming back. And these were the sorts of expectations that continually pulled diner operators back to traditional formulas.

The diner industry may have predicated its expansion strategy on the narrowing earnings gap between blue-collar and white-collar workers, but there was no getting around the fact that people on the upper end of the statistical middle majority had a lot more money to spend than those on the lower end. Even at the height of postwar prosperity, when the economy hummed along at full employment, there were many families in the middle-income range, especially those saddled with heavy car and house payments, who struggled to get by. Fancier diners meant higher prices, which was all well and good if they translated into higher profits. But proprietors who upgraded their diners always ran the risk of pushing customers beyond their financial limits and thus losing a significant share of regular revenue.

The issue of menu prices came to a head in the debate over the nickel cup of coffee. Perhaps no single menu item was more closely linked in the popular mind to the diner than the venerable cup of java. According to a 1949 survey, over 90 percent of all diner checks included coffee. The beverage was especially popular among truck drivers, some of whom spent hours at the counter nursing one or two cups. Since the 1930s, the five-cent cup of coffee had been a diner tradition. By the late 1940s, however, many operators calculated that five cents no longer covered their costs. In order to make the transition to the ten-cent cup of coffee as painless as possible, the operators of the Lackawanna Diner and the University Grill in Morristown, New Jersey, urged their local competitors to raise prices simultaneously. They didn't get very far. As the owner of the Morristown Diner explained, many patrons in his establishment were clerks at local retail stores and simply could not afford the new price. Fearful of losing their business, he refused to budge on the five-cent tradition. Through the 1950s, many like-minded operators preferred to sell coffee at a loss in deference to their poorer customers.

On some occasions, customer resistance prevented proprietors from dismantling specific features of the workingman's diner. When Harry Zelin opened his sixth Market Diner on the West Side of Manhattan in 1958, he wanted an up-to-date operation. So he dispensed with the traditional overhead sign boards and relied exclusively on individualized menus. But the longshoremen and truckers who frequented the establishment demanded that Zelin install the old-fashioned menu boards so the place "would be more like a diner." Afraid of losing a significant portion of his business, Zelin complied. Even as the diner industry tried to construct a more virtuous image around the customer who, as one manufacturer put it, "wants no liquor but wants quick meals in a clean place," particular circumstances often dictated less wholesome types of service. As a concession to the aircraft workers who frequented their Long Island diner, Phil and Joe Roy added bottled beer to their menu to go along with their kiddie menus and soda fountain service.

Another vestige of the workingman's diner that survived into the 1950s, largely due to the preferences of factory workers and truckers, was the counter. While counter space was incrementally sacrificed for more comfortable booth and table seating over the course of the 1950s—in some diners it was not uncommon for counters to extend only half the length of the unit—no manufacturer eliminated the counter and stool arrangement entirely. By retaining the counter, even in a truncated form, proprietors preserved a male domain within the diner. While booth seating, lighter fares, and redecorated interiors increased female patronage substantially, with some proprietors reporting nearly even numbers of women and men, male customers monopolized the counter stools. As the preferred point of congregation among truckers and solitary workers, the counter remained the one place in the diner where one could still engage in coarse banter and argue about an upcoming prize fight. For women experiencing the diner for the first time, it was not just the discomfort of the stools that made the counter forbidding. Kathy Corbett recalled her visits to the Westfield Diner in the late 1940s as an act of rebellion against her status-conscious high school friends and parents. Yet although Corbett had no trouble ordering a tuna fish sandwich and a cup of black coffee from the comfort and safety of a booth, she was too intimidated by the rough workers to take a seat at the counter.

Erecting an invisible barrier between the counter and the booths was one way to handle customer diversity. Indeed, the policy of spatial segregation proved an effective way of diffusing all sorts of social tensions. Compartmentalizing the diner into different sections and rooms allowed for customers to use the diner in a variety of different ways. More importantly, it kept people who had no desire to associate with one another at a distance. If the diner achieved a diverse following, it was as much the result of proprietors' efforts to keep people apart as to mix them together.

Consider the ways that some proprietors handled the problem of disruptive teenagers. The teenage market was a lucrative one and the installation of jukeboxes and soda fountains testified to proprietors' interest in capturing it. But a national preoccupation with juvenile delinquency, fueled by the "threatening" music of Little Richard and Elvis Presley and the defiant images of James Dean and Marlon Brando, raised the possibility that in opening their doors to local rebels without a cause, diner proprietors might merely be trading a disreputable working-class reputation for one that was equally undesirable. Hence, some proprietors sequestered youths in separate dining sections. Gaston Wiley set up a small patio behind his McAllen, Texas, diner, dubbed it "teen town," and reserved it for the use of young adults during after-school hours. Eugene Dusenberry's variation was a teenager impoundment on the roof of his building. To the relief of many diner owners, the potential clash of generational cultures was averted by conflicting schedules. Teenagers tended to use diners late at night or just after school, times when families were unlikely to stop in for dinner. Barry Levinson, who wrote and directed the film *Diner*, based on his adolescent experiences in Baltimore, remembered how he and his high school friends used the Hilltop Diner as a late-night rendezvous after they had dropped off their dates for the evening. This routine indicates both the time-specific use of diners by certain types of customers and the persistence through the 1950s of the notion among some consumers that the diner was a predominantly male and often unsavory social space.

The clock also turned out to be a convenient tool for segregating diner patrons by class as well as age. At noon and then again at midnight, workers from the Curtiss Wright plant in Lodi, New Jersey, streamed into Doyle's Diner for quick lunches. In between, however, the Doyles sold meals to families from the surrounding neighborhood. Likewise, when Eunice Fisher, a waitress at the Beach Haven Diner on the Jersey shore, arrived for work at 5 A.M., the place swarmed with commercial fishermen wolfing down quick breakfasts before heading out to sea. Only much later in the morning did vacationers from New York and Philadelphia arrive for their morning meal. Yet even this split schedule did not fully reconcile conflicting class orientations. The crude language and insult trading that formed the basis of Fisher's repartee with the commercial anglers often offended the sensibilities of the middle-class tourists.

Of all the varieties of social friction that vexed diner owners, none was more complicated or explosive than the antagonism between customers who differed according to the color of their skin. Even before his diner opened for business in 1954, John Vonetes had a decision to make about how to handle the touchy matter of race relations. The Lee House Diner was situated on a stretch of highway that connected the town of Petersburg, Virginia, with Fort Lee, a large military installation. Anticipating heavy patronage from servicemen on a limited budget, Vonetes planned his operation around the concept of simple food at reasonable prices. But he also wanted to bolster his business with trade from people who lived in town. He concluded that a "family-style" restaurant would take care of the needs of both types of customer. After a good deal of soul searching and financial calculation, Vonetes concluded that an integrated establishment would not be viable. He assumed that the culinary needs of black and white customers were incompatible, that black patrons would demand dishes such as chitterling pizza and ungarnished fried chicken sandwiches that white customers would find offensive. Moreover, he was convinced that the type of clientele he aimed for simply would not patronize an integrated establishment due to the prevailing social mores. So the Lee House Diner opened as a restaurant for whites only. African-American customers who entered the diner, including military personnel, were shown the door and instructed to leave the premises.

However incomplete the blending of class, generational, and gender cultures was within the 1950s diner, its relatively high level of integration of disparate white socio-economic groups contrasted sharply with the almost universal persistence of racial segregation. A sharp rise in the number of middle-income black consumers posed a conundrum for diner owners. Constituting 11 percent of the nation's total population, African Americans represented a huge consumer market in the 1940s and 1950s—one roughly the same size as Canada in terms of dollar volume. Although the median income of African Americans lagged well below that of whites, the opening of employment opportunities in unionized industrial jobs and white-collar professions pushed ever larger numbers of black households across the threshold of the middle majority market. While the patronage of middle-income black families held out the prospect of additional revenue, in the eyes of diner owners, it also meant trouble. In some cases, waitresses refused to serve black customers. Undoubtedly, some proprietors harbored similar prejudices and were all too willing to turn African Americans away at the door. Yet, their most pressing concern, at least judging from comments made in public forums, was the possibility of a hostile reaction from their regular white customers, a consumer version of the real estate phenomenon of white flight. Diner owners feared that increased revenue from black patronage would be offset by an even larger loss of patron-

age from regulars who were not prepared to tolerate racial democracy in the diner.

These fears were not entirely unfounded. The years after
World War II were a time when the nation's racial boundaries
were very much in flux. Whereas white workers who joined industrial unions had recently endorsed the principle of racial equality
in the workplace for the purposes of forging a united front against
corporate management, their disposition became more selfish
when it came to sharing private consumer privileges. Indeed, to
the extent that status rested upon activities and practices performed outside work, upwardly mobile whites perceived the presence of blacks in their residential neighborhoods, schools, stores,
and diners as a threat to their recently won social gains. Sociological research conducted during the 1950s revealed that outward
expressions of racial prejudice were strongest among groups experiencing rapid mobility, either upward or downward. At a time
when it became more common for blacks and whites to hold
equivalent jobs, the temptation to highlight social distinctions in
the realm of consumption was powerful. For second- and third-
generation Americans anxious to claim the privileges of whiteness, the stakes involved were quite high.

It bears remembering that before World War II, immigrants
from Asia, Latin America, and southeastern Europe were not considered fully white. Yet, by constructing home lives that were
barely distinguishable from the blond, fair-skinned families on
television shows and advertisements, second- and third-generation
Americans of southern and eastern European ancestry climbed
America's racial hierarchy and became more "white." Jews, once
barred from elite residential subdivisions and exclusive country
clubs along with Asians, Mexicans, and African Americans, may
have been the greatest beneficiaries or this racial revision. In most
parts of the country by the 1960s, Jews were seen less as a distinct
race than as yet another white ethnic group in the nation's pluralist
mosaic.

Race could only retain its effectiveness as a social sorting device, however, as long as certain groups were permanently relegated to the "nonwhite" category. Those who had most recently attained white status were reluctant to jeopardize their gains by extending those privileges to other minority groups. Thus, Italians, Jews, Greeks, Irish, Hungarians, and Poles eagerly embraced a more simplified meaning of race based exclusively on skin color so that they could conveniently distinguish racial minorities such as Mexicans, Chinese, and African Americans from culturally based ethnic groups like themselves. In diners and other places where upwardly mobile Americans of recent European extraction sought to celebrate and announce their arrival in the white middle class, this new color line would be vigorously enforced.

In the chummy atmosphere of the diner, customers were not shy about notifying proprietors of their unwillingness to tolerate racial integration. John Vonetes heard plenty of commentary, usually phrased euphemistically, about how people would no longer "come up" from the community if the Lee House Diner ever became integrated. Some customers were blunter. When one truck driver was asked by a reporter what he would do if Maryland diners along Route 40 began to serve black customers, he quipped, "I'd pack a box lunch, that's what I'd do."

How then to reconcile the desire for African-American dollars with the intense hostility toward interracial mingling from regular white customers? In one form or another, the answer involved the physical separation of black and white customers. This was more easily achieved in southern states, where Jim Crow practices were underpinned by both law and custom. Southern blacks as well as those from elsewhere who made pilgrimages to the South to visit friends and relatives, were routinely denied table service but allowed to order food to take away with them. Some diner operators offered African-American travelers the humiliating option of ordering food to go from a side door or rear entrance. African Americans passing through Woodstock, Virginia, could get served inside the

At Lucy's Diner (since renamed the Broadway Diner) in Columbia, Mo.,
African-American patrons were required to order and receive food from the
take-out window shown at the right.

Blue Star Diner but only at a small table in the kitchen. The Johns-
Mansville Diner in Jarratt, Virginia, was one of the few that allowed
black customers to eat inside. In the heart of Jim Crow territory, the
Johns-Mansville Corporation purchased a diner in 1943 to feed its
employees. Because a substantial number of them were black, and
because the dining car was the only facility available to workers,
black employees were admitted inside the diner, but only as long as
they sat in a rear section reserved for their use.

Segregated service was by no means exclusive to diners located in
the Deep South. Luncheonettes, coffee shops, and diners in the
Middle Atlantic and midwestern states resorted to many of the same
practices that prevailed in the old Confederacy. Eddie Warner, for
instance, ran a chain of diners in suburban Maryland on the outskirts

of Washington, D.C. Warner instructed his employees to notify black patrons that they could not be served inside the diner, but that take-out service was available. Warner made no exception for the African-American cooks and dishwashers he hired periodically. Company policy dictated that they take their meals alone in the back kitchen. At the Meadowbrook Diner in Indianapolis, African Americans who wished to purchase food were required to place their orders through a separate back door. In other midwestern and northeastern cities, lunch-counter proprietors were not beyond serving spoiled food, overcharging, or offering discourteous service in order to discourage black patronage inside the restaurant.

In most metropolitan areas, however, even in those parts of the country where overt racial discrimination was not practiced, residential segregation eventually freed diner owners from the dilemma of whether to serve black customers and effectively preserved diners as white institutions. Through the 1950s, suburbanization was primarily a white phenomenon; hence, as diners migrated to the outskirts of cities, their owners were not required to formulate any official policy of discrimination. And although prosperous African Americans established beachheads in certain suburban communities such as Jamaica, Queens, on the outskirts of New York City, and the Roxbury district of Boston, diners rarely found their way to such neighborhoods, perhaps because proprietors deliberately avoided locations where they were likely to confront the volatile issue of racial mixing. Moreover, African Americans were well aware that they were not welcome in diners located in white residential suburbs. When the owners of the Club Car Diner opened a new establishment on one of Pittsburgh's suburban thoroughfares, they found little reason to institute any formal segregation policy because, as one of the managers put it, "blacks would have been reluctant to walk into a place like that." Likewise, the all-white clientele at the Chuck Wagon Diner in Gary was less a product of formal segregation than the widespread reputation that the neighborhood had as being off-limits to African Americans.

Few diners were moved to change their policies by the rising tide of social protest in the 1950s and early 1960s, even though the integration of restaurants had been a long-standing goal of the postwar civil rights movement. Indeed, direct-action protests against segregated restaurants predated the Montgomery Bus Boycott of 1955, which is often viewed as the movement's first act, by almost ten years. During the late 1940s, and increasingly in the 1950s, civil rights organizations such as the Congress of Racial Equality (CORE) staged demonstrations outside segregated restaurants in selected parts of the country and tested the resolve of culpable restaurant owners by sending interracial parties inside to dine. In general, the victories won through the use of these tactics came slowly. Yet by the end of the 1950s, CORE and other local civil rights organizations could cite significant progress in cities like St. Louis, Washington, D.C., and Baltimore. Few diners were integrated by these campaigns, however, largely because CORE ignored them. Striving to gain maximum effect and publicity for their efforts, early civil rights activists tended to target restaurants that were either located in downtown districts or associated with national chains. Even when a more aggressive and effective student sit-in movement burst on the national scene in the early 1960s, activists kept the focus on downtown lunch counters run by chain stores like Woolworth's and Kress's. The reasoning behind their choice of targets was sound. Downtown establishments, if integrated, were more likely to be patronized by African Americans, who lived and worked nearby, than were diner-type establishments located in white residential neighborhoods. Moreover, restaurants associated with national chains were vulnerable to consumer boycotts from sympathetic consumers in more progressive parts of the country. Consumer boycotts against Woolworth's in northern states, for example, were instrumental in getting the company to capitulate to sit-in protesters south of the Mason-Dixon line.

In instances where civil rights activists aimed their organizational resources at diners, the results were mixed. In 1962, about half a dozen prefabricated diners came under close scrutiny in CORE's campaign to desegregate restaurants and bars along Highway 40 in northern Maryland. Although some of these diner owners, fearful of adverse publicity, volunteered to adopt an open-door policy toward racial minorities, others objected to what they called "outside interference" and defended their constitutional right to deny service to whomever they wished. Interracial groups dispatched to "test" the diners in the latter category were greeted with a stern reading of Maryland's trespassing law and asked to leave the premises. To its dismay, CORE discovered that even some of the diner owners who had pledged their support for racial integration in the press, changed their minds the moment the first African American walked through their front door.

Through the 1950s, and in many places into the early 1960s, then, African-American families who wanted to partake in the adventure of commercial dining had little choice but to patronize local restaurants that bore little resemblance to the domesticated diner. People in the diner business wanted no part of the inner-city African-American market. John Vonetes probably spoke for many other diner owners when he insisted that African Americans would not support a modern family style diner. Black entrepreneurs eager to serve their own communities, on the other hand, did not buy prefabricated diners because they had no background in the business and no connections to the people who manufactured them. Instead, they placed sandwich shops, snack shacks, and small cafes behind unassuming storefronts and in crudely constructed freestanding buildings. The difficulty of securing credit for businesses in minority neighborhoods meant that many of these ventures were severely undercapitalized. Outside observers characterized them as dingy and dull. Because many of these minority-owned restaurants operated on slim profit margins, proprietors frequently developed adjunct businesses on the premises. On the South Side of Chicago, for instance, one restaurateur supplemented his food service with a coal-hauling operation while a rival proprietor ran an exterminating service in conjunction with his sandwich shop. Another point of departure from diners was cuisine. Some menu items overlapped; hamburgers, frankfurters, and fountain drinks were ubiquitous, for example. Yet the restaurants that lined the major commercial streets of Harlem, Chicago's South Side, St. Louis's North Side, and Cincinnati's West End also featured dishes rarely found on diner menus, such as barbecued ribs and pig ears. African-American consumers certainly enjoyed a variety of dining options in their neighborhoods, yet few of the establishments they had to choose from displayed the glitzy exteriors, domesticated interiors, or elaborate menus that were so integral to the diner's ability to project social success.

The Diner in Decline

By the time George Yonko retired from the diner business in 1965, the industry was in the throes of a decline. The explosion of fast-food outlets and chain restaurants across the metropolitan landscape soon penetrated suburban markets everywhere and cut deeply into the diner's trade. Diner proprietors complained of patronage lost to McDonald's, Burger King, Kentucky Fried Chicken, Howard Johnson's, and Bob's Big Boy. The desertion of younger customers proved particularly damaging. The diner had been transformed into a safe and inviting middle-class institution, but in straying from its traditional social niche it also became more vulnerable to competition. As restaurants with diverse regional and class lineages converged on the middle-income family market, a variety of commercial dining formulas and styles were synthesized into a uniform standard. This was not good news for the diner industry; as the diner lost its distinctiveness it also lost its competitive edge.

By the 1960s, a plethora of restaurant chains and independent family-style restaurants descended on the middle-majority market, from the West Coast to the East Coast, each operating under the same basic formula: casual atmosphere, reasonable prices, and wholesome domesticity. Most followed the example of the diner in offering customers a choice of counter seating, booth seating, and table service. Drive-ins complemented their carhop service with indoor seating. Formal full-service restaurants abandoned rigid formalities and turned casual, perhaps even adding a counter for solitary patrons. Whether one ate lunch at Howard Johnson's, Denny's, Steak 'n' Shake, or the Chuck Wagon Diner, the dining experience was comparable in terms of menus, prices, and decor.

While the chain restaurants shared many characteristics with the modern suburban diner, and while those similarities intensified as they adopted comparable marketing strategies, they remained products of very different social backgrounds. None carried the diner's burden of trying to shed an urban industrial heritage. As a result, they had an edge over the diner in attracting members of the established middle class as well as upwardly mobile working-class patrons who were intent on leaving behind their humble origins.

The first of the big chains, Harvey House, originated as a catering service for long-distance passengers at railroad depots. With a requirement that male customers attire themselves in dinner jackets, Harvey House cultivated an aura of upper-class respectability that lingered even after it relaxed its dress code in the 1930s. In the face of declining railroad ridership in the 1950s, the Fred Harvey Company took its tradition of "fine dining" to the nation's new interstate highways, opening a series of "oases" along the newly constructed Illinois tollway. In pursuing the interstate highway trade, it followed a strategy that had been pioneered by a much younger company, Howard Johnson's. In contrast to the Fred Harvey Company, Howard Johnson's gained its reputation as a purveyor of high-butterfat-content ice cream at New England seaside resorts during the 1920s and 1930s before branching out to key locations along the Pennsylvania Turnpike in 1940. The company's highway strategy, which later expanded to include toll roads in Massachusetts, New Jersey, Ohio, Oklahoma, and several other states, coincided with a decision to fuse its soda fountain and ice cream operation with full menu service. It was also at this juncture that the restaurant chain assumed its distinctive appearance. Decorated in the style of a middle-class living room, the restaurant's interior design featured knotty-pine wall paneling, window curtains, and small table lamps. A neo-colonial exterior paid homage to the nation's pre-Revolutionary heritage; its featured menu items—hot dogs and ice cream—were quintessentially American. With its uniformed waitresses, extensive soda fountain service, and unique architecture, Howard Johnson's grew to become a familiar beacon to middle-class families on the road who wanted simple food in a homey yet dignified atmosphere.

Then there were the California coffee shops, popularized on the West Coast in the 1950s before spreading eastward. With their flamboyant space-age architecture—panoramic windows, angled canopies, and zigzagging parapets—they spoke not only to a vision of technological progress but to a culture steeped in excess as reflected in their heavily stylized interiors and exteriors. If they resembled the Space Age diners of the East Coast it is because they courted an audience with similar aspirations of mobility. Unlike the diner, however, the California coffee shop was thoroughly suburban in its origins. Sambo's and Denny's, two of the most popular restaurants of this variety, shared similar backgrounds. Although both aimed explicitly for an affluent, blue-collar clientele, their first units opened in suburban settings, Denny's in the mass-produced suburb of Lakewood, about thirty miles south of Los Angeles, and Sambo's on the Santa Barbara beachfront. Initially Denny's specialized in doughnuts while Sambo's built its reputation on pancakes. Both businesses, however, expanded to twenty-four-hour service and full lunch and dinner menus as they built up their chain operations, first in California and by the 1960s, across the country.

The diner industry responded to the competition by incorporating elements of these other eateries into their own designs. In 1955, the Kullman Dining Car Company announced "the newest idea since diners began . . . the Kullman Drive-In Diner," a unit that combined counter seating, table service, and carhop stations. At the same time, interior design moved further toward the standards established by the middle-class family restaurant chains. By the end of the decade, builders were finishing their dining room annexes with knotty-pine wall paneling that bore a striking resemblance to a Howard Johnson's interior. Reflecting the near obliteration of distinctions among the various eateries and the diner's particular trajectory, the industry's trade journal changed its name from *The Diner*, to *Diner, Drive-In, and Restaurant* in 1954.

Imitation may have staved off the diner's demise temporarily. At first, people who had grown up with the working-class diner were intimidated by the newer restaurants where they were unsure of how to dress or what codes of conduct were acceptable. Pat Fodero, a major postwar dining-car builder, recalled that one of his favorite strategies in the 1950s was placing a diner off the highway next to a Howard Johnson's. Fodero reasoned that billboards painted by the national chain would lure motorists off the highway and then confronted with a choice, many would select the diner, a restaurant type to which they were more accustomed. As people became familiar with the national chains—a process that was propelled by national advertising campaigns and exclusive contracts for superhighway food service—Fodero's strategy failed; more people began to choose Howard Johnson's and eventually McDonald's.

The behemoth of the fast-food industry, McDonald's, was born in rather unremarkable circumstances. A San Bernadino drive-in owned by two brothers, Maurice and Richard McDonald, McDonald's was one among many drive-ins that catered to the trend-setting motorists of southern California. Its menu was extremely limited: hamburgers, french fries, milk shakes, and soda. The business was also extremely successful. The McDonald brothers prided themselves on their ability to serve large numbers of customers quickly. By eliminating carhops in favor of a self-service walk-up system in 1948, they were able to churn out hundreds of 15-cent hamburgers at a time. Despite their huge popularity on the remote outskirts of Los Angeles, in 1955 there was no reason to think that the enterprise had a brighter or dimmer future than any of its competitors.

That was the year that Ray Kroc came on board. Kroc was in the business of selling milk-shake mixers, and the McDonald brothers were among his best customers. When he visited their small San Bernadino hamburger stand, he was astounded at the crowds that waited on line for the mass-produced burgers. Kroc signed on with the company as its national franchising agent. His job was to sell the McDonald's system to investors, each of whom would open and operate his or her own McDonald's hamburger stand according to a strict set of rules and regulations. Kroc was a relentless promoter and a tireless worker. Six years later, when Kroc bought out the McDonald brothers for $2.7 billion in 1961, he was responsible for adding over 250 units to what had become a truly national chain.

What made McDonald's a household name and a threat to diner owners everywhere was a prescient marketing strategy built around suburbs and children. Kroc gave simple marching orders to his real estate scouts: "Look for schools, church steeples, and new houses." In contrast to diners that tended to cluster in transitional suburban neighborhoods, McDonald's franchises were more likely to appear on undeveloped land on the very fringes of urban settlement, as much in anticipation of suburban growth as in response to it. Moreover, these locations, what one McDonald's executive referred to as "tricycle and bicycle neighborhoods," tended to attract families with above-average incomes and very young children, precisely the clientele that Kroc wanted.

McDonald's, Downey, Calif. This 1953 vintage McDonald's walk-up was the third unit built by the company.

In contrast to diner owners who devised kiddie menus and distributed toys to secure the loyalty of children, McDonald's used national advertising. A cheerful clown named Ronald McDonald dominated television advertisements for the chain. Ronald assumed the role of corporate spokesperson, making public appearances throughout the country and participating in parades and shows. Corporate executives crowed that as a result of the media saturation, Ronald McDonald had attained a higher name recognition among American children than any other public figure save for Santa Claus. The assertion was dubious but without question, as more and more children pleaded with their parents to take them to the "place with the clown," the company's growth rate reached astounding levels. By 1970, the McDonald's empire consisted of 1,500 franchised outlets. In terms of sales volume and reputation, McDonald's had established itself as the undisputed leader of the fast food industry.

Indeed, McDonald's set a standard for fast food that was widely emulated. Its most successful competitors followed the same basic formula with only slight variations in decor and food preparation. Keith Cramer and Matthew Burns opened their first Insta-Burger King in 1954 shortly after visiting the McDonald brothers' stand in San Bernadino. With a limited menu and a self-service ordering system, the Jacksonville, Florida, restaurant was a virtual carbon copy of the McDonald's operation. There were only two noticeable differences: Burger King broiled, rather than grilled, their hamburgers, and it charged three cents more per sandwich.

Most of the fast-food imitators pursued the same customer base as did McDonald's. Some, like McDonald's, originated as drive-ins and thus were already entrenched in places where people relied heavily on automobile transportation, namely, the suburbs. Although none was as effective as McDonald's in winning the loyalty of children, their marketing strategies placed a heavy emphasis on families. During the late 1950s, Burger King devoted most of its advertising budget to the sponsorship of the *Jim Dooley Show*, a children's television program. On each episode, a character named Mr. Moke made a spectacle of himself by devouring a Burger King Whopper, much to the delight of the young live audience.

Having secured a beachhead in the far-flung suburbs, the fast-food franchises, California coffee shops, and family restaurant chains began to make inroads into diner territory—the transitional neighborhoods closer to the urban core and eventually inner-city neighborhoods. What had loomed as a dark cloud on the horizon for diner owners in the 1950s became a threat to their very survival in the 1960s.

Certainly, one factor that gave the national chains a critical edge over the diner was the franchising system. Franchising supplied a mechanism for extraordinarily rapid cloning of successful operations. Because the franchisee supplied the funds for opening new units, the system excelled in raising expansion capital. Companies such as McDonald's and Howard Johnson's underwrote their growth through hundreds of separate bank deals, thereby dispersing financial risk among hundreds of individuals. The growth rates of franchised chains could assume astronomical proportions. McDonald's, which oversaw 1,600 units in 1972, was the largest of the fast-food hamburger chains, but Burger Chef, established in 1958 as a carbon copy of McDonald's and bought out by Hardee's in 1982, trailed fairly close behind with 1,200 outlets while Burger King boasted no less than 800. The number of retail outlets franchised by these three companies alone roughly equaled the total number of diners in operation at the time. In less than twenty-five years, then, fast-food hamburger chains were born, grew, and came to outnumber the venerable diner. When one takes into account the full range of franchise chains, hamburger chains, family-style coffee shops like Denny's and Sambo's, and the growing number of fast-food firms that specialized in pizza, chicken, and tacos in the 1970s, the odds against the diner's survival appeared grim.

The franchising system, in addition to facilitating the rapid replication of individual units, also allowed the chain restaurants to amass huge budgets for national advertising. As individual, independent, and small-volume enterprises, diner owners could only afford to publicize their businesses through inexpensive local media. The vast majority of diner owners did no advertising at all. Those who did generally relied on highway billboards, hand-distributed fliers, or modest blurbs in local newspapers. Radio advertising was unusual; television was out of the question due to its high cost. The national chains, on the other hand, could afford to be more ambitious. Pooling their resources through an advertising fee levied on each franchisee, the chains raised enough revenue to saturate local and national media with publicity. Most of the larger chains devoted a substantial portion of their marketing budgets to network television. By the early 1970s, for example, McDonald's was spending more than $20 million annually on the production of television commercials.

Most importantly, franchising ensured a degree of reliability and consistency that eluded the diner industry. As prefabricated structures, diners were standardized to a certain extent. They were certainly the defining mass-produced restaurants of their era, and much of their popularity can be attributed to the mental associations that issued forth from a distinctive architectural design. The motorist who passed a stainless-steel diner along the roadside had a fair notion of what he or she would find on the inside: what kind of food, what kind of seating arrangements, what kind of prices, and what kind of clientele. But the motorist who passed a Howard Johnson's or a McDonald's had an even clearer idea and ran a smaller risk of being unpleasantly surprised by the food, service, or premises. For in addition to standardizing the architecture of their restaurants, the franchised chains imposed uniformity on their menus, recipes, and prices. McDonald's even went so far as to require all franchisees to attend its training center, Hamburger University, for instruction on scraping grills, blanching french fries, and mixing milk shakes.

The diner industry simply had no means of imposing that level of conformity on its operators. Builders might try to impress upon their clients the benefits of running a wholesome establishment, and trade journals might hold up countless examples of diners that became more profitable after revamping their businesses, but in the end it was up to each individual operator whether or not to follow such advice. Industry leaders worried, with good reason, that all the hard-won popular approbation associated with the newly domesticated diner would be undermined by the anomalous and aberrant greasy spoon, that all the goodwill generated by progressive diner owners would be swept away by the occasional sloppy operator who refused to clean toilets on a regular basis, allowed cockroaches to crawl across the counter, and insisted on hiring gruff and sullen countermen to cook and serve food. There were just enough sloppy operators out there to give such fears credence.

While the precise impact of the national chains varied from one locality to another, many diner operators could date the decline of their businesses to the opening of a nearby Burger King, Denny's, or Burger Chef. For the Tastee Diner in Laurel, Maryland, the culprits were Denny's and Big Boy. For Dean's Diner in Blairsville, Pennsylvania, it was Burger King. Bill Komondorea recalled how high school students stopped patronizing his diner almost immediately after McDonald's opened its first restaurant in Newburgh, New York, even though the franchise was located on the other side of town, several miles away.

In response to the fast-food onslaught, some diner owners simply jumped ship. Jim Aldom owned the only diner in Salem, Ohio, during the 1950s. Hoping to expand his business opportunities in the early 1960s, Aldom purchased a Burger Chef franchise and placed the fast-food outlet in direct competition with his diner. The Burger Chef did so well that over the next few years he signed contracts for several more franchises and sprinkled southeastern Ohio with Burger Chef outlets. Meanwhile, Aldom neglected his diner, turning over management responsibilities to his employees. The diner's business deteriorated badly, and eventually Aldom had it carted away to another Ohio town for a fresh start under new ownership.

Other diner owners struggled to survive where they were, but, in general, the results were disappointing. The most successful were those who distinguished themselves from the upstart chains by emphasizing home cooking, wide menu choices, and ever more flamboyant decor. Especially in the New York City and Philadelphia regions, diner builders accommodated proprietors with architecturally distinctive buildings that featured Greco-Roman statuary, ornate fountains, and massive glass chandeliers. Some owners who could not afford such lavish improvements tried to modernize their appearance by covering their stainless steel exteriors in a veneer of brick. While these strategies paid dividends in some instances, the overall trend for the industry was disheartening. Thousands of diners went belly up during the 1960s and 1970s due

Sales brochure, Kullman Diners, circa 1995. To distinguish themselves from chain restaurants, diners built in the 1970s and thereafter adopted more flamboyant interior designs.

to the competition from national chains. Some were gutted and re-fashioned for other purposes. A Staten Island diner was converted into a bank. A New Jersey diner became a record store. Others simply rusted and rotted by the side of the road. Diner manufacturers suffered a similar fate. With production down to only a handful of diners annually, most of the major postwar diner builders had gone out of business by the 1970s.

Ironically, by narrowing the cultural distance between blue-collar and white-collar dining milieus, diners paved the way for the ulti-

mate triumph of the national chains. Franchised formulas that placed
a premium on fast service, rock-bottom prices, informality, and attention to the needs of families enabled the fast-food chains to replicate much of what diners offered but with even greater consistency
and without any unsavory traces of a working-class lineage. Standardizing food and service in addition to architecture, they offered
an experience that was acceptable and familiar to patrons of diverse
class backgrounds and, above all, identical everywhere from Maine
to California. By introducing a large segment of the market to this
very type of consumer experience after the war, diner owners and
builders sowed the seeds of their own demise twenty years later.

Diners, Democracy, and the Persistence of Social Division

The fact that diners entered a period of prolonged decline after
1960 in no way diminishes their historical significance. For many
Americans, diners represented a link between ethnic neighborhood saloons and franchised chain restaurants. Diners helped millions of Americans translate material prosperity into activities that
made life easier, brought small pleasures, and affirmed some measure of social success. In guiding upwardly mobile Americans into
a world of mass consumption, diners encouraged them to adopt
new social rituals and new standards for social conduct. Indeed, in
the drive to capture the widest possible market, they challenged
Americans from all walks of life to deny the relevance of class.

This challenge was met with only partial success. Diner builders
and owners invoked the concept of public domesticity to draw
middle-income people from various backgrounds and with various
occupations out of their homes at mealtimes and congregate in
one common dining space. Although affluent blue-collar workers
and young white-collar families with eastern European surnames

may have approached middle-class standards of domesticity in the diner, they did not meld harmoniously into an undifferentiated middle class. The invisible barrier between the counter and booth, the clashes between fishermen and tourists, and the distinction between diners that served coffee for a nickel and those that served the same cup for a dime reminded patrons that class mattered. The domesticated postwar diner succeeded by presenting a democratic face while still accommodating, even enforcing old prewar social divisions, a practice that was highlighted with insidious clarity every time a black patron was turned away at the door. The ultimate triumph of the national chains was due not to their ability to resolve these social tensions but rather to their ability to finesse them even further. Even if fast-food outlets and family restaurant chains received patronage from a wide variety of classes, a large gulf separated the businessman who stopped in to McDonald's for a quick lunch from the family that ate Sunday dinner there. Despite rhetorical commitments to equality, family restaurant chains continued to privilege their white consumers in subtle and sometimes not-so-subtle ways. Until it folded in 1982, Sambo's clung stubbornly to a name that offended many African Americans on account of its obvious reference to the unflattering fictional character of children's stories, "Little Black Sambo." In the 1990s, the highly successful coffee shop chain of Denny's, faced charges of blatant discrimination against African-American customers.

The diner was only one among many institutions that guided upwardly mobile Americans into the unsettling and tantalizing world of consumer affluence after World War II. A wide range of retailers and manufacturers who before the war had developed commodities for a working-class clientele attempted to broaden their market after World War II by pitching their product to the new and vast middle majority. But there were unforeseen consequences, some of which threatened to explode a theoretically homogeneous mass market into fragments. The attempt to forge a unified market around the ideal of the classless nuclear family brought new social tensions to the surface, particularly those associated with gender and generation. The problem of meeting evolving standards of domestic behavior encountered by diner proprietors proved to be equally vexing to one of the most successful postwar consumer venues to make the transition from working-class diversion to middle-majority institution, the bowling alley.

2

Bowling Alleys

BILL SLOCUM, an old-time newspaper reporter, was taken aback by the swanky scene laid before him at the grand opening of Gil Hodges Lanes in Brooklyn. It was the winter of 1961, and it had been twenty years since Slocum had last set foot in a bowling establishment. To his dismay, he encountered none of the shady characters or illicit activities he had come to expect. Searching for the customary back room where local bookmakers posted winning horses, Slocum stumbled upon a play room where parents could deposit their children while they bowled. As far as he could tell, there were no scratch sheets or pornographic materials being passed from one person to another. When several police officers entered the premises to take a look around, Slocum was surprised and a bit chagrined that nobody bolted suddenly for the back door. Even the alleys themselves had changed; mechanized equipment now set pins, returned balls, and kept score. In Slocum's view, these new contraptions seemed to take the spontaneity out of the game and, more importantly, made it that much harder for him to cheat his opponents.

While the clean and modern bowling alley of the 1960s disappointed Slocum and a few grizzled veterans of the game, its sanitation was largely responsible for the popular resurgence of the sport. America fell in love with bowling after World War II. A 1946 study counted the number of bowlers at somewhere between 10 and 15 million, a higher figure than for any other competitive sport. Less than twenty years later, in 1964, the number of bowlers had more than doubled, to 39 million. More important than the sheer increase in the number of bowlers were the changing demographics of the sport. What had once been a men's activity was now pursued almost equally by male and female participants, including a large number of young bowlers. And what had once been a sport dominated by working-class people of modest means had attained significant popularity across occupational categories and income levels.

In many ways the transformation of the bowling alley paralleled the postwar transformation of the diner. Both the diner and bowling trades sought to rehabilitate their images and broaden their constituencies by conforming to emergent standards of domesticity and appealing to the new "middle majority." Like the diner, the bowling alley entered the postwar era with a rather seedy reputation. In the popular mind, it was associated with dreary basement dives where the poor and shiftless congregated to drink beer, spit tobacco, and make wagers on their bowling scores. But in contrast to the diner's transformation, which was effected by a number of culinary and design changes, the domestication of the bowling alley can be traced almost exclusively to a singular technological innovation, the invention of the automatic pinsetting machine. By eliminating the need for surly and reprobate young men manually restoring pins in the pits, the mechanical pinsetter gave proprietors an opportunity to reorient their appeal to women and children in spectacular new bowling centers that people in the industry referred to as "the people's country clubs."

The tricky part was finding a formula that would accommodate the conflicting desires of men, women, and children without destroying the basic integrity of the family. Bowling alley proprietors recognized that what compelled participation in the world of consumer abundance was the promise of liberation, not only from the agony and drudgery of hand-to-mouth existence, but from the confining social relationships of the past. In their promotion of separate women's leagues and children's leagues, they played relentlessly on the theme of liberation. At the same time, however, proprietors addressed fears of social instability by devising new methods of integrating Americans into family and community life. To reassure parents who worried that too much free time and a little pocket change would turn their children into juvenile delinquents, bowling alleys developed youth bowling programs that instructed youth in the principles of good behavior and responsible citizenship. Responding to fears that consumer abundance would distract women from their domestic obligations, bowling alleys provided baby-sitting services, installed laundry facilities, and sponsored shopping expeditions for busy mothers. If the supposed racial purity of white families was threatened by a widening circle of social contacts outside the home, bowling alleys would enforce a policy of racial segregation. Most importantly, the modern automated bowling center assured its customers that family fun, as experienced through mixed bowling leagues and tournaments, could serve as the new basis for harmonious household relations.

The cumulative message imparted by these novel services, policies, and promotions was that meaningful and virtuous social relationships could be purchased. In the lavish bowling palaces that appeared in suburban shopping centers across America in the 1950s, newly affluent consumers could enjoy the good life, establish connections to their new suburban communities, and above all else, nurture families that were both wholesome and cohesive.

The Bowling Alley's Humble Origins: Tenpins and Saloon Culture

The postwar bowling alley's origins lay in the saloon and its male, working-class, immigrant culture. The game itself had long been associated with foreigners and their offspring. During the Middle Ages, Germans perfected the sport of kegling, in which contestants tossed round stones at anywhere from three to nine standing clubs. Travelers spread the ninepin version of the game to the Netherlands, Spain, and England, where it flourished among the very wealthy. Although information on the history of bowling in America prior to the eighteenth century is sketchy at best, it is certain that variations of the game were imported from England and northern Europe in the earliest days of colonial settlement. We know that colonists in Jamestown, Virginia, whiled away their hours bowling in the streets when they should have been planting corn in the fields. Dutch settlers brought the game of ninepins to New York shortly thereafter—an event that achieved literary renown when Washington Irving described Henry Hudson's ghost crew bowling in the story "Rip Van Winkle."

Subsequent immigrant communities continued to infuse the sport with vitality over the next two centuries as the game evolved from ninepins to tenpins and as play moved from outdoor lawns to indoor alleys. The heavy migration of Germans to American cities in the 1840s and 1850s gave bowling a substantial boost, and for the remainder of the nineteenth century, German Americans were largely responsible for the sport's growth. Turnvereins, gymnastic and cultural centers supported by German immigrants, often housed several bowling lanes. In New York, German Americans organized specialized bowling clubs shortly after the Civil War. These clubs, however, functioned more like fraternal organizations than modern-day bowling leagues. In addition to sponsoring annual bowling tournaments that stretched from fall until spring every year, these clubs arranged picnics, dances, and other social events that promoted cultural cohesion within the German-American community. This is not to imply that German immigrants did not take their bowling seriously. The avid "keglers" within the clubs were instrumental in opening indoor bowling establishments in New York and in organizing the first regional bowling association in the country in 1885, the United Bowling Clubs of New York. It is significant to note that the first two bowling periodicals published in New York City were printed in German.

The sport of bowling enjoyed a certain measure of respectability for much of the nineteenth century. Elite antebellum summer resorts from Saratoga to New Orleans invited guests to cavort on their outdoor bowling lanes. Some of the earliest indoor bowling lanes were to be found in elegant gentlemen's clubs, while private lanes were installed in the homes of some of the nation's wealthiest business magnates during the late nineteenth century, including Jay Gould, R. J. Reynolds, and George Vanderbilt. Bowling was also fashionable among high-society women, who attended matches in their most stylish outfits and occasionally heaved wooden spheres side by side with their gentlemen companions.

In general, however, bowling was developing a reputation as a sport of the masses. While well-heeled aristocrats and business magnates bowled in the privacy of their mansions and social clubs, they rarely frequented the numerous public bowling halls that catered to a very different clientele and fostered a very different kind of social interaction.

In high-society circles during the late nineteenth century, men and women usually bowled in private clubs and residences.

Outside genteel circles, bowling had become intimately associated with the central institution of working-class immigrant social life, the saloon. Bowling had always been associated with merriment and alcohol consumption, but as it became a popular urban sport, saloons were the primary means by which it was introduced to the masses. Indeed, the company that would come to dominate the manufacture of bowling alleys and equipment, the Brunswick Balke Collender Company, developed the trade as a sideline to its major business of selling billiard tables to tavern owners in the 1880s. Many saloon proprietors had installed billiard tables and bowling alleys in their establishments to boost alcohol sales. Two of the first indoor bowling establishments in Chicago were taverns that used bowling as a novelty in the hopes of attracting more customers and getting them to buy more beer than they would otherwise. With every two beers purchased, the patron was entitled to bowl a free game. Moreover, the standard procedure of play was designed to encourage alcohol consumption. Three teams competed on two alleys in a round-robin series, thereby ensuring that

A typical bowling establishment housed in a saloon, Galena, Ill., circa 1900

one team would always be sitting out with nowhere to wait but at the bar. A 1918 survey of Toledo bowling establishments found that almost half were located inside saloons, while most of the others were "strategically located in close proximity to a saloon."

More often than not, the saloon areas set aside for bowling were shabby, dark, and dreary. When Joe Thumm built a pair of lanes in the basement of his lower Manhattan saloon in 1886, he established a precedent. Tavern owners in cities across the country adopted the practice of burying their bowling lanes in dingy underground spaces. Whereas subterranean alleys suffered the worst reputations, those on upper floors were not much better. The Toledo survey, which covered both above-ground and below-ground facilities, found most lacking in basic amenities. Wash-

Basement bowling in LaCrosse, Wis., circa 1890

rooms were inadequate, lighting was poor, and there was little in the way of ventilation, a particularly acute problem given the heavy volume of tobacco smoke. In addition, the Toledo investigators were aghast at the spectacle of public expectoration upon the floor. In most bowling alleys in the early part of the twentieth century, the lanes themselves were of crude construction, built by the hands of individual proprietors. Only as bowling became a more profitable part of their operation and the sport became more standardized around the turn of the century, did saloon owners come to rely more heavily on major manufacturers such as Brunswick to properly outfit their alleys.

Like cockfighting, billiards, dice, and other recreational activities associated with the saloon, bowling became an important element in an emerging masculine bachelor subculture. Bowling halls earned a reputation as places where outcasts and criminals congregated. Gambling was rife; indeed, bookies made regular rounds to saloons with bowling alleys, not only to take bets on the bowlers and billiard players in the house, but to generate action on local horse races and boxing matches. Prior to the use of standardized equipment, betting on bowling could be a precarious enterprise; crafty hustlers were known to use loaded balls and make secret arrangements with the pinsetters to rig the score.

It was these unsanitary conditions and disreputable activities that elicited the condemnation of middle-class reformers in the early part of the twentieth century and kept away patrons who considered themselves respectable citizens. By World War II reform interests had achieved success in securing local legislation designed to prevent the worst sorts of offenses. Virtually all major cities required alley operators to apply for licenses, thereby giving law enforcement agencies an opportunity to weed out shady characters from the business. Many municipalities also had laws on the books restricting hours of operation, banning minors from the premises, and prohibiting gambling in the form of card playing, dice games, or roulette. These laws tended to suffer from selective enforcement, however, and ultimately did little to upgrade the status of the sport.

Within middle-class Protestant reform circles, the poor reputation of urban bowling parlors was exacerbated by an association of the sport with newer immigrant groups from eastern and southern Europe. For recent immigrants, bowling was one of the few commercial amusements that was both affordable and accessible. In Chicago, bowling was especially popular in the Polish community. Fraternal societies such as the Polish National Alliance were active in organizing leagues as a means of perpetuating ethnic solidarity. The Toledo survey cited earlier found that most bowling halls were located in neighborhoods populated by recent eastern European immigrants. In addition, the survey determined that eastern European immigrants dominated the proprietary end of the business. According to D. H. Johnston, a Toledo minister, the "foreign element" in the bowling trade was a major source of corruption among the city's youth. Along with other moral reformers, Johnston urged churches and Christian organizations such as the YMCA to establish alternative bowling centers for Toledo's adolescents.

Cleaning up Its Act:
Early Attempts to
Domesticate the Bowling Alley

The reformist zeal reached its zenith with the imposition of Prohibition in 1920. What should have been the death knell for bowling alleys paradoxically provided for their renaissance. Prohibition severed the connection between bowling alleys and saloons and launched bowling on its slow but steady trajectory toward respectability and wider social appeal. For virtually all alley operators, the immediate effects of the Eighteenth Amendment were sobering. Whether or not alleys were operated in conjunction with saloons, alcohol sales constituted an important part of proprietors' revenue stream. Deprived of liquor sales, many taverns that featured bowling simply went out of business. Some saloon keepers and alley managers, however, kept afloat by converting their businesses into full-fledged bowling parlors. While the total number of bowling venues fell precipitously during the 1920s, the decade saw the growth of a smaller number of unusually large facilities designed specifically for bowling. In Chicago, to cite one example, a sharp drop in the number of bowling alleys between 1919 and 1933 was compensated for by an increase in the average number of lanes per establishment from 6.5 to 10.6.

Proprietors who now relied exclusively on bowling had both an opportunity and a vested interest in elevating the status of the sport and broadening its social appeal beyond the sort of people who usually frequented saloons. Brunswick Balke Collender faced the same imperative as Prohibition cut deeply into its sales of bar fixtures. In an attempt to resurrect bowling's sullied reputation and develop what was only a sideline business prior to Prohibition,

Brunswick distributed promotional literature that touted the moral attributes of the sport. According to one brochure, "followers of this game consciously or unconsciously are developing such character building qualities as self-control, patience, honesty, courtesy, unselfishness." To complement this rhetoric, Brunswick urged proprietors to refurbish their establishments. In particular, the company encouraged the construction of multistory recreation centers that featured a first-floor restaurant, a second-floor billiard hall, and a third-floor bowling parlor.

Although few proprietors went to such elaborate lengths, a great many spruced up their joints in the hopes of enticing not only a better class of male patrons but more women as well. Indeed, the most forward-thinking operators recognized that expanding the bowling market across gender lines was the best strategy for survival in an era when the traditional source of revenue, alcohol sales, was prohibited by law. Prior to the 1920s, women in bowling alleys had been a rarity. Few women felt comfortable or welcome in the all-male bastions where cuspidors overflowed with tobacco juice and drunken men swindled one another out of their weekly wages. Myra Evans recalled that when she first started bowling in Montana in 1926, she had to make special arrangements with the manager of the pool hall where the alleys were housed to let her in after the regular patrons had left for the night. Some women may have been inspired by bowlers like Floretta McCutcheon of Pueblo, Colorado, who took up the sport in 1925 as a way to lose weight. Two years later she gained national publicity by defeating Jimmy Smith, who was reputed to be the nation's top male bowler, in a three-game match.

For proprietors, the first step toward cleaning up their establishments entailed making a few aesthetic modifications to the physical structure, such as splashing colored paint on the walls and masking unsightly pipes and water drains with curtains or plaster. Others went further and equipped their alleys with soundproofing, overhead lighting, and spectator seating. Brunswick did its part to attract the female trade by marketing a lighter ball, the Whelanite, that was designed especially for women. At the end of the 1920s, the Bowling Proprietors' Association of America gloated over its achievements. Acknowledging that in the past "bowling alleys were no place for a woman," the national trade association bragged, "We now have recreation establishments featuring bowling that compare favorably with our best theatres. . . . Many cities claim that thirty and some say forty per cent of their bowlers are women."

As more women took to the sport, they formed their own leagues under the auspices of the Women's International Bowling Congress. Although the Congress was founded in 1916, four years prior to the advent of Prohibition, it was not until the dry years of the 1920s that the organization assumed national proportions. In one city after another, "ladies leagues" appeared where before there had been none. By 1923, the Women's International Bowling Congress was active in twenty-nine cities, most of them located in the Middle West, where bowling was most popular. And by 1928, the national organization could boast that its membership had increased more than tenfold, from 641 to 7,757, over the previous decade. The number of women's bowling leagues continued to increase in the 1930s. A 1939 tournament for women bowlers held in Chicago drew over a thousand teams from across the country. By this time the national organization claimed over 50,000 members.

The extent of women's participation in the sport of bowling during the 1920s and 1930s should not be exaggerated. Just prior to America's entry into World War II, men still represented two out of every three bowlers, according to the most conservative estimates and, more importantly, about four out of five league players. As dramatic as the appearance of women toting bowling balls must have been, most bowling alleys remained predominantly male domains. And despite the construction of a few upscale recreation

centers, the sport continued to be dominated by blue-collar workers with recent immigrant origins.

Working-Class Heroes:
Class and Ethnicity
and the Growth ofBowling's Popularity

It is significant that two Italian immigrants were probably the most
prominent bowlers in the 1930s. Their initiation into the world of
bowling provides a glimpse of the role that the sport played in urban immigrant communities at the turn of the century. Hank
Marino was born in Palermo, Italy, in 1889. With a guitar, a small
money pouch, and directions to Chicago sewn into his underwear,
his parents sent him across the Atlantic at the age of ten to live
with his brother. He worked in his brother's barber shop, lathering
faces before graduating to haircutting. Five years after his arrival,
at the age of fifteen, he went into business for himself, opening a
seven-chair barber shop. Chicago at the turn of the century was
one of the nation's bigger bowling towns, in large part due to the
presence of the Brunswick Balke Collender Company. Thus, it was
not unusual that Marino would spend much of his free time at
places like the Aurora Lanes downtown. By the age of twenty, he
had achieved local renown in the city's bowling alleys. A long
string of victories at national and international tournaments in the
1920s and 1930s won him recognition as the nation's top bowler.
Like many stars of the sport, he would later go on to open his own
bowling emporium. In 1951, the National Bowling Writers Association dubbed Marino "Bowler of the Half Century."

Andy Varipapa earned his celebrity status largely as a result of
his appearance in a series of short bowling-related films and his nationwide bowling exhibitions. Like Marino, Varipapa left Italy at
the age of ten, his final destination being Brooklyn, New York. He

found work in a foundry that made door hinges. At quitting time, he usually strolled to Fraternity Hall to bowl a few games. Studying the more accomplished bowlers, Varipapa perfected his skills and developed a penchant for performing trick shots. He threw a boomerang ball that reversed direction halfway down the lane and spun back to the foul line. Consistently, he was able to knock a pin into the air and have it topple another pin in the adjoining alley. Varipapa's most famous stunt involved converting the difficult seven-ten split by rolling two balls consecutively from either side of the lane at different speeds so that they crossed paths and knocked down the two standing pins at the same moment. These shenanigans earned Varipapa local acclaim and, as word spread, eventually landed him his movie deals and cross-country publicity tours. After World War II, however, Varipapa decided to get serious. Affronted by a general lack of appreciation for his legitimate bowling skills, he devoted his energies to formal tournament play, an effort that paid off with two consecutive All-Star national championships in 1946 and 1947.

In contrast to the German Americans who dominated the sport during the nineteenth century, eastern European immigrants rarely imported their skills from overseas. Most learned the game from scratch in the United States in neighborhood joints like Aurora Lanes and Fraternity Hall. The preponderance of bowlers of eastern European extraction in the early part of the twentieth century was more than anything a product of their material circumstances; bowling was ideally suited to urban dwellers with restricted incomes and limited time.

Unlike boating, skiing, hunting, and golf—sporting activities that enjoyed popularity among the well-to-do—bowling required little in the way of financial expenditures. The fee of 20 or 25 cents per game just prior to World War II may have been prohibitive to the destitute, but it presented no great hardship to those with steady jobs in the industrial sector. Most alleys made free house balls available to their patrons; those that required special shoes, and there were many that did not, either rented them for a nomi-

Women's teams took up much of the slack in league bowling created by the entry of 6 million men into the armed forces during World War II.

nal fee or provided them free of charge. Many regular bowlers preferred to purchase a bowling ball and a pair of shoes of their own, an investment that would set them back less than $25 in 1941. With the rich pot games and private wagers that remained rampant in most places, a bowler even held on to the possibility of leaving with more money than he had when he arrived.

Biographies of the nation's premier bowlers at mid-century reveal a disproportionate number who developed their prowess while working at manual trades during the 1920s and 1930s. Walter Ward, who was known for smoking his trademark crooked cigar on the alleyways, grew up in a poor household in Cleveland at the turn of the century. His father assembled and installed stoves, and his mother took in laundry. Initiated into the bowling world at the age of twelve by a customer on his newspaper delivery route who owned a bowling alley, Ward honed his skills when he began bowling on a regular basis as a member of the McKinney Steel Company team in 1920. Ward had been hired to work fourteen-hour shifts as a paint boy in the company's shipping department four years earlier, and he continued to work in the mill until 1940. In the intervening years, Ward racked up some of the highest bowling scores in the Cleveland area. In 1937, he made a big splash on the national scene by rolling the fifth highest score ever in the American Bowling Congress's All-Events competition. Joe Ostroski, on the other hand, practiced his craft whenever he was not toiling away in the coal mines of western Pennsylvania. After taking a job as the manager of a bowling alley in 1938, Ostroski devoted even more time to league play. By the 1950s, the "Swoyerville Socker," as he was known in the Pennsylvania circuit, was recognized as one of the top bowlers, not only in Pennsylvania, but in the United States. Frank Benkovic, an immigrant from Austria-Hungary, was introduced to the game of bowling when two of his co-workers at the Blumenfeld Locker Hosiery Company in Milwaukee invited him out for an evening at Plankinton Arcade. Before long he was hooked, bowling as many as 100 games weekly, a pace he continued to maintain when he found a new job at the Schlitz Brewery in 1935. By that time, Benkovic had already established the record for the highest score ever in the American Bowling Congress's All-Events tournament.

Ward, Ostroski, and Benkovic, while exceptional in their skills, were typical of the kind of people who dominated local bowling circuits prior to World War II. Most bowlers held blue-collar jobs and a great many of them bowled regularly with their co-workers under the auspices of industrial leagues. Thousands of industrial firms sponsored bowling teams for their workers; leagues that carried these teams were the bread and butter of most bowling businesses. In heavily industrialized cities where many factories operated around the clock, it was not uncommon to find alleys hosting leagues on three separate shifts during weekdays. Exceptionally large plants, such as the Lockheed Aircraft and the Douglas Aircraft facilities, both in Los Angeles, supported over two hundred teams each. The thirteen alleys at the Sports Center in Cleveland were kept busy with leagues run by a wide variety of industrial firms including Republic Steel, Sohio Oil, the American Steel and Wire Company, the Mooney Iron Works, the Grabler Manufacturing Company, Leonard Electric Company, E. F. Hauserman Company, and Ferro Foundry and Machine. A few miles away the twenty teams that made up the Motor Transport Bowling League, composed primarily of truck drivers, shared the lanes at St. Clair-Ontario Recreation with the Cleveland Twist Drill Company, Weldon Tool Company, and the East Ohio Gas Company.

Bowling During Wartime: The Game Continues to Grow

World War II disrupted the bowling business just as it disrupted so many facets of American life. The entry of many avid young bowlers into the armed forces deprived proprietors of their best customers. A war economy operating at full throttle provided some compensation, however. Bowling establishments benefited from the combination of high wages that encouraged discretionary spending on much-needed recreation and gasoline rationing that confined people to their immediate neighborhoods. In addition, bowling halls attracted an unprecedented number of women who were brought into the sport under the same organizational framework as men, that is, as industrial workers. As women replaced men on the assembly line, they created their own industrial leagues, some of which could be quite sizable. The Curtiss Wright bomber plant in Columbus, Ohio, purportedly had the largest circuit with 370 female war workers rolling for seventy-four teams. Some bowling alley managers claimed that women represented 60 percent of their customers during the war years.

While proprietors welcomed the additional business provided by female customers, they considered women bowlers a poor substitute for their male patrons at best and a headache at worst. Proprietors claimed that their newer customers did not bowl as frequently as their former patrons. And when they did bowl, they bowled at a leisurely pace. Slower games meant fewer games, which translated into a smaller take for proprietors. Editors of the *Woman Bowler* attempted to short circuit this criticism by reminding readers to keep their focus on the task at hand, rather than engage in social interaction when they were on the lanes. "Once the game is under way," preached a 1943 editorial, "the player should remain with her team and be ready to take her turn as it comes instead of visiting her friends, perhaps several lanes down, or running off to the refreshment stand, making telephone calls and other time killing stunts." One wartime proprietor was so exasperated with this type of behavior that he vowed never to take on another "damned" women's league even if he never filled his house again.

These criticisms notwithstanding, the biggest setback confronting wartime proprietors was neither insufficient patronage nor dawdling customers but rather a shortage of pinsetters, due to the tight labor market. Without young men to set the pins, some bowling establishments were forced to curtail operations, even when demand remained high. Typical was the scene at Chester House in the Bronx, where twelve teams arrived one winter night to bowl in a local tournament. Only two pin boys were on hand, so the management solicited volunteers from among the spectators and substitute players. A few men offered their services, but not enough, and the tournament was canceled. Thus, the war represented a lost opportunity for the bowling business just as the sport's popularity and respectability were on the upswing. As one proprietor explained, "With all the money around, with all the hankering to bowl, if pinboys had been available, what a nice volume of business we could have done."

Meanwhile, the installation of more than 3,000 alley beds at military bases in the United States and overseas ensured that soldiers away from home would not lose interest in the sport. In the war-torn cities of Europe and the remote jungles of the South Pacific, soldiers cobbled together makeshift alleys out of available materials—felled trees, spare bits of wood—so that they could enjoy some home-style recreation and relaxation. Military bowling not only allowed seasoned keglers to maintain their skills, but introduced the pastime to thousands of men to whom the sport was unknown. According to one estimate, 4 million new bowlers were drawn to the sport because of their experience in the armed forces.

The Postwar Market and the Importance of League Bowling

With the resumption of peace, bowling proprietors expected to surpass the attendance records set during the brief surge in business that preceded the attack on Pearl Harbor in December 1941. They were buoyed by the anticipated return of young bowlers— both longtime players and recent converts—who served in the military, and they were hopeful that they could retain the many women who had taken up the sport during the war. For the most part, their strategy remained the same as it was before the war: Retain the loyalty of enthusiasts by providing clean and respectable venues. Marketing efforts continued to target the regular bowler through the mechanism of leagues and tournaments.

Consistent with their efforts before the war, proprietors relied heavily on industrial leagues to fill their alleys. Typically, alley operators took advantage of the slow summer months to drum up business for their fall leagues. First, they urged companies that sponsored teams in the previous year to renew their contracts. To fill any remaining slots, operators approached the plant managers of other nearby firms and outlined the merits of a recreation program than included bowling. At a time when labor strife was at an all-time high, alley proprietors pitched bowling, first and foremost, as a means of improving worker-management relations. Brunswick advised proprietors to let executives know that a corporate-sponsored league not only contributed to goodwill among employees but alleviated class tensions by giving "department heads and employees, both men and women, a chance to meet on an equal basis and develop an understanding of each other's problems." Many corporations concurred with this logic. Hurlburt Smith, the president of L. C. Smith & Corona Typewriters, organized five leagues to encourage his employees to "know each other in a friendly way." Company officials at the Fashion Park–Stein Bloch corporation in Rochester, New York, subsidized worker bowling to smooth relations between front-office personnel and factory workers.

The editor of a New York City bowling newsletter went even further, arguing that bowling was guaranteed to forestall the development of radical ideology among workers. According to the editor's logic, there was a good reason why "no bowlers ever turn Communist": Bowling simply took up too much time and energy that might otherwise be devoted to the consideration of dangerous Marxist doctrines. And should any worker succumb to the temptations of "Moscow ideals," bringing workers and foremen together in a bowling league would surely "be the end to any feeling of class consciousness." By pursuing this line of argument, the bowling industry aligned its self-interest with more lofty national ideals; leagues that joined workers and managers championed bowling as an incubator for democratic values and upheld the ideal of a classless society. The strategy certainly paid off at the cash register. Industrial leagues dominated organized play through the early 1950s, providing proprietors with nearly 50 percent of their business.

If business executives sponsored bowling teams to improve labor relations, workers had their own reasons for devoting their time and energy to the weekly routine. At the local alley, wage earners could fraternize with one another informally, outside the supervised factory setting. They might also come home with a little extra pocket money, no small consideration for workers whose earnings barely kept pace with mounting consumer expenditures. Players commonly bet among themselves. Winning teams were rewarded with a distribution from the prize fund. Certainly the lure of cash prizes motivated the bowlers who signed up for the sweepstakes tournaments held at the end of each season. In some cases the awards could be quite substantial. Among the most extravagant tournaments held on a regular basis in the immediate postwar years was the one hosted by Hank Marino's Recreation in Milwaukee. For an entry fee of $25, bowlers vied for a grand prize of $2,500, not a bad draw for a week's worth of flinging bowling balls.

Bowling proprietors appealed to women on the same basis as they appealed to men. A major dilemma faced by proprietors was how to retain those female customers who had worked in defense plants during the war and had bowled in industrial leagues. For the most part, industrial leagues reverted to their male orientation after the war, along with the industries that sustained them. By the late 1940s, there were precious few women's leagues to be found under the sponsorship of factories. To compensate for the decline in women's industrial bowling, proprietors tried to organize merchants' leagues around retailers that catered primarily to women. In places where alley managers were successful, the postwar period saw new "ladies' leagues" composed of teams sponsored by florists, jewelers, sportswear stores, and the like. Another possibility was the office league, which drew upon the many women who remained in the workforce performing clerical tasks. The female employees who worked for State Farm Insurance in Bloomington, Illinois, organized such a league in 1945. When the office closed for the day at 5 P.M., fifty women marched the two blocks to McCarty Brothers Bowling Palace where they monopolized the ten alleys. At seven o'clock they were replaced by another fifty keglers from the same firm. Although proprietors salvaged some of their women's trade through the creation of new office leagues and merchants' leagues, men came to outnumber women in bowling alleys once again, as they did before the war.

In satisfying die-hard bowlers and continuing to improve the image of the sport by maintaining clean, attractive, and re-

The Tower Bowl in San Diego used the lure of food and live music to attract new patrons in the years immediately after World War II.

spectable establishments, people in the bowling business were cautiously optimistic about the future. As expected, lineage, the number of games bowled, increased after the war and more leagues signed up for play. Moreover, the prosperity enjoyed by their patrons enabled alley managers to charge higher prices. Despite grumblings, dedicated bowlers were willing to absorb the price hikes as long as these were kept within reasonable bounds. When in the summer of 1946 operators in Schenectady announced their intention of raising fees from twenty-five to thirty cents a game, 150 league representatives vowed to boycott the sport, insisting that the financial burden of the nickel increase was too onerous. Yet one bowler at a protest meeting who vehemently charged that "Bowling in this town isn't worth more than 25 cents a game" was spotted later that night "spilling the maples" at Woodlawn Bowling Alleys, where he had apparently paid the thirty-cent fee. Another bowler acknowledged, "I can also realize how the increase may be very expensive to those who do a lot of bowling and may have more than one kegler in the family" but added that the nickel increase would not impose any hardship on him.

Although the immediate postwar years were kind to most bowling alley operators, they did not meet the industry's highest expectations. The 1945–46 season was a disappointment. League membership was well below the comparable figure for the 1941–42 season, a difference that was attributed to the fact that many young men in the armed services remained at their overseas posts despite the end of hostilities. Moreover, proprietors were still hobbled by shortages of both labor for pinsetting and materials for routine alley maintenance. League play was more robust the following year, although business varied considerably from one city to another. In most parts of the country, proprietors could count on two shifts of league play each weekday evening, with the first round beginning at six o'clock and the second at eight o'clock. In Cleveland, however, a dramatic surge in bowling, combined with a shortage of venues, allowed operators to inaugurate a three-shift schedule on weekdays. Some Cleveland operators reported that they were taking reservations for weekend leagues as well. By 1947, nationwide attendance had reached such unprecedented levels that a representative from the Bowling Proprietors Association of America recommended that the National Bowling Council discontinue its publication "How to Book Your Alleys Solid" because "proprietors have no accommodations to take care of any more leagues."

Still, for those who took a long-term view, there were troubling signs on the horizon. One was the decline in open bowling, that is, unstructured play outside the rubric of any league. While lanes were packed with league players during the evenings, they were often empty during the day and the wee hours of the morning. If full leagues reflected the industry's efforts to cater to the regular bowler, the decline of open play reflected the industry's inability to attract the casual bowler who may not have had much prior experience with the game. Some farsighted proprietors fretted about the fact that few new bowlers were taking up the hobby. By 1951, the decline in open bowling had reached such alarming proportions that the Bowling Proprietors of America Association (BPAA) spent several thousand dollars in hiring an advertising agency to research the problem and suggest solutions.

The Pinboy Problem

Owners knew that the biggest impediment to the growth of bowling was the pinboy problem. A shortage of workers willing to work for modest wages under onerous and even dangerous conditions, which had assumed dire proportions during World War II, persisted into the late 1940s and early 1950s. The same prosperous conditions that brought bowlers back to the alleys in record numbers also robbed proprietors of their supply of unskilled labor. Jobs were plentiful, and, for most people, pinsetting was a last resort.

The work itself was not terribly complicated. After the bowler rolled his or her first ball, the pinboy shoved it back along a return ramp and cleared the fallen pins from the head of the alley. After the second ball was rolled, the worker reset the pins in their proper arrangement and again returned the ball to the bowler.

For such unskilled work, pinboys did not make much money unless they worked one of the major tournaments. Moreover, pinboy earnings were unreliable. Pinboys were paid according to the number of games they worked, or in bowling vernacular, by the line. Hence, earnings could vary dramatically not only from one place to another, but from one night to another. During the late 1940s and early 1950s, the prevailing rate per line ranged anywhere from five to thirteen cents. At seven cents a line in 1950, the standard rate in New England was slightly below average. In New York City, workers earned the same wage but could usually count on supplementary five-cent tips from players. Elsewhere, a lineage rate of between eight and ten cents without a tip was standard. By the early 1950s, however, West Coast pinboys were bringing in as much as thirteen cents a line.

At times, the pinboys turned the labor shortage to their advantage by using it as leverage to secure higher pay. During World War II, for example, pinboys around the country began demanding gratuities prior to service. Although the practice of tipping pinboys was common in the New York City, it was unheard of elsewhere. But because bowlers and proprietors were so dependent on the few hired hands they could scrounge up, workers were able to demand prearranged fees from the bowlers under the threat of refusing to set the pins. Although pinboys did not have quite as much leverage after the war, when they were organized in labor unions, they continued to assert demands for higher wages. When a Manhattan local of the Building Service Employees International Union picketed five bowling establishments, their demands included a contract with all New York City proprietors that would include a raise of two cents per line for all pinboys.

Still, pinboy labor was never especially lucrative. During league play, when work was steady, pinboys might make a decent wage; a pinboy setting thirty or forty games each night might expect to

Unknown pinsetter, Des Moines, Iowa, 1926

bring home anywhere from $3 to $5. But during slack times, when leagues were not in session, a pinboy was lucky to make thirty cents an hour.

However simple the job, it was nevertheless unpleasant and hazardous. Pinboys spent most of their time behind the alleys in the small, cramped spaces known as the pits, spaces about four and half feet wide, depressed about a foot below the level of alley beds so workers would have just enough room to maneuver without having to do much squatting or kneeling. The job involved constant stooping to lift the sixteen-pound balls and the three-pound pins. Servicing more than one lane required the pinboy to leap across the partition separating one alley from another after each roll of the ball. Ideally, proprietors had pinboys on hand equal to the number of alleys, but when labor was scarce, the boys might have to service multiple alleys simultaneously. During league bowling it was quite common for pinsetters to work an entire match, which took place over two adjacent lanes.

Moreover, the pinboy continually faced the danger of being hit with flying pins and sixteen-pound spheres of compacted rubber traveling at high speeds. These risks meant that the pinboy had to be on constant alert, especially when handling more than one alley at a time. Grogginess could lead to serious injury, as a twelve-year-old Connecticut boy learned when the impact of a fast ball cost him two fingers. Mashed fingers, split lips, lost teeth, broken noses, and concussions were the occupational hazards of the trade.

Pinboys might be responsible for performing additional menial duties on the premises, when not cooped up behind the pins, such as emptying sand urns, changing towels, and picking up empty bottles. At the very least, pinboys were responsible for routine maintenance on the alleys—cleaning the pins and sweeping the alleys.

Menial pay combined with arduous work deterred many job-seekers from filling out applications at the local bowling alley. Even those without job skills had plenty of other alternatives available. Able-bodied men who didn't mind hard and dirty work could find unskilled jobs in the construction industry that paid much higher wages. Teenagers might not be able to find more lucrative work, but certainly could find lighter jobs—ushering in movie theaters, serving customers at hamburger stands, stocking shelves at drugstores.

Faced with this situation, proprietors took what they could get, which tended to be young teenagers and older itinerants. Proprietors claimed that they would have preferred more reliable adult workers but that such labor was unavailable. Instead, they turned to all sorts of drifters. For wandering vagabonds, pinsetting was an attractive job not simply because it required little in the way of skills but because proprietors often supplied lodging for those in need. Pitrooms, next to the pits, often contained a few cots for vagrant workers who needed a place to sleep. According to the prevailing stereotype, pitrooms were the site of heavy alcohol consumption and gambling, largely due to the influence of these pinsetters. The pinsetters' reputation was further undermined because, as a job situated near the bottom of the urban occupational hierarchy, it drew many African Americans, both young and old. The mere presence of black workers degraded a job in the eyes of white customers who saw their own social status vested in the enforcement of a color line.

For the late afternoon and early evening shifts, labor-starved proprietors turned to adolescents. Whenever possible, proprietors hired older teenagers whose employment was sanctioned by law. But this was not always possible; the hiring of underage youths was rampant. During World War II, many states, responding to pressure from influential bowling industry lobbyists, relaxed child labor laws so as to allow children to work in bowling alleys at all hours of the day. After the war, bowling industry leaders lobbied to prevent states and localities from raising age requirements back to prewar levels. In states where the wartime laws were rescinded, the bowling industry pushed for new legislation that would bring down the minimum age once again. While child labor organizations, the American Federation of Labor, and the U.S. Department of Labor pushed for stricter legislation, bowling interests were sometimes joined by police departments and parole boards, which argued that it was better for young kids to be at work than on the streets. In most cases, the bowling industry managed to secure passage of laws that permitted the employment of teenagers as young as sixteen. But in many cases, even the supply of sixteen- and seventeen-year-olds was insufficient, prompting proprietors to flout the law. When a young man entered a bowling alley and offered his services for pinsetting, proprietors were reluctant to ask for much information beyond the boy's first name. Although an Ohio law prohibited the employment of minors under the age of sixteen, it was estimated that 90 percent of all pinboys in the state were under sixteen. Cleveland alone employed 100,000 underage pinboys over a five-year period in the mid-1940s. To evade law enforcement officials, proprietors resorted to all sorts of subterfuge. Some alleys, for example, were reported to have buzzer systems to warn youngsters when an inspector was on the way, giving the illegal workers ample time to scamper to secret hiding places. A 1953 government report noted that it was not uncommon to find boys as young as nine setting pins in some establishments.

A reliance on mostly underage teenagers and itinerant adults imposed a number of constraints on the bowling alley proprietor. The bowling alley was a labor-intensive business, with pinsetters making up the bulk of the alley's labor force. A typical twelve-lane establishment might employ twelve or thirteen pinsetters. Dependence on this labor in addition to the drastic variability in demand for pinsetting services meant that proprietors had to locate their establishments where they could be assured of a pool of workers who would be available on short notice. During the daytime, the demand for pinsetting labor could fluctuate dramatically from one hour to another, depending on the flow of customer traffic. Proprietors encouraged youngsters and vagrants to loiter on the premises so that in a pinch there would be plenty of free hands around. It was not unknown for desperate managers to venture out on the streets to corral idle bodies inside for an hour or two of work in the pits. These labor requirements kept proprietors tied to inner-city neighborhoods where young people could commute by foot or public transportation and where idle workers could be easily found. This restriction became especially frustrating as more and more families moved to suburbs where these sorts of labor arrangements were difficult if not impossible to sustain. The unavailability of schoolchildren during the daytime and late-night hours forced many proprietors to curtail operations at these times, thereby limiting their income and inhibiting the growth of the sport among recreational non-league bowlers.

Perhaps most important, pinboys intimidated the casual bowler, a fact that was especially detrimental to the fostering of open-play business. The relationship between regular league bowlers and pinboys was hostile enough. Matches were rife with mutual recriminations hollered across the lanes. League bowlers became irritated when they had to wait for the pinsetter, either because the worker was busy servicing another lane, or even worse, taking a break in the middle of a game to use a rest room or to get a drink of water. Some bowlers vented their frustration, deliberately trying to hit pinboys in the knee by rolling when the pinsetters were still in the alley head clearing pins.

While league bowlers sometimes complained about dawdling behind the pits, the pinboy was even more likely to deride the slow bowler. As one poetic proprietor noted in 1945, "Bowlers fiddle and fool around talking with their girlfriends, run to the bar, pose for the general public to admire, while the ambitious pinsetter frets and fumes as the minutes, sands of time, float by, forever lost, likewise his piece work compensation." Impatient pinsetters commonly taunted bowlers to speed up their game so they could make more money. This verbal harassment could be intimidating to women bowlers and novices. As a general rule, women preferred to bowl at a more leisurely pace than men. And, of course, beginning bowlers of either sex were likely not only to prefer a slower pace and a more leisurely experience but also to be more tentative approaching the foul line. As such, they were easy targets of pinboy taunts. Many women and casual bowlers cited belligerent pinboys as the major reason for shying away from bowling alleys.

As if these impediments to business and growth were not damaging enough, pinboy labor also generated unfavorable publicity in the press. Social reformers who raised the issue could care less about the anxieties of bowlers. They contended that there was a much larger danger lurking behind the pins, the corruption of American youth. Dreary pit conditions and onerous work routines harkened back to the horrid era of child sweatshops that proliferated in the poor immigrant quarters of turn-of-the-century cities.

Pinboys outside a bowling alley, New Haven, Conn., 1909. Photographer and social reformer Lewis Hine documented the morally degenerating effects of jobs that required children to work late hours under onerous conditions.

At worst, pinboy labor frayed the moral fiber of America's young and set them on the path to delinquency. Deprived of fresh air and sunlight, diverted from their schoolwork, and exposed to the most degenerate elements of society, pinboys were bound for a life of crime, according to several child welfare experts. At best, pinboy labor was inconsistent with a middle-class understanding of adolescence as a stage in life that required parental supervision and nurturing to ensure passage into responsible adulthood.

Condemnation from reformers and journalists reached a peak during World War II, when proprietors often resorted to the use of very young children to set pins in bowling alleys. Teachers complained about students who came to school late or fell asleep in class on account of their late-night employment in bowling alleys. Of particular concern was the interaction between innocent youth and the older workers who were characterized by one report as "older men of weak character and bad habits." Exposure to alcohol consumption and gambling in the pitrooms was noted as a corrupting influence. And it was thought to be just as bad outside the alleys, where youths were supposedly targets for roving gangs and susceptible to initiation in their delinquent activities.

The bowling industry was stung by this criticism that threatened to derail efforts to upgrade the sport's reputation and attract new customers. To counter this adverse publicity, leaders in the bowling industry and individual proprietors pledged to mend their ways. John Canelli, representing the American Bowling Congress, noted that unless proprietors demonstrated some good faith in cleaning up alley conditions, they were not likely to be successful in their legislative efforts to secure the young labor they needed. As a demonstration of its determination to correct the worst abuses, in 1953 the BPAA sent its members a folder, "Fair Play for Pinsetters," together with a report, "What Proprietors Can Do to Improve Conditions."

Some proprietors went to great lengths to create both better conditions and positive publicity for the pinboys in their establishments. Milford Wickstrom inaugurated the Baird Recreation Pinsetter Scholarship in 1953 to publicize his most outstanding pinboy, the one who attained the best academic and scholastic record each year. John Schuck, who won the first award in 1953, played violin for the school orchestra, attained the rank of Star Scout in the Boy Scout troop at his church, and was named to the Honor Society at his school. Several proprietors built model dormitories so that their young workers could spend their off-hours in clean and wholesome surroundings. Still others pledged to lighten their pinboys' workload and even help them complete their homework assignments.

Promises to treat pinboys more humanely, the provision of tutors, and offers of special scholarships may have warded off public criticism to a limited extent, but they did little to address proprietor woes associated with pinboy shortages and offensive pinboy behavior. The human pinsetter remained a painful thorn in the side of the bowling industry, a bottleneck in the long-standing effort to attract new adherents to the sport.

The Coming of Automation

For many years, alley managers had turned to architectural and technological solutions to reduce the damage attributed to pinboy labor. Early in the twentieth century, Brunswick redesigned its ball returns to eradicate the problem of pinboys who threw balls back to customers so hard that bowlers' fingers were broken. The new returns looped the balls back to bowlers against a heavy strap situated at the end of the chute. As a Brunswick catalog from around 1920 explained, "It makes no difference how hard the pin boy pushes the ball, the speed is retarded by the loop and the strap."

One fairly simple way to minimize friction between bowler and pinsetter was to erect a physical barrier between them. Proprietors hid unkempt or surly pinboys behind curtains, blinds, or steel screens that extended from the ceiling to a point just above the top of the pins at the rear of the alley. The masking units sold by the American Bowling and Billiard Corporation during the early 1950s promised to "conceal pit and pin boy" from public view. With the use of such masking devices widespread by the 1950s, pinboys were visible only from below the knee, making it more difficult for bowlers and pinboys to engage in acrimonious shouting matches.

For many years, the industry had also been moving toward greater mechanization of pinsetting. By the outbreak of World War II, few pinboys set pins without the aid of some mechanical device. Most establishments used a contraption that held pins in their proper position and lowered them onto the alley. The pinboy was simply required to collect the fallen pins, load them into the machine, and then pull a handle or bar to lower the pins. Vaunting the simplicity of their "Backus Automatic Pin Setter" in 1920,

Brunswick Balke Collender assured potential buyers that "it can be operated by any boy twelve years of age." By the 1950s, Brunswick was also marketing an automatic ball lift that enabled pinboys simply to kick the bowling ball into a hole at floor level, at which point a mechanical arm raised it to a sufficient height to allow gravity to propel it down the return chute. According to a Brunswick advertisement, the new device saved pinboys from "lifting over two tons every hour," thereby enabling proprietors to "get and hold the best pinboys." More important, the advertisement continued, "The C–20 Automatic Ball Lift means no slowing down in final frames because of tired pinboys."

Brunswick had considered the possibility of a fully automatic pinspotter as early as 1911. In that year, Benjamin Bensinger, the company's president, hired an inventor specifically for the purpose of building such a contraption. The inventor was unsuccessful, and, due to the abundance of cheap pinsetting labor during the 1920s and 1930s, Brunswick lost interest in the scheme. Thus, top company officials were unenthusiastic in the late 1930s when a fellow by the name of Fred Schmidt claimed to have figured out a way to pick up standing pins and reset them in their proper position through the use of mechanical suction cups. They refused to finance the project.

When executives at the American Machine Foundry Company, a maker of industrial machinery with no previous experience in the bowling business, learned of Schmidt's breakthrough, however, they immediately recognized the potential value of the invention. They purchased the patents from an intermediary company that had bought them from Schmidt and set about engineering the device. It took six years to translate Schmidt's ideas into what AMF thought was a viable product. In 1946, the company unveiled its new machine at the American Bowling Congress's annual tournament in Buffalo. Although most observers were duly impressed, the machine had serious defects. Weighing over two tons, it was cumbersome. Moreover, it malfunctioned frequently. AMF took the product off the market almost immediately and sent its engineers

The AMF Pinspotter, circa 1952

back to the drawing board. After another five years passed, the company finally emerged with a reliable machine, based on Schmidt's original concept, which reset pins accurately without the aid of human hands.

AMF's Pinspotter was a fairly simple device. The machine was activated the instant the bowling ball crashed against a cushion behind the pit. After the first roll, suction cups descended to grab and lift the standing pins while a bar swept the fallen pins into a wheel-like conveyor. With all "deadwood" cleared from the lane, the suction cups then deposited the standing pins back in their appropriate positions. After the second roll, the sweeper raked all the remaining pins into the conveyor while a second set of pins descended for the next bowler. Meanwhile, the conveyor fed all ten fallen pins into a rack, ready for the following frame. The only intervention required of the bowler was pressing a reset button after the third roll in the tenth frame.

Having been convinced that such a machine would never work, executives at Brunswick were stunned by AMF's accomplishment. Suddenly faced with the prospect of being displaced as the leading supplier of bowling equipment, the company launched a crash program to develop its own device. In 1956, Brunswick announced the arrival of the automatic Pinsetter. The Brunswick machine worked on the same basic principles as the AMF Pinspotter, although it relied less on electronic wizardry and more on mechanical contraptions. The primary difference, however, lay in the method of distribution; AMF leased its machines by the line while Brunswick sold its machines outright, usually on an installment plan.

The invention of the automatic pinsetter occurred in the context of other technological innovations that further mechanized the sport. AMF's Radaray Foul Detector worked in conjunction with its automatic pinsetter. Like the pinsetter, it was a labor-saving device that in this case eliminated the need for someone to watch for bowlers who crossed the foul lane before delivering the ball. With the electric-eye foul detector, a signal alerted the pinsetter when the bowler performed the illegal action so that the pins would be reset as if the bowler had rolled a gutter ball.

Then there was the AMF Pindicator, which not only "pindicated" the number of pins left standing diagrammatically on a large screen at the end of the alley, but also noted strikes, spares, and whether the ball rolled was the bowler's first or second. Customers supposedly liked it because "No longer does the bowler have to stand on tip toe and crane his neck to look for that 'sleeper.'" (A "sleeper" was a term used to denote a pin that was hidden behind another.) Proprietors found it saved bowling time by eliminating costly time-consuming discussions about how many pins were still standing.

Another electronic innovation that helped to modernize and upgrade the bowling alley was the electric air-blown hand dryer, usually mounted on a pedestal, scoring table, or the terminus of the ball return. For years, it had been customary simply to tie a towel to the end of the ball rack with which patrons could dry their sweaty hands. Brunswick's Electric-Aire Hand Dryer was promoted as a sanitary improvement, which was probably true given the fact that the towels were shared by many bowlers and were not always changed between matches.

The other major postwar innovation in bowling alley technology, the underlane ball return, did not rely on electronic gadgetry. Since the early days of saloon bowling, balls had been returned to bowlers along chutes that ran alongside the lanes. The rattling and rumbling of returning balls contributed to the high noise levels that people associated with bowling alleys. In an effort to create a quieter atmosphere, AMF developed an underground chute in conjunction with its Pinspotter, along with a mechanism that gently lifted incoming balls to a rack several feet behind the foul line. Now bowling balls hummed softly as they sped back to their owners.

The adoption of these various electronic and mechanical devices by bowling alleys was swift. By 1960, automatic pinsetters, foul detectors, hand dryers, and underground ball returns were all standard features. For example, according to one estimate nine out of ten alleys had already converted from pinboys to automatic pinsetting machines.

The Pinsetter Revolution

Industry leaders identified the mechanical pinsetting device as the major factor responsible for an increase in the number of women bowlers and the even more spectacular surge in youth bowling in the decade following its invention. Mechanized equipment, by cutting loose often surly and disreputable pinboys, allowed proprietors to build lavish bowling emporiums in suburban areas that catered to all members of the family. Millions of new bowlers were initiated into the sport as mechanized bowling gave fun and sociability preeminence over the competition and cash prizes that characterized older urban alleys.

The mere appearance of the AMF Pinspotter, however, did not make the transformation of the bowling alley a foregone conclusion, nor did it set the history of the bowling alley on any sort of predestined course. Indeed, failing to appreciate the revolutionary potential of the automated bowling alley, proprietors and industry leaders were slow to change their ways. Even when the industry finally settled upon a marketing strategy built around the concept of family fun, it continued to grapple with difficult issues: How would it convince Americans that the bowling alley was now an appropriate place for women and children? How would it allay fears that recreational bowling would divert women and children from their primary family responsibilities? How would it accommodate customers who preferred to bowl with their peers than with other members of their family? What additional modifications in decor and service would be required to align the bowling alley experience with customers' expectations? Consumers, of course, had an important voice in answering each of these questions. If the bowling industry took the lead in recasting the bowling experience, bowlers—as individuals as well as members of organizations—contributed to the restructuring of the sport by embracing or rejecting particular innovations and by responding in unanticipated ways.

Prior to the advent of mechanized bowling, proprietors typically wooed new bowlers to their establishments by promising better performance. With so much business coming from hardened bowling addicts, people who bowled regularly and took the game seriously, it made sense for proprietors to emphasize playing conditions. Serious bowlers gave their allegiance to places where they consistently rolled high scores. Hence, proprietors made sure their alleys stayed in tiptop condition, resurfacing them regularly with fresh shellac, and even keeping the pins in good shape so bowlers would be assured of lively action. Jack Garay, manager of the Boulevard Lanes in Cleveland, lost business because bowlers complained that his alleys were producing low scores. To win back his clientele, Garay ripped out all of his old alley beds in 1948 and installed new ones with much higher-grade lumber. Then he hired an "expert alley sander" to manicure his new beds to ideal condition, a process that involved cleaning, smoothing, and polishing the surface of each lane. Scores improved and bowlers stopped complaining; Garay credited the renovation for saving his business.

Out on the West Coast, Ed Hartnett, who managed the Pasadena Bowling Center, also attributed the high scores rolled at his house to meticulous upkeep. He prided himself on using just the right type of wood on his lanes and manicuring his alleys enough so they would neither be too fast nor too slow. In his mind, "high scores, concocted [sic] on well kept courts, are the things that reach the newspapers and publicize the sport." Alluding to the depressed state of the bowling business in the early 1950s, Hartnett added, "It needs promotion these days, especially out here on the coast. What better and healthier manner to promote the game is there than by giving the bowler the conditions for better scoring?"

Following the prevailing marketing wisdom, AMF initially promoted its revolutionary pinsetting device by emphasizing the benefits that would accrue to the accomplished bowler, in particular, speed and reliability. One of the company's first advertisements for its Pinspotters noted that the devices made it possible "to bowl more games without interruption. That's because they *always* set up pins perfectly—eliminating delays. And AMF pinspotters will work 24 hours a day." Another early advertisement claimed: "More and more enthusiastic bowlers are now enjoying the exhilarating experience of *Rhythm Bowling* provided by AMF Automatic

Pinspotters. With the prompt regularity and consistent action of the 'automatics,' bowlers find they can concentrate more on their game . . . develop peak form and added smoothness which is bound to produce higher scores."

Other technological innovations were likely to be touted for their ability to improve performance as well. All-star bowler Jack Aydelotte, in an advertisement for AMF's Underlane ball return, raved about how the new contraption eliminated once and for all the distraction of incoming balls hurtling toward bowlers as they approached the foul line. "I don't care whether you're a 150 bowler or a 210," read the advertising copy in a Cleveland bowling gazette. "The Underlane ball return . . . keeps the returning ball out of sight, sends it back to the rear of the approach area. Believe me, it really helps your score!"

Bowlers seemed to concur with such claims, although the adjustment to mechanized bowling sometimes took awhile. Occasionally, bowlers who forgot to reset the automatic Pinsetter in the tenth frame were found hollering at the device for not clearing deadwood from the alley. Some league bowlers also griped about the fact that the machines denied them the luxury of a free practice ball prior to the start of matches. For the most part, however, bowlers gave glowing reports, impressed by both the efficiency and dependability of the machines. Some regular bowlers agreed with AMF that the machines helped them establish a smoother rhythm and roll higher scores.

The response from proprietors was even more enthusiastic, despite the fact that automation entailed slightly greater expenditures. At first, AMF's automatic pinsetter cost the operator between fifteen and sixteen cents per game. AMF received twelve cents; the remainder covered routine maintenance and any remodeling that had to be done to accommodate the machines. Brunswick sold its machines for about $8,000 apiece, a hefty expense, even though purchasers did not have to pay all costs up front. Moreover, neither company's device eliminated the need for labor entirely; operators of large establishments had to keep a mechanic on hand to tend to any malfunctioning machine. Still, proprietors considered the added reliability worth the expense.

For some proprietors, the simple elimination of all the headaches associated with hiring and managing pinboys was enough to make the automated equipment worthwhile. Ken Kushner, who managed the Metro-Forest Bowling Academy in Queens, New York, was initially reluctant to invest in the new AMF product. But he was quickly won over when he discovered that the new machines meant the removal of his "Pin-boy ulcers" and his "sleepless nights."

Kushner was equally impressed with the "tremendous increase in business" that followed the installation of the AMF machines. For those proprietors who were among the first to install the Pinspotters, the machines translated into immediate profits. Jewel City Bowl in Glendale, California, was the first West Coast recipient of the AMF machines. Within two weeks of their installation, business at Jewel City had increased 30 percent, according to the proprietor Hugo Kohn. Anticipating a similar increase in patronage, Frank Hoefler doubled the capacity of Airport Bowl in Buffalo, from twelve lanes to twenty-four. It was not enough to meet the heavy demand; within a year, Hoefler was "forced" to add another dozen. By 1956, the number of lanes at Airport Bowl had increased to fifty, a growth that Hoefler attributed directly to the Automatic Pinspotter.

To some extent, these dramatic upturns in business derived from curiosity seekers who had to see the mechanical marvels for themselves. Proprietors deliberately capitalized on the novelty of the automatic machines. The Fairview Bowling Center, one of the first establishments in Cleveland to employ the new AMF product, advertised in 1954: "The AMF machine picks up and returns the ball . . . sets up the pins . . . clears the lanes of dead wood. . . . Seeing is believing . . . so come in and see for yourself."

In the Wee Small Hours:
Automation and the
Twenty-Four-Hour Bowling Alley

But it was not simply curiosity that brought more business to the automated bowling centers. No longer dependent on a scarce labor supply, proprietors were able to operate at full capacity around the clock. Twenty-four-hour-a-day operations, while not unheard of, were a rarity before the advent of the mechanical pinsetter. During World War II, a number of operators experimented with extended hours to accommodate the recreational needs of night-shift workers; some operators extended this practice into the post-war era. For the most part, however, proprietors kept their alleys open during hours when they could count on pinboys, typically from late afternoon until midnight.

Automation, however, made twenty-four-hour operation the norm. Proprietors consistently cited the increased business at odd hours of the day as one of the most outstanding benefits of automated bowling.

Les Miller was the first proprietor in Des Moines, Iowa, to install automatic pinspotters, a move that allowed him to stay open around the clock. Almost immediately, Miller sought to capitalize on his new opportunity by running radio advertisements at 11 P.M., midnight, and 1:30 A.M. urging people riding around in their automobiles to drop in for open bowling at his Capitol Lanes.

The thirty-two-alley Cascade Bowling Center, the seventh Chicago establishment to go automatic, experienced a similar surge in after-hours business, helping offset the initial investment in automation. In addition to the expense of leasing equipment from AMF, the owner, Lloyd Weaving, was forced to spend $60,000 to re-lay all of his alley beds to make room for the under-alley ball returns that sliced each pair of lanes. Still, Weaving thought the investment well worth it. In addition to shaving an average of ten minutes off of each league session, the automatic equipment stimulated open play at odd hours. "At 2 A.M. our alleys used to be deserted," noted Weaving; "now we have all we can do to get the bowlers out at 5 o'clock in the morning. Already I've picked up a couple of odd hour leagues."

Like Weaving, proprietors with the automatic pinsetters eagerly recruited leagues to fill empty slots in mornings, afternoons, and late nights. Upon installing thirty-two robotic pinboys in September 1952, the managers of Amherst Recreation in Buffalo were able to sign up 156 additional teams that competed in the early afternoon and the early hours of the morning, times when pinboys were previously unavailable. As a relieved secretary-treasurer of Amherst Recreation explained, "We won't have to turn anybody away with the excuse that we don't have any pinboys." In North Arlington, New Jersey, the Bowl-O-Drome began scheduling leagues at four o'clock in the morning for night-shift workers from surrounding industrial plants in Newark, Jersey City, and Paterson.

League play structured around work schedules, however, could not possibly fill all the available time. Thus, the development of the automatic pinsetter created not only an opportunity, but an imperative, to open the sport to novices, particularly women and children. The bowling industry was not oblivious to the possibilities of expanding its customer base prior to AMF's invention, but for most proprietors, there was little incentive to do so given the shortage of pinboys. Suddenly, proprietors found themselves in a situation where they needed to drum up business at times when their regular customers were unavailable. In the newer, round-the-clock suburban establishments that opened for business in the wake of automation, the thought of all those dead hours on weekday mornings and afternoons was enough to change the minds of proprietors who had once balked at the prospect of thirty lanes filled with dawdling women or screaming children.

New Recruits: Courting Women
and Children in the Suburbs

Moreover, the disappearance of the pinboys gave greater ur-
gency to arguments emphasizing the need to cultivate a new
generation of bowlers. Prior to automation, proprietors counted
on pinboys to pass through the ranks from employee to customer. With ample opportunity to polish their skills—lulls in
business might well allow for fifteen or twenty practice games a
day—pinboys often developed bowling addictions that carried
into their adult lives. With the demise of this pinboy "apprenticeship," the next generation of recruits would have to come from
elsewhere. Especially for establishments that were located in residential neighborhoods, the obvious candidates for new customers were women homemakers and schoolchildren, two
groups who had free time during those periods of the day when
bowling alleys tended to be vacant.

Proprietors received assistance in their attempts to court these
customers from the major manufacturers of bowling equipment.
AMF and Brunswick recognized that with the advent of automated
bowling, their fortunes were tied to proprietors' success in attracting new patrons. AMF's leasing formula, in which proprietors paid
the company per game bowled, ensured that greater lineage translated into greater company profits. For Brunswick, the stakes were
even higher; the Chicago company held the promissory notes on
all the pinsetters sold on installment. To recoup its money,
Brunswick depended on the financial success of its clients. With a
direct interest in the overall fortunes of the bowling business, both
manufacturers poured thousands of dollars into promotional campaigns—television shows, bowling clinics, and advertisements—
designed to spread the popularity of bowling among the uniniti-
ated. Television programming emerged as the most novel medium
used to demonstrate the ease and fun of bowling during the 1950s.
Not only did weekly television broadcasts showcase the nation's

star bowlers in professional tournaments, but they also demonstrated how quickly novices could master the craft. Among the more popular shows in the latter category was *Bowling for Dollars*, on which amateur contestants introduced themselves to the viewing audience and then rolled for prizes.

To further encourage the participation of beginners and, of course, to cash in on their expanding patronage, manufacturers developed special lines of bowling accessories for women and children. In addition to marketing a lighter ball for women, the nation's oldest manufacturer of bowling equipment decorated its "Lady Brunswick" in mottled patterns of "cornflower blue" and "explosive pink." With its "Junior Mineralite" ball, weighing only eight pounds, Brunswick promised youngsters that they could "bowl just like dad." In 1957, the John E. Sjostrom Company of Philadelphia announced that it was manufacturing a series of lightweight bowling balls for children and teenagers. Youngsters could choose from weights in intervals of nine, eleven, twelve, thirteen, fourteen, and fifteen pounds. The eleven-pound ball, called the "teenager," was sold in three colors. In addition to the lightweight balls, Brunswick, Sjostrom, and other companies sold miniature sized shoes and bags for young bowlers.

Ultimately, however, the burden of expanding the industry's clientele fell to those on the front lines of the business, the thousands of bowling alley proprietors across the nation. Advertisements for particular bowling houses exhorted people in the surrounding neighborhoods: "Bowl Close to Home." Savvy proprietors opened establishments in suburban shopping centers to draw business from women making their daily shopping rounds. Ben Mason, for example, used his shopping center location in Kansas City to his best advantage by enlisting adjoining merchants in the distribution of fliers that announced free bowling instructions, free coffee, and free nursery service at his Mission Bowl. Neighboring retailers cooperated, hoping that regular bowlers would become regular shoppers at their adjacent stores.

The People's Country Clubs:
Suburbanizing and Glamorizing
the Bowling Alley

The imperative to expand clientele was particularly strong in the suburban bowling centers that sprouted in the 1950s as a direct result of automation. No longer tethered to inner-city districts where casual labor that could be channeled into pinsetting was most abundant, proprietors were free to follow the stampede of middle-income families to residential developments on the metropolitan periphery. It was not just that large numbers of people were moving to the suburbs, but that the suburbs were capturing the largest share of America's most affluent consumers, providing enormous business opportunities for retailers and entrepreneurs of all kinds, including bowling alley proprietors. Hence, the 1950s witnessed a rash of suburban bowling alley construction. Frank Caprise recalled that when he opened his first bowling alley several miles east of New York City in the Long Island town of Mineola in 1940, there were only about three other competing establishing in all of Nassau County. Fifteen years later, the market in the county was "saturated." This proliferation of suburban alleys was occurring nationwide.

Automated bowling centers tended to make their appearance in the same type of neighborhoods that supported modern diner-restaurants, that is, transitional suburbs populated by upwardly mobile, middle-income families. Due to the convergence of markedly similar marketing strategies, it was not uncommon to find new diners and new bowling alleys sitting side by side in the 1950s, or at least, in close proximity to one another. Just as suburban diners established new standards in the field of commercial dining, suburban bowling alleys took the industry lead in recrafting the bowling experience.

By adding a degree of reliability to the enterprise of bowling, the automatic machines encouraged the investment of venture capital in new bowling alleys on an unprecedented scale. Lending institutions were willing to finance million-dollar establishments, especially in populous suburban areas where the bowling market was largely untapped. Moreover, because labor requirements were no longer a major consideration and because space was both abundant and relatively inexpensive in these suburban areas, there were few limits to bowling alley size. Hence, suburban establishments tended to be larger and more elaborate than their inner-city counterparts. Vast one-story, free-standing structures comprising forty, fifty, or sixty lanes became the norm.

These large investments in suburban locations, often in excess of a million dollars, enabled proprietors not only to build large facilities but also to decorate them lavishly. Investors hired prominent architects to design sleek buildings with cantilevered roofs, beveled ceilings, glass curtain windows, and jutting outdoor pylons covered with large neon lettering. Not dissimilar in appearance to the Space Age diners that were opening for business in the same places at the same time, the new automated bowling centers of the late 1950s conformed perfectly to the aesthetic of glitz that was coming to dominate the commercial thoroughfares of suburbia. In making their interiors more colorful and ornate, suburban bowling alley proprietors again paralleled the prevailing trends in diner design. Huge sums of money were spent on lobby areas by laying thick wall-to-wall carpeting in eye-catching colors and designs and by dispersing tropical plants around the premises. Proprietors commissioned artists to paint murals of rustic scenes on their walls, installed floodlit fountains alongside their entrances, and embellished their exteriors and interiors with large modern sculptures.

California architects took the lead in crafting the new look in bowling alley design. One firm in particular, Powers, Daly, and DeRosa, was credited with pioneering the "California style" that set the standard for bowling center architecture in the late 1950s, both within and beyond the Golden State. Known for its "lavish lounges, cavernous concourses, high-beamed ceilings, and flam-

Covina Bowl was one of many lavish bowling centers built by Powers, Daly, and DeRosa in the 1950s.

boyant exterior architecture," the firm designed nearly fifty bowling centers between 1955 and 1962. Each building expounded upon an exotic theme. Java Lanes in Long Beach, California, with its exotic wall decorations and its East Indies Lounge, employed a Polynesian motif. Covina Bowl evoked the spirit of Antony and Cleopatra with a pyramid entrance and Egyptian statuary in the cocktail lounge. With a towering totem pole gracing its entrance, the Bel Mateo Bowling Center featured the imagery of Pacific Northwest Native American culture. The highlight of the Persian-themed Futurama Bowl in San Jose, California, was its "Magic Carpet Room," a cocktail lounge adorned with 470,000 hanging beads.

Willow Grove Lanes was the most ambitious project undertaken by Powers, Daly, and DeRosa. Located next to an amusement park in a North Philadelphia suburb, Willow Grove was like a theme park unto itself. The 800-foot-long V-shaped building took fifteen months to build. Viewed from the outside, it was noth-

ing if not breathtaking. The main entrance was highlighted by a
solid parabola that swung skyward 116 feet and hovered over a
multicolored water fountain situated in a miniature lake. When
you entered the building, your eye was drawn to a rotating
turntable display of bowling paraphernalia. To accommodate the
disparate needs of different types of customers, the architects provided a variety of ancillary social spaces. Their nursery boasted a
life-size rocking horse. Teenagers fraternized at a soda bar called
the "Hutch." Adults were invited to sample the German fare at the
"Hofbrau," a full-service restaurant.

Architectural critics dismissed the work of Powers, Daly, and
DeRosa, condemning their buildings as garish and far too expensive to build and maintain. The three California architects did not
deny that their designs were extravagant and fanciful. As Pat
DeRosa, the youngest member of the architectural trio explained,
"Frankly, we don't want a client who is trying to get by as cheaply
as possible. It's our feeling that a really attractive building *will* bring
in business." The automatic pinsetter attracted big-money investors to bowling, people who had both the capital and the will
to finance the construction of expensive and attractive buildings
that screamed, "Have fun here!" The eye-popping decor seemed to
strike a chord among suburban bowlers, many of whom were experiencing material affluence for the first time. Thus, despite the derision they elicited in architectural circles, Powers, Daly, and
DeRosa became the darlings of the bowling industry. Their designs were widely emulated, not just in California but across the
country.

The investors behind the Mages Sporting Goods Company did
as much as any other individuals to disseminate the California
style across the bowling world. In 1959, the company announced
its intention to build fifty architecturally uniform Mages Bowlare-
nas across the country. The first among them, a pilot project located on the northwestern edge of Chicago, was designed by
Richard Barancik. Its façade was sheathed in a highly stylized

rough marble aggregate. For the entrance, highly regarded sculptor Abbot Pattison designed a 200-foot precast concrete frieze in an abstract design. Stone was used liberally inside and outside the building; the entrance lobby featured crab orchard floors. The countertops in the ladies rooms and the color-coordinated Italian tile in the drinking fountains were overlaid with marble. The billiard room was paneled in walnut. Describing the overall effect, Irving H. Mages proclaimed, "The design of our first bowling center strikes a motif of gaiety and flamboyance in keeping with its recreational use."

To be sure, the swanky new bowling palaces served primarily as places to bowl, but the elaborate architecture suggested they were much more. Indeed, they had to be if the industry intended to reach out beyond the die-hard competitive bowler. Part of the strategy involved creating a psychic distance between the automated suburban establishments and the older, inner-city variants housed on decrepit second stories or in dingy basements. For starters, modern proprietors almost universally dropped the word "alley" from the names of their businesses, preferring more snazzy titles such as Bowl-O-Drome, Wonder Bowl, and Bowlero. More commonly, owners simply affixed the name of their suburban locality to the word "lanes" or "recreation center," as in Bayside Lanes or Hillcrest Recreation Center. As Norma Kirkendall, editor of *The Woman Bowler* explained, "Isn't it a lot nicer to hear 'lane' than 'alley' which smacks of garbage cans and trash? A 'lane' has a romantic tinge and 'going down the lane' sounds like the fun that it is."

While suburban bowling alley proprietors had no trouble defining what their establishments no longer were—inner-city dives— they struggled to define their new function in contemporary suburban society. Finding the right formula for success required that they address the peculiar aspirations and anxieties associated with the upwardly mobile, middle-income residents who lived nearby, many of whom had arrived in the suburbs only slightly earlier than the automated bowling center.

The families who lived in the inner suburban rings of Chicago, St. Louis, Indianapolis, and Detroit may have enjoyed a measure of material comfort, but they were still not in the same economic league as upper-crust elites who whiled away their hours at yacht basins, country clubs, and debutante balls. The bowling alley tried to present itself as a reasonably priced alternative to these tony leisure activities. In the words of one successful proprietor, the automated bowling centers of the 1950s were "the people's country clubs." The "country club for the public" theme was employed frequently to suggest that the elegant trappings and wide range of amenities that typified exclusive and private leisure venues could be found for a modest price in a modern bowling establishment. At the 64-lane Holiday Bowl Recreation on the outskirts of Chicago, "country club luxury and atmosphere" consisted of a sunken-garden cocktail lounge, an Olympic-sized swimming pool, a sun deck, and tennis courts. Such extravagance was surpassed by the Kansas City establishment that included an art gallery and an aviary which required the services of a full-time bird-keeper. What made these "people's country clubs" so extraordinary was not simply the profusion of fancy cocktail lounges, swimming pools, and aviaries, but the fact that these amenities could be obtained without a private membership and in fact cost very little to enjoy. Luxuries and comforts of the sort that were once restricted to the very rich were now open to all; the modern bowling center made a version of the lush life available to the average suburban family.

While bowling alley proprietors sought to attract new customers by evoking the glamour of the leisure class, they also sought to integrate their establishments into the civic life of the communities in which they were located. The modern bowling alley often came to serve as a community center, a place where local civic leaders and groups could gather and make community decisions. By 1960, Fred Magee had invested in twenty-eight bowling centers throughout the Midwest. Committed to making his bowling houses pillars of the community, he convened a meeting with

Victory Bowling, late 1950s. Bowling centers built in the wake of automation used distinctive architecture and amenities such as coffee shops and cocktail lounges to draw a more diversified clientele.

local church leaders to coincide with the opening of each establishment. These meetings were held to determine how his business could best contribute to the community's mores: whether alcohol should be served, when schoolchildren should be admitted, and so forth. When Northfield Lanes in Cleveland, Ohio, announced that its meeting rooms would be available for church groups and civic organizations on a permanent basis, it followed the example of many other bowling centers across the country. Ranch Bowl, on the other hand, may have been unique in offering its facilities to the sixty-piece Omaha Symphony Orchestra for Monday night rehearsals. Whether hosting Boy Scout gatherings, church group meetings, or symphony orchestras, bowling centers that integrated themselves into community affairs helped customers—most of them recent arrivals—establish a connection with their communities, an appeal that may have resonated among those who felt a sense of rootlessness in their new suburban settings. Its new role as a community center also went a long way toward rehabilitating the seamy reputation of the bowling alley in the eyes of its upwardly mobile customers.

A Place to Take the Wife and Kids: Fostering "Family Togetherness"

Above all else, the bowling establishments of the 1950s were promoted as centers of family fun that fostered a spirit of togetherness outside the home. Coined by *McCall's* magazine in 1954 and employed liberally in the popular press throughout the rest of the decade, the slogan "family togetherness" embodied the ideal of domestic social relations and priorities to which responsible Americans aspired. "Togetherness" implied that parents would center their lives around the needs of their children and that husbands and wives would share household duties more equally. Time spent away from work would be devoted to the children. Dad would help Mom change diapers, wash dishes, and shop for groceries. Mom might even assist Dad with simple home improvements. Elevated by the popular media to cult status, the ethic of family togetherness governed the marketing strategies of advertisers and retailers who wished to push consumption to new extremes. The bowling industry had good reason to believe that tenpins could succeed as a family activity since equivalent skill levels could be easily attained by all members of the family. Especially if the ultimate objective was fun rather than competition, there was no reason that Mom, Dad, and kids could not find a focal point for their recreational energies in bowling.

It was fitting that the Wonder Bowl corporation chose a site adjacent to Disneyland for the first of its six southern California establishments that aimed at "welding family life." Walt Disney had built his entertainment empire on the concept of wholesome family fun, with not so subtle prescriptions for proper social behavior encrypted in his cartoons, movies, and theme parks. Bowling pro-

moters would attempt much the same. When an American Bowling Congress official asserted, "The number one reason for the
bowling boom . . . is that Mama has accepted it as a wholesome
recreation, not only for her husband but for herself and her whole
family," he expressed the core principle that underlay the strategy
of the bowling industry in the mechanized era. Mama was indeed
the key. As was the case with the diner, the bowling alley was domesticated in order to convince women that it was an appropriate
place, not only for themselves, but for their husbands and children. The once exclusively male preserve would open up to a far
wider constituency: men, women, children, and whole families.

To counteract the lingering antipathy felt by many toward
bowling alleys due to the churlish antics of pinboys, the industry
went out of its way to remind potential suburban customers that
automation made bowling alleys family friendly. Within a few
years after inventing the Automatic Pinspotter, AMF was making
explicit connections between its machines and family bowling.
Most of the company's promotional material featured "Mr.
Pinspotter," a smiling metallic robot who offered a stark contrast
to the surly pinboy of the past. With a bowling pin gripped in one
pincer while the other waved a friendly hello, Mr. Pinspotter
could not have appeared less threatening when he proclaimed,
"Bowling is fun for the entire family . . . anytime[,] automatically."
Alongside Mr. Pinsetter, AMF usually set drawings or photographs of families enjoying themselves at the bowling alley,
cheering one another on.

In an instructional brochure distributed at bowling centers
across the country, AMF used the example of the Taylor family of
Long Island to illustrate bowling's potential for improving family
relations. There was a time when Saturday mornings saw all members of the Taylor family go their own way. Joe played cards with
the "gang," presumably his male buddies, while Alice, his wife, performed household chores, twelve-year-old Bobby went to a cow-
boy movie, leaving nine-year-old Diane with nothing better to do

than stand on the front lawn waving at passing cars. While not an atypical family situation, neither was it a particularly healthy one. Everything changed when one rainy Saturday morning, young Bobby asked his dad to drive him over to the new automated neighborhood bowling center. Dad decided to stick around and bowl a few games with his son. He enjoyed the activity so much that he insisted the entire family return the following week. Thereafter, Saturday morning bowling became a regular routine for the Taylor family. The result, according to Joe, was that "ever since, we've all been a lot happier."

While AMF and Brunswick did the most to publicize in local and national media the pleasure and harmony to be gained from family bowling, it was left to individual proprietors to determine the right mix of ancillary services and amenities—concession stands, banquet halls, lounges, pro shops, nurseries, instructional programs, and so forth—that would ensure the loyalty of families once they were lured inside and create the atmosphere that would be most conducive to wholesome family fun.

In particular, they had to decide how to handle the long-standing association between bowling and alcohol consumption. Gone were the days when most bowling took place in saloon basements; Prohibition abruptly terminated that phase of the sport's history. Well into the 1940s, however, alcohol consumption remained an integral part of the game. On any given night it was quite common to find league bowlers chugging beer on the bench before staggering up to the foul line while bartenders scurried from one party to another balancing trays of bottled beer. Beer was a lucrative sideline, and few proprietors were eager to forsake the revenue it brought them. At the same time, proprietors as a group recognized that lingering associations between bowling and the saloon posed a threat to the sport's viability as a family activity. As early as 1940, Brunswick Balke Collender, which was as concerned with the sport's reputation as any proprietor, recommended a solution: restrict drinking to a separate room cordoned off from the playing area. By the 1950s, this solution had become standard practice, with most of the automated bowling centers abandoning the crude bar and stool arrangement in favor of plush cocktail lounges with table service and tightly controlled public access. The removal of liquor sales to secluded confines inverted the traditional relationship between spaces for play and drink in bowling alleys. Whereas turn-of-the-century alleys functioned as adjuncts to the saloon, by the 1950s, the saloon functioned as an adjunct to the bowling alley. Now the real money was to be made on the lanes, not in the bar. Alcohol merely served to boost bowling profits.

Some proprietors were not satisfied with segregating alcohol and bowling. They went further and discontinued liquor sales altogether. When Max Newman made the decision to orient his Northfield Bowl around families and young children in 1955, he chose not to serve any alcohol. Admitting that "revenue from a bar would be a boon financially," he nevertheless continued, "we get a certain satisfaction out of operating without liquor on the premises. Northfield Bowl is like a recreation center. . . . It's an ideal spot for young people and youngsters can come here and bowl in an entirely wholesome atmosphere."

Likewise, some proprietors decided to divorce billiards from bowling. Although the two sports shared a common origin in turn-of-the-century saloon culture, billiards never escaped its association with hustlers and criminals. Thus, when Nielson Harris opened Orchard Twin Bowl just outside of Chicago, he feared that a billiard room would attract the wrong type of patron and thus decided not to include one. As he explained it, "We didn't want that type of hoodlum hanging around." Harold Weber, on the other hand, decided to retain a billiard room when he opened All Star Bowl, just a short drive away from Harris's establishment. But access to the room was restricted to members of the billiard club, thus giving Weber a means of weeding out undesirables.

The biggest difficulty facing proprietors involved reconciling the popular ideal of family togetherness with the preference among many of their customers to bowl with their peers rather than other family members. The concept of family bowling was more complicated than it appeared on the surface. Creating a suitable space for family activities did not mean that proprietors were uninterested in men, women, and children bowling independently of each other. Quite the contrary, especially in light of the fact that conflicting school and work schedules made it impossible for men, women, and children to bowl together much of the time. More than anything else, "family" became a code word designed to generate acceptance for bowling among a broad range of customers, men and women, old and young, seasoned and novice. As far as proprietors were concerned, the success of family bowling would be measured by the sheer volume of paying consumers rather than the number of customers passing through their doors in family units. Proprietors discovered, if they did not already know, that appealing to men, women, and children on an independent basis was just as vital to a good marketing strategy as promoting collective family leisure.

As part of their effort to secure the loyalty of this potentially large group of recreational bowlers—both families and their individual members—proprietors began to offer an array of services at their alleys. Among these was free or inexpensive instruction. The impatient and sometimes antagonistic pinboy had long been a source of intimidation for the inexperienced bowler. Automation not only made parents feel more comfortable allowing their children inside bowling alleys but often eased their anxieties as well if they had not reached a certain level of proficiency. Still, new bowlers were fearful of looking foolish on the lanes, prompting proprietors to inaugurate instructional programs. From the proprietors' point of view, the incentive for providing lessons, even if offered free of charge, lay in the potential for cultivating a devoted clientele. The idea was that in creating good bowlers, they would produce regular bowlers and eventually league bowlers. In many cases instruction programs channeled students directly into regular leagues.

This was the technique used by John Smith at Cloverleaf Bowl in Miami. Smith employed a team of four female canvassers who went door to door in the surrounding neighborhood, inviting women to attend free classes at his establishment. When the classes ended, the students were urged to join open-bowling clubs that ran for five weeks. Smith hoped that by this time they would become addicted to the game and ripe for recruitment into his daytime and evening leagues. While few proprietors were as methodical as Smith, by the late 1950s most had full-time instructors on hand to provide one-on-one tutoring or group instruction.

Bowling academies were an integral part of Milton Raymer's scheme to get children and teenagers off the street and into the bowling alley after school. No individual in the country did more to promote the sport to this group than Raymer, whose work on behalf of youth bowling dated to 1935 when he organized a four-team league for his students at Tilden High School in Chicago. From there, the concept expanded, first to include teams from other schools in the Chicago area, and later to involve competition among high schools throughout the nation. In 1941, Raymer formalized inter-scholastic competition on the national level under the organizational auspices of the American High School Bowling Congress. Raymer did not stop there. After World War II, he proposed a plan to bowling industry leaders that would expand the program to include children of all ages and to encourage sponsorship from church groups, fraternal organizations, and civic groups, in addition to high schools. With liberal financing from the Brunswick Corporation and the National Bowling Council, Raymer organized the American Junior Bowling Congress in 1947.

Over the next decade, Raymer traveled energetically from city to city, visiting proprietors to publicize the Junior Congress and encouraging them to contribute their alleys to the program. Invariably, these visits coincided with demonstration schools where Raymer instructed young neophytes in the fundamentals of bowling. The schoolteachers who chaperoned the children were encouraged to assist the program by integrating bowling into their physical education curriculum. Proprietors were asked to donate their alleys and the services of pinboys free of charge for the demonstration schools. The pitch made to proprietors was that the bowling schools would lead directly to the formation of leagues during after-school hours. In addition, youth bowling was sold as a good long-term investment; by molding good bowlers at a young age, the program would ensure a dedicated stream of customers for many years to come.

In addition to offering lessons for beginners, proprietors devised a variety of promotions targeted at women, children, and teenagers. Special deals for children's birthday parties were particularly popular. The managers of Walnut Bowl in Walnut Creek, California, for example, sent flyers to parents in the area notifying them of their offer to host a birthday party for the price of $1.50 per child. In addition to two games of bowling, the children received a slice of decorated cake, a soft drink, and a portion of ice cream. Some proprietors turned their facilities into dating venues to attract young adults. In Stockton, California, Lloyd Bloom organized a Sunday morning singles competition where teams, composed of one man and one woman, were drawn at random each week. Following the game, all bowlers sat down for a singles breakfast.

Other promotions clearly based their appeal to women on traditional feminine grounds. It was obvious that the owners of Pike Lanes anticipated women's patronage; at their grand opening in April 1961, they gave away orchids to the first 500 women who entered. To provide an added incentive for his newer female bowlers who tended to bowl in the morning, the owner of Fairview Lanes in Rockford, Illinois, set out a breakfast spread of pastries and coffee on the last Tuesday of each month. Late one spring, Fairview Lanes chartered a bus trip to a shopping center just outside Chicago where women were invited to a luncheon and fashion show. In 1959, Brunswick developed its Something for the Girls Program in conjunction with local bowling businesses. Proprietors sent coupons for free bowling and instruction to women within a prescribed area. Once the coupons were redeemed, the women were automatically entered into a sweepstakes competition for a Mercedes-Benz sports car, a full-length mink coat, an Esther Williams swimming pool, and other prizes.

Proprietors also found it necessary to further refurbish their establishments to suit the practical needs and aesthetic sensibilities of the growing number of women customers. Even before World War II, proprietors who wished to a cultivate the female trade had lavished attention on decor. Certainly the extravagant designs of the postwar suburban bowling palaces aimed in large part at attracting female customers. Sometimes, however, the physical adjustments made to bowling houses could be quite subtle. The women who patronized Phil's Recreation in Manhattan compelled the management to install purse hooks on the ends of every scoring table. Since many of the beginners did not own their own bowling bags, they had little incentive to rent lockers. Instead, women kept their purses on the spectator benches just behind the play area. But this arrangement was also convenient for thieves, and several purses were pilfered. So that bowlers could keep a closer eye on their possessions while they played, one league secretary contrived simple hooks made from wire hangers and attached them to the scoring table. Observing the need for a more permanent solution, the proprietor screwed in hooks. Although only a minor alteration, one that probably passed unnoticed by many of Phil's male customers, the example of the hooks illustrates how new customers could take the initiative in transforming the modern bowling alley.

Modifications were made for the benefit of young bowlers as well. To assist juniors who had trouble pushing the ball the full length of the alley, some owners built new approaches beyond the foul lane to reduce the distance to the pins. Presumably, they dismantled the electric foul detector prior to play. If they had not done so before, proprietors stocked up on candy and gum and dispensed them from the main counter to supplement their profits. Jukeboxes and soda fountains represented more significant investments on behalf of young customers.

A League of Their Own: Organized Women's Bowling

Free instruction, special promotions, and refurbished interiors bore fruit in the form of increased casual patronage and eventually tournament and league play for women and children. Although open-play bowling rose dramatically with the advent of automation, proprietors much preferred to see their lanes occupied by leagues that guaranteed them a steady flow of business. Thus they eagerly welcomed the growing number of tournaments and leagues sanctioned by the American Junior Bowling Congress and the Women's International Bowling Congress. During the daytime hours, suburban bowling centers filled with homemakers' leagues, while juniors monopolized the lanes in the afternoons. Some of these "alternative" leagues were strictly for beginners. The 151 teams entered in the Columbus Housewives Tournament at Olentangy Village were composed exclusively of women who had enrolled in the establishment's free daytime bowling clinics. Most of the grandmothers who rolled in the Grannies Bowling League on Friday afternoons at Hialeah Bowling Lanes, near Miami, were beginners, as were the hundred nuns who bowled in a special morning tournament at the Ames Bowling Center in Omaha, Nebraska. Few of the sisters had ever set foot in a bowling hall. Dressed in their full habits, the nuns apparently had difficulty hitting the pins, but claimed to have enjoyed themselves nonetheless.

For many women, daytime leagues provided a break from a hectic routine of cooking, cleaning, and child care. The Housewives League of Parkersburg, West Virginia, was formed in 1945 by women who found themselves with a block of free time in the early afternoon. By 1:30 P.M., the Parkersburg homemakers had fed their husbands and children, washed the dishes, and sent the kids back to school. Bowling provided a diversion for two hours until they were needed back home once again to care for their returning children. To establish a symbolic link between their work and their recreation, the women named every team in the league after a kitchen utensil, so that the Egg Beaters squared off regularly against the Coffee Pots, the Rolling Pins, and the Can Openers.

For millions of women trapped in isolated suburban settings, daytime leagues like the one organized by the Parkersburg housewives provided a much-appreciated outlet for socializing with peers. Bowling was a tonic for suburban loneliness, a malady that was particularly tough on women who were accustomed to very different work and social routines before the war. In the extended family households that characterized congested inner-city neighborhoods, domestic work was often performed in the company of other women—sisters, aunts, mothers, and nieces. The nuclear structure of postwar suburban households, on the other hand, virtually assured that housework would be performed alone. Companionship would have to come through recreation. For Sara Turner, that meant weekly bowling, an activity that dramatically transformed her social life. "I used to sit around at home while my husband was out working . . . feeling sorry for myself," she explained. "But now my phone is ringing all the time."

Allaying Fears:
Keeping Women in the Domestic Sphere

The concept of daytime women's bowling seemed harmless enough. But if bowling brought women out of the house, might it not encourage other types of independent behavior that ran against the cultural grain? The idea would not have seemed so far fetched to the editor of *The Woman Bowler* who proclaimed that the "bowlerette" of the 1940s was a "woman of action," and while interested in the "latest coiffeur," she was also vitally engaged in "the activities of her community, her city, yes, and her nation. As such, she is naturally interested in price controls, longer skirts, [and] cancer-research." The implication here was that the female bowler had a mind of her own and a set of interests that extended beyond the customary orbit of hearth and home. The modern "bowlerette," in other words, was unlikely to remain content in the traditional role of docile and obedient homemaker.

The prospect of women abandoning their familial responsibilities for the bowling alley did not sit well with many husbands. The ideal of family togetherness encouraged husbands and wives to spend more time together, but as disillusioned wives and mothers were quick to point out, it rarely approached full equality. Husbands still expected their wives to assume the lion's share of domestic burdens, whether or not they also held down full- or part-time jobs in the paid labor force. Thus, we can imagine the vexed and alarmed response of husbands when one of the participants in the Parkersburg, Virginia, Housewives League asserted, "When housework interferes with bowling, to heck with housework." We do not have to imagine the response of husbands to the Women's Greater Houston league. Incensed that their bowling-obsessed wives left them with the household chores on Friday evenings, the husbands sought revenge by organizing their own league on the same night. To make their point they arrived at Palace Recreation with placards reading, "We Want to Bowl Too. No More House-work." Although these men articulated their frustration with a dash of humor, their "revolt" spoke to underlying tensions that could and did take on more acrimonious manifestations.

Nothing was more threatening to men than the likes of LaVerne Haverly. Wife of a Los Angeles police investigator and mother of a thirteen-month-old child, she was also known as the "blond bomb-shell . . . for the way she has thrown pin-fans throughout the coun-try into a tantrum." According to one sportswriter: "You'd never guess, however, that she is a domesticated thing after the manner in which she has carried on in this game. Her bearing on the lanes is something to behold. Having both beauty and skill, she can af-ford to be rambunctious and fiery in action." A far cry from the idealized docile homemaker, Haverly openly flaunted her sexuality and displayed a level of competitive aggression that struck many men as unseemly. When she arrived in Chicago for an exhibition with Ace "Clown Prince" Calder, the Chicago bowler felt com-pelled to raise the stakes to a full-fledged war between the sexes. Said Calder: "No blonde or brunette or even a red-head is gonna beat a man of my stature . . . it's still a man's world." Haverly ended up beating Calder roundly, besting him in six of seven matches. Perhaps it was not a man's world after all.

If the bowling industry was to encourage independent women's bowling, it had to be careful not to incite a cultural backlash. First and foremost, proprietors had to ensure that bowling would not jeopardize the rearing of children. To this end, virtually all of the elaborate suburban centers built in the 1950s incorporated nurs-eries. The nurseries proved quite popular and were often filled to capacity with frisky tots during daytime hours. Sam Levine, a Cleveland sportswriter, spent an entire afternoon at the Clover-leaf Lanes day-care center to observe the phenomenon firsthand. Regardless of whether parents enjoyed their bowling outing, the children appeared to be having a good time. To keep the young-sters occupied, the proprietor had invested $300 in toys, includ-

Nursery, Paramus Lanes, Paramus, N.J., late 1950s

ing popper-rollers, building blocks, plastic telephones, a riding horse, and, always on the lookout for an opportunity to mold future customers, a miniature plastic bowling set. The $300 was not a one-time expense; the toys took considerable abuse and suffered from short life spans. Within a few hours, one boy ripped the legs from a teddy bear and a girl ravaged one of the plastic pins. Possibly due to its resemblance to an ice cream cone, she chewed hungrily on the top. According to Levine, the most popular toys were the noisiest.

Day-care facilities ensured that parents would not be derelict in their duties while they indulged their personal consumer appetites. Most of the nurseries kept matrons on duty so that, in effect, the bowling alley acted in loco parentis. As an added precaution, bowling centers like the Cloverleaf also placed closed-circuit television monitors and intercom pagers on the lanes so that mothers could keep a watchful eye and an attentive ear on their children while they bowled. Yet Harold Weber discovered that the women who bowled at All Star Lanes in Skokie, Illinois, paid no attention whatsoever to his television monitors. The mothers saw bowling as a respite from their maternal obligations and preferred to leave the child-watching entirely to the supervisor on duty in the nursery.

In 1958, AMF came up with a concept that would prevent women's bowling from intruding upon another domestic obligation, food shopping. The company suggested that proprietors offer a grocery shopping service on Fridays, the day most homemakers made their largest food purchases. Prior to bowling, the women would submit a grocery list to the clerk. By the time they were ready to leave, shopping bags filled with the requested items would be waiting for them. It is not known how many proprietors, if any, adopted AMF's suggestion. A similar line of reasoning, however, prompted a Missouri proprietor to install washers and dryers in his establishment so that women could take care of their laundry while they bowled.

The bowling industry used the media to dispel fears that women's league bowling would loose mothers and wives from their domestic moorings. Articles and editorials in bowling periodicals, many of which reached a national audience, publicized the views of experts who insisted that women's bowling was beneficial for families. A 1953 article in *The Woman Bowler* directed readers' attention to the opinions of Madge Taggart, a judge from Buffalo, who was a strong advocate of women's bowling. According to Taggart, league bowling made women better homemakers because "it gives the housekeeper a chance to get away from the oftentimes monotony of daily household chores for a bit of relaxation. . . . The hour or two supplies a break in the week. The competition injects new spirit in her. . . , bowling helps keep a woman active. And if she bowls consistently, it might help to keep her figure trim. . . . The score really doesn't matter, but, the competition, the exercise and the hour out could send her home actually refreshed and ready for the next day's household chores."

Another article, appearing in *The National Bowlers Journal and Billiard Revue*, explained that even when husbands and wives bowled on separate teams, in separate leagues, at separate venues, women's bowling enhanced marital bliss because the shared avocation helped "hubby and wife" develop a "deeper understanding" of one another. Perhaps, but this formulation certainly stretched the concept of family togetherness, which was supposed to involve joint activity, to its limits.

To counter the threatening images of women like LaVerne Haverly, the blond bombshell, magazines glorified female bowlers who were skilled at their craft but also seemed to know their proper place. Indeed, upon divorcing her first husband and wedding all-star bowler Don Carter, Haverly consented to a thorough revision of her image in the bowling media. No longer portrayed as the sexy firebrand who challenged male bowlers in head-to-head competitions, Laverne Haverly, as Laverne Carter, was transformed into the dutiful wife who knew her proper place. In a 1959 interview for *The Woman Bowler*, the transformed Laverne insisted: "Bowling isn't actually my life—my family is." To drive the point home, the magazine's profile deferred coverage of her bowling feats to an extended discussion of her views on cooking (her favorite recipe was macaroni and cheese) and fashion (she preferred sheaths and tailored sports clothes to the briefly popular sack dresses).

Clothes and the Woman

Clearly, the former blond bombshell was now safely and rightly ensconced in the domestic sphere, where family, meals, and fashion were paramount. In fact, fashion played a large role in reassuring an uneasy public that women who bowled were still "ladies." The difference between sack dresses and tailored sports clothes was no small matter; the question of attire went to the very heart of the social implication of women's participation in bowling. Women who took their bowling seriously preferred clothing that facilitated high scores. Gladys Dempsey recalled the formal outfit her mother wore when she bowled in one of the earliest women's leagues in Detroit before World War II. Dressed in a white middy blouse, a Kelly green scarf that hung down in a large bow, an ankle-length full-pleated skirt, long black stockings, and white tennis shoes, her mother could only attain an average of 125. Dempsey attributed her mother's meager accomplishment to her constricting attire. Even those who valued leisure over competition wanted to bowl in comfort. Neither form-fitting nor cumbersome outfits would do.

Hence, Paul Prescott, an apparel firm, emphasized that its bowling dresses were "designed for freedom and action; with extra deep armholes and deep action-pleats front and back." Gladys Dempsey expressed appreciation for the shorter skirts and looser blouses that had become acceptable since her mother's day but feared that some women carried the trend to an unacceptable extreme. "Some women even wear shorts and slacks," she complained, "but I'll reserve comment on these except for mentioning that there is a time and place for everything and the individual should choose sensibly for herself." Indeed, in the conservative social environment of the 1950s, one could go too far in the direction of the casual. An advice column in a 1959 issue of *The Woman Bowler* counseled, "Any outfit that is too tight or short or mannish and one that would

Bowling fashion, 1963. This outfit, part of AMF's Magic Triangle International Collection, assured women that they would retain their femininity while bowling.

cause comments unfavorably should be avoided on the lanes. Bowling is a respectable sport and should not be cheapened by vulgar dress when in public."

Designers went to great lengths to ensure that their outfits, while comfortable and conducive to high scores, also allowed customers to retain their femininity. Thus, the bowling dress designed by Paul Prescott facilitated not only quick movement but "graceful movement" as well. Moreover, it was "so lovely to look at." Typically, retailers boasted that their bowling outfits were sufficiently fashionable to be worn for social outings; they were as attractive at parties and luncheons as they were on the alley. Parade Fashions in Chicago sold an extensive line of women's bowling wear. One of its dresses, the "Big League Bowler," was advertised as a "Best fitting, Most comfortable dress made for Bowling and Casual Wear, Too!" To convert the outfit from sport to social or office use, the individual needed only to snap off the plaque designating the team name on the back. Lazarus denied any conflict between the objectives of fashion and proficiency, maintaining that its "Ken-Master" bowler dress for $8.99 "makes your game better because you *look* better."

In Mixed Company: Men and Women Bowling Together

The boldest attempt to accommodate women's leisure demands while maintaining traditional, nonthreatening gender roles, was to foster mixed play. By encouraging men and women to bowl together, proprietors promised to bring women into the game within the framework of marital or courtship norms. Nonetheless, pairing men and women as partners implied some measure of equality between the sexes. Mixed-play bowling presumed that marriages were becoming based more on consensual than patriarchal relations. As such, it tested people's commitment to the ideal of family togetherness as well as the bowling alley's ability to improve family relations through consumer activities.

Barriers between the sexes crumbled gradually in the years following World War II. Nineteen forty-six marked the first time that the men in the Scotia A.C. bowling league invited their wives and girlfriends to attend the end-of-the-season banquet at the Green

Lantern. Other leagues in the area decided to maintain the tradition of annual dinners as "stag" affairs. It was around this time that a few bowling proprietors began to experiment with leagues that brought men and women together in various formats. In 1947, Chicago's Cascade Bowling Center hosted an All-Star League composed of eight men's teams and eight women's teams. Although the men and women shared the same bowling venue, they did not compete against one another: Women bowled on one set of alleys while the men bowled on another. A Little Rock, Arkansas, proprietor took the concept a step further the following year in a league that saw women's teams compete head to head with men's teams.

When the Woodlawn Bowling Center in Schenectady, New York, announced its first mixed doubles tournament in April 1946, it established itself as a pioneer of the style of mixed play that would come to predominate by the 1950s. In this three-day affair, teams composed of one man and one woman competed for a first prize of $50. By the early 1950s, quite a few bowling houses sponsored leagues of this sort with teams composed of members from both sexes. The Queens Center Mixed Major League elicited enough popular interest in 1953 to fill all twenty-eight lanes of a suburban New York establishment. Across the East River, at the Port Authority Bus Terminal, the Midcity Mixed Major anticipated an enrollment of twenty teams, up from twelve the previous year.

The integration of sexes in the bowling alley was fraught with tension. Not all men were thrilled about the prospects of bowling side by side with women. Despite the high scores that demonstrated women's proficiency, the scuttlebutt in male bowling circles consisted of jokes about the deficiencies of women bowlers and how they would only interfere with the efforts of their more serious male counterparts. Typical was the cartoon published in a 1959 issue of *The National Bowlers Journal and Billiard Revue*, which showed a young woman approaching the foul line in what appeared to be fine form only to fling the ball backwards at the last moment, hitting her poor male partner square in the face. Jack Brown of Chicago undoubtedly spoke for other ordinary male bowlers when he stated unequivocally, "Bowling with women is no bowling at all. What's the matter?" he scoffed. "Those guys afraid to bowl with the men?"

The issue of proper decorum was another sore point. Apparently, many men took exception to the upgrading of manners required by the presence of the opposite sex. In particular, they worried that they would no longer be able to "talk it up" with the boys. Women, on the other hand, expressed reservations about sharing lane space with men on account of the foul language used by some men in bowling alleys.

At the very least, mixed bowling required certain adjustments on the part of both men and women to prevent togetherness on the alley from destroying rather than improving conjugal relations. A 1959 article in a popular bowling magazine offered advice on the thorny questions of etiquette that arose when married couples bowled. Should husbands carry their wives' bowling bags? Should the husband teach the wife to bowl? In mixed leagues is it improper for the husband and wife to be on different teams? Is it good for the husband and wife to make side bets between themselves? On the matter of bowling bags, the article warned husbands that they had better carry their wives' bowling equipment or else "she might find a new caddy." This response spoke directly to fears that exposing their spouses to other members of the opposite sex in consumer venues, if not handled carefully, might do more harm than good. One wonders, for instance, about the consequences of Harold Weber's special promotion at All-Star Lanes in Skokie, Illinois. During the evening mixed league, any bowler who rolled three consecutive strikes was permitted to kiss all members of the opposite sex in attendance.

Mixed bowling marked a new style of play, one that emphasized sociability over competition. As such it was an important element in the transformations of the sport and of the bowling alley as a social space. By 1958 mixed leagues constituted about 26 percent of the total, a remarkable statistic given that they were almost unheard of ten years earlier. Nonetheless, it is significant to note that nearly three-quarters of all bowlers continued to bowl with members of their own sex. Since by this time the total number of female bowlers almost equaled the total number of male bowlers, this figure also included the majority of women bowlers. When Mary Hoyt, one half of a successful husband-wife team on the West Coast, insisted that "almost all wives like to bowl with their husbands," she may have well overstated the case. The data suggest that a woman identified only as Betty more closely approximated the predominant motivation for women's bowling when she explained to a magazine reporter, "I get to be with women I like. I get out of the house and meet new people." For millions of bowlers like Betty, the sport was, first and foremost, a vehicle for developing broader social contacts with other women.

Heading off Trouble: Getting Teens off the Streets and into the Bowling Alley

Selling junior bowling required as much ingenuity and dexterity as selling independent women's bowling, and perhaps more. The in-

A school bus waits outside the Bird Bowl. Note the figure of AMF's Mr. Pinspotter featured on the building facade to advertise the new phenomenon of automated bowling.

flux of so many women bowlers was instrumental in transforming the postwar bowling alley, but female participation was not nearly as novel as organized junior bowling, which was quite rare prior to automation and virtually unheard of before World War II. Efforts to draw youngsters to the sport ran up against a legacy of the pin-boy era: the notion that the bowling alley was no place for unsupervised children. The national preoccupation with juvenile delinquency after World War II made it all the more difficult for proprietors to justify the expansion of the bowling market to include young consumers. Even as Milton Raymer hopscotched about the country drumming up support for his Junior Bowling Congress, several states and municipalities were attempting to ban children from bowling alleys altogether. Ultimately, the success of junior bowling hinged on the ability of Raymer and other industry leaders to turn the common wisdom about bowling and juvenile delinquency on its head, to make the case that bowling actually made children and teenagers better citizens and more responsible family members.

The idea that bowling might serve as a weapon in the war against juvenile delinquency dated back to the years immediately after World War II. Georgia Veatch, a columnist for *The Woman Bowler*, insisted that the sport had "a boundless offering to make to the reconversion of youth to a less delinquent stage. . . . Neighborhood clubs should corral its street urchins and divert their interests from doubtful means of self-amusement and organize them into teams and leagues in the nearby recreation center." Her advice was heeded. In both Detroit and St. Louis, police officers organized bowling leagues to keep troubled youth off the streets. The value of this selling point was not lost on Milton Raymer. In 1946, he contacted FBI director J. Edgar Hoover to solicit his support for the national youth bowling program on the grounds that it tied in with the agency's anti-delinquency efforts. Hoover subsequently endorsed Raymer's Junior Bowling Congress.

In developing the guidelines for participation in the American Junior Bowling Congress, Raymer went to great lengths to remove any potential corrupting influences associated with bowling alleys. All play would be supervised by adults, usually by schoolteachers who volunteered their services or by sanctioned AJBC instructors. AMF urged proprietors to shuttle students back and forth from the bowling alley in school buses, so they would never be beyond the watchful eye of adults. Proprietors were not allowed to sell alcoholic beverages on their premises while junior leagues were in session. Bowlers were forbidden from smoking or playing pinball machines (it was somehow assumed that teenagers who gathered around pinball machines were up to no good). To remove any lingering taint of gambling from the game, trophies, badges, and ribbons were awarded in lieu of cash prizes.

Some proprietors went beyond ensuring the wholesomeness of the bowling experience and tried to instill positive values in their young bowlers. J. Henry Aronson, known to Chicago's South Side youths as "Uncle Henry," donated his thirty-two lanes to neighborhood kids every Wednesday, Saturday, and Friday. Occasionally, Aronson chaperoned them to free movies and sporting events. By 1957, over a thousand children were taking advantage of Aronson's program. In order to join the "Uncle Henry Club," however, each member had to sign a pledge to be good. Pepsi-Cola sponsored an equally large junior bowling program in Detroit for boys of the "dangerous age." Walter Dossin, owner of the Pepsi-Cola franchise, used the opportunity to lecture the boys on proper code of conduct, including exhortations to "Honor Your Father and Mother" and to "Have Fullest Respect for Law and Order."

On one level the strategy was a smashing success. Especially with the disappearance of pinboys, parents proved receptive to the concept of supervised bowling as safe, wholesome, and even uplifting. Sally Tinner was convinced. Although her three sons, ages six, eight, and ten, were quite young, she had already begun training them as bowlers in the hopes that as teenagers they would "spend their time and money in the bowling alleys," thereby precluding the possibility that she would have to "pull . . . them out of 'Pool Halls' where the scum hangs out after school is over."

Advocates of youth bowling could not have been more delighted when Paul Harvey, the staccato-voiced radio commentator, endorsed the idea on a March 1957 broadcast. Harvey confessed that prior to the day his son dragged him to the Bowler's Club in suburban Forest Park, Illinois, he had assumed that bowling alleys were nothing more than juvenile delinquent hangouts. Upon observing the wholesome surroundings and taking up the sport with his wife, he became convinced that, on the contrary, supervised youth bowling held forth the promise of diverting troubled teens from "smoking dope" and "stealing cars." This was no small matter to Harvey, who identified the threat of teenage "internal combustion," ignited by the "undisciplined emotion" of youth, as an even more pressing danger to American society than all the political and social turbulence abroad.

Statistics reveal the fervor with which both customers and proprietors embraced the concept of youth bowling during the latter half of the 1950s. Youth bowling had already enjoyed significant increases in the late 1940s and early 1950s. By 1952, Raymer had signed up more than 31,607 students in the Junior Congress, a considerable achievement given the obstacles he faced. By 1955, Raymer had added another 17,000 members to the rolls. Thereafter, as bowling houses rapidly converted to automated equipment, the ranks of the Junior Congress swelled dramatically. In 1956 membership reached 93,767. In 1959 alone, the organization's membership tripled, bringing the total close to 400,000.

The Family That Plays Together Stays Together: The Formation of Family Leagues

With the successful introduction and growth of men's, women's, mixed, and youth leagues, the next logical step for the bowling industry, intent on burnishing their new family-friendly image, was the formation of family leagues. The organization of family

Promotional material distributed by the bowling industry, such as this 1962 photo, emphasized bowling as an activity that could be enjoyed by the entire family.

leagues represented the most direct attempt to keep youth tethered to their family responsibilities. By the late 1950s, many bowling houses sponsored special family tournaments where fathers competed against their sons or mothers battled their daughters, usually under a handicap system where scores were adjusted to compensate for dissimilar skill levels. Often these tournaments were held at the end of a junior bowling league season. On other occasions tournaments and leagues paired parents with their children. The AJBC encouraged proprietors to hold annual tournaments where different combinations of family members bowled together on the same team. A Davenport, Iowa, tournament offered different competitions for mother-son, father-daughter, and father-son combinations. Such events came closest to matching the ideal of family togetherness that the bowling industry promised to deliver in its public relations campaigns.

By 1960, children were thoroughly integrated into the formerly adult and unsavory world of commercial bowling. In 1961,

Brunswick estimated that roughly one-third of all bowlers in the nation were under the age of nineteen.

The dramatic increase in the number of young bowlers and the tremendous profits that accrued to proprietors and manufacturers certainly testified to the success of youth bowling on one level. If, however, youth bowling was to be judged on its ability to solidify family bonds and restrain the independent and potentially deviant impulses of America's youth, the results were more ambiguous. A 1960 market survey of bowlers conducted for AMF was revealing. About 19 percent of parents reported that they had bowled with their children at least once during the previous year, not an insignificant figure, but not a wholesale turn to bowling in family units either. When asked why they bowled, only a few adult respondents, about 5 percent, replied that it was a good activity for the entire family. Teenagers were even less motivated by the desire to spend time with their families, with more than 98 percent supplying alternative reasons, such as the chance to socialize with friends, exercise, and the pure enjoyment of the sport. And for all the youth that were drawn to bowling alleys through supervised programs, many more came independently and bowled without direct supervision. According to the 1960 AMF survey, fewer than 20 percent of teenagers were introduced to the sport through structured leagues. Indeed, most industry experts agreed that the large gains made in the area of unstructured, open bowling, was due to the increased patronage of young adults.

Only the Ball Was Black:
The Segregation of Bowling Alleys

The lanes at Terry Moore's Bowling Alley in north St. Louis were filled to capacity on June 5, 1962, but the sound of falling pins was conspicuously absent. Most of the men and women on hand that day were members of CORE, a civil rights organization that had recently launched a campaign to desegregate St. Louis bowling alleys. While many of the protesters sat patiently at the vacant scoring tables waiting their turn to bowl, others stood in line at the service counter. Outside, another contingent marched with placards that urged regular customers to take their business elsewhere. St. Louis was only one of many cities that saw the sit-in tactic spread from lunch counters to bowling alleys in the early 1960s. The drive to desegregate bowling alleys, however, preceded these nonviolent, direct-action protests by almost two decades. Thus, the bowling sit-ins of the early 1960s stood as a testament to both the resolve of African Americans and other racial minorities to establish a presence in the mainstream consumer world and the equally strong resolve of white business owners and patrons to keep them out.

Prior to 1920, in the days when bowling was an adjunct to the saloon business, racial discrimination was not systematic in the sport. A survey of bowling parlors conducted in Toledo, Ohio, just after World War I, for example, noted that racial mixing was quite common in the establishments located in the downtown business district. As bowling moved out of the saloon and became more competitive in the 1920s and 1930s, however, it also became more segregated, largely because both the American Bowling Congress and the Women's International Bowling Congress explicitly barred African Americans, Asian Americans, and Native Americans from participating in their leagues. The American Junior Bowling Congress followed with a similar segregation policy in the 1940s, conferring eligibility only on applicants who met the requirements of the adult organizations. In order to keep in good standing with the governing bodies that sanctioned league play, bowling alley operators toed the line; those proprietors who veered from official policy risked decertification and the loss of their league business. Well into the 1940s, there were few places where people of color could bowl save for the pair of lanes that might be located in the basement of a YMCA hall.

Excluded from the nation's major bowling tournaments, a group of African Americans from Michigan, Illinois, and Ohio formed the National Negro Bowling Association in 1939 to sponsor leagues around the country on a nondiscriminatory basis. Although membership in the organization was open to men and women of all races, it functioned primarily to coordinate league play for racial minorities. Like the American Bowling Congress, the National Negro Bowling Association, which later changed its name to the National Bowling Association, sanctioned alleys for structured competition and organized national tournaments for its top players. Its main challenge, however, was finding a place for them to bowl.

In some cities, National Bowling Association officials worked out agreements with alley proprietors that gave them access to bowling facilities late at night, after business hours. Typically, when the last white league finished for the evening, the proprietor hung a "closed for private party" sign on the front door and admitted National Bowling Association league members through a rear entrance. This arrangement allowed bowling alley owners to capture the business of racial minorities without violating the bylaws of either the American Bowling Congress or the Women's International Bowling Congress, much in the same way that take-out service enabled diner operators to profit from African-American consumerism without risking backlash from their white customers. It was not, however, a satisfactory solution for the men and women who had to wait around until midnight to begin their bowling. Hence, at the same time that they were negotiating for limited access to existing bowling establishments, National Bowling Association officials scoured the country for individuals who might be interested in building new bowling facilities for a predominantly African-American clientele. The problem they ran into here was that in many parts of the country, including cities like Cleveland and Indianapolis, banks were unwilling to lend money to African-American investors. In cases where proposed bowling alley projects enjoyed the backing of famous black athletes like Joe Louis or the ex-Harlem Globetrotter Sonny Boswell, banks were sometimes willing to take the plunge. More commonly, however, the only recourse available for African Americans who wanted to invest in bowling was to purchase decrepit bowling halls that white owners were anxious to abandon. So although by the 1950s, most cities contained alleys where African Americans could bowl, they were undercapitalized and outdated, nothing like the swanky bowling palaces becoming so common in white residential suburbs.

In addition to providing African-American bowlers with a mechanism for league competition, the National Bowling Association sought to strike down the discrimination clause in the American Bowling Congress constitution. Not only did segregation bar African Americans, Asian Americans, and Native Americans from the most up-to-date bowling facilities, it denied them the opportunity to compete against the top white bowlers, a situation they resented deeply. In the years immediately following World War II, this struggle to desegregate organized bowling gained momentum due to critical support from organized labor. In 1947, the United Autoworkers threatened to withdraw its sponsorship of leagues and tournaments if the white bowling association did not allow open competition among people of all races. The following year the International Ladies' Garment Workers Union informed industry leaders on the National Bowling Council of their refusal to participate in the Industrial Bowling Program on account of the fact that the color line violated both their rules and their traditions.

Initially, the white bowling world resisted change. According to the president of the American Bowling Congress, there was a vast difference between political and social rights, and while there were statutes that ensured equal rights before the law, people were free to choose whom to associate with in their recreational ventures. In the view of American Bowling Congress officials, if there were a civil rights issue at stake, it was the "impending peril to the rights of [white] bowlers" to choose their own bowling partners.

The obstinate will of the American Bowling Congress finally cracked under the pressure of a legal assault that began in the late 1940s. Relying on antidiscrimination statutes, civil rights groups and labor unions tried, unsuccessfully, to prevent the American Bowling Congress from holding tournaments in Michigan, New Jersey, and Ohio. The decisive blow, however, came in 1950, when Illinois judge John Sbarbaro fined the American Bowling Congress $2,500 and threatened to revoke its Illinois-based charter if it did not remove the discriminatory clause from its bylaws. At its annual meeting several months later, the fifty-year-old organization relented, and integrated competition was initiated in the following year. The first African-American team to bowl in ABC competition was from Allen Supermarkets in Inkster, Michigan. Thomas Pollock, anchorman on the team, was the first to roll an ABC-sanctioned 300 in the Detroit City Tournament.

Despite this major breakthrough, racial segregation within bowling alleys persisted in many areas well into the 1960s, thus providing impetus to the sit-in campaigns. Margaret Lee recalled an incident in the early 1950s when the proprietor of a Philadelphia establishment refused to let her bowl with her white high school classmates on account of her race. The experience did not deter Lee; by the 1960s she had become an avid bowler. Even at this time, however, there were few places she could bowl with white people. The major national bowling organizations, having deleted discriminatory language from their bylaws, did little to police the actions of individual proprietors, who set their own racial policies. In Brooklyn, where Lee resided, bowlers who competed at the modern and glitzy "white houses", such as Gil Hodges Lanes, discouraged black participation, thereby leaving African Americans with no other alternatives than the inferior "black houses," such as Fitzsimmons Lanes and Bedford Bowl. As she toured the country, entering one competition after another, she discovered similar patterns of segregation elsewhere, especially in the South. When she competed in New Orleans, for example, she suffered the indignity of being forced to enter and exit through a back door. In Ohio, proprietors maintained the practice of forbidding black customers from competing until late at night after all the white bowlers had finished.

By the early 1960s, the patience of black bowlers had worn thin. Under the direction of national civil rights organizations like CORE and the Student Non-Violent Coordinating Committee (SNCC), they renewed their war against segregated bowling by visiting offending bowling alleys en masse and stubbornly refusing to leave until served. This time, the results were more encouraging. After three rounds of sit-ins over the span of a week, the proprietors of Terry Moore's Bowling Alley in St. Louis had seen enough disruption to their business. On the afternoon of June 9, 1962, the manager announced that everyone in the building would be allowed to bowl regardless of his or her race. Fearful of similar disturbances, other bowling proprietors in St. Louis fell into line and opened their facilities to African Americans.

CORE's sit-in tactics proved equally successful in other large cities where proprietors feared the adverse consequences of negative publicity and disrupted business. Still, there remained pockets of white intransigence where achieving racial progress required much higher levels of dedication and sacrifice on the part of civil rights activists. Even after passage of the 1964 Civil Rights Act, which outlawed racial segregation in public accommodations, some proprietors clung stubbornly to what they asserted was their right to serve whomever they pleased. Harry Floyd, owner of the only bowling alley within forty miles of Orangeburg, South Carolina, was one such individual. Insisting that his establishment was not covered under the national civil rights law because he did not engage in interstate commerce (Congress justified federal intervention on the basis of the Constitution's interstate commerce clause), Floyd vowed to maintain his policy of segregation as long as he remained in business. This stance did not sit well, however, with the growing number of black students who had taken up league bowling in their hometowns before enrolling at Claflin College and South Carolina State College, both located in Orangeburg. Moreover, it rankled students who, though they had little interest in bowling, recognized Floyd as an intolerable remnant of Jim Crow and an ugly reminder of how easily local custom could subvert the nation's expressed commitment to racial equality in consumer venues.

Having staged successful sit-ins at segregated lunch counters earlier in the decade, students on Orangeburg's two college campuses renewed their fight for racial justice by initiating a series of "bowl-ins" at Floyd's All-Star Bowling Lanes in the winter of 1968. Floyd would not cave, however, and the stand-off between students and local police called out to protect Floyd's property grew tense over the week of February 5th. And then, in what came to be known as the "Orangeburg Massacre," the confrontation between students and local police escalated into a full-fledged melee in which three young men were shot to death and 27 others were wounded. In the end, All-Star Bowling Lanes was integrated, but only after the publicity generated by the massacre moved the U.S. Department of Justice to bring the full weight of the government's legal authority to bear on Floyd's illegal practices in a federal lawsuit.

That an incident of such tragic proportions should have originated in a dispute over access to a 16-lane bowling alley in 1968 indicates just how contentious the issue of expanding the middle majority market across racial borders remained even by the end of the postwar period. At the same time it confirms the extent to which that particular institution, the bowling alley, became a marker of success in postwar America. Indeed, to bowl in a modern bowling alley was to assert one's identity as a full-fledged American just as patronizing a diner signaled one's arrival in the affluent mainstream of America. From the perspective of racial minorities, second-class status as bowlers was tantamount to second-class status as American citizens.

The Final Frame:
The Bowling Boom Cools

By 1960, the bowling boom was over. The rash of bowling alley construction in the wake of automation saturated suburban markets in the major metropolitan areas. Proprietors complained that too much competition was eroding their patronage, forcing them to reduce prices to untenable levels. After a brief period of retrenchment in the late 1950s and early 1960s, business revived. Yet although the sport continued to gain new adherents into the 1970s, the pace of growth never again reached the dizzying heights of the 1950s. There would be no more dramatic innovations along the lines of the automated pinsetter to attract large numbers of curious novices.

The mechanized pinsetter revolution was instrumental in changing the face of bowling in much the same way that the removal of the front grill, the appearance of waitresses, and the emphasis on table service transformed the diner. In both cases, the overarching marketing strategy was identical: eliminate all associations with blue-collar labor by domesticating the consumer experience. Neither the bowling industry nor the diner industry was completely successful in this regard. Certainly by the 1960s, the bowling alley had become thoroughly incorporated into the routines of millions of suburban Americans: the sport's demographic profile conformed closely to that of America's suburbs: white, married, occupationally diverse, above average in income, predominantly homeowners. Yet, just as the diner never fully shook off its reputation as a workingman's hash house, popular culture continued to assign a working-class designation to the bowling alley. From *The Honeymooners* in the 1950s, to *Laverne and Shirley* in the 1970s, and up through *Rosanne* in the 1990s, television programs used the bowling alley to broadcast the working-class status of their protagonists. If not entirely middle class in the minds of many, the bowling alley nonetheless had attained an aura of re-

Richard Nixon bowling

spectability. As the "people's country club," the automated bowling center of the 1950s stood for the simple pleasures of hard-working, honest Americans, so much so that Richard Nixon, who as vice president deliberately cultivated the persona of the unpretentious middle American, frequently advertised his affection for bowling. At a 1958 visit to Wichita, Kansas, Nixon proudly confessed that he much preferred watching a good bowling match to a stuffy panel discussion.

If bowling enjoyed something of a noble status in the postwar era in spite of its working-class reputation, it was because it enabled customers to shed their class identities in favor of their familial affiliations. Adults entered the bowling center, not as welders or pipefitters but as fathers and mothers. Children arrived, not to set pins, but to partake in the joys of knocking them over. If the nuclear family was the vehicle through which Americans climbed the rungs of the social ladder, the bowling alley assisted the ascent by appealing to customers on the basis of their familial roles, even when men, women, and children bowled separately.

Indeed, the genius of the marketing strategy developed by AMF, Brunswick, and thousands of individual proprietors lay in the ability to stretch domestic norms to accommodate varied patterns of social interaction. The bowling industry projected an ideal, one borrowed from the consumer world at large, of family togetherness. But as proprietors and customers worked out its meaning in the formation of leagues and the provision of services, the concept took an unanticipated form. In practice, bowlers were more likely to play with peers than family members. Separate leagues for men, women, and children certainly gave the concept of family togetherness an ironic twist: the entire family may have bowled, but rarely did they do so together. To reconcile, or at least finesse, the contradictions between the image and reality of family togetherness, proprietors became surrogates. The bowling alley would supervise the toddlers, keep teenagers out of trouble, do the food shopping, and even link individuals to their larger communities. It would be father, mother, husband, wife, older sibling, and civic leader. Having successfully domesticated the once rough-and-tumble bowling alley, transforming it into an institution where the entire family could enjoy themselves and celebrate their entry into a world of affluence and leisure, the industry now found itself propagating the radical idea that domestic bliss and social stability could be commodified and purchased.

3

Trailer Parks

TWO RESIDENTIAL DEVELOPMENTS arose from the farms and fields of Bucks County, Pennsylvania, in 1951. Situated less than twenty miles northeast of Philadelphia, the two suburban communities had much in common. Both benefited from mass production construction technologies that lowered the price of housing to the point where it became affordable to families of modest means. Both contained a high percentage of blue-collar workers. The first community was filled primarily with construction workers and their families. The neighboring development contained a high percentage of steel workers employed at the nearby Fairless Works. In each residential enclave, home owners placed a high priority on nurturing stable families and strengthening the bonds of neighborhood community.

The similarities ended there. The steelworkers lived in Levittown, the second in a series of sprawling suburban subdivisions built by William Levitt using assembly-line techniques. Following the system he pioneered in building his Long Island community several years earlier, Levitt knocked out thousands of nearly identical three-bedroom ranch homes, at the rate of 150 a week by dividing the work into discrete steps and sending specialized labor crews from house to house performing discrete tasks. The construction workers, on the other hand, lived in a trailer camp. Unlike the Levitt homes, which were built on site, the trailers were made in factories and then hauled by automobile to the concrete slabs upon which they rested. The reception encountered by the two communities could not have differed more markedly. By this time, Levitt had already earned acclaim for making affordable and respectable housing available to honest, hard-working families. While some longtime residents of Bucks County worried that the influx of 16,000 families would destroy the region's rustic landscape of quaint farmhouses and churches, most civic leaders, merchants, and property holders welcomed the arrival of the Levittowners. The construction workers, on the other hand, were derided as "trailer trash," and their community was labeled a slum. Citing the threat to property values and the anticipated strain on local resources—schools, roads, sewer systems, police and fire departments—surrounding Bucks County towns passed ordinances to drive trailer parks from the area.

In the years after World War II, some two million Americans found themselves in the same besieged position as the trailer colonists of Bucks County. The phenomenon of long-term trailer living was still in its infancy, and the concept met with scorn in many circles. Even some trailer manufacturers scoffed at the notion that their product was suited for anything other than vacation travel. But for families who could not afford conventional homes, and for individuals whose occupations required constant relocation, trailers for year-round living made a good deal of practical sense. By 1965, trailers constituted one out of every ten new houses constructed in the United States, and it was estimated that roughly 3 percent of the American population lived in mobile homes.

Despite their evident popularity, trailer coaches were not what postwar Americans had in mind when they imagined their suburban dream homes. But then neither were Levitt's cookie-cutter boxes, at least not initially. In the decades after World War II, the question of how to house the masses cheaply and comfortably preoccupied the minds of manufacturers and developers across the country. Through the mid-1950s, housing was in short supply as there had been little new construction over the previous twenty years despite rapid population growth in many cities. If home builders were to lower housing costs through the magic of mass production, they would have to modify the look and design of the middle-class home. By shrinking domestic space to a bare minimum to meet the pocketbooks of working-class consumers, covering it in sheet metal, and mounting it on wheels, trailers tested how far Americans were willing to extend the concept of middle-class housing in an age of supposed consumer democracy.

Ultimately, trailer park communities fixed the lower boundary of the middle majority market. Although house trailers, much like the mass-produced homes built by Levitt, gave moderate-income families the opportunity to realize the long-standing American dream of private home ownership, external prejudices and internal spatial constraints made it difficult for trailer park residents to pre-

The Traveleze (1937) was an early version of a manufactured travel trailer.

sent their trailer coaches as emblems of social success. Assigned a cultural niche far beyond the middle majority mainstream, trailer parks exposed the notion of a classless nation as illusory and highlighted the consequences for consumers of failing to meet prevailing norms of postwar domesticity.

Travel Trailers

Prior to World War II, trailers were used almost exclusively for camping expeditions. As the automobile opened new possibilities for travel after the turn of the century, thousands of middle-class city dwellers took to the nation's roadways to "See America first," as a popular marketing slogan went. Weekend jaunts into the countryside and longer trips to explore the nation's scenic wonders promised rest and relaxation for the harassed urban worker along with an opportunity to admire the country's natural treasures. For all its virtues, auto-camping generated a host of practical problems, among them, a demand for basic overnight lodgings. Well before

The Schult Aristocrat of 1939 was slightly larger and more elaborate than the Traveleze.

the invention of the motel, there were few places outside the major cities where families could rent a room for a night. While the hardiest travelers simply pitched tents in the woods, those who wanted a slightly more refined experience began to haul their accommodations with them. With a few planks of wood, some nails, a sheet of canvas, and a set of wheels, a resourceful individual could piece together a crude travel trailer fairly quickly and hitch it to the back of a car.

In the late 1920s and early 1930s, manufacturers simplified the task by selling the first prefabricated units. First in northern Indiana and then in southern California, dozens of converted carriage factories and blacksmith shops churned out camping trailers that mimicked the homemade pull-trailers. Although a few companies catering to the upscale market built stylish and commodious "motor yachts" modeled on Pullman sleeping cars, the majority manufactured modest accommodations that were anything but glamorous. Resembling inflated bread boxes on wheels, they rarely contained more than 100 square feet of interior floor space, enough room for a small coal-burning stove, an icebox, a few cupboards, and a bed that, when turned over, became a kitchen table. Some likened trailer travel to living on a small boat; to foster this slightly exotic and adventurous association, a few models included windows in the form of portholes. Cramped, uncomfortable, and flimsy, they served a purely utilitarian function for spirited vacationers whose primary interest lay in spending as much time as possible out of doors.

The travel trailer may have solved an accommodation problem, but it simultaneously created another one: a massive parking headache for townsfolk and farmers. When time came to rest for the night, campers stopped wherever they found a convenient clearing: an open space by the side of the road, a corn field, or perhaps a parking lot on the edge of town. As the number of auto campers multiplied in the 1920s, haphazardly parked vehicles became a major nuisance for roadside property owners. Campers left trash, picked flowers, and raided orchards for fresh fruit. The countryside swirled with stories of farmers brandishing shotguns and attack dogs to shoo away carefree and unsuspecting auto campers.

Some cities tried to avert hostile confrontations by establishing public camping grounds on large tracts of vacant land within municipal boundaries. Early on, campers could settle for the night at many of these sites free of charge. Cities not only provided space for parking, but afforded a few amenities such as electric outdoor lighting, washrooms, kitchen facilities, and potable water. Local merchants were strong advocates of these camps, as they constituted a boon to local commerce.

One of the earliest municipal trailer camps of this sort was founded in Sarasota, Florida, a mecca for sun-seeking trailerists. Each winter, beginning in 1919, a convoy of 1,500 ramshackle trailers from a wide swath of northern states descended upon this small Gulf Coast community. With their temporary homes and belongings hitched to the rear of their Model T's, the mass of "tin-can tourists," as they called themselves, scouted for locations to set up camp. Sometimes they negotiated agreements with private property holders; sometimes the city found vacant parcels for their use. Searching for a more permanent arrangement, in 1931 city officials decided to convert a thirty-two-acre tract of land into a municipally owned and operated trailer camp. Lined up in neat but densely packed rows, the trailers formed a self-contained village, complete with electricity hookups, a post office, a recreation hall, and an athletic field. Strict rules and regulations governed the behavior of the campers: No liquor was allowed on the premises, vile language was prohibited, and fish were not to be cleaned beyond the bounds of one's assigned lot.

Roadside property owners adopted a more sanguine view of invading tin-can tourists than they previously held once they recognized the potential for profits. If trailer campers flocked to free municipal sites, might not the more discriminating tourist be willing to part with a small fee to cover the cost of a few extra amenities such as electric exterior lights, attractive landscaping, and playgrounds? Among middle-class tourists who wished to distinguish themselves from the riffraff who camped at the free sites, the answer was a resounding yes. Indeed, privately owned pay camps proved so popular that by the eve of World War II, the free municipal sites had disappeared. Cities that remained in the trailer camp business followed the lead of their privately owned counterparts and began charging nominal fees in return for basic services and amenities.

Almost any undeveloped parcel of land located along a well-traveled thoroughfare might be divided into lots and converted into a profitable trailer camp, or trailer park, as some of the more elaborate called themselves by the 1930s. For the individual who already owned roadside property, a trailer park required little in the way of capital investment, just enough for the installation of electrical wires, lights, toilets, and whatever extra amenities were deemed necessary. A property owner did not necessarily have to make these improvements all at once; typically they were introduced incrementally over several years. In many cases, trailer courts operated as adjuncts to roadside gas stations, fruit stands, and tourist cabin courts. Some were simply carved out of large yards in front of or beside privately owned homes. As a rule, these prewar pay camps were "Mom and Pop" enterprises where the owners lived on the premises and managed the park themselves.

Trailer Parks for Workers

While trailer camps catered primarily to vacationers through the 1930s, the Great Depression introduced a new element to the trailer park, the transient worker. Although it was not unheard of for park managers to lease space to the occasional traveling salesman, itinerant construction worker, or seasonal crop picker during the 1920s, such visits were rare. As increasing numbers of individuals and families took to the road in search of scarce work during the 1930s, however, the migratory worker became a more familiar type of customer. For all the migrants who traveled like the Joads in John Steinbeck's *The Grapes of Wrath*, with belongings piled high on pickup trucks, there were others who built or purchased crude trailers and hitched them to the rear of their jalopies. Less interested in leisurely discovering nature than desperately seeking work, this breed of traveler altered not only the character but the geography of the trailer park business, introducing the phenomenon to urban centers. By the latter part of the 1930s, trailers occupied by migrant workers and hopeful job seekers could be found on parking lots in almost any large city. Like the rural roadside property holders of the preceding decade, individuals who owned vacant urban land in the 1930s found that easy profits could be made by installing electric lines, toilets, and water, and then charging rent for parking privileges.

Bennett Simmons was one such individual. Simmons owned a ten-acre parcel of land on the outskirts of Los Angeles in the 1930s when a Works Progress Administration project to channelize the Los Angeles River brought hundreds of temporary workers into the area. Because there was more work than there was housing, many of the migrant workers brought their homes with them in the form of tiny trailers. Besieged with requests to use his land for trailer parking, Simmons knew a good opportunity when he saw one. He built rest rooms, installed overhead lighting, and opened for business under the name Bell Trailer City. Initially, the park operated without a sewage system. Wastewater from kitchen sinks drained into five-gallon buckets that were emptied by hand, twice daily, into the nearest city sewer intake. Sewers or no sewers, the park filled quickly. Within a year, over 100 trailers arranged in a horseshoe pattern supported a community of about 200 men, women, and children.

Although hundreds of communities like Bell Trailer City sprang up during the 1930s, it was not until World War II that the use of trailers for year-round housing became widespread. Military operations and defense production uprooted thousands of Americans and channeled them into new locations. If not overnight, then within a matter of months, sleepy towns such as Pascagoula, Mississippi, Orange, Texas, and Ypsilanti, Michigan, were transformed into bustling centers of war production. Industrial metropolises such as Detroit, St. Louis, and Philadelphia enlarged their already sizable populations with thousands of additional war workers. Military bases produced the same effect: The streets of Norfolk, San Diego, and Mobile now overflowed with soldiers, sailors, and pilots. In all of these places, the supply of existing housing was insufficient to meet the surging demand.

Trailers rapidly emerged as the most popular type of stopgap housing. They had the advantage of being cheap, portable, and above all, easy to build. Although trailers were not designed for permanent habitation, defense workers had few alternatives. Rationing and material shortages precluded any prospect of alleviating the housing crunch through the construction of conventional

housing. Most of the trailers manufactured privately during the
war, about 35,000 of them, were purchased directly by the federal
government and then rented to defense workers and military personnel. In Richmond, California, alone, the federal government
provided 2,500 trailers to house shipyard workers whose services
were deemed vital to the war effort. To accommodate this swelling
population, the National Housing Agency laid out hundreds of
makeshift trailer camps on the parking lots and fields surrounding
military installations and defense plants. According to one estimate, about 200,000 trailers were in use during World War II, with
about 60 percent of them located in defense areas.

Disavowing the Trailer Home

When the war ended, the future of the trailer industry remained
uncertain. Would the experience of the Depression and World
War II set a precedent for widespread use of trailers for permanent
habitation? Or would the return to normalcy revitalize the market
for vacation trailers? Initially, camp operators and trailer manufacturers were leery of diving headfirst into the permanent housing
market, largely because the previous fifteen years of economic
hardship and war had tarnished the reputation of trailer living. The
humble trailers that had provided desperately needed shelter during two periods of national emergency had become associated in
the public mind with down-on-their-luck itinerants and migrant
defense workers.

During the Depression, for instance, trailer living spawned fears
of the development of a parasitic class of wheeled hobos who
would suck resources from host communities and menace respectable citizens. It was one thing to be visited by middle-class
vacationers who spent money at local shops and restaurants, but
quite another to be invaded by vagabonds who neither boosted
commerce nor paid real estate taxes. Resentful citizens and civic

leaders resorted to a variety of means to drive trailer court denizens from their midst. When a Detroit man leased parking space to nineteen trailers, adjoining property owners sought redress from city government on the grounds that he had created a public nuisance. The matter was turned over to the city's Board of Health. An investigation concluded that the makeshift trailer village was unsanitary and all occupants were evicted. Elsewhere, cities passed ordinances to discourage the practice of turning travel trailers into semi-permanent homes. An Oakland, California, law limited trailer camp parking to 90 days within any six-month period. Similar legislation in Toledo, Ohio, restricted trailer stays to three months out of the year. Several cities went further, outlawing trailer camps altogether.

Although the emergency nature of wartime trailer housing forestalled additional restrictive legislation in the 1940s, the reputation of trailer parks continued to suffer. Many of the units manufactured during the war were constructed hastily with cheap materials. Thin walls offered scant insulation against either bitter cold or searing heat. Roofs were fashioned from sheets of painted canvas, and moisture condensed on the ceilings. In most cases, the park grounds were no better. Overcrowded and poorly planned, they resembled higglety-pigglety squatter camps more than orderly communities. Sanitary facilities were inadequate and the absence of paved roads turned many parks into pastures of mud after heavy rains.

Fearing adverse financial repercussions from negative public opinion, industry leaders openly discouraged the idea that trailers were suitable for fixed housing. As the war drew to a close, manufacturers prepared consumers for the proper postwar behavior with promotional literature depicting their products in vacation settings. Typical was a March 1945 advertisement for the Schult Luxury Liner, which illustrated how the "convenient, livable HOME FOR TODAY," could be easily converted to "the RESORT of TOMORROW," beside the "mountains, . . . the seashore," or a "favorite lake." Into the early postwar years, trailer manufacturers continued to design their products accordingly, giving simplicity and mobility priority over comfort, durability, or size.

Meeting the Need: Trailers in the Tight Postwar Housing Market

The best intentions of industry leaders notwithstanding, the requirements of an affluent, housing-starved postwar population locked manufacturers and park operators into the market for residential housing. Not that the vacation market vanished. As middle-class Americans resumed the practice of taking annual holiday trips, the demand for old-fashioned travel trailers rebounded from low wartime levels as did the demand for camping space in resort areas. At the same time, however, more Americans were discovering the trailer as a practical and affordable alternative to conventional housing. It was not long before the demand for residential trailers outstripped the demand for travel trailers. The incompatible needs of the two constituencies posed a serious dilemma for manufacturers and camp operators alike. Ultimately, divergent imperatives forced the industry to split into two branches.

City officials in Huntington Beach, a coastal community about thirty miles south of Los Angeles, expressed a marked preference for vacationing trailerists over those who used their coaches as a form of permanent housing. Shortly before the war, the city had established a small oceanfront trailer park to accommodate trailering tourists in the hopes that vacationers would inject money into the community. During the war, priorities shifted and the park filled with workers from nearby aircraft plants and shipyards. To the horror of local business leaders who had assumed that this was only a temporary and provisional arrangement, many of these blue-collar workers stayed on after the war ended. Local lawmakers were appalled to learn that several people who owned homes in the community had sold their property and had moved into the

Pennsylvania Trailer Show, 1947. Trade shows such as these enabled manufacturers to showcase and sell their latest models.

park as semi-permanent residents in order to reduce their tax burden. This would not do. To arrest the trend, the City Council raised rents more than 50 percent and prohibited tenants from erecting small porches on the side of their coaches, a measure intended to discourage the sort of structural improvements that might make long-term occupation more attractive. In possession of an ideal beach front location that offered breathtaking views of the Pacific Ocean, Huntington Beach officials could afford to be choosy about the social caliber of their tenants. Elsewhere, the overwhelming demand for permanent housing compelled park owners to adopt the opposite course by reorienting business around the use of house trailers, or what would later come to be called mobile homes.

The atomic explosions in Hiroshima and Nagasaki in August 1945 summarily ended the war against Japan, but the termination of hostilities by no means alleviated the housing shortage. The population dislocations set in motion by the wartime economy rolled over into the postwar years. Jobs remained plentiful in the defense production boomtowns due to the high levels of military spending associated with the emerging Cold War. Likewise, industry's relatively smooth conversion to civilian production sustained the demand for labor in the nation's major manufacturing cities. In Los Angeles, for example, over 85 percent of the city's 782,000 defense workers remained there after the war ended. In certain sections of the country, the housing shortage was compounded by internal migration flows during the late 1940s. In what came to be known as the "second great migration," African Americans left the rural south for large urban centers like Chicago, St. Louis, Pittsburgh, Philadelphia, and Detroit. Meanwhile, Sun Belt cities of the South and West filled with retirees in search of milder climates. Aided by the advent of air-conditioning in the late 1940s, Miami, Tucson, Phoenix, and San Diego, to name a few popular retirement destinations, suddenly abounded with elderly empty-nesters.

The severity of the postwar housing shortage was illustrated by dramatic acts of desperation on the part of housing-starved families. Stories circulated in the media about people who had no choice but to make apartments out of chicken coops, boxcars, and portable tents. According to *Life* magazine, some house hunters made the rounds at local mortuaries to get first crack at homes and apartments that were about to appear on the market. A brazen couple in New York City set up house in a department store display window to attract attention to their plight.

The housing shortage was particularly acute for returning veterans and their families. Servicemen who were occupied overseas when existing housing units filled had the most trouble finding accommodations in the immediate postwar years. They also had the greatest need. Veterans streamed home from the war eager to start new families, sending birthrates soaring to levels that were unprecedented by twentieth-century standards. With so few apartments and homes on the market, many settled reluctantly for a spare room in the homes of parents or in-laws. By the spring of 1946, an estimated 1.2 million families were doubling up with other families in houses or apartments.

Dreams of Home: Trailers as Temporary Housing

A living room sofa, a spare room in the basement, or an inner-city tenement apartment provided little consolation for families that dreamed of owning their own suburban home. The privately owned, detached suburban home with a lawn had a powerful hold on the American middle-class imagination. Indeed, scholars have traced the widespread American preference for privately owned detached homes in rustic settings to an English tradition that predated European settlement of the New World. The wide open spaces of North America allowed colonial settlers to make a scaled-down version of the English country estate available for ordinary townsfolk. The earliest New England settlements, for instance, consisted largely of detached single-family structures clustered around a town church and village common. When William Penn laid out his eighty-block grid for Philadelphia in 1783, he made sure that every house plot would be large enough to accommodate a free-standing home and a small garden. It was not until the second half of the nineteenth century, however, that ideals of domesticity and suburbanization converged to make the privately owned detached home a hallmark of middle-class status in the United States. Around this time, the developers of planned suburban communities such as Llewelyn Park, New Jersey; Riverside,

Illinois; Bronxville, New York; and Overbrook Farms, Pennsylvania, offered elite families a haven from urban vices. Laid out on curvilinear, tree-lined streets, provisioned with ample open space, and filled with multi-storied homes surrounded by expansive front and back lawns, they became early models for the countless middle-class subdivisions that would spring up on the periphery of metropolitan areas around the turn of the century. In rushing to fill these new communities on the periphery, businessmen and white-collar professionals secured the reputation of the suburbs as middle-class edens.

Into the twentieth century, political commentary reaffirmed the centrality of private home ownership to the American ethos. While serving as Secretary of Commerce in the early 1920s and then later in the decade as president, Herbert Hoover extolled private home ownership as a bulwark against social pathology and an essential ingredient in the recipe for responsible citizenship. Hoover reasoned that only people who sank permanent roots in a community would have a vested interest in socially responsible behavior and active engagement in civic affairs. Hoover's successor in the White House, Franklin Roosevelt, carried the concept even further. His New Deal rhetoric held up stable and secure housing as a basic right in the modern liberal state. New Deal policy made the meaning of this prerogative concrete with home mortgage refinancing and insurance programs that facilitated ownership of detached single-family houses. By the time of World War II, therefore, most Americans conflated home ownership with both citizenship and social success. Suddenly apartment dwelling and house renting were no longer sufficient for those hoping to realize the American Dream.

What made the postwar housing squeeze so frustrating for young couples was the fact that one of the long-standing obstacles to ownership had been removed: It was no longer necessary to accumulate ten or twenty years' worth of savings to buy a home. New Deal housing programs enabled families to secure long-term mortgages with minimal down payments. The government tendered especially juicy deals to those who had recently fought in the war; under the provisions of the Serviceman's Readjustment Act of 1944, also known as the GI Bill of Rights, the returning veteran could purchase a new home with the meager outlay of one dollar. The remaining obstacles to home ownership now lay in the realm of supply. Material shortages, labor scarcity, and government restrictions imposed a bottleneck on housing construction. As the first full year of peace approached, experts estimated that it would be three years before the housing industry would begin to make significant inroads into alleviating the shortage, an assessment that turned out to be correct.

It was in this context of postwar scarcity that families like the Stuffts turned to trailer living as a stopgap measure. In February 1946, during the worst of the national housing shortage, Forrest Stufft received notice that he had just one month to find a new home. His landlord had just sold the house that he and his family of four had been renting, and the new owners were about to take possession. Not having amassed enough savings to buy their own place—the only homes they could find for sale were well beyond their price range—the Stuffts searched out affordable apartments. No luck. Landlords who did not object to their two small children refused to accept dogs, and the Stuffts were unwilling to part with either their children or their pet collie. Under normal circumstances, the Stuffts would not have considered a trailer as a viable option. Friends they spoke with were aghast at the prospect. With three days left on their lease, however, and no prospect of acquiring conventional housing, the Stuffts adopted the only remaining course of action left available to them. With a $680 down payment, the Stuffts purchased a used trailer, hauled it to a vacant plot of land on the edge of town, and prepared to wait until the housing situation eased.

For the Stuffts, as for most families, trailer living was viewed as an interim arrangement. Thousands of defense workers who had purchased trailers during the war thought it prudent to hold on to them a little while longer just in case they couldn't find affordable permanent housing. Others who had no prior experience with trailer living either picked up second-hand units, sometimes for as little as a few hundred dollars, or bought one of the new models that streamed out of the factories of northern Indiana and southern California. The demand for new trailers was so heavy immediately after the war that trailer coach manufacturers, like suburban housing developers, reported difficulty in meeting it. The 60,000 units manufactured in 1947 set an all-time production record. Indeed, the rush to buy trailers was so great by 1948 that, according to one estimate, trailers supplied housing for 7 percent of the American population, a remarkable figure even if exaggerated given the fact that only ten years earlier, year-round trailer living was virtually unheard of.

Returning veterans composed the largest segment of the immediate postwar market. It was not at all unusual to find trailer courts filled entirely with ex-GIs. In some instances, government assistance facilitated the transition to trailer living among returning soldiers and their families. Milwaukee County, for example, cleared 45 acres of undeveloped land just beyond the city, purchased 550 trailer coaches from local dealers, and then leased them to homeless war veterans. Trailers were also used extensively on college campuses, where the influx of students benefiting from the government tuition subsidies authorized by the GI Bill of Rights quickly outstripped dormitory space. In the area around the University of Illinois in Champaign-Urbana, trailer coaches overflowed from saturated trailer parks into the yards of private homes. Anticipating the enrollment of more than 400 war veterans and their families, Rutgers University, in New Brunswick, New Jersey, purchased several hundred trailers and rented them out to students who could not find homes or apartments in the area.

If southern California was at all representative, American trailer owners in the immediate postwar years did not fit the prevailing stereotype of the broken-down hobo or destitute migrant worker; instead they were well-educated, fairly affluent, and eager to move out of their trailers into conventional houses as soon as possible. A 1948 survey conducted in a ten-county area of California that stretched from Los Angeles to San Diego showed that the majority of trailer coach inhabitants, almost 60 percent, consisted of veterans and their families who were unable to find more suitable housing elsewhere. Skilled tradesmen earning over $4,000 a year made up the largest category of breadwinners in the survey. Although most responded affirmatively when asked if they enjoyed trailer life, a whopping 85 percent admitted that they planned to abandon their trailers when they could find newly constructed, affordable single-family houses.

On the Outside Looking in:
The Continuing Housing Crunch
for Working-Class Families

By the mid-1950s, the mass-produced construction techniques pioneered by William Levitt enabled the housing industry to meet much of the pent-up demand for conventional homes. Financed by government loans designed to spur development and alleviate the housing shortage, several manufacturers experimented with the concept of factory-built homes after the war. The most famous of these prefabricated dwellings was the squat, metallic Lustron House. Weighing 12.5 tons, the Lustron House consisted of over 3,000 separate parts, which were manufactured in a former aircraft factory near Columbus, Ohio, assembled on site, and mounted on a concrete slab. Because its walls, along with its roof and ceiling, were made of enameled steel, interior pictures were hung with magnets. Despite a lot of hype and over $37 million in federal government loans, the Lustron House was a flop. Consumers thought it was ugly, and more importantly, high material and labor costs inflated the price beyond what many working families were able to afford. It was not until large-scale developers like Levitt entered the picture that mass-production techniques translated into considerable cost savings. In essence, Levitt converted the entire building site into a factory. In what some observers likened to an "assembly line in reverse," work crews with specialized skills moved in sequence from one home site to another performing specific tasks: laying foundations, erecting frames, installing plumbing, mounting roofs, and so forth. The crucial factor contributing to Levitt's success was that he sold not just individual homes but a planned community. By filling an entire subdivision with his mass-produced homes, he could assure prospective home buyers that all properties were eligible for FHA or VA financing, something that prefabricated house manufacturers could not possibly do. Even if a Lustron home, to take one example, met all the requirements for low-cost government loans, a buyer might place it in a run-down neighborhood deemed too risky for by FHA appraisers. In this case, the loan application would be denied. By placing each of his homes in a planned "Levittown," Levitt avoided this problem.

The Levitt formula, with minor variations, was widely imitated. The central feature was the emergence of an entrepreneur who assumed responsibility for coordinating all aspects of community development from start to finish: purchasing the land, dividing it into lots, building the houses, marketing the development as a community to prospective buyers, and selling individual parcels to the final consumer. By controlling each step in the process, the developer could assure lenders that all building in the subdivision would conform to FHA standards, thereby making all properties eligible for low-cost loans. Moreover, by planning communities in accordance with government standards, developers were able to secure the financing necessary for building on an incredibly large scale. The two Levittowns outside New York City and Philadelphia were among the largest, with over 16,000 homes in each. Using comparable building techniques and financing strategies, other developers approached this large volume of building. Eichler Homes was able to churn out 500 homes a year in its various subdivisions in the San Francisco Bay area. Further south along the California coast, the industrialist Henry J. Kaiser developed Panorama City, a community of 2,000 homes for the sort of people he employed in his shipyards and steel mills. On the outskirts of St. Louis, Charles Vatterot planned and built a 500-home community expressly for large Catholic families that held blue-collar jobs and had outgrown their cramped city apartments. By the close of the decade, the creation of sprawling residential subdivisions on the metropolitan periphery had increased the stock of single-family homes by well over six million, many of them filled with veterans and other working-class families who had just begun to taste the fruits of postwar affluence.

The impact of these developments on the trailering population was profound. The increasing availability of moderately priced conventional homes slowly drained tenants from trailer parks. For those fortunate enough to move into one of the newly constructed split-level ranch homes, or perhaps an older detached home in an already established transitional suburban neighborhood, trailer living functioned only as a stepping stone along the path to the American dream. Yet a sizable proportion of the trailering population was still not in a position to realize that dream just yet. Indeed, two out of three respondents in a California survey conducted in 1956 indicated that they planned to live in their trailers "indefinitely." It was not that they necessarily wished to remain in their trailers forever, but, for the foreseeable future at least, trailer living offered them certain advantages of either cost or mobility.

Despite their best intentions, the liberal mortgage insurance programs sponsored by the FHA and Veterans Administration left a large segment of the American population outside the orbit of affordable private housing. During the early 1950s, the full cost of most homes purchased with the help of FHA mortgages fell somewhere between $9,000 and $20,000, a price range that was well within the means of white-collar professionals and skilled factory workers. There remained many working-class families, however, including those whose livelihood depended on menial labor or non-union jobs, for whom these homes remained just out of reach. For the very poor, the federal government subsidized the construction of public housing projects, usually in inner-city neighborhoods. But to avoid competition with the private developers and builders, Congress denied direct public assistance to those slightly higher on the socio-economic ladder, those whose housing needs were not being met by private enterprise. The unskilled, though employed, laborers and their families were falling between the cracks of housing policy, which favored the destitute and the new middle class.

For people who fell in this unfortunate in-between category, house trailers remained the only viable alternative to older inner-city apartments. In 1948, one could purchase a thirty-foot trailer for about $3,000, significantly less than the $7,500 that ranch-style homes were selling for in Levittown. Usually trailer buyers received financing from a bank, not on terms as liberal as those home buyers who received FHA loans, but on terms that were quite affordable given the lower list price. Most financing packages required the buyer to put down about one-third of the cost with the remainder amortized over a one- or two-year period. Moreover, the absence of real estate taxes meant a real cost savings that offset lot-rental payments to park owners. As conventional housing costs rose over the course of the mid-1950s, while trailer costs remained fairly stable, the price differential between the two only increased. By the mid-1950s, the average price paid for a house trailer was $4,500 while Levitt's homes in Bucks County, Pennsylvania, still considered a bargain, were going for upwards of $10,000. According to a 1960 estimate, trailers sold from between one-fourth to one-third the cost of a conventional home.

Anderson Mobile Homes Park, Portsmouth, Ohio, circa 1955. Forty-seven trailer parks in the vicinity of Portsmouth housed the 16,000 construction workers that came to the area to build an atomic energy plant.

On the Road Again:
Trailer Living and Itinerant Workers

Trailers continued to serve as the most practical housing option for men and women who worked in occupations that required mobility. Indeed, many of the industrial laborers who took up trailer living worked in the construction trades. The men who built pipelines, roads, dams, and bridges stayed at a given work site from anywhere between six months and five years. Trailer ownership saved them the trouble of finding apartments or rental properties in each successive location. The Cold War defense build-up funneled construction crews to remote areas of the country where existing housing could not possibly accommodate the influx of workers. The construction of the Savannah River hydrogen bomb project, for example, drew 40,000 workers to a sparsely populated section of Georgia, creating a housing crunch that was eased somewhat by the importation of 5,000 trailers. In 1949, construction workers nationwide purchased 20 percent of all manufactured trailer coaches, a percentage that would increase over the course of the 1950s.

In addition to construction workers, the transient trailer population also included a large contingent of military personnel, carnival hands, and seasonal agricultural workers. Because many husbands and wives preferred trailer living to the dismal alternative of military barracks, trailer parks surrounded most army and navy bases. In the event of a transfer to another installation, which was a fairly common occurrence in the armed forces, trailer ownership greatly simplified the process of relocation. Trailer living was equally popular with migrant farmhands whose work routines varied with the seasons. While seasonal farmwork supported many trailer parks in rural locations, there were other occupations that brought transient workers and their trailers through cities. Carnival workers and circus performers traveled from town to town in trailers, setting up temporary campsites adjacent to fairgrounds. Sarasota, Florida, the winter home of Ringling Brothers, Barnum, and Bailey Circus, contained several trailer parks in its environs that filled for half the year with acrobats, tightrope walkers, trapeze artists, and clowns. The St. Charles Trailer Court, located about twenty miles west of St. Louis, did a large volume of business with traveling wrestlers and men who made their way across the country painting water towers.

In the case of the Hanasaki family, the needs of mobility and the constraints of economic deprivation converged. Frank Hanasaki, a Japanese immigrant, landed a job operating a game booth with a traveling carnival troupe shortly after World War II. In order to keep his wife and two daughters with him as he completed the annual circuit from Minnesota to Louisiana, he purchased a tiny house trailer. The arrangement worked well enough until his daughters reached school age; at that point, the Hanasakis decided to establish a permanent address. A house was out of the question, however. Carnival work paid poorly, and the odd jobs that Frank took in the off-season—driving taxis, working in factories—did not pay any better. So the Hanasakis continued to live in their trailer, mooring it permanently at a trailer court just beyond the St. Louis city limits. For many years, it was as close as they would ever get to the suburban ideal.

Trailers and Trailer Courts for Permanent Living

The dramatic rise in long-term trailer occupancy forced the industry to revise its earlier assumptions about the viability of trailer living and alter its business methods accordingly. Trailer coaches, accessories, and courts currently designed for tourists met neither the needs nor budgets of people who looked to the trailer to fulfill basic housing requirements. Although the tourist and residential trailer markets still overlapped in some places—as late as the 1960s, some trailer coach models could function as either vacation vehicles or year-round homes—the overall trend was unmistakable. An industry that once discouraged the use of trailers for permanent living increasingly oriented its products around the preferences of consumers who left their trailers on one site for an extended period of time and lived in them throughout the year.

At the close of World War II, roughly fifty firms manufactured trailers. The astronomical expansion of the permanent housing market required manufacturers to modify their product lines accordingly. In contrast to their prewar counterparts, postwar trailers were larger and sturdier. Architects divided interior space into discrete rooms to afford individuals more privacy, an important commodity

The southern California company Trailer Coach Specialties primarily built units for permanent living, although this 1953 Fleetwood model was ideally suited for tourist travel.

for families with children. Because migrant workers comprised a substantial portion of the market, mobility remained an important feature in trailer design, keeping the units compact. For families that had no intention of relocating, however, smallness was no longer a virtue. For these customers, manufacturers offered super-size models that ranged up to fifty feet in length by 1952. Another revolution occurred in the late 1950s when the ten-foot-wide trailer replaced the standard "eight-wide." With two or even three bedrooms, a living room, and a dinette, these jumbo models were a far cry from the humble travel trailers introduced by manufacturers twenty years earlier. Equipped with full-size appliances—four-burner stoves with roasters and broilers, garbage disposal units, seven-cubic-foot refrigerators—the deluxe house trailers of the mid-1950s boasted nearly all the conveniences of a conventional suburban home.

The inclusion of built-in bathrooms marked the most important departure from the tourist trailer. During the prewar period and into the 1940s, trailer dwellers relied on common washrooms provided by park managers to satisfy their sanitary requirements. Long treks to the toilet in cold weather, waiting lines at the showers, and rank odors from washroom mildew made the absence of bathrooms one of the biggest drawbacks of trailer life, especially for those who had to endure these inconveniences day in and day out. Portable potty stools that were made available in many trailers shortly after World War II alleviated the problem somewhat. Still, the daily ritual of emptying the pots in the community washroom was a source of embarrassment to homemakers with any sense of modesty. Thus, full-time trailer dwellers hailed the advent of the interior bathroom, which by the mid-1950s had become a standard feature. By this time, top-of-the-line models offered full-size bathtubs along with flush toilets and sinks. These manufacturers made provisions for convenient hookups to sewer lines, as well as electrical power lines, just as in conventional homes.

The shifting nature of the consumer market also altered the formula for operating a successful trailer park. By the early 1950s, about 12,000 trailer parks lay scattered across the country, most of them catering to the long-term tenant who stayed for a minimum of eighteen months. While the tourist-oriented camps continued to provide a variety of recreational amenities—for instance, swimming pools, tennis courts, and playgrounds—such features added more expense than long-term tenants were willing to pay for. Unlike the vacation camps that sprung up in scenic settings near mountains or large bodies of water, the residential parks benefited from close proximity to sources of employment. By the 1950s, the majority of trailer parks were located in urban areas.

Residential trailer courts varied widely in terms of what they offered. The most primitive lacked paved roads or street lighting and provided tenants only with a place to park and hook up to a source of electricity. Renting a space in a park like this was cheap, sometimes as low as $15 a month in the early 1950s. Higher-priced parks, in which rents might run four times as high, provided lots with concrete patios, sewer connections, carports, storage sheds, and attractive landscaping. Some of the larger parks functioned as self-contained communities with their own churches and shops.

Regardless of whether one paid rent in a well-planned, well-provisioned mobile home community or a crude, ramshackle trailer camp, the effort and ingenuity on the part of the proprietor necessary to create an environment that satisfied social expectations in an age of affluence were extraordinary. The people who took up residence in trailer parks were neither very rich nor exceptionally poor. Most breadwinners found steady employment in blue-collar jobs that paid decent wages. The culture of abundance that beckoned from television advertisements, billboards, and shop windows was not far beyond their reach. Close as they were to joining the ranks of the middle majority, trailer life conflicted with some of the most central tenets of postwar consumer culture, most notably the ownership of a fixed single-family suburban home. Postponing the purchase of the split-level ranch house did not prevent trailer owners from seeking out the good life in the products they purchased and the activities they pursued. In their trailer courts, they hoped to realize the American Dream, or some version of it. Yet, for two million Americans, living in a trailer community involved a constant struggle to affirm their own social success and earn the respect of outsiders despite their humble homes.

Promoting Trailer Life

The most effective publicity for the trailer industry in the postwar era came in the form of the blockbuster film *The Long, Long Trailer*, starring Lucille Ball and Desi Arnaz. Based on a novel by Clinton Twiss, the 1954 movie featured Lucy and Desi as a pair of newlyweds who spend their honeymoon in a trailer that is, if nothing else, very, very long. As the madcap couple journey across majestic mountains and meander through small towns, assorted mishaps put their marriage to the test. Overly gregarious neighbors in a trailer park interrupt their wedding night. Lucy makes a mess in the kitchen trying to cook dinner while clattering down the highway. Later on, after the trailer gets stuck in the mud, Lucy's rock collection nearly causes the coach to overturn and sparks a bitter fight that brings the couple to the brink of divorce. In the end, however, they learn that it is their own stubbornness, rather than the trailer, that stands in the way of marital bliss. When they embrace behind a trailer door flapping in the wind in the final scene, viewers are left with the impression that trailers are as good as any other type of housing at nurturing successful marriages and families.

This was precisely the message that the industry sought to impart to the American public in the 1950s. To judge from the promotional literature generated by manufacturers, dealers, park operators, and their trade associations, there was nothing inferior or degrading about living in a trailer. In fact, the experience could be exhilarating. Carrying forward a prewar marketing strategy, industry publicists cultivated a mystique around the carefree nomad who took off in a trailer to explore the scenic wonders of the continent. Advertisements linked small travel trailers with the romance and adventure of long cross-country journeys.

As the vacation market diminished in importance, the industry spent more energy trying to convince the American public that trailers were a perfectly suitable form of permanent housing for families. Both national and regional trade associations launched public relations campaigns to dispel the negative impressions of residential trailer parks left by the Depression and the war. Industry representatives took to the road, speaking at service club luncheons and visiting trailer parks to ensure that managers were complying with the basic sanitary and hygienic standards promulgated by the trade associations. The Trailer Coach Manufacturers Association, headquartered in Chicago, developed a ranking system to prod park operators to upgrade their facilities. The Trailer Coach Association of California went even further by developing and operating its own model parks. Of particular concern to both organizations was the quality of sanitary services—washrooms, garbage collection, and sewer connections, in trailer parks.

Monthly magazines written for the occupants of trailer homes championed the virtues of trailer living most aggressively. *Trailer Life* and *Trailer Topics,* which had the largest circulations during the postwar era, painted trailer life in glowing terms. Reports about the latest mobile home communities emphasized the modern facilities, the abundant amenities, and the legions of satisfied tenants. Trailers invited the inevitable comparisons with both conventional suburban housing and inner-city apartments; invariably, the trailers came out ahead. Regular columns like "Why I Like Trailer Living" and articles like "There's No Crack in Our Picture Window" featured families that were drawn to trailer life by happenstance and won over by the experience. Morris Horton cherished the day his suburban ranch-style house burned down, compelling him to take refuge in a modern mobile home. Leona Proctor had always wanted to settle down in a large house but after financial difficulties forced her and her husband into a twenty-seven-foot unit, she became a convert. Testimonials from satisfied customers like Mrs. Fred Stephens of Bedford Heights, Ohio, who insisted that she "would not trade [her] . . . trailer for the best house ever built," not only presented a positive image to outsiders, but assured subscribers that in adopting the trailer lifestyle, they were wise consumers and successful Americans.

Among the benefits of trailer living touted by the industry, freedom of movement overshadowed the rest. While residential mobility offered obvious advantages for people engaged in transient work, it was also touted as a potential benefit for owners whose work did not require relocation. If conditions at any given trailer park proved unsatisfactory, families needed only to rehitch their units and drive to a more suitable place. Thus, mobility provided a safeguard against greedy and irresponsible landlords. Trailer living, so the argument went, enabled families to attain the goal of home-ownership without the burden of being shackled to a particular piece of property.

Trailer living also freed homeowners from onerous financial obligations. Comparisons with conventional suburban housing in-variably stressed the substantial cost savings achieved through lower purchase prices, cheaper utility costs, and lower mainte-nance expenditures. This argument had to be crafted carefully, however, as industry boosters did not want to portray trailer own-ers as financially strapped individuals who adopted their way of life out of economic necessity. So, they took pains to emphasize that mobile-home parks catered to people from all walks of life; what distinguished trailerists from their stationary brethren was that they preferred to spend their money on consumer luxuries such as television sets, sports cars, and pleasure boats, and trailer living allowed them to do so.

Occasionally, defenders of trailer living went to absurd lengths to make their case. A 1951 article appearing in *Trailer Top-ics* explained how trailers offered families greater protection against nuclear attack than conventional homes. While a fixed home was likely to collapse from the pressure of an atomic bomb blast, a trailer was "more apt to roll with it," according to the au-thor. "After all," the writer added, "trailers are built to absorb a great deal of knocking about on poor roads." And in the event of an evacuation, trailer dwellers were spared the "thousand deci-sions" about what belongings to take with them; all that was re-quired was hitching their home-on-wheels to the back of their car and driving off.

Of all the subjects addressed by trailer publicists, none received more complete coverage than whether or not mobile homes were

Trailer court in Augusta, Ga., near the Savannah River atomic energy plant, circa 1953. The trailer industry promoted an image of trailer living that was consistent with prevailing middle-class norms about family life.

suitable places to raise families. During the Depression and war, it was most often single men—construction workers, defense laborers, military personnel—who converted tiny travel trailers into semi-permanent homes. The popular image of the trailer park as a rough, male-dominated space—like the diner and bowling alley before it—was not far off the mark in many cases. Into the postwar years, these impressions remained etched in the public mind even as trailers grew large enough to accommodate three or four people comfortably and park operators upgraded their establishments. Manufacturers were careful not to reinforce these outdated impressions in their brochures and advertising copy. Typical were advertisements that showed families of three or four relaxing in a front yard, gathered in a living room or sitting around a dining room table. Editors of the trailer magazines were equally vigilant on the subject. Articles like "Children Can Be Happy in Trailers," "Trailer Children Are 'All-American' Kids," and "Teen-ager in a Trailer," upheld the advantages of mobile homes for raising virtuous children and nurturing healthy families.

It was not sufficient to demonstrate that trailers were large enough to accommodate families. To convince families about the benefits of trailer living, manufacturers, dealers, and park operators had to persuade consumers that prevailing domestic norms could be attained in trailer park communities. This was a tall order. The practical advantages of mobility and cost notwithstanding, trailer life imposed severe spatial constraints upon residents. Spatial confinement made it difficult for families to meet the standards of domesticity that had evolved in the context of detached single-family homes surrounded by vast expanses of lawn. Although promoters of trailer life did their best to present the hidden benefits of limited space, the interior design of trailers and the layout of trailer parks posed real challenges on both a practical and psychological level.

There's a Hitch to It: Meeting the Domestic Ideal

Sally Skyline was a huge hit at regional and national trade shows in 1958. Employed as a spokesmodel by Skyline Mobile Homes, Sally dazzled prospective home buyers with her unusual performance. The company's display featured a trailer with one side completely removed so that the interior was exposed to viewers At an appointed moment, the interior lights of the model trailer brightened and piped-in music swelled. Into the spotlight waltzed Sally. "Whirling gracefully," she pointed out the fine furniture, fixtures, and drapery in the living room while singing to a catchy melody, "Skyline is my line . . . " From the living room she pranced through the kitchen, bathroom, and bedroom, changing her costume as she went from an apron to a bathrobe and then, a nightgown. For the grand finale, Sally returned to the living room to perform an interpretive dance that summed up all the advantages of owning a Skyline Mobile Home.

The mobile home through which Sally Skyline waltzed was one of the largest on the market. Had she attempted a similar performance in an average-sized postwar trailer, a simple pirouette might well have sent her crashing against a wall. With 500 square feet of interior floor space, even the largest mobile homes manufactured in the late 1950s were puny by the standards of conventional single-family tract homes. When William Levitt built his first sprawling postwar subdivision, he achieved much of his cost savings by paring down the prototypical middle-class house to its bare essentials. Dispensing with the guest room, sun porch, pantry, and den, Levitt offered only a basic kitchen, a small living room, two bedrooms, and a bath, all on one floor. Although Levitt offered a minimum of rooms, his floor plan remained loyal to the conventional room arrangement in terms of their placement and relative size. Moreover, from the outside, the Levittown house looked like a miniature version of homes in white-collar neighborhoods. With mass-production techniques, Levitt was able to produce a stripped-down version of the middle-class home for blue-collar wage earners.

Trailer manufacturers had a lot less to work with in trying to accomplish the same goal. Architects could not possibly design narrow trailer interiors according to the blueprints used for squarish houses. Indeed, the only realistic room plan was a shotgun pattern, that is, a linear arrangement of rooms one after another from front to rear. Normally, one entered a trailer from a side door that opened into the kitchen. Toward the front of the trailer, the kitchen flowed into a living room, usually furnished with a couch, a table, and an armchair. In the other direction, a narrow hallway, fringed by a bathroom on one side and a closet on the other, led to a rear bedroom.

Manufacturers offered only minor variations on this basic floor plan. A few reversed the location of the living room and kitchen. Units over 35 feet in length might contain a small secondary bedroom wedged between the master bedroom and the kitchen. Frequently these children's rooms were outfitted with bunk beds. One manufacturer squeezed a loft-style bedroom into the front of the trailer, accessed by a narrow staircase. Skyline Mobile Homes introduced a most unusual floor plan in 1958 that featured a bedroom followed by the living room, another bedroom, a bathroom, and a rear kitchen. American Coaches boasted no less than forty-eight different arrangements for its living room, kitchen, and dinette, in 1953. No matter how innovative, all of these variations conformed, to a large extent, to the prototypical shotgun layout.

Privacy was the major casualty of this ubiquitous floor plan. Except for the rear master bedroom, each room doubled as a passage way to yet another room. Folding screens might be employed as partitions, but still it was difficult to engage in any sort of activity without advertising it to everyone else in the household. Spatial deprivation could be especially maddening for youngsters. School children had difficulty finding a quiet study nook; teenagers had no place to entertain their friends. In tiny trailers, makeshift sleeping arrangements for children might consist of a mattress that folding out from a living room wall or an overturned breakfast table. Where four or more people shared a trailer, siblings almost always shared bedrooms, if not beds. Doris Brundage set her newborn baby to sleep at the foot of a bed occupied by her four-year-old daughter. By alternating the direction of their bodies, a mother from Reading, Pennsylvania, managed to squeeze four children, ranging from three to fifteen years of age, into one double bed. Even the staunchest advocates of family togetherness would have had problems with this solution to overcrowding. Although experts on domesticity recommended that parents and children devote much of their time to shared activities, they acknowledged that parents and children alike needed solitude once in a while to cultivate independent interests. Trailers living made it difficult, if not impossible, for families to strike the appropriate balance between family togetherness and individual privacy.

Defenders of trailer life went to great lengths to demonstrate that cramped quarters were no handicap to the maintenance of perfectly normal domestic relations. Sure, tiny rooms and railroad car floor plans eliminated privacy, but spatial confinement bred intimacy and warmth among family members. While doubling up in beds might create some inconvenience, at least there was a good excuse for keeping the in-laws from making weekend visits—a proposition certain to invite ruin to any happy family.

The trailer industry's sales pitch, like those of diners and bowling alleys, was aimed at women. In all three cases, the reasoning was that if women could be won over, the rest of the family would follow. When it came to addressing the problem of spatial limitations, trailer boosters invariably trotted out the argument, aimed at women, that compacted space simplified housekeeping chores. Less interior space meant less floor to scrub, fewer windows to wash, and less furniture to dust. In contrast to the typical suburban home, trailers were a breeze to clean. Liberated from time-consuming cleaning chores, homemakers were freed to pursue more enjoyable activities: taking music lessons, joining a bowling league, enrolling in an adult education course. Trailer living thus promised women a carefree style of life that did not encroach upon their domestic responsibilities.

At the same time, however, articles and advice columns on trailer housekeeping acknowledged that spatial constraints posed certain difficulties, namely, avoiding clutter. No matter how rooms were arranged within a trailer, they afforded little space for storage. Living rooms, which tended to be the most spacious, rarely exceeded 100 square feet and most were about half that size. Beds consumed nearly the entire space available in most bedrooms. Trailer kitchens boasted full-size refrigerators, ranges, and sinks, but little in the way of counter or shelf space. Especially when people moved into trailers from larger accommodations, the volume of personal belongings often exceeded existing storage space. For large families living in small trailers, it required constant vigilance to keep bicycles, toys, sports equipment, tools, hobby materials, and magazines from spilling out of closets and shelves onto living room floors and overflowing from house interiors into carports and front lawns.

The tendency to clutter in trailer homes conflicted with prevailing middle-class norms regarding cleanliness and tidiness. As labor-saving household appliances such as vacuum cleaners, garbage disposal units, and automatic washing machines became commonplace after World War II, advertisers and manufacturers raised standards of cleanliness in order to sell more products. The antiseptic and tidy home validated the dutiful homemaker. More so than in a conventional house, meticulous housecleaning in a trailer was imperative because clutter was so noticeable. Even a few items strewn around inappropriately could make a trailer appear slovenly.

Then there was the problem of finding room for consumer possessions. The postwar home was supposed to be a showcase for material possessions, the modern appliances, toys, and amenities that signified attainment of the good life and one's arrival in the wonderful world of consumer abundance. But where to place the hi-fi system, the television set, and the washing machine in a tiny trailer? Large furniture sets were out of the question. A small piano might be wedged against a living room wall, but that meant no room for the reclining lounge chair or dinette set.

Always prepared to put the best face on any perceived deficiency, industry boosters maintained that mobile-home dwellers were, in fact, on the cutting edge of the consumer revolution. They reminded customers that manufacturers installed the "latest appliances, decorating innovations, and up-to-the-minute utilities" in trailers months before they made their appearance in conventional homes. Picture windows, wall-to-wall carpets, natural wood paneling that might cost thousands of dollars in a house—all had become standard features in trailers by the 1960s. Trailer residents were likely to be trendsetters in the consumption of miniature

Mobile-home interior, late 1950s. Trailer buyers displayed a preference for the same kitchen appliances that graced conventional suburban homes.

products, such as the portable, battery-operated transistor television set and the 45-rpm phonograph player. They were likewise assured that they were in the vanguard of fashion because the aluminum that surrounded them on four sides would soon become the material of choice for all sorts of commodities ranging from jewelry to furniture to dresses. According to a writer for *Trailer Topics* magazine, the acoustics within small trailer homes enhanced the sound quality of hi-fi systems. A 1950 article in the same publication explained that trailer colonists were in the best position to take advantage of the new phenomenon of television. If one disliked the programming in one city, one could pick up and move to another locale where the shows were better.

Trailer dwellers were not so easily mollified, however; the issue invariably came back to the items that were just too large for a small trailer. Upon viewing a set of maplewood furniture for a young boy's bedroom that "Jimmy would love," a woman who had recently moved from a house into a trailer expressed her biggest regret: "That's what I miss most, I think—no place to put the things you want, the things you just *ache* to buy." A few manufacturers catered to a specialized market by selling miniature versions of standard products. The Acme-National Refrigeration Company advertised its "Space Master" as "the smallest kitchen in the world with the largest capacity." Taking up less than five square feet, the "three-in-one kitchen" consisted of a two-burner stove and sink that sat atop a refrigerator-freezer unit. It did not sell particularly well. Especially when it came to kitchen appliances, trailer buyers preferred the same full-sized units that graced middle-class suburban homes. Anything smaller carried the dangerous suggestion that the woman of the house was something less than a full-fledged homemaker.

To make the best of a bad situation, homemakers and their families found ingenious ways to maximize what little interior space they had. Pots and pans were kept in the stove or hung from hooks on a wall; extra blankets were stored between boxsprings and mattresses. One resourceful couple saved room by fashioning an infant's cradle from a laundry basket and hanging it from an overhead cabinet on springs and hooks. Trailer tenants quickly learned to put furniture to multiple uses whenever possible. A record cabinet might double as an end table; a short cedar chest might be covered with cushions and used as a small bench.

Mobile-home park near the Savannah River atomic energy project, mid-1950s. Trailer owners attempted to follow middle-class norms regarding lawn arrangements by erecting picket fences and planting flower gardens.

When finances permitted, trailer owners who still lacked the wherewithal or desire to buy a small house, traded in their existing models for larger units. Over the course of a twenty-year period, families who lived in trailers permanently might pass through three or four different units, each one larger than the previous one. Another popular alternative was the built-on addition. Most trailers had concrete patios on the side that could be enclosed with walls and covered with an aluminum awning, thus converting it into an extra room. For those who lacked the time or skill to build their own addition, several firms sold prefabricated cabanas that latched on to the side of prefabricated trailers. In 1949, for example, a Miami firm introduced a detachable metallic "Alum-O-Room" that doubled as an extra living room and porch. By means of such cabana attachments, trailer colonists could easily double their interior floor space. When all else failed, one could simply stretch a sheet of canvas from the trailer roof and create the equivalent of a poor man's cabana. By means of a few chairs and a table, the strip of property alongside the trailer could be converted into an extra living room.

Unfortunately, the more that living quarters spilled beyond the trailer coach, the more that trailer living violated middle-class

Evergreen Trailer Park, Aurora, Minn., 1955. With only a few feet of space separating coaches, congested trailer parks inhibited the attainment of privacy.

norms about the proper use of the lawn. For the typical postwar suburbanite, front and back lawns provided a buffer between private and public worlds, between one's family and one's neighbors. It is quite telling that the one item that Levitt refused to skimp on when he designed his communities was the lawn; each of his homes appeared as islands in a vast sea of grass. Expansive front lawns and spacious backyards, especially when enclosed with fences or hedges, allowed families to maintain a certain amount of privacy outside as well as inside. The typical trailer dweller enjoyed no such luxury. Trailer owners might use their small lawns in conventional middle-class ways: cultivating flower gardens, hanging bird feeders, and erecting white picket fences around the borders of their lots. Some went further with their decorating impulses, planting munchkins, jockeys, or pink flamingos in the soil next to their butane tanks. But for trailer colonists, lawns were not merely canvases for creative expression; they were a relief from congested living quarters and functioned as extensions of the home. Families spent much of their time outdoors. Christmas might be celebrated around an outdoor Christmas tree. Baby's playpen might find a more or less permanent location under the shade of a trailer awning. Indeed, the near necessity of using the lawn as living space was one of the main reasons that mobile-home living flourished in warm climates.

The arrangement of trailer coaches within trailer parks severely undermined the attainment of privacy. In most parks, developers laid out lots in the most economical way so that trailer coaches lined up one after another with only a few feet of intervening space. The view from a kitchen window was likely to be a neighbor's living room. Picture windows that spanned five or six feet gave trailers a more spacious feel and conveyed the impression of a ranch-style suburban house. At the same time, however, they turned living rooms into theaters that staged a premiere performance every night. The fact that families spent so much time out of doors only heightened this neighborly visibility. Trailer parks may have been a voyeur's paradise, but they were less than ideal for those who valued their privacy. The woman who complained that she "couldn't dress up without being conspicuous," only scratched the surface of complaints that derived from densely packed dwellings. Another disenchanted trailer dweller captured the larger dimension of the problem when she sighed, "Everybody is on exhibition like in a zoo."

No Pets, No Kids: Trailer Park Resistance to the Domestic Ideal

Just as trailers could neither accommodate the full range of consumer commodities that people expected to find in prototypical middle-class homes nor meet prevailing middle-class standards of privacy, trailer parks were often unable to accommodate two vital components of the prototypical middle-class household, pets and children. Robert Bross recalled how his father came up with an unusual solution to this problem common to trailer colonists. Shortly after the outbreak of World War II, the Bross family of St. Charles,

Missouri, packed their belongings into a tiny travel trailer and relocated to Arizona. Upon arrival, they found plenty of trailer courts but few that would take their dog, Rodney. After being turned away numerous times, Henry Bross became exasperated. The next time a park manager told him, "Sorry, we don't accept pets," Bross was prepared. He returned to the car, collected Rodney, sat him down on the front-office lawn, and to his family's amazement and horror, "blew him away" with a shotgun. Bross then knocked on the manager's door and inquired politely, "Now will you rent us a space?" This time, Bross family, minus the dog, was accommodated.

The household pet was a staple of postwar middle-class family life. Dogs were particularly popular as they were well-suited to suburban living. Ranch-style homes with large back yards provided plenty of scampering space, while suburban streets and parks created a safe and pleasant environment for morning and evening walks. In trailer parks, however, where owners left their dogs outside much of the time, pets could easily become pests. Unless kept constantly on a leash, frisky canines roamed onto adjoining lots, trampled flower gardens, and terrified innocent children. Where open space was limited, dogs often relieved themselves on adjoining lawns, much to the consternation of neighbors. And late-night bouts of barking could drive an entire trailer colony to the brink of madness.

Complaints from aggrieved residents prompted park managers to establish a variety of regulations to keep the pet problem to a minimum. At the very least, parks required dogs to be leashed at all times. A few parks established quotas on the number of pets in a park. Besieged with complaints about dogs running loose on the property and biting tenants, a Detroit park manager, levied a monthly fee of five dollars on each pet owner. In the effort to reach a workable compromise between pet lovers and pet haters, some park operators divided their property into two sections, one that would accept tenants with cats and dogs and one that prohibited them. By the 1950s, the concept of separate pet sections gained favor among park operators and most trailer parks that admitted pets confined them to one end of the park property.

But there were just as many parks that forbade large pets altogether. Many proprietors experimented with milder forms of pet regulation only to find that tenants flouted the rules. "I posted a set of rules that specifically stated that dogs should be kept on a leash or confined to the boundaries of the owner's space," lamented a Florida park owner. "Dogs still ran loose all over the place." Like many other owners, he concluded that the only permanent solution was a ban on pets. And while some continued to look the other way when it came to small indoor pets such as parakeets or goldfish, the line was frequently drawn at dogs, and almost as frequently, cats. In the end, things turned out all right for Robert Bross. He was content with the companionship of a pet duck he won at a carnival. Indeed, Rinkameyer the duck was so loyal that it followed Bross to school every morning. For thousands of other trailer park children, however, Rinkameyer was a poor substitute for Lassie.

It was one thing to hold up a petless trailer park as a model of domestic bliss, quite another to make the same claim for a trailer park that prohibited children. Yet many postwar trailer parks did just that, thereby erecting the most formidable barrier to the attainment of middle-class domestic ideals. "If a park is going to be an example of a good American way of living," declared a suburban Chicago proprietor, "then you *must* have children in your park." Determined to uphold an all-American image, many operators struggled to maintain livable communities for families with children. Certainly, there was no shortage of business for trailer courts that welcomed kids. Among families with small children, the demand for trailer park spaces remained heavy through the 1950s. Apartment landlords who refused to take small children sent families scouring for inexpensive alternatives, including trailer parks. Likewise, newlyweds who had set up house in cozy trailers were not always financially prepared to purchase a private home when newborns made an appearance. For construction workers and military personnel, house trailers were a means of keeping families intact as they traveled from one location to another.

Park managers who accepted large families were overwhelmed with applications. Eager to lease lots as quickly as possible, the owners of the Wiggins Trailer Court in Gardena, California, posted a large sign at their front entrance reading, "Children Welcome." Within four months, the park was filled to capacity. All but one trailer housed families with youngsters. On a compact parcel of property designed for 29 coaches, there were no less than 65 children scampering about on a daily basis.

Parks like the Wiggins Trailer Court, overflowing with babies, toddlers, young children, and teenagers, no matter how All-American, created nightmares for proprietors and tenants alike. Squealing babies and rambunctious children could be just as irritating as pesky dogs, and many tenants, especially older ones, would just as soon do without them. As one park manager explained, "Our retired residents have had their fill of children in their lifetimes. . . . Children make them nervous." Playful children were equally annoying to night workers trying to catch some sleep during daylight hours. For Howard Greenlee, who had a son of his own, the "mischief, noise, and confusion," created by unruly youngsters constituted the worst feature of trailer life.

Herman Smith owned a park in Florida where a third of his sixty spaces were occupied by families with children, and he was fed up with them. "They break up everything," he complained, "windows in the recreation room; windows of mobile homes, they fill up the sewer outlets; toilets in the washrooms have had to be torn out to remove stuff they've thrown into them." Such juvenile mischief drove proprietors to distraction. Some park managers singled out teenagers as the primary source of mayhem and destruction. "They think it is smart to aggravate the neighbors and vie with each other to see who can do the most damage," recounted a custodian based on his experience in several trailer parks located in different parts of the country. Others blamed parents for poor discipline. Weighing in against the parents, one trailerist blamed mothers who allowed their children to roam freely through the community, assured that they would remain secure while in the confines of the park. "They give the children something to eat, send them outside to eat it and forget about them for hours," she observed, adding, "naturally, these children will do as they please until someone stops them."

Whether the fault lay with parents or the children, many park managers insisted on taking steps to prevent restless youth from dragging down the quality of life in their communities. While indifferent park owners left it to children to create their own play spaces amid the streets, service yards, and communal laundry facilities, most found it prudent to keep youngsters out of mischief by setting aside prescribed play areas. Thus, many family parks contained small playgrounds consisting of slides, swings, and perhaps a sandbox. Some park owners went even further and programmed regular recreational activities—storytelling hour, costume parties, sports tournaments, and so forth. F. V. Thiess, who ran a park in Orlando, Florida, had a different technique. Convinced that he had a knack for screening out brats, Thiess made a habit of inviting prospective tenants into his mobile home for an interview. "It doesn't take long to find out whether the parents pay any attention to what the kids do," he claimed. Presumably, families with suspect children were sent back out on the road.

To ensure the happiness of all tenants at the Happy Hollow Trailer Park in National City, California, B. J. Olsen ran a fence through the center of his property. On one side of the chain-link barricade, Olsen placed all families that had small children. Empty-nest households were assigned to spaces in the other half of the park. Youngsters who transgressed the boundary received a stern reprimand and an escort back to their half of the park.

By the 1950s, most parks that accepted children adopted a similar policy, setting aside a special section of the park for them, just as they did for pets. Indeed, the pet and children sections of the park were often identical. In these situations, families with small children and pets were usually quarantined in the rear of the park, separated from other tenants by a buffer zone that might consist of a playground or a shuffleboard court. Isolated family and pet sections gave trailer parks a schizophrenic character; crossing over the boundary into the family section meant leaving tranquil homes and well-ordered lawns into the cacophony of toy-littered yards, bicycles zipping through the streets, and screaming parents. Dual parks, however, enabled park owners to reap the profits from the family trade without alienating those tenants who insisted on peace and quiet.

For many proprietors, however, the costs of admitting children outweighed any benefits, regardless of the park's configuration. No matter how carefully proprietors screened prospective tenants or how well large families were sequestered, the presence of children entailed additional expenses and responsibilities. There were locks to install, fences to erect, and more often than not, windows to repair. As many as a third of all trailer parks refused to accept children outright. In parts of the country where retirees predominated, the percentage could be much higher. In San Diego, about half of all parks prohibited children. A disgruntled trailerist in Phoenix griped that he visited about fifteen courts before he found one that would take both his kids and his dog. While many "adult only" communities were restricted to men and women beyond child-bearing age, usually above 45 or 55, others were geared toward younger working couples. The latter approach involved a certain amount of risk as childless couples, if they were young enough, might receive an unexpected visit from the stork once comfortably ensconced and then be faced with eviction.

Laying Down the Law:
Restricting the Freedoms of
Trailer Park Residents

Prohibitions on pets and children imposed the most severe constraints on the attainment of the middle-class domestic ideal, but
most parks also issued a wide variety of rules and regulations that
collided with the liberty that families expected as a corollary to private home ownership. Like the buyers of conventional homes, pur-
chasers of trailer coaches looked forward to the freedom of arranging their domiciles as they wished. As one champion of trailer
living put it, "It's a great comfort to know that we can hang up a picture, paint a cupboard, or put up a shelf without getting permission
from a crotchety landlord." In fact, however, this freedom was circumscribed by deed restrictions and park bylaws that went beyond
those established in conventional suburban subdivisions. The parks
constructed hurriedly to relieve the housing shortages of the 1940s
imposed few restrictions on their mostly temporary occupants. As
long as tenants paid their rent on time, park owners rarely meddled
in their affairs. The trend toward longer-term occupancy in the
1950s, however, led tenants and managers alike to seek a more
structured experience.

Most of the regulations promulgated by park management were
designed to maintain an attractive environment, thereby preventing any depreciation in the status of the park. There were rules
proscribing the days of the week on which tenants could hang
their laundry out to dry, and where tenants could store paraphernalia that did not fit inside the trailer coach. Some park managers
shouldered the responsibility for lawn care, while others left the
task to tenants as long as they followed rigid guidelines regarding
the placement of hedges and shrubs and the types of trees and
flowers that could be planted. Likewise, regulations stipulated
what materials, if any, could be used for the fencing of house lots.

Park owners who permitted fencing usually required the wooden picket variety, painted white. Other regulations aimed to minimize auto and truck congestion in the park. Park managers, for example, often restricted to a designated few the companies that could deliver milk, bread, laundry, and packages to individual homes. Some parks banned home delivery altogether.

These well-intentioned regulations often served only to frustrate trailer park residents. Exclusive contracts with delivery companies made it impossible to get home delivery from certain stores that did not make the cut. Laundry room schedules prevented crowding but aggravated tenants who wished to wash a few items in between their assigned time slots. Regulations prohibiting the erection of unsightly television antennae annoyed those who yearned for better reception. While a tenant might sympathize with the spirit behind these regulations, they could also become a source of disgruntlement when they conflicted with individual preferences.

Gone with the Wind: The Perils of Nature in Trailer Parks

Regulations were useless, however, when it came to protecting trailer dwellers from the harsh elements and vagaries of nature. Among the advantages of trailer life cited by its advocates was that it brought people closer to nature, allowing them to live in settings removed from the concrete, congestion, and artifice of the inner city. Much like suburban subdivisions, trailer parks enticed prospective tenants with idyllic names that conjured up images of pastoral utopias: Tall Pines, Pine Oak, Oak Grove, Shady Grove, Shady Acres, Green Acres, Green Meadow, Meadow Lark, and so on. The use of the term "park" to describe a community of mobile homes, suggested, at the very least, some tenuous connection with nature. But whereas the conventional suburban community brought residents close to a nature that was carefully controlled and well ordered, trailer colonies often stood in the path of a nature that was chaotic and destructive.

September 13, 1960, was a tense day for residents of the Sarasota City Trailer Park. Weather bulletins had alerted them that Hurricane Donna was heading in their direction. Park management convened a morning meeting to advise a mass evacuation from the premises. In a park that held close to a thousand trailers, only forty-one intrepid, or perhaps foolhardy, tenants decided to remain. In preparation for the worst, work crews made their way around the property tying down loose objects; all electrical power was shut off to prevent fires and accidents from falling wires. As predicted, the storm hit with full force that night. Dozens of trailers were damaged. Hurricane Donna demolished carports, stripped awnings from their moorings, poked holes in trailer coach roofs, and engraved dents into trailer coach walls.

A mixture of emotions accompanied tenants as they returned to their homes to assess the hurricane's damage. Those who had purchased insurance counted their blessings and began to fill out the necessary claim forms. Those without policies cursed their luck and started to make repairs. These particular trailer park residents had reason to be grateful. As trailer disasters went, this one was relatively minor. It paled in comparison to the 1947 tornado that razed an entire forty-two-home trailer park in Findlay, Ohio, or the hurricane that sent trailer coaches flying through the air around Miami three years later.

Contrary to popular belief, hurricanes and tornadoes contained no built-in homing devices guiding them to trailer park targets. Rather, trailer parks were exceptionally vulnerable to damage from extreme weather conditions. Many were located on flat and low-lying land that was susceptible to flooding and wind damage. Most importantly, the structures were not as sturdy as conventional homes built of bricks and mortar or wood frame. Trailer advocates might like to think that their homes could withstand nuclear attacks better than other types of housing, but the experience of hurricanes and tornadoes suggested otherwise.

When the inevitable heavy rains and rising winds came, trailer parks burst into a frenzy as residents prepared for the worst. Old hands counseled novices on the proper way to chain down propane tanks, remove awnings, and arrange interior furniture so that the coaches were weighted against the wind. Those who had completed these tasks roamed the park, offering their assistance to others. Then came time for the crucial decision to either take refuge elsewhere or tough it out at home, to risk looking foolish for panicking unnecessarily or to risk life and limb in metal compartments under the siege by the elements.

Innocence and Experience: Childhood in the Trailer Park

Despite the claims of the trailer industry, then, living in a trailer park was not at all like living in a conventional suburban subdivision. The inconveniences and hardships associated with trailer park life—rigid rules, destructive storms, congested living arrangements—prompted tenants to undertake a constant reevaluation of their housing options. If many transient workers and families on limited incomes concluded that trailers represented their only means of realizing the dream of home ownership, there remained a large contingent of young couples who saw trailer parks as a temporary way station along their journey from an inner-city apartment to a suburban ranch-style home. For those in the latter category, it was invariably the issue of raising children that prompted the most serious questions about trailer living.

To be sure, parents appreciated those features of trailer park life that eased the burdens of child care. High-density residential arrangements facilitated parental or other adult supervision. As long as children remained in the trailer compound, they rarely left the sight of some watchful adult. In the event that a husband and wife wanted a night out for themselves, baby-sitters were easy to come by. In the Florida trailer park where Ray Millard and his wife settled in the mid-1950s, the abundance of teenage girls looking for extra spending money made it easy to find someone to take care of their two daughters when they decided to go out for an impromptu night on the town. A few progressive parks even established day-care centers where working mothers could deposit their children before heading off for their jobs. More often, informal day-care networks crystallized among the many trailer families that depended on two wage earners for financial support. At the Birmingham Trailer Village in Van Nuys, California, for example, working mothers left their youngsters under the charge of volunteers from the trailer park who signed up for playground duty in two-hour shifts.

Nor did parents have to worry about any shortage of playmates for their young ones in a family-oriented park. Children growing up in trailer courts were rewarded with rich social lives. Tight friendships, often lasting a lifetime, formed as children spent their leisure hours in the open spaces of the court building train sets, playing ball, and riding bicycles. On occasion, playtime rituals took strange twists. Boys and girls playing house might act out scenarios involving replacing butane tanks or repairing stopped-up sinks. At the Greater St. Louis Trailer Park, teenagers amused themselves on summer evenings by trying to peer over the fence of an adjacent drive-in movie theater that showed adult films. But for the most part, trailer park children played much like children in conventional suburban subdivisions.

These advantages notwithstanding, many parents deemed trailer parks inappropriate settings for raising families. Where recreation space was not provided, parents worried about children getting injured while playing in the streets of the trailer court. Some parents worried about disreputable neighbors with whom their children might come into contact. Allan Berube, who grew up in a trailer park in Bayonne, New Jersey, remembered the strict instructions he received from his mother never to visit any trailer unaccompanied, a rule he violated on occasion without her knowledge. Above all else, however, it was lack of space that led parents to the conclusion that trailers were unsuitable for small children. For Carolyn Wilson, who was brought up and married in a trailer park, the issue was privacy. "When I had kids," she explained, "I wanted to make sure that they had their own room, that they could have their own room and close the door, that they could have some privacy." For Thomas Crouthamel, it was simply a matter of congestion. He remembered, "when we were going to have our first kid we realized that the trailer was not big enough for two adults and a kid even though it was a thirty-five footer. . . . Kids take up the space of three adults. So we sold it and bought a house." The difficulties associated with raising children was the most common reason cited by tenants for wanting to abandon trailer life; the arrival of a newborn was the event most likely to precipitate an exit.

Pulp Trash:
Trailer Parks in the Mass Media

The difficulties of meeting middle-class domestic norms in trailer parks were real enough, but they became magnified out of all proportion when projected through the distorted lens of the mass media. In mass-circulation magazines, pulp fiction novels, and B-movies, trailer parks were not presented merely as hard places to raise children but as breeding grounds for dysfunctional families. In the popular mind, trailer parks were synonymous with poverty, filth, and pathological behavior. The people who lived there were drunks, sex maniacs, wife beaters, and child abusers. Despite the efforts of progressive proprietors and trade associations to build model parks and publicize the wholesome virtues of trailer living, the negative stereotypes propagated by the media were the ones that stuck.

This distorted public perception was partly due to the enduring image of the ragtag parks built during the Depression and World War II. Improvements in the quality of trailer parks did not easily register in the public consciousness. Trailer subculture was largely invisible to outsiders. Few people saw the interior of trailer courts. Those that lay partially exposed to public streets tended to be among the shabbiest.

In the absence of firsthand knowledge, most people relied on unfavorable media stereotypes. Some of the most damning portrayals of social life in trailer park communities came in the form of pulp fiction novels. Trailer parks were among the most popular settings for titillating story plots that revolved around sexual debauchery and passed themselves off as documentary truth. According to the blurb on the back cover of one such novel, *Trailer Park Woman*:

> Today nearly one couple in ten lives in a mobile home—one of those trailers you see bunched up in cozy camps near every sizable town. Some critics argue that in such surroundings love tends to become casual. Feverish affairs take place virtually right out in the open. Social codes take strange and shocking twists. . . . "Trailer Tramp" was what they called Ann Mitchell—for she symbolized the twisted morality of the trailer camp . . . this book shocks not by its portrayal of her degradation—rather, by boldly bringing to light the conditions typical of trailer life.

If trailer life turned housewives into wanton women, it was thought to exert equally ruinous effects on the morals and well-being of young children. Typical was the journalistic exposé of a camp on the outskirts of Pittsburgh where twenty-three trailer

Unidentified trailer park, mid-1950s. Ragtag trailer parks continued to drag down the reputation of the industry through the postwar era.

coaches were crammed onto a parcel of property roughly the size of a square city block. Seventy-five tenants, about a third of them small children, shared one toilet and a shower stall no larger than a telephone booth in the basement of the owner's house. In the absence of adequate sanitary facilities, young girls routinely squatted behind trailers to relieve their full bladders; presumably young boys resorted to similar measures. Tenants hiked a quarter of a mile to dispose of their garbage in an open dump. Not surprisingly, the park was infested with "hundreds of rats." Trying to put a positive spin on an incident whereby an aggressive rodent bit a young girl on the arm while she slept, a neighbor asked rhetorically, "Good thing it wasn't her face they chewed, wasn't it?" What galled the reporter most of all was that tenants seemed to accept these abject living conditions as a matter of course.

Certainly, there were plenty of shoddy parks to which critics could point as evidence of the deplorable physical conditions of trailer living. Even by the 1950s, many parks lacked adequate sanitary facilities. Rat infestation was an ever-present menace wherever people and their garbage amassed in such dense settings. As inadequate as many parks may have been, generalizations about trailer life were invariably drawn from worst-case scenarios. Stories about trailer park inhabitants invariably highlighted the most deviant types of behavior. Given the widespread dissemination of this overwhelmingly negative image, it was difficult to escape the conclusion that social depravity was endemic to trailer living.

Serious attempts to explain the pathological effects of trailer parks usually focused on the one feature that was intrinsic to trailer housing, mobility. The long-standing celebration of home ownership in American culture was based on the idea that fixed residence would generate stable communities, and thus, responsible citizens. Residential mobility, on the other hand, was thought to discourage those feelings of civic obligation that were vital to the functioning of a democracy. Critics were particularly troubled by the perceived long-term effects on children. How could children possibly learn the principles of good citizenship while being pulled in and out of schools? How could they ever develop stable social relationships when their playmates were recycled every few years if not every few months?

Never mind that by the early 1960s, trailer residents moved only once every five years, right on par with the rest of America, and probably less frequently than families headed by young corporate executives. When William Whyte conducted his sociological study of transient life in the upper-middle-class suburb of Park Forest, Illinois, a community where frequent corporate transfers produced a continuous turnover in the population, he expected to find families struggling with psychological instability and loneliness. Instead, he discovered a community of spontaneous joiners capable of forming meaningful friendships and social organizations. Thrust into a new setting with people of similar backgrounds previously unknown to one another, the settlers of Park Forest impressed Whyte with their determination to manufacture a cohesive and friendly community from scratch. While most Americans had little troubling swallowing the concept of manufactured belongingness in white-collar suburbs, they could not fathom the possibility that transient tenants could form equally stable and social bonds in working-class trailer parks. In the public mind, conventional suburbs produced wholesome families no matter how often people moved in or out, a perception that was certainly reinforced by popular television shows such as *Leave It to Beaver, Father Knows Best,* and *The Donna Reed Show.* Trailer courts were different, the American public was told, and the people who lived in them were a breed apart. Indeed, they were often referred to as "gypsies," a slur that not only questioned their morals but cast suspicion on their status as Americans.

Trailer Trash: Race, Class, and Shifting Notions of "Whiteness" in Trailer Parks

"Gypsy" was not the only derogatory term that scorched the ears of trailer tenants. Eleven-year-old Peggy Lou Haner was so insulted by a remark made by one of her classmates that she whacked him on the head with her doll, sending him running home in tears to his mother. The boy had called her "trailer trash."

Vivian Tucker was among the forty-three tenants who presented a petition to Huntington Beach City Council protesting the city's plan to raise rental fees and prohibit the construction of cabanas in the municipal trailer court. Above all else, what incensed Tucker was the park manager's threat "to have the rent raised to get rid of the white trash."

Just as the term "gypsy" set trailer park dwellers apart from authentic Americans, the designation "trash" classified them as less than middle-class and less than white. If taking a meal in a modern diner-restaurant or spending an afternoon in an automated bowling center conferred an American identity, some semblance of middle-class status, and above all, whiteness on the descendants of European immigrants, there were other types of consumer behavior that could just as easily compromise these attributes. Living in a trailer park was among them.

In fact, it was difficult to find people in trailer parks who would not otherwise have been considered fully white. There were a few parks that admitted the occasional Asian or Latino family. Jose Palacios and his three brothers came to the United States from Mexico to join the circus as trapeze artists. During the off-season they made their home in a tiny trailer, and although living conditions were not always ideal, they encountered little difficulty finding rental spaces. At the Sunset Trailer Park in Bayonne, New Jersey, the succession of white trailer households was interrupted by a Chinese-American family, who stayed there largely because discrimination prevented them from buying a private home in the area. African Americans, on the other hand, were almost universally barred, thus severely limiting their access to inexpensive private housing.

Even if physical appearances suggested that the vast majority of trailer park tenants were white, outsiders found it difficult to assign them the same racial status as the white people who raised families in fixed suburban homes. In some cases, the withholding of white status could be quite stark. Allan Berube may have had a deep tan from playing in the outdoors without a shirt, but there was no mistaking him for an African American. Nevertheless, he was called "nigger-boy" when assaulted by the neighborhood boys who lived in conventional homes. Even *Life* magazine could not resist the temptation to link the debased social status of trailer park dwellers with inferior racial status. When the mass-circulation periodical profiled a cross-section of American society in the "typical American town" of Rockford, Illinois, it selected a trailer dweller to represent the lowest of all social ranks, the "lower-lower class." Sam

Sygulla moved to Rockford after the war and shifted from one job to another before landing steady employment in a wood products plant. Unable to find affordable conventional housing, Sam, along with his wife, daughter, and puppy settled for a spot in a primitive trailer court where they cooked meals on a hot plate and bathed in a communal shower. Of all the varieties of housing found in Rockford, trailers ranked lowest on the scale of social prestige. To underscore the deprivation faced by the Sygullas, *Life* noted that their "neighbors include Negroes who are moving in to take unskilled jobs." The implication was clear: In their choice of housing and neighbors, the Sygullas had compromised their white status.

Popular discourse about trailer living revealed the extent to which one could not talk about class without talking about race. In a culture that correlated racial status with social standing, trailer park dwellers who violated prevailing norms of domesticity found their whiteness constantly called into question and qualified. Thus, the labels "white trash" and "trailer trash" stuck to them wherever they went. Moreover, if the middle majority was to be built upon racial separation, then racially suspect trailer parks would have to be isolated from respectable housing developments. The trash would have to be removed.

Trash Removal:
The Legal Assault on
Trailer Communities

Marshaling dubious evidence of their destructive influence, middle-class communities across the country commenced a relentless legal assault on America's trailer park settlements in the postwar years. Civic leaders condemned trailer colonists as parasites who drained municipalities of resources and contributed nothing but headaches in return. Trailer coaches, like other vehicles, were assessed only as personal property. Because they paid no property taxes, trailer tenants were derided as freeloaders and blamed for overburdened hospitals, schools, law enforcement agencies, fire departments, and other public agencies. Even where municipalities attempted to cover expenses by establishing registration fees for all trailer park occupants, or where school boards levied an extra tuition fee on children who inhabited trailer homes, the perception persisted that mobile home owners did not pay their own way.

Curiously, civic officials rarely applied these arguments or supplemental levies to apartment dwellers, even though apartment tenants were in an analogous situation. Although William Levitt and other builders of conventional homes encountered mild community opposition to their housing developments on the grounds that their massive subdivisions would overwhelm public facilities, such opposition never approached the bitterness that attended condemnation of new trailer park developments.

Trailer owners were also thought to be poor consumers, adding little in the way of revenue to local commerce. The operative logic was that trailer dwellers were poor to begin with and, thus, would not support local merchants as did "normal" families. Without sufficient space in their homes for furniture, rugs, curtains, and framed pictures, it was assumed that they frittered away their earnings on frivolous ornaments for their cars, or worse yet, on gambling. The fact that many merchants discriminated against trailer families, refusing them credit on the grounds that they were temporary residents, only made it harder for trailer park residents to prove their value to communities as buyers of local goods and services.

The mobile home industry funded and publicized studies on trailerist spending habits to dispel the myth of the poor consumer. The residents of Sarasota's municipal trailer park spent nearly half a million dollars on new automobiles, $295,000 on local entertainment, and $647,000 on prescription drugs, gifts, clothes, and other sundry items from local merchants in 1957. According to a more comprehensive survey, the average trailer resident spent $62 a week in their communities. These studies were of little avail as they rarely resulted in Chamber of Commerce officials clamoring for new trailer camps for their towns.

Behind the rhetoric of trailerists' limited contributions to commerce and tax coffers was the fear that trailer parks would bring ruin to the larger communities in which they were situated. Arguments levied against them invariably included vague references to the threat they posed to community health, safety, and morals, or the "bad element" they introduced to the community. Trailer courts were viewed as the most recent incarnation of the urban slum, and their presence in the vicinity of stable middle-class suburbs was interpreted as a blighting influence. Perceived as a cancer that needed to be checked, trailer residents felt the full weight of a sustained legal assault on the part of middle-class communities across the country.

On a summer day in 1954, police swooped down upon the Ideal Trailer Park, just outside Cleveland, Ohio, and carted thirteen tenants off to jail. The Ohio Supreme Court had recently upheld a local ordinance limiting trailer occupancy to sixty days. The violators were well aware of the legal proceedings, but assumed that they would be given some advance warning prior to prosecution. City officials, however, wanted it to be known that they planned to take a hard line against the trailer menace.

The litany of objections against mobile home dwellers inspired many such systematic attempts to rid communities of the trailer parks. Many municipalities, such as the one in Ohio cited above, employed time limits on trailer parking so as to distinguish the "good" vacationing trailerist from the "bad" permanent inhabitant. Other communities banned trailer parks from their jurisdiction altogether. The targets of these legal assaults, both trailer park owners and residents, fought back when they could, and in some instances managed to mount effective counteroffensives. When the local lawmakers in Bell, California, threatened to banish all trailer courts from the city, residents of three large parks joined forces and fielded their own slate of candidates for mayor and city council in the next election. Wielding a large bloc of votes, they won at the polls, and the campaign to eliminate trailer parks came to a swift end. Elsewhere, where park residents lacked enough votes to challenge their opponents at the polls, they contested anti-trailer ordinances in court, with some success. Although courts invariably upheld the right of communities to regulate trailer housing, they usually rejected the notion that trailers constituted a nuisance, per se.

Faced with uncertain legal ramifications and in some cases, electoral backlashes, most communities used their legitimate zoning authority to contain the anticipated damage from the trailer menace. By the postwar era, most incorporated cities enjoyed the power to designate the types of activity that could take place on particular parcels of property. City planners divided the territory within their jurisdiction into zones that would accommodate three basic types of land-use: residential, commercial, and industrial. The purpose of zoning was to protect property values by preventing the siting of undesirable activities in the vicinity of desirable ones. Trailers were relegated to areas where they could do the least damage, in other words, as far away as possible from respectable middle-class communities. In the scheme of zoning classifications, this usually meant they were placed within commercial or industrial areas. Zoning trailer courts in commercial districts might have made sense in the days when they functioned primarily as temporary resting places for tourists. By the 1950s, however, equating trailer parks with commercial, let alone industrial, land uses said more about people's prejudices and fears than about what they really were, which was residential housing.

Hostile legislative and zoning maneuvers had a profound impact on trailer park geography. Excluded from prime residential areas, trailer parks were shunted to marginal locations on the metropolitan periphery, places that promised no other productive use. In the Pittsburgh area, trailer courts were built atop abandoned slag dumps, refuse pits, and coal mines. In Baltimore, zoning officials agreed to let an operator establish a park in an area that was surrounded by old houses, a gas station, a welding shop, and a school for African American children. Elsewhere, it was not uncommon to find trailer colonies abutting airports, adjacent to noxious factories, or wedged between railroad tracks and arterial highways. In stark contrast to diners and bowling alleys, which had improved their reputations by moving out of seedy urban districts, trailer parks relegated to the hardscrabble margins of the city continued to suffer by association with their surroundings. At the same time that diners and bowling alleys were becoming domesticated, trailer parks were being treated as anything but homes.

External community opposition and regulatory pressures hindered the ability of park owners to create within the confines of their property the sort of environment that might translate into greater social prestige. In the eyes of many tenants, labeled as white trash and blamed for the slovenly appearance of their parks, dilapidated parks were the fault of greedy, lazy, or indifferent owners. Usually, the truth was more complicated. Property located in industrial or commercial districts, however unappealing from an aesthetic standpoint, was not necessarily cheap. Trailer parks were often only marginally profitable enterprises to begin with. Recouping an investment on an expensive piece of property often led the trailer park operator to skimp on physical improvements and squeeze as many coaches as possible onto a small plot of land. To avoid hassles with zoning officials, park operators moved out beyond the city limits into unincorporated areas where regulatory authority was weaker and land was cheaper. These were usually undeveloped areas, inhabited by the poor and bereft of basic municipal services. In many cases, unsanitary conditions derived from the lack of water and sewer systems rather than the indifference of landlords.

While long-term parking regulations and zoning restrictions betrayed the prejudices of local authorities, discrimination against trailer parks also operated at the highest level of government, where it was equally effective in undermining the efforts of trailer court tenants and owners to create the sort of communities they might have desired. No single factor was more instrumental in stimulating the fantastic growth of suburban subdivisions in the postwar years than the federal housing policies that insured mortgages for the buyers of new single-family detached homes. Yet, it was not until 1971 that the FHA extended such privileges to buyers of mobile homes. As long as the FHA maintained the distinction between fixed and mobile homes, banks saw mobile homes and mobile home parks as relatively risky investments.

Had lending institutions been more generous, mobile home parks might have evolved into settlements that were much closer in appearance to conventional suburban subdivisions. There was no shortage of architectural plans for low-density trailer parks arranged around curvilinear streets and buffered with abundant green space. The problem was raising funds for the construction of these idyllic trailer courts. Even the inauguration of an FHA program of mortgage insurance for trailer park developers in 1955 did little to loosen credit. Strict eligibility requirements and limited governmental liability—loans were insured only up to 75 percent of their value, in contrast to the 90 percent that was standard for new suburban homes—scared lenders and investors as much as it enticed them. In the end, the program attracted few takers. Their access to capital severely restricted, mobile home park developers remained frustrated in their attempts to build the sort of settlements that both their tenants and neighboring communities would have preferred.

Dream Parks by the Sea: The Retiree Market and the Subdivision Formula

There was one significant exception to this general rule, the trailer park for retirees. By the 1950s, elderly couples represented a sizable and rapidly growing segment of the market for house trailers. One of the most striking developments of the postwar era was the concept of retirement as a distinct stage of life. Medical advancements and the disbursement of social security benefits meant that for the first time, retired couples could quit work at age sixty-five and look forward to a period of extended leisure. The prospect of passing one's twilight years under the shade of palm trees inspired a mass migration of senior citizens to warm-weather resorts in Florida and the southwest region of the United States. For elderly couples on reduced incomes, low-cost trailers made the retirement dream affordable. By the end of the 1950s, it was estimated that retired couples occupied one out of every ten mobile homes.

Indeed, the nation's largest mobile home park, with approximately 3,000 residents, was populated almost entirely by retired men and women. Located on Florida's Gulf Coast, the Bradenton Trailer Park had been owned and operated by the local chapter of the Kiwanis Club since 1936. Although the park was initially set up to accommodate vacationing tourists, by the 1950s the Kiwanians were promoting it as an ideal retirement alternative for couples forced to live on monthly pensions that fell below $100. To maintain the homogeneity of the population, management forbade residents from securing paid employment. This regulation virtually guaranteed that families with noisy children would be excluded. A full schedule of recreational and educational activities—dances, card parties, Bible classes, and plays—kept tenants occupied throughout the daytime and evening hours. Very quickly, this formula of creating self-contained retirement communities with an active recreational program spread to other trailer parks in Florida and then other warm-weather settings.

Retirement trailer courts departed dramatically from those that catered to younger families, largely because they escaped the stigma commonly associated with mobile home living. Civic leaders and local authorities rarely raised fears about the threat to community health, safety, and morals, when the people in question wore dentures and ambled about with the assistance of walking sticks. Because visiting grandchildren were likely to be the only youngsters on the premises, retirement trailer courts did not violate prevailing norms of domesticity, in that elderly couples were not expected to have children in their households. Freed from the usual forms of community opposition, developers of retirement parks had a much easier time raising investment capital, thereby enabling them to embellish their parks with a wide variety of amenities: swimming pools, auditoriums, and the obligatory shuffleboard court. Indeed, the rich potential and readily available capital for building retirement parks was the source of an inspiration that one developer hoped would revolutionize the entire trailer park business.

Sydney Adler had a novel idea while visiting the west coast of Florida on a business trip in the early 1950s. A young Miami lawyer, Adler had no previous experience in the mobile home business. Yet he was struck with the abundance of trailer parks in the region, many of which were filled with retirees from northern states. Why, he wondered, didn't developers sell lots for trailers as they did for houses? The question lodged in his mind and the more he thought about it, the more he became convinced that trailer owners, particularly older couples who were not looking to relocate again, would jump at the chance to own their own lot rather than subject themselves to the vagaries of tenancy. Pooling some money with two other interested investors, Adler decided to test his theory. In 1954 he purchased property in an undeveloped area midway between the towns of Sarasota and Bradenton and began selling lots for trailer owners.

Trailer Estates, the community that Adler designed and developed, was a far cry from the typical trailer park of the times. The lots were large: 2,400 square feet, enough room for a fifty-foot trailer, a cabana, a small garden, and a carport. The herring-bone pattern of trailer coaches departed dramatically from the traditional barracks-like grid. To further sweeten the bait Adler provided amenities galore: a private beach, a marina for 140 boats, a grocery store, shuffleboard courts, and a full schedule of organized recreational activities ranging from square dancing to bingo. While Adler expected the majority of buyers to be older couples in their retirement years, he also anticipated a demand among families with children, and, hence, he set aside a portion of the park exclusively for their use.

Claude and Pearl Mallory were among the first five families to buy property at Trailer Estates. They had retired to Florida several years earlier and were living in a rental park in Sarasota. Frustrated with annual rent increases, they jumped at the opportunity to purchase their own lot when they learned of Adler's enterprise. They knew that at their current stage of life, they weren't going to be doing a lot of moving around. At $895, the price for lots seemed so reasonable that the Mallorys bought two, one for their trailer and one for an expansive garden.

Other families were recruited directly from northern locales. Adler sold lots off a plat map displayed in Grand Central Station in New York City and set up a booth at the Michigan State Fair decorated with orange and palm trees. To ease the psychological transition to Florida living, Adler named his streets after northern states—Ohio, Michigan, Indiana, New York, and so forth. He envisioned that migrants from the North would gravitate to the streets named after their home states, thus providing an immediate common bond among neighbors. The novel concept, combined with aggressive marketing, paid dividends. By 1960 the park was full with a population that approached 2,000.

Adler may not have been the first person to come up with the idea of what became known as the subdivision park, one where trailer owners purchased their lots. At least one other park in Florida claimed to have preceded Adler. Nonetheless, Adler was the first to employ the concept on a large scale. Flush with his initial success, Adler proceeded to develop a series of parks built on the Trailer Estates model. By the early 1960s, Adler and his company, MobilLife, operated six subdivision parks in the states of Florida, Arizona, Nevada, California, and Michigan, some of which were even more luxurious than the original venture, boasting swimming pools and eighteen-hole golf courses. The idea behind the Michigan park, the only one located outside the Sun Belt, was that some of his Florida customers might want to spend the hot summer months up north, where another mobile home awaited them.

Within a few short years of the opening of Trailer Estates, dozens of park operators around the country picked up on the idea and built their own subdivision parks. The concept was especially popular in Florida, where 12 percent of all mobile home parks were of the subdivision variety by 1960. Like Adler's communities, these parks were developed in almost identical fashion to conventional residential suburbs, with land developers purchasing a large section of land, dividing it into lots for mobile homes, putting in streets, sewers, gas, water, and electrical lines, and then offering the lots for sale to individual owners. In this type of development, each mobile-home owner had his or her own property deed and the right to sell the lot. Annual assessments on each property owner, usually around $100, funded maintenance and common facilities. In Florida, prices for lots ranged anywhere from $500 to $5,000.

In common with most rental parks, and for that matter most middle-class suburban communities like Levittown, subdivision parks strove for racial homogeneity. Deed restrictions limited occupation to whites in no uncertain terms. Typical was the provision in the title deed signed by every property holder at Bar-J Estates in Tampa, Florida: "No property shall ever, at any time, be owned or occupied by any person of Negro descent." In other subdivision parks, including Adler's Trailer Estates, exclusion also extended to Asians and Mexicans.

As exciting as the subdivision idea seemed to Adler and other developers, the limits of the concept soon became apparent. The idea of owning one's own trailer lot held little appeal beyond the retirement market. When selling lots for Trailer Estates, Adler had the most trouble turning over property in the family section. Indeed, in some of his later parks, he abandoned the idea of a family section altogether. Other subdivision park operators who sought the family trade reported similar difficulties.

Looking back, Adler speculated that the "own your own lot" concept failed to take hold among working couples and younger families with children because it denied them the psychological security afforded by mobility. Even though most trailer park residents were sedentary, the freedom to pick up and move when opportunities arose elsewhere held enormous appeal. Financial investment in a piece of landed property complicated the prospect of relocation. For retirees with only a limited number of years in front of them, residential anchorage was more a positive attribute than a burden.

In addition, lot ownership, though far less expensive than purchasing a house, was nevertheless often prohibitively expensive for young families. When Adler first proposed the idea for Trailer Estates, he heralded the venture as "moderate cost living for families on a moderate income." True to Adler's prediction, few among the residents at Trailer Estates or his subsequent subdivisions could count themselves among the extraordinarily wealthy. Most were reasonably prosperous, however, certainly better off financially than the typical trailer dweller of the times. Many of the retirees in Adler's parks kept trailers as their second homes, retaining houses in the north for use during the summer months. For younger couples struggling from paycheck to paycheck, on the other hand, the deluxe subdivision park was simply too expensive. Even though the purchase of a trailer lot might prove more economical than renting in the long run, the cost of the initial down payment was daunting, especially when added to the annual maintenance fees levied in "own-your-own-plot" parks.

No doubt, subdivision parks stood out as the most well-maintained and exclusive mobile-home parks of the postwar era. With their attractive landscaping, recreational facilities, and innovative layouts, they represented a stark contrast to the dismal and disheveled trailer parks that had been banished to the city's grimy margins and seared into the public consciousness. For the most part, only rental parks that catered to older couples approached the standard set by the subdivision parks. Although retirement parks—both the rental and subdivision varieties—constituted an increasingly large segment of the market, they remained a clear minority. As of 1960, retirees represented about 10 percent of the total market for mobile homes. The parks that catered to them flourished primarily in warm climates, the sort of places where Adler located his establishments (with the exception of his Michigan park, which turned out to be a bust because, as it turned out, few retired couples wanted to own two mobile homes).

Ultimately, the subdivision parks made an important cultural contribution to the American middle class by introducing the concept of active retirement. Their schedule of round-the-clock activities—hobby classes, drama clubs, movie screenings, shuffleboard—served as a model for the exclusive and self-contained retirement communities developed by Del Webb and others in the 1970s. Within the mobile-home industry, however, their influence was more limited. Few of the progressive design and lifestyle features filtered down to the parks catering to working families, which remained in the majority and remained under a cloud of suspicion and derision.

Minorities Need Not Apply: Embattled Trailer Parks Close Ranks

Whether populated by working families or retirees, whether adorned with swimming pools and golf courses or stitched to-

The Spruces, Williamstown, Mass., 1960. Mobile-home communities built expressly for retirees tended to be more lavishly appointed than those built for working families.

gether with gravel roads, drainage ditches, and overhead electrical wires, mobile-home parks muddled through the postwar era as little universes unto themselves. Within the gates that enclosed rows of rectangular homes on wheels, residents who stayed anywhere from several days to many years forged tight social networks that sustained viable communities. To the outside world, they assumed a defensive posture. Among themselves, they took great care in constructing codes of etiquette and modes of cooperation that provided some semblance of the good life even as they struggled in vain to meet prevailing norms of domesticity.

According to surveys taken in the late 1950s and early 1960s, many mobile-home dwellers still hoped to move into conventional homes at some point in their lives. Yet, in contrast to returning veterans who filled trailer courts in the 1940s, they were less prepared to make a quick exit when new housing opportunities presented themselves. Over the intervening decade trailer park tenants had become poorer relatives to the population at large, less educated, and more blue-collar in their occupational profile. For these families, many of whom did not qualify for FHA mortgages, trailer living was as likely to become a trap as a springboard into the middle class.

Trailer homes, although cheap, were not conducive to the accumulation of savings. Indeed, they were lousy long-term investments, depreciating in value much faster than conventional homes. Banks charged high interest rates on loans and demanded repayment within three to five years as opposed to much lower rates and much longer repayment terms (of up to 20 years) for fixed-site homes. On top of the obligation of mortgage payments, trailer park tenants were subject to monthly rental payments on their lots. Calculating the costs of mortgage payments, rent, and utilities, *Consumer Reports* determined that the average trailer tenant was saddled with monthly payments that ranged between 15 and 50 percent higher than the buyer of a new suburban home.

The relentless legal assault on trailer communities and the persistent projection of degrading images of their residents in the mass media only compounded the financial constraints on upward mobility. Perhaps most alarming of all from the perspective of trailer owners was the fact that by the 1960s the thin line that separated white trash from blacks in the American psyche was echoed in the shifting social geography of trailer parks. The demographic dislocations that plagued American cities during the 1960s and 1970s posed a new threat to the status of trailer park colonists. As industrial districts once situated on the urban fringe found themselves absorbed into expanding metropolises, trailer parks relegated to these districts now occupied ground zero of sudden racial transitions, the precise dynamics of which varied from one city to another. In north Miami, the 79th Street corridor that planners had once set aside for trailers witnessed an influx of Haitians and Central Americans. In the industrial districts bordering Los Angeles to the east, Mexicans and other immigrants from Latin America began appearing. More typical was the situation in East St. Louis, where African Americans moved into neighborhoods that were once monopolized by working-class whites.

One man whose salary precluded the purchase of a new house in a far-flung suburban community explained that trailer living provided more security against racial transition than a conventional house in an urban neighborhood, which would have been his alternative. "We'd tie up everything we've got in a house," he explained, "and then lose out when the area changed." Yet, in an ironic twist of history, mobile-home dwellers discovered they had less geographic flexibility than those who lived in fixed abodes. The tightening of zoning restrictions made it difficult to build mobile-home courts in the newer suburbs, and thus made it harder for mobile-home owners to relocate to lily-white areas. Families who had no alternative to mobile homes were severely limited in the types of neighborhood in which they could find housing. A reflection of increased immobility, by the early 1970s, mobile-home dwellers changed their residential address less frequently than the average American.

So they stood their ground and defended their turf, even after the passage of civil rights legislation made the task more difficult than ever before. In the past, park managers had been quite blatant about their exclusionary policies. Over the course of the 1960s, rejected applicants filed a series of lawsuits against trailer park owners for violation of state and national civil rights statutes. Increasingly, park managers turned to subterfuge to evade the spirit if not the letter of the law. Some quoted exorbitantly high rates to dissuade minority applicants from renting space in their parks. More commonly, however, minority applicants were simply told that no spaces were available. When an "undesirable" customer, which presumably included African Americans, Latinos, and Asians, applied for a space at a San Diego park, the manager pointed to a row of stored mobile homes and explained, "See all those? They're waiting for a lot, just as soon as we have a vacancy." It was an outright lie. The applicant was invited to place his name on a waiting list, although the manager had no intention of making future contact. Trailer park waiting lists were full of the names of Mexican Americans, Puerto Ricans, and African Americans who were never called back.

Placed on the defensive, park owners and tenants justified their exclusionary practices on the grounds that integration would undermine the "mutuality of interests and backgrounds" that sustained their tight-knit, congenial communities. Race, they maintained, was simply one among many criteria employed in the tenant selection process to ensure homogeneous, and by extension harmonious, communities. There were parks designed primarily for workers, for retirees, for people with families, and for people with pets. If African Americans or Hispanic Americans wanted to enjoy the benefits of trailer living, they would be better off in their own parks, or so the argument went. The fact remained, however, that mobile home parks that catered exclusively to racial minorities were few and far between. As a last resort, park owners cited financial reasons for their refusal to accept minority applicants. A park manager who claimed to "have no race prejudice whatever" explained that if he admitted one minority family, "at least two of my old tenants, perhaps more, will move." Determined to hold the line against racial transitions, mobile-home parks became white islands in a darkening sea.

Island Castaways: The Increasing Isolation of Trailer Parks

The price that trailer park residents paid for their territorial ways was invisibility. As the 1950s bled into the 1960s and 1970s, mo-

Unidentified trailer park, mid-1950s. Trailer parks of the postwar era supported rich networks of both formal and informal social relationships.

bile-home colonies became increasingly withdrawn from the larger social communities that contained them. Social interaction took place almost exclusively within the confines of trailer park borders. Tenants invented their own version of the town center in the mail room where letters were distributed and gossip exchanged. Participation in civic affairs was as likely to involve a position on the trailer park tenant council as it was to involve any sort of formal role in the larger body politic. Where parks contained their own groceries, restaurants, beauty shops, service stations, and chapels, there was little need to interact with the outside world. When tenants ventured beyond trailer park gates, they often did so in the company of neighbors. Children who boarded the school bus together at the trailer park entrance tended to cling together in their classes and after school. Trips to the local bowling alley or municipal softball field were likely to occur under the auspices of park-sponsored teams. Outings to the local diner were often made in conjunction with a park-organized social club. If nothing else, trailer park communities were insular.

In a culture that increasingly alienated them, in places where they were besieged by people unlike them, mobile-home owners created tight-knit communities that assured safety and security. Communal laundry rooms, washrooms, recreation halls, and mail rooms created a profusion of collective spaces that had no counterpart in other housing developments. News traveled quickly, sometimes aided by crude community newsletters that reported on the most trivial details of people's lives: a visit from a relative, a birthday gathering, a second-degree burn from an overturned vaporizer. Trailer park residents knew each other's business and watched out for one another. Strangers and intruders were conspicuous and were regarded with suspicion. The high visibility and corresponding lack of privacy for trailerists that impeded the attainment of middle-class domestic norms also came to serve as a bulwark against falling any further down the social scale, at least in their own minds.

Fear of falling further down the socio-economic ladder also accounted for the hypersensitivity that trailer tenants displayed about subtle distinctions of status within their circumscribed world. Even if most trailer park tenants worked in comparable blue-collar jobs and earned similar incomes, they constructed fairly elaborate social hierarchies that permitted upward mobility within the trailer park world. At the Sunset Trailer Park in Bayonne, New Jersey, families able to support a full-time homemaker looked down upon families in which both husband and wife worked outside the home and refused to associate with them. In the larger parks, different sections developed into the equivalent of separate neighborhoods. Not only were parks divided into family and pet sections, but sections for large trailers and small trailers. Social credit accrued to families who traded in their dilapidated coaches for larger models and relocated to the "neighborhoods" reserved for supersize trailers. From there, the chain of upward mobility might lead to another trailer park altogether. Trailer tenants recognized a hierarchy of trailer parks that was based on the physical appearance of trailers, the landscaping surrounding them, and the size of tenant families (an overabundance of either single drifters or children was viewed as undesirable and suspect). As the term "mobile home park" came into widespread use after 1960, the older expression "trailer park" was reserved for the more run-down settlements. A woman who considered herself a member of an elite mobile-home community put the matter bluntly, "You wouldn't want a place with a lot of *trailers*. That's a whole different class of people."

However important these distinctions may have been to people who lived in trailers, they were lost on outsiders. A trailer park was a trailer park (even when it was called a mobile-home park) and the people who lived there were all located well beyond the bounds of the middle majority mainstream. A 1971 article published in *Horizon*, a mass-circulation magazine, classified the average trailer dweller as "a notch below the widely publicized 'Middle American.'" According to the author of the article, their status was reflected in a distinctive subculture that was slightly out of step with the times. Trailer park fashion, which seemed strangely static and consisted of clean-shaven faces, peaked caps, and string ties for men, and sprayed hair and girdles for women was more reminiscent of the 1950s than the post-Beatles era in which they lived. Moreover, the author insisted, there was little deviation from the norm. Within any given park, one could stroll the streets on a Sunday evening and "not miss a turn on the Ed Sullivan Show." Visiting homes in one park after another, one encountered the same TV dinners thawing in kitchen drainboards and the same "America, Love It or Leave It" pasted across living room windows. Undergirding this cultural uniformity was a population that displayed a remarkable degree of homogeneity in terms of income, occupation, race, ethnicity, and educational attainment.

Trailer courts may well have defined the lower boundary of the middle majority mainstream, and by the 1970s trailer parks may have indeed harbored a segmented subculture. Yet for all the impediments to realizing the middle-class domestic norms of postwar America placed before them and for all the external attacks upon their status and moral character, it would be wrong to assume that people who lived in trailer parks lived wretched lives. Far from it. Through frequent face-to-face contact and cooperative ventures, they forged meaningful and lasting relationships. Tenants came together to ward off social threats, defend themselves against political attacks, and rebuild their communities in the aftermath of natural disasters. More so than in most types of communities, people depended upon one another for assistance in finding employment, arranging day-care services, and learning the ins and outs of unfamiliar environs. The sharing of scarce resources extended from communal lawn mowers to car-pool networks. As friendships formed and romances blossomed, people exhibited an unusual level of compassion for one another. The death of a tenant was likely to result in the delivery of a lavish flower arrangement to the doorstep of surviving family members. The arrival of a newborn baby was likely to be the cause for a park-wide celebration.

No question, life in a trailer was often difficult. Tenants were well aware that living in trailer parks was different than living in the bucolic suburbs shown on television programs or even the mass-produced Levittowns featured in the popular press. Perhaps they would eventually get there. Yet, if that supposedly ideal life was beyond their reach, they would strive for social success within a more circumscribed world, and transfer their broader social aspirations to the next generation. At least a trailer was a home you could own, and a trailer court was a community that afforded a scaled-down version of the American Dream. Even if few outsiders confused trailer homes with middle-class housing, many who lived in them took solace in the knowledge that their home life was better than any alternatives would have provided had trailer parks never existed.

CONCLUSION

Giving Chase

IN HIS FINAL ECONOMIC REPORT to Congress, delivered in January 1960, President Dwight Eisenhower took the opportunity to assess the nation's progress since the end of World War II. Above all, what impressed the five-star general was the widespread distribution of material abundance. For almost all Americans, the quality of housing had improved. Consumer commodities once considered luxuries were now commonplace in middle-income homes. Summer vacations had become the norm. To drive the point home, the president rattled off the statistical evidence: Three-quarters of all families owned cars; 90 percent of homes wired for electricity had television sets; 6.5 million people enjoyed air-conditioning in their homes; over eleven million had refrigerators with built-in freezers. Fifteen years of uninterrupted prosperity had rewarded the average American family with a standard of living that was the envy of the world.

Only a few months earlier, Eisenhower's vice president, Richard Nixon, had offered a similar set of observations in a well-publicized debate with the Soviet premier, Nikita Khrushchev, at a trade fair in Moscow. Roving among displays of automatic floor sweepers, cosmetics products, plastic baby bottles, sports clothes, cooking ranges, and a mammoth IBM computer, the two political leaders debated the relative merits of Soviet communism and U.S. capitalism. Rather than make the case for U.S. superiority with reference to its military might or abstract principles of democracy and freedom, Nixon extolled the attributes of American-made kitchen appliances and color television sets. To the Soviet premier and to the world, Nixon proclaimed that America's greatness lay in a standard of living that enabled the average steelworker to purchase a six-room California-style ranch house and a freedom of choice that enabled housewives to select from among many brands of automatic washing machines.

The notion that consumer aspirations, capabilities, and choice were fast enlarging and unifying the American middle class held tremendous appeal among defenders of the Cold War political consensus. Indeed, the premise became a kind of party line among nationalistic pundits who sought to distinguish the United States from its communist rivals. A consumer culture that denied class distinctions evinced proof of the nation's enduring democratic character. Its ability to absorb people from working-class backgrounds and foreign ancestries testified to the superiority of the American way, namely free-market capitalism. By permitting men and women of modest means to claim membership in the middle class and to feel vested in the nation's democratic destiny, consumer abundance salvaged an American Dream that seemed imperiled by the shrinking of entrepreneurial opportunities.

For many Americans, diners, bowling alleys, and trailer parks were testaments to the perseverance of the American Dream. The transformation of these three institutions marked the enormous cultural distance their patrons had traversed since World War II. For millions of families who once struggled on the brink of poverty, they symbolized a life that was easier, more enjoyable, and more secure. Stripped of their associations with the world of work and refashioned as extensions of the happy suburban home, diners and bowling alleys allowed men, women, and children to meet a standard of domestic relations that connoted middle-class status. With all its drawbacks, trailer housing enabled transient workers and low-income families to own their own homes. For people formerly on the margins of society, these three institutions provided assurance that their customers were as American as anyone else.

For many people, especially those who had recently jumped the collar line or had landed high-paying industrial jobs, the postwar era marked an introduction to mass consumer culture. Diners, bowling alleys, and trailer parks all served as vehicles that guided upwardly mobile families into that world of consumer abundance. It is important to emphasize that upwardly mobile families initiated into the world of mass consumption for the first time after World War II did not automatically adopt middle-class styles and standards. They did not forsake bowling alleys for tennis courts. They did not abandon diners for fancy tea rooms. Nor did they move immediately from inner-city apartments to suburban ranch homes. Instead, they encouraged manufacturers and retailers to re-tool familiar blue-collar institutions to fit the rhythms of suburban life and the optimistic temper of the times. Dining cars became diner-restaurants, bowling alleys became bowling centers, and trailer courts became mobile-home parks. Through lessons learned from the daily give-and-take between buyers and sellers, businesses devised strategies to enlarge their customer base and absorb people from widely divergent backgrounds. The cumulative result was a new consumer culture that projected powerful standards of personal behavior and new benchmarks for social success. First and foremost, the new consumer culture celebrated an ethic of family togetherness that enabled newly affluent Americans to derive an immediate sense of "moving up" by piling into the station wagon for a weekend getaway to the Catskills, installing a pool table in the basement rumpus room, or simply gathering around the living room television set to watch Jackie Gleason.

This is not to suggest that blue-collar families took vacations or furnished their homes with pool tables and televisions merely to claim membership in the middle class or that the immediate gratification derived from consumer purchases necessarily clashed with more lasting strategies for pursuing social advancement. The men and women who raised families in the prosperous decades following World War II carefully aligned their consumer expenditures with longer-term financial strategies designed to ensure a better future for themselves and their children. It was not just the status associated with home ownership that convinced many families to buy trailer coaches, for example, but the notion that they constituted a good financial investment, or at least a better investment than paying rent for an apartment. Diner meals, while allowing moderate-income families to adopt the upper-class custom of eating away from home, also made it a little easier for them to send two adults into the paid labor force by relieving homemakers of their cooking and dishwashing chores. Many parents appreciated the modern bowling alley because they believed it kept their children off the rough-and-tumble streets and on the straight and narrow path leading through high school and college to a white-collar job. As consumer commodities that were reasonably inexpensive, diner meals, youth bowling leagues, and trailer homes appealed to families on limited budgets who wanted to reap the immediate rewards of affluence without mortgaging their future, or more importantly, their children's chances of occupational mobility.

Nonetheless, the unrelenting pressure that forced diner, bowling alley, and trailer park owners to update their products underscored the danger of measuring success in terms of consumer activities and possessions. Beneath the smooth veneer of mass consumer culture lay a web of contradictory messages about class relations, race relations, and family relations. Eliding these contradictions required that the purveyors of goods and services continuously revise standards of appropriate behavior. In a consumer society, the meaning of the good life was always in flux; it was always ambiguous. For many families clinging to the American Dream by their fingernails, success was ultimately elusive. Moreover, what had appeared as a source of unity through the 1950s was exposed as one of discord by the end of the 1960s. Ambiguous messages from advertisers and the mass media fanned the flames of the social conflagrations of the 1960s: the civil rights movement, the counterculture, the women's movement, and a devastating series of urban riots.

The Ascendance of the Classless Family Ideal

In the efforts of diner, bowling alley, and trailer park owners to take consumer traditions with strong working-class roots, repackage them, and deliver them to more diversified customers, the predominant strategy was to downplay class distinctions and to add prestige to the product by cloaking it in the mantle of family respectability. This marketing strategy was employed time and time again by manufacturers and retailers in the postwar era as a means of selling more products and drawing new adherents into the world of commercial abundance. The new consumer culture had to downplay class differences if both blue-collar and white-collar households were to be included. Hence, traditional distinctions between the classes and masses collapsed into a more amorphous middle-class prototype, one based less on ethnicity and occupation than on the attainment of a certain level of affluence and the adoption of certain protocols concerning family arrangements and goals.

Family-oriented marketing was not an entirely novel concept. Earlier in the century, advertisers routinely depicted their products in domestic settings and emphasized the contribution they made to harmonious family life. The lure of the suburban middle majority market, however, catapulted family fetishism to the heights of absurdity after the war. This was, after all, the era of the family car, the family room, the family film, the family vacation, and the family-size carton. Products and services that could be shared and experienced by entire families gained a special legitimacy as well as a practical competitive advantage in the marketplace. Even products that lacked any intrinsic connection to the structure of nuclear households were packaged accordingly and promoted as elixirs of family happiness. Ivory Soap saturated the media with images of wholesome mothers and babies. An advertisement appearing in *Life* magazine for the soft drink SQUIRT showed a mother, father, and daughter sipping the beverage joyfully from the same glass, through individual straws. Readers of the *Saturday Evening Post* learned that "Families have more fun together in a home that has a Hammond Organ." Meanwhile, ChapStick was advertised as the "all-family lip balm."

Businesses discovered the magic of family marketing in a variety of ways: through trial and error, by noting novel patterns of behavior among their customers, and by reading advice columns in trade journals. For trailer park operators, the decision to court families was thrust upon them in the late 1940s by the large influx of young couples with children who were desperate for housing. In the bowling and diner industries, a reevaluation of marketing strategies followed their geographic dispersal to suburban loca-

If sweet soft drinks leave you thirsty... SWITCH TO *SQUIRT*

TANGALIZED FOR COMPLETE REFRESHMENT

Never an after-thirst

THE NEW TANGALIZED SQUIRT IS A SPARKLING MIXER, TOO!

Advertisement, SQUIRT, 1956 (SQUIRT is a registered trademark under license © 2000 Dr. Pepper/Seven Up, Inc.)

tions, places where an exclusive reliance on male customers no longer made sense. In the case of bowling, a technological breakthrough, the mechanical pinsetter, functioned as a catalyst to attracting family business. In the diner industry, the dwindling opportunities for profit in inner-city locations provided the necessary impetus to move to the captive audience of families in the newly settled suburbs.

It was in the transitional suburban neighborhoods inhabited by the newly affluent where family marketing found exceptionally fertile soil. In contrast to inner cities and rural towns, suburbia nourished higher fertility rates, higher percentages of married couples, and a higher proportion of households arranged in nuclear-family units. Moreover, the placement and design of suburban subdivisions guaranteed that families would operate as the primary unit of social organization. Low-density development and a paucity of public space inhibited socialization beyond the confines of the

Advertisement, Hammond organ, 1956

backyard. The endless chores associated with the maintenance of suburban property conspired to keep suburban residents home-bound for much of the day. Removed from the distractions and enticements of the city, suburbs gave families an opportunity to set the standards for appropriate behavior and conduct. As long as retailers assured all family members that their products contributed to the creation of happy and efficient suburban households, they stood poised to capture a huge market composed of people from widely divergent backgrounds. Thus, the convergence of household structures around the standard nuclear arrangement, as much as the flattening of the income pyramid, made it possible for retailers and manufacturers to collapse class and ethnic distinctions in crafting a mass market.

Confronted with a homogeneous national market in which the bulk of spending power was spread across a vast middle-income group, American businesses extended mass-production technologies to a host of new products designed for the suburban market. In addition to automobiles, which had been mass-produced for decades, factories churned out oodles of nearly interchangeable blue jeans, sling chairs, automatic dishwashers, and one-story ranch houses. Prepackaged frozen foods filled supermarket display cases; Swanson made a big splash with its compartmentalized meat, potato, and vegetable meal that could be baked quickly and consumed without muss or fuss while watching television (hence the name TV Dinner). Sales of lawn and porch furniture nearly tripled between 1950 and 1960. Advances in the manufacture of small engines created a new market for household power tools and encouraged many a tinkering father to set up a workshop in his basement or garage.

The explosion of labor-saving devices for housework was a direct response to the dearth of domestic help in suburbs. Heavy lifting, vigorous scrubbing, and the bending and reaching involved in dusting and sweeping may have been acceptable when it was performed by an Irish or African-American maid, but it was out of the question for the middle-class suburban housewife, who, in many cases, wished to put some distance between her present life and her more humble origins in the inner city. Manufacturers responded to the plight of the suburban homemaker with a host of new and improved products that promised to minimize the drudgery of housework. Not every one of these new products caught on; the thermoelectric baby bottle, the self-shaking mop, and the oven that could be activated by a remote telephone call never lived up to their manufacturers' expectations. By the end of the 1950s, however, few middle-income homes lacked an electric vacuum cleaner, an automatic washing machine, and a cupboard full of "miracle" cleansers. The garbage disposal unit and the automatic dishwasher were not yet standard items but were gaining favor among women who cooked and cleaned on a daily basis. Not all labor-saving devices were targeted at women, however. Husbands charged with the responsibility of manicuring expansive suburban lawns certainly welcomed the advent of power lawn mowers, hedge trimmers, and Rototillers.

Suburban children were by no means overlooked in the drive to mass-produce new products. Toy manufacturers offered a wide array of recreational equipment that was perfectly suited for backyard and front lawn use, such as swing, badminton, and croquet sets, plastic wading pools, and wiffle balls and bats. Bicycles were a near necessity for maintaining a network of friends in sprawling suburban subdivisions; by the mid-1950s, companies like Schwinn were selling close to half a million two-wheelers annually. The bicycle was to the younger generation what the automobile was to adults, a way to get around and a possession to show off. The kid on the block with the new Black Phantom flaunted it with all the swagger of the grownup bragging about the shiny Ford Fairlane convertible sitting in the driveway.

To the extent that the consumer landscape extended beyond the bounds of the private home, family-oriented marketing domesticated public space. The places where consumers spent their money—shopping centers, vacation resorts, restaurants, and automobile service stations—were redesigned and refurbished to accommodate all family members, reproduce a homelike environment, and replicate the social relations of the suburban household. Upon relocating to the suburban commercial strip, consumer venues once restricted to men were refashioned to win the approval of women and children. It was here, for example, that Midas Muffler pioneered the family-oriented auto repair shop by outfitting its franchised units with playpens and scrupulously clean waiting rooms. Race tracks located on the metropolitan periphery hosted fashion shows and garden tours to lure women through the gates on slow afternoons. Meanwhile, traditionally feminine consumer spaces—most notably department stores—were redesigned to entice male shoppers, many of whom found themselves with more leisure time due to shorter work schedules. When opening branch outlets in suburban shopping centers, stores added hardware and sporting goods departments. In suburbia, shopping became a family affair.

Family marketing meant more than just selling commodities separately to men, women, and children; it meant appealing to customers as specific constituents of nuclear households, acknowledging the role that each one played. Soliciting customers by referring to their status as caring spouses and responsible parents proved to be an effective strategy for goading men and women into unfamiliar cultural terrain as it enabled consumers to justify all sorts of expenditures that might otherwise have seemed frivolous or selfish. Marketing strategists exploited this tendency mercilessly, using children and spouses as emotional levers to influence family decisions about where to take vacations, what cars to buy, and which brands of prepackaged foods to choose at the supermarket. Moreover, by marketing goods and services to families, retailers in transitional suburban neighborhoods invited their upwardly mobile customers to adopt consumer habits that were indistinguishable from their counterparts in the established middle class.

When Blue-Collar Met White-Collar

This attempted melding of the new and old middle class led to the development of interesting, if not bizarre, product and entertainment hybrids. The prospect of more uniform spending habits encouraged the architects of a domesticated consumer culture to borrow heavily from a variety of class and ethnic traditions. The resulting fusion of working-class and middle-class forms was one of the most outstanding and initially disorienting features of postwar consumer culture: diners that sold lobster, bowling alleys that rented space to symphony orchestras, and trailer parks designed with curvilinear streets and cul-de-sacs.

Certainly, the process of cross-class cultural diffusion through the mechanism of mass production and mass consumption had precedents earlier in the century. In the past, however, the expansion of consumer culture usually involved the filtering down of consumer habits from the rich to the not-so-rich. Automobile ownership, jewelry adornment, and cosmetic application were all forms of consumer behavior that had their origins in upper-class circles. The downward filtration of consumer commodities continued unabated into the postwar years, such that by the 1950s it was not so strange to find affluent workers playing golf, jetting across the bay on motorboats, or hanging reproductions of famous artworks on their living room walls.

Cultural flow in the opposite direction, however, was more a novelty of the postwar era, and, as was the case in the diner, bowling, and trailer industries, it often coincided with the domestication of working-class consumer traditions. Disneyland was the example par excellence. The idea for this wildly successful theme park was born out of Walt Disney's frustration with the seedy fairgrounds that dotted the Los Angeles area in the 1940s. Escorting his two daughters from one kiddieland to another, the cartoonist bemoaned the lack of places where both parents and children could enjoy themselves in clean and friendly surroundings. Determined to rectify this unfortunate state of affairs, Disney took it upon himself to build a vast entertainment complex that would provide wholesome fun for the entire family. Set in one of the fastest-growing suburbs of America's most suburbanized metropolis and promoted aggressively through the new medium of television, Disneyland opened with great fanfare in July 1955. Gone were the sideshow freaks, carnival barkers, and surly ride operators whom one found in the older Coney Island–style amusement parks. In their place, Disney paraded his familiar cast of cartoon characters alongside a well-coached staff of clean-cut, smiling attendants. Rides, performances, and theatrical sets brimmed with nostalgia for an already bygone era of small-town friendliness. Disneyland lived up to its hype. One million visitors arrived within seven weeks of its opening, and they continued to pour in as the park became a popular destination for vacationing families bounding across the country in their station wagons. In time, Disneyland became the prototype for the family theme park, its formula replicated in cut-rate form on the periphery of virtually every major metropolitan area.

Television also crawled into the cultural mainstream on the back of the suburban middle-class family. We tend to forget that television made its initial splash in blue-collar households and that early programming was consciously orchestrated to conform to working-class sensibilities. Early hits like Milton Berle's *Texaco Star Theater* and Sid Caesar's *Your Show of Shows* came directly out of the vaudeville tradition with their heavy reliance on crude sight gags, rough slapstick, and sexual innuendo. Other favorites such as *The Goldbergs, Life with Luigi, Mama,* and *The Honeymooners* (which originally appeared as a regular sketch on Jackie Gleason's variety show) highlighted distinctly ethnic and blue-collar themes. Although the immigrant-based, blue-collar humor of Milton Berle and Molly Goldberg may have struck a responsive chord among working-class audiences in large northeastern cities, it played poorly in Peoria. As network executives sought to capitalize on television's penetration into midwestern, rural, and suburban markets, they searched for entertainment formulas with more universal appeal. By the mid-1950s, they had settled on the antiseptic family sitcom. Molly Goldberg moved to the suburbs where she joined the Cleavers (*Leave It to Beaver*), the Nelsons (*Ozzie and Harriet*), the Andersons (*Father Knows Best*), and other thoroughly middle-class families. On virtually any night of the week, viewers could tune in to watch wise fathers, loving mothers, and good-hearted, if slightly rambunctious, children resolve their minor domestic mishaps within thirty minutes. If the Cleavers, the Nelsons, and the Andersons did not faithfully represent the behavior of many families in their audience, they nonetheless projected a model of home life to which viewers from different backgrounds could aspire.

Had the politics of the era been much different, the drive to homogenize popular culture might have collided against a stubborn defense of regionalism, ethnicity, or class privilege. Yet Cold War rhetoric reinforced the egalitarian thrust of postwar consumer culture by acting as a cudgel against those who turned up their nose at mass forms of comfort and leisure. Drawing attention to class differences through conspicuous extravagance was not only pompous, but un-American. Any behavior that might be considered highbrow, smacked of subversion. The juiciest targets for rabid Red baiters like Senator Joseph McCarthy were intellectual dandies who flaunted their privileged pedigrees in their comportment and attire. In casting suspicion on Secretary of State Dean Acheson's loyalties, McCarthy needed only to call attention to the aristocratic statesman's "cane, spats, and tea-sipping little finger."

To be a real American hero, on the other hand, was to reject any impulse toward privilege or pretension, to be middle-of-the-road in all respects. No one understood this better than Richard Nixon. As the vice president insisted to television viewers in his famous Checkers speech, he was just an ordinary American. Like the average Joe, he drove home from work every afternoon, parked his two-year-old car in the garage, shepherded the cocker spaniel to the backyard doghouse, and sat down in the living room to wrestle with the mortgage bills. As for his wife, she kept no mink coat in her wardrobe; instead one made of plain "Republican" cloth was good enough for her.

The celebration of the center in both the political and economic realms had profound implications for the nature of social conflict in postwar America. A more homogeneous consumer culture, undergirded by a Cold War populist ethos, conspired to mute class conflict in both the workplace and the political arena. As class consciousness became more nuanced, or at least complicated by affluent workers adopting a dual identity of members of the working class on the job and of the middle class at home, outward manifestations of class conflict receded. There were no Bonus

Army melées or Memorial Day Massacres to inflame class animosities. Instead of fighting over who should control the production process, labor and management engaged in less ideological squabbles over the content of benefit packages. In the halls of Congress, debate over how best to ensure full employment gave way to discussions about how to prevent inflation from eroding increasingly affluent consumers' purchasing power. Yet if class differences appeared to be dissolving under the universal solvent of consumer abundance, that appearance was deceptive. People learned quickly how to translate class suspicions into a language that was more consistent with Cold War ideology and consumer values. Rather than address the underlying causes of social inequality, mass consumer culture shifted the locus of conflict from the factory floor and the polling booth to the living rooms, streets, and shops of suburban America.

The Invisible Strains in the Classless Consumer Culture

It was one thing to promote a class-neutral ideal of family harmony, quite another to expect people to abide by its precepts. Indeed, the possibility that the new consumer culture would turn the nation into one big happy family frightened people as much as it inspired them. Mainstream consumer culture was built upon a shaky set of contradictions; the center could hold only as long as the insiders maintained the charade and outsiders failed to expose its hypocrisies.

If cursory observation and Cold War rhetoric suggested that class differences were eroding, closer inspection and more sophisticated critiques revealed an integration of classes that was tenuous at best. Several sociological studies conducted in the decades after World War II suggested strongly that, despite acquiring the outward trappings of middle-class status, manual workers and their families continued to live apart and move in different social circles from their white-collar counterparts. According to sociologist Bennett Berger, who spent several years investigating the lives of auto workers in Milpitas, California, even after purchasing private suburban homes, blue-collar families continued to behave in distinctly working-class ways: avoiding membership in social clubs, rejecting the advice of child-care experts, and voting for Democratic candidates. Another sociologist, Burleigh Gardner, noted in 1955, that while working-class families might mimic white-collar consumption habits, they had little desire to socialize with white-collar families. "Chicago," he wrote, "is full of factory workers who given a winning ticket in the Irish sweepstakes, would still not dream of moving to an upper-middle-class suburb, although they might well move to a new housing development filled with people like themselves."

Perhaps the most scathing refutation of middle-class homogeneity flowed from the pen of Harvey Swados, a left-leaning novelist and social critic. Excoriating what he termed "the myth of the happy worker" in a 1957 essay, Swados depicted the typical factory hand as an overworked, overtired, debt-ridden casualty of capitalism who felt and appeared more like a trapped animal than a contented member of the middle class.

Despite his vitriol, Swados's point was well taken. More than any other segment of the mainstream middle majority market, affluent workers internalized the values of consumer culture. Because their daily passage through the factory gates reminded them that they did not possess the occupational credentials for membership in the middle class, they felt the greatest pressure to demonstrate their status through the accumulation of things. Moreover, a naïve faith in the promise of consumer acquisition rendered them susceptible to the "hard sell" and rapid fluctuations in fad and fashion. These psychological factors operated in conjunction with the wider availability of credit to encourage many affluent working-class families to buy more than they could afford. Although debt accumulation was by no means exclusive to blue-collar families, it could be more debilitating from both a financial and psychological standpoint. And unlike the indebted junior executive, the factory worker in arrears did not have a high-prestige occupation to fall back upon when mounting expenditures and debts forced him to violate prevailing domestic norms. Paying the bills on time meant having to choose between Mother finding a part-time job or Father moonlighting as a bartender in the evening or a cab driver during the night.

Upwardly mobile families from working-class backgrounds also distinguished themselves with a set of consumer preferences that was, in the opinion of the established middle class, crass. The visual exuberance that characterized much of mainstream consumer culture—the Las Vegas architecture of the commercial strip (including the California-style bowling centers and Space Age diners), the superfluous ornamentation on cars and appliances, along with the excessive mounds of whipped cream on pies in diner pastry display cases—reflected a strong faith in the promise of consumer society to deliver social prestige and a better way of life. Those who attempted to ride the postwar economic juggernaut across class boundaries embraced an aesthetic of glitz most eagerly. Surveys of consumer preferences revealed that while those well-ensconced in the middle class favored subdued tones and austere designs, upwardly mobile blue-collar families sought to distance themselves from the bleak and grimy inner-city tenements they came from by surrounding themselves with brightly decorated products that exuded the attributes of cleanliness and modernity. The liberal application of bright coloring in products ranging from gelatinous desserts to men's shorts seems to have been a direct appeal to working-class sensibilities, one that fed the seemingly insatiable blue-collar appetite for more, bigger, and better.

The aesthetic associated with newly achieved affluence became the basis for re-erecting status barriers as differences in consumer style were translated into hierarchies of taste. An evaluation of consumer choices rather than information about family lineage, line of work, and income served as the primary means by which members of the white, Anglo Saxon, Protestant (WASP) middle class attempted to drive a wedge between themselves and the children of immigrants and affluent laborers who were making claims upon their status prerogatives. The new snobbery emphasized the value of the critical eye, denigrating the ostentatious and esteeming artistic motifs that required education to gain a sense of appreciation. The hierarchy they devised was not organized as a simple division between cultural connoisseurs and philistines but rather as finely graded distinctions such that those who collected Eames chairs could disparage those who furnished their living rooms in neo-colonial decor, who could in turn look down upon trailer park dwellers who decorated their lawns with pink flamingos. As the group most excited about gadgets, fashions, and fads, recent initiates to the world of consumption, whether they lived in trailer parks or conventional homes, risked social isolation even as they adopted lifestyles that were less distinctive than ever before.

Suburban Subdivision: Rupturing and Repairing Family Relations Through Consumerism

In the end, class tensions proved less volatile for the architects of mass consumer culture than did the shifting dynamics at work within middle-income families. The happy suburban family provided a model of social relations that helped businesses expand the mass market for goods and services. Yet family togetherness implied a measure of equality between husbands and wives and a more permissive approach to child rearing that could easily give rise to demands for greater consumer autonomy among women and youth. Indeed, the vendors of mass goods and services recognized that men, women, and children were as likely to seek refuge from the straitjacket of family hierarchies and responsibilities through their consumption activities as they were to seek togetherness. Through the 1950s, marketing strategists walked a delicate tightrope as they sought to capitalize upon individuals' independent yearnings without violating the sacred conventions of a proper family life. The endeavor became more difficult as time wore on and the centrifugal pull of peer-group pressure and individual expression overwhelmed the centripetal lure of family togetherness. In contrast to the economic dependencies that bound families in previous eras, consumption rituals fashioned a weak integrative net. Moreover, to the extent that retailers and manufacturers positioned themselves as surrogate families, they encouraged men, women, and children to find fulfillment and pleasure beyond the family circle.

For one Chicago homemaker, the frustrations of domestic life came to a head over footwear. She complained that in contrast to the eleven pairs of high-heeled shoes she had purchased when single, she had not bought one pair since. She, and many others like her, looked forward to the day when the kids were out of the house so she could once again indulge her consumer whims. Herein lay a problem, not just for frustrated mothers, but for the makers and sellers of shoes. The wider availability of credit, the profusion of labor-saving appliances that supposedly lightened housework, and the income derived from full- or part-time jobs gave women unprecedented opportunities to enlarge their participation in the consumer economy in the decades after World War II. Yet, as the case of the Chicago woman made clear, at some point familial responsibilities could easily act as a brake on consumer spending. It was in the interest of manufacturers and retailers to demonstrate that proper family behavior need not always entail personal sacrifice. If women's emancipation could be turned into a motivation for unrestrained buying, the purveyors of consumer commodities would proudly push for greater equality between the sexes.

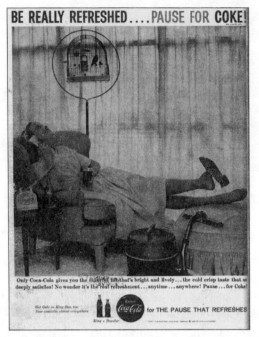

Advertisement, Coca-Cola, 1959. Advertisements such as this one deftly appealed to women in their conventional role as homemakers while simultaneously goading them to find relief from their household chores through consumer products. Courtesy of the Coca-Cola Company.

At the same time, manufacturers and retailers were careful not to push cultural boundaries too far. Even if husbands were willing to grant their wives greater control over household budgets, they still expected to wield an all-important veto power and were more likely to make final decisions about big-ticket items like cars, air conditioners, and vacations. Moreover, they were as likely as ever to scoff at what they considered to be frivolous expenditures on clothes, cosmetics, and jewelry. Hence, the architects of mass consumer culture faced the challenge of devising a model of women's emancipation that would not incite a backlash among men.

The concept of the "balanced homemaker" seemed to fit the bill. The balanced homemaker, a term coined in 1945 by a market researcher for electric appliances, was a woman whose primary motivations revolved around domestic concerns—she was a wife and mother first. Yet she also held outside interests. Perhaps she belonged to a garden club. Most likely she enjoyed a wide network of friends. Almost certainly she was active in the PTA. Thus, she was an ideal customer for businesses that hoped to increase their sales of paperback books, airline tickets, afternoon bowling leagues, and weekday lunches. Moreover, in order to pursue these outside interests without sacrificing her housework, the balanced homemaker was always looking for ways to discharge her chores more creatively and efficiently. Thus she was also the ideal customer for labor-saving appliances, cake mixes, and easy-to-clean trailers that took the drudgery out of housewifery. If the vendors of these products and services had their way, she would be the sort of woman who would equate social progress with spending.

By actively encouraging women to develop outside interests and broader social contacts, manufacturers and retailers gently but actively manipulated the reins of social change. There were too many women who still clung to the sharply circumscribed role of the traditional housewife, many of them in working-class households. Their horizons had to be expanded; their latent desires had to be stimulated; their purse strings had to be loosened. Still, it remained quite rare for businesses to appeal to women, or for that matter men, outside the context of their familial responsibilities. Even when encouraging women to develop outside interests and broader social contacts, they stressed the benefits that would accrue to family life. Every household needed a second Chevrolet so that Mom could, among other things, complete her chores twice as fast. At the very least, the bowling alleys that provided nurseries and shopping services encouraged women to pursue independent leisure without any guilt about neglecting their domestic duties.

Appealing to men outside the context of their familial obligations was equally rare. Businesses that sold automobiles and automotive parts knew that men made most of the purchases in this area, yet they routinely addressed men in their capacity as husbands and fathers. Tire makers, for example, advised fathers to think first and foremost about the safety of their children when selecting a brand, while illustrations in advertisements for Quaker State and Pennzoil motor oils suggested that the entire family would appreciate the smoother ride assured by their products. Likewise, banks urged fathers to open savings accounts so that they would have money put away for a future fishing trip with their sons, and correspondence schools assured men that their wives and children would think more highly of them if they received one their diplomas. The balanced homemaker, of course, required a male counterpart who was willing to tolerate a certain amount of independent activity on the part of his wife. Thus, postwar advertisers refined the concept of the good husband to mean someone who not only provided income and security for his family but also allowed his wife to pursue outside interests and to defer certain household chores to the consumer economy. Certainly, this impulse lay behind the diner advertisements that encouraged husbands to grant their wives an occasional night off from their meal preparation duties.

The extent to which businesses could effectively market products to men outside the context of their familial obligations received its most serious test when *Playboy* magazine hit the nation's newsstands in 1953. The brainchild of Hugh Hefner, a young husband and father with little experience in the publishing business, *Playboy* openly celebrated the unrestrained gratification of male sexual and consumer desires, blurring the line between them in the process. Hedonistic to the core, the quintessential playboy, a bachelor living in a Space Age bachelor pad, surrounded himself with a bevy of beautiful women and a surfeit of beautiful products: fine whisky, expensive cigarettes, hi-fi equipment, and modern furniture. He was not a family man, and *Playboy* was not a family magazine.

Predictably, Hefner came under fire from a number of religious leaders for espousing a debauched and decadent lifestyle that veered far from mainstream conventions. Yet public admonition was surprisingly mild and the magazine encountered very little in the way of censorship. In part, public criticism was blunted by Hefner's emphasis on good taste; his nude models were displayed more like works of art or fancy consumer products than overt sexual toys. In addition, the threat to public morals was mitigated by Hefner's explicit appeal to unmarried men. His intended audience consisted of affluent, college-educated gentlemen who consciously rejected the model of the happy suburban family in favor of urban apartments and eternal bachelorhood. The quintessential playboy may not have been a family man, but neither was he a home wrecker.

But were the typical reader and the typical playboy one and the same? Apparently not. Whether by design or good fortune, the magazine's allure extended well beyond its purported constituency. Surveys showed that at least half of its readers were married. For husbands who stashed a secret stack of *Playboys* in the office or garage, the magazine offered escape from the constraints of marital responsibilities through fantasy. Its wide readership among married men, some one million of them by the early 1960s, exposed a fundamental contradiction in the terms of family togetherness, a contradiction of their own marketing strategy that some purveyors of consumer commodities were happy to cultivate on the sly.

Just as vendors of consumer commodities began to target mothers and fathers separately, the 1950s also witnessed the expansion and crystallization of a distinct youth market, as the purveyors of mass culture capitalized on the growing number of teenagers with independent income derived from generous allowances and part-time jobs. Moreover, business leaders came to recognize that the internalization of consumer values among youth amounted to a long-term investment. Hence, teenagers became the object of specialized advertising and merchandising campaigns (an unintended consequence of which was a sharp rise in juvenile shoplifting).

The allure of the independent teen market was the source of tremendous innovation in the marketing world, especially during the latter half of the 1950s. Independent appeals to youth were dramatized by the introduction of "junior" lines of apparel, for example. In 1957, four prominent corporations—Schrank Dreamwear, Canada Dry, Coty, and RCA Victor—collaborated on an advertising campaign to promote teenage pajama parties. They anticipated that more overnight teen get-togethers would translate into higher sales of ginger ale, perfume, records, and, of course, pajamas. Portable transistor radios became all the rage late in the decade, in large measure because they liberated teens from the "square" music piped through the heavy wooden radios that sat in family living rooms. In the privacy of their own bedrooms they could tune out Benny Goodman and tune in Elvis Presley. Presley, in fact, became the center of a merchandising bonanza that accounted for $22 billion in sales during the mid-1950s. Attempting to cash in on the singer's popularity, especially among young girls, product designers imprinted his likeness on sofa pillows, bracelets, and socks. Girls intent on buying lipstick were invited to choose from Houndog Orange and Heartbreak Hotel Pink. For starstruck teens who wished to convert their bedrooms into Elvis shrines, one canny manufacturer offered a complete line of Elvis lamps and furniture.

Daring as these marketing gambits may have been for their time, they did not portray commodities as overt symbols of rebellion. Pajama parties may have promised a night of excitement for young girls, but it was understood that these gatherings were to take place under parental supervision. Retailers had reason to be wary about pushing the idea of adolescent autonomy too far. They knew that parents still held the upper hand in households when push came to shove; most of the merchandise returned to stores by teenagers consisted of items of which their parents disapproved. When it came to commodities of a potentially controversial nature, producers and vendors tread lightly over the minefield of parental concerns. Hence, when the American Tobacco Company aspired to increase sales of Lucky Strike cigarettes among teenagers, it eschewed direct overtures in print and television advertisements. Instead, it opted for the slightly more subtle approach of sponsoring the popular teen television program *Your Hit Parade* and introducing a new brand of cigarettes with the same name.

Although most adults were willing to tolerate a certain amount of adolescent autonomy, they drew the line where teenage behavior was interpreted as an outright rejection of mainstream mores. Older Americans became nervous when adolescents twisted mass culture to their own ends or, even worse, improvised their own deviant forms of popular culture. Teenagers proved far more willing than their parents to fuse class, racial, and ethnic traditions, particularly in the areas of music and fashion. From the perspective of many adults, they took the concept too far. For a while, however, the damage was contained. Through the early 1960s, a dynamic corporate economy managed to corral wayward youth back into the fold by appropriating teenage cultural initiatives and delivering them back to the mass market shorn of their defiant and subversive edges.

The rise and demise of hot rodding exemplifies this process. For older teenagers navigating the social relationships in sprawling suburban developments of the 1950s, the automobile emerged as the most definitive expression of both individual personality and collective identity. Yet the desire to project an independent identity through automobility was frustrated by the staid selection of cars available on the market. Detroit produced cars that were too heavy, too slow, and, in the minds of most teenagers, too ugly. Their solution was to rip them apart and rebuild them anew. By lowering the frame, adding more horsepower, and making the car look more like something from outer space than something Dad drove to work, teenagers had a vehicle they could show off to friends and, if they were so inclined, race in the streets. The hot rod craze spawned a parallel automotive industry consisting of spare-parts dealers and chop shops that rebuilt custom cars for those who lacked the skill to do the job themselves. By 1952, *Hot Rod* magazine claimed a circulation of half a million enthusiasts.

In this overt rebellion against adult automotive styling, Detroit sniffed an opportunity. But rather than replicate the chop shops that elicited the admonition of elders, leading car manufacturers borrowed a few features—high compression motors, low-slung bodies—and used them to embellish mainstream models. The results were the Detroit muscle cars and sports cars of the early 1960s, for instance the Studebaker Avanti and Ford Mustang. For customers who wanted to go further, the major auto makers were happy to oblige, furnishing a wide range of additional options that essentially replicated the amateur hot rods part for part. Faced with this competition from corporate America, the informal hot rod economy shriveled, serving only a small cadre of specialized racing aficionados.

One can detect the same dynamic at work in the corporate commercialization of rock 'n' roll. By hiring white groups like Bill Haley's Comets and even straight-laced, "square" white crooners like Pat Boone to rerecord, or cover, raunchy and defiant tunes originally written and performed by black artists like Chuck Berry and Little Richard, record companies attempted to strip the genre of its incendiary character. More often than not, the songs heard on middle-of-the-dial radio stations and nationally syndicated television shows, such as *American Bandstand*, elaborated on the decidedly uncontroversial themes of marriage and consumer acquisition, even if the protagonists drove fast cars and played loud electric guitars. Commercial rock 'n'roll, in the hands of corporate America, affirmed the basic values of family-oriented consumer culture and, like much of mainstream commercial youth culture, sought to guide potentially reckless youth into respectable adulthood.

Not all businesses were so successful at controlling the independent impulses of adolescence. The unhappy fate of two venerated postwar institutions, the drive-in movie theater and the drive-in restaurant, served as a cautionary tale. Originally, the drive-in concept was marketed as an alternative to conventional restaurants and movie theaters that discouraged the patronage of young children. With the entire family confined to their automobiles, parents had no need to worry about the nuisance created by their screaming babies and scampering toddlers. Some drive-in theater proprietors offered additional inducements: small kiddie playgrounds, animal parks, and free admission to children under twelve. Through the 1940s and early 1950s, the meteoric growth rate of drive-in restaurants and theaters was attributable to their appeal to families with young children.

By 1960, however, teenagers who had grown up with the drive-in, converted them into their exclusive playgrounds. The privacy created by dark nights and fogged windows made drive-in theaters ideal for unsupervised romance and revelry. More than a few proprietors abetted the shift from family venue to adolescent hangout by showing schlocky films that only someone in the throes of puberty could appreciate. Meanwhile, the drive-in restaurant emerged as a popular late-night rendezvous for teens who wanted to show off their hot rods and carouse with friends. Bored high school students spent hours loitering in the drive-in parking lot, blaring rock 'n' roll from their radios, and shouting even louder to converse with passengers in adjacent cars. In the public mind, drive-in culture had become a breeding ground for juvenile delinquency. Aghast at such indecent behavior, many families began to shun both institutions, and revenues declined commensurately.

The Assault on Mass Consumer Culture

The universal and largely illusory standard of success that mass marketers worked so hard to uphold in the 1950s was shattered by

the social disruptions of the 1960s. The civil rights movement brutally exposed the fallacy of a democratic consumer culture. The
women's movement and the counterculture shattered the myth of
the happy suburban family. If the center no longer held, however,
the architects of the mass consumer market were as much responsible for its undoing as were the marchers in the streets. Historians
have rarely interpreted the social turbulence of the 1960s as a response to the consumer aspirations cultivated over the previous
decade. Yet to a large extent, the contradictions exposed by the
very act of attempting to create a homogeneous mass consumer
culture gave rise to each of the social and cultural upheavals that
defined the decade.

Young men and women affiliated with the 1960s counterculture
tendered the most radical critique of mainstream consumer culture
and its materialistic values. The adult world's obsession with the
latest car models struck children who had never known economic
deprivation as shallow. Peering behind the rhetoric of consumer
freedom in advertising copy they saw only a new form of enslave-
ment, one in which conformist consumers walked in lockstep to
the directives of manipulative corporations and individuals became
increasingly alienated from nature and their innate carnal impulses.
The hypocritical messages delivered by advertisers epitomized the
immorality and corruption of corporate capitalism. As an alternative, hard-core hippies, many of whom abandoned the city for
rural communes, espoused a doctrine of liberation from the trap of
consumer conformity through spiritual transformation. Outside
the channels of mainstream goods and services, countercultural
purists pursued self-realization through sex, love, meditation, and
illegal drugs.

As these countercultural ideas filtered through a broader segment of open-minded young people in cities, the quest for spiritual
liberation from a postwar conformist consumer culture intersected
with commercial culture. Yet this emergent commercial counterculture stood well apart from the mainstream middle majority. In

the retail strips of Greenwich Village, Venice Beach, and Haight Ashbury and the numerous shopping districts abutting large college campuses, vendors catered expressly to the bohemian impulses of youth. Pipeshops peddled a plethora of paraphernalia that promised to deliver the perfect drug trip. In addition to pipes, roach clips, and other practical gadgets, consumers were invited to browse through a selection of incense, chimes, and paste-on diffraction gratings, which when affixed to one's forehead, projected a spot of prismatic color. So-called psychedelic shops distributed underground publications that preached the virtues of free love and hallucinogenic drugs, while experimental theaters provided demonstrations in the flesh, quite literally. Among the bead shops and hippie boutiques that were ubiquitous in countercultural enclaves, one could purchase all the accessories necessary to artfully construct the standard hippie uniform: fringed leather vests, headbands, body feathers, moccasins, and of course, beads.

The women's movement was equally harsh in its condemnation of mainstream consumer culture, although it did not go so far as to reject materialism per se. Rather, it exposed the ways in which the values propagated by the mass market stifled women's psychological development and sustained unequal power relations between men and women. The frustrations articulated by Betty Friedan on behalf of millions of suburban homemakers in her 1963 best-seller *The Feminine Mystique* were grounded in the empty promises of fulfillment extended by the purveyors of consumer goods and services. Under the pretense of promoting family togetherness, they asked women to feel good about their role as self-sacrificing martyrs. In the name of emancipation, they enticed women with products that supposedly eased the burden of domestic chores and with recreational outlets that afforded new possibilities for extra-familial socializing. But as Friedan illustrated so pointedly, emancipation through washing machines and bowling expeditions was no emancipation at all as long as women were still expected to measure their self-worth according to the shine of their kitchen floors and the taste of their tuna casserole. Although Friedan and the activists who founded the National Organization for Women (NOW) devoted their early energies toward opening employment opportunities for women and securing equal pay for equal work, consumer culture persisted as a target for feminists throughout the 1960s. The activists who protested the 1968 Miss America Pageant filled a Freedom Trash Can with consumer instruments of male oppression, among them a dishcloth, a girdle, and a brassiere.

Equal pay for equal work, on the other hand, while rarely articulated as a consumer issue, nonetheless owed much of its drawing power to contradictions that arose out of the postwar consumer economy. Even if the ethic of family togetherness stipulated slightly more egalitarian relations between husbands and wives, it only applied to behavior at home. Outside the home, manufacturers and retailers had a vested interest in maintaining sexual inequality so they could hire women as waitresses, clerks, stenographers, and door-to-door sales representatives at wage rates far below what they would have paid to men. The same businesses that encouraged more autonomous consumer spending among women also kept them dependent on a male breadwinner for income, a situation that became increasingly intolerable for women who sought to chart a truly independent course outside the bounds of conventional family relationships.

In the wake of the countercultural and women's movements— which divided the generations and sexes, which set parents and children, husbands and wives in opposition to each other—the utility of family marketing dwindled precipitously. To the extent that major corporations tried to exploit these insurgent sensibilities for profit, they were compelled to drop any references to family ties and obligations. Appeals to youth embraced rebellion unabashedly, a shift in strategy that was most evident in the music industry. Major record companies that once shied away from any topics more controversial than courtship and consumption suddenly sponsored artists such as Jimi Hendrix, Sly and the Family

Stone, and Jefferson Airplane, who all sang openly about sex, drugs, and the hot political issues of racism and war. It was also around this time that women's liberation found a home on Madison Avenue. Virginia Slims' "You've come a long way, baby" campaign, inaugurated in 1968, was the first to encourage pride in independent consumption, but it was not the only one. Under the helm of Helen Gurley Brown, *Cosmopolitan* magazine not only projected the image of the sassy single woman who spent money on herself but also filled its advertising pages with plenty of items to buy. Feminists rightly attacked such bold appeals to self-centeredness as a perversion of feminist principles. Nonetheless, the success of these marketing ploys indicated that they struck a responsive chord among women who had too long watched their children and husbands indulge their consumer desires while they scrubbed the floor. Never again would the vast majority of Americans rally round the happy suburban family as a model for appropriate consumer behavior.

Ironically and perhaps tragically, the people most likely to remain faithful to the model were among those who had the hardest time gaining access to it. Blue-collar families struggling from paycheck to paycheck clung fiercely to the paradigm of family relations projected by the mass media in the 1950s and looked warily on the cultural convulsions of the 1960s. The counterculture's rejection of materialism was an insult to families who had only recently escaped the clutches of poverty. Women's liberation was even more threatening. Women from a wide variety of social backgrounds relished the idea of outside employment as an opportunity to develop wider social contacts and acquire some independent spending power. Yet what established middle-class families took as a sign of more egalitarian household relations became a reflection of a husband's inadequacy as breadwinner in working-class families. The issue of the working wife was a source of tremendous friction in blue-collar households. Grasping for a center that was rapidly disintegrating, white working-class families on the margins of the middle class grew increasingly defensive about the domestic arrangements that had brought them comfort and respectability in the years since World War II. Their sense of being under siege only intensified as African Americans stepped up their bid for inclusion into the American mainstream, a perception that was deftly manipulated by a new cadre of rising political stars including Ronald Reagan and George Wallace.

Desegregating Consumer Culture

The civil rights movement took on mass consumer culture on February 1, 1960. That was the day that David Richmond, Franklin McCain, Ezell Blair, Jr., and Joseph McNeil, students at the North Carolina Agricultural and Technical College, sat down at the Woolworth's lunch counter in downtown Greensboro and ordered coffee. Informed that they could not be served on account of the color of their skin, the four young men announced their intention to remain at the counter until the store changed its policy. As promised, the students returned the following day to resume their protest, this time with nineteen reinforcements. On the third day, the number swelled to eighty-five, thereby allowing the students to monopolize the counter stools in shifts. Only after three months had passed, and the students had extended their protest to a number of downtown variety stores, did white merchants capitulate and agree to serve black customers on the same basis as whites.

The Greensboro episode marked an important shift in the way that consumer activities intersected with civil rights protest. In the past, African-American activists had used their economic power as consumers as a lever to secure better jobs and to integrate public transportation systems. The "Don't Buy Where You Can't Work" campaigns of the 1930s were designed to pressure white store owners who did business in black neighborhoods to hire more black workers. The Montgomery Bus Boycott of 1955 demonstrated how the withdrawal of consumer spending could bring an entire city to its knees. Not only did the boycott deprive the Montgomery City Lines of 70 percent of its revenue, but it cut deeply into the profits of downtown businesses that relied on commuting black shoppers. Confronted with a local economic crisis and then an unfavorable Supreme Court ruling, Montgomery's business and civic leaders reluctantly capitulated to the demands of boycott organizers for an end to Jim Crow seating arrangements on city buses, whereby blacks were allowed to sit only in the rear section. The lessons of Montgomery were not lost on the Greensboro students. In conjunction with their sit-in demonstrations, they also launched a consumer boycott of downtown stores. Where they broke new ground, however, was by making the extension of consumer privileges an end in itself.

The effects of the Greensboro sit-in on the civil rights movement were immediate. Within two weeks, students at nearby campuses in Durham and Raleigh, along with young men and women in more remote locations—Nashville, Tennessee; Tallahassee, Florida; and Portsmouth, Virginia—launched their own acts of civil disobedience at local lunch counters. Very quickly the targets expanded beyond food service establishments. The tone was set by Atlanta demonstrators who staged a sit-in at Rich's Department Store just one month after the initial Greensboro incident. Like their predecessors in North Carolina, the Atlanta activists insisted on the right to enjoy a meal like any other customer. But their list of demands also included the desegregation of movie theaters, concert halls, and other public venues. Elsewhere, activists staged "sleep-ins" at segregated motels, "play-ins" at segregated parks, "stand-ins" at segregated amusement parks, and "watch-ins" at segregated movie theaters. By September 1961, the assault on segregated consumer facilities had reached more than a hundred cities, mostly in the South but in other parts of the country as well.

Nowhere were the contradictions of mass consumer culture more blatant than when it came to the treatment of racial minorities, particularly African Americans. Blacks were no less eager than white Americans to participate in the postwar consumer bonanza, and to some extent they did. By 1960, television sets, radios, and washing machines were commonplace additions to African-American homes, although the rates of black ownership for these items still lagged behind the comparable rates for white Americans. But most businesses that sold products to racial minorities tried to have it both ways—that is, enticing them with promises of material abundance on the one hand and then treating them as second-class consumers on the other. Securing the allegiance of anxious white families on the threshold of the middle class—usually considered to be the more lucrative market—compelled manufacturers and retailers to clarify social boundaries in what they determined was the most expeditious means, by privileging the patronage of customers with white skin.

From the perspective of mass marketers, it was one thing to sell African Americans television sets, washing machines, soft drinks, and automobiles that would be used in the privacy of their homes and segregated neighborhoods that whites never ventured into, and quite another to identify national brands with African-American consumers. Fearful that visible overtures to minority audiences would depreciate the value of their products in the minds of white customers, major manufacturers rarely, if ever, showed African Americans, or for that matter Asian Americans or Latinos, using their products in advertising copy. Razors shaved white faces, dresses hung on white models, and television sets sat in the living rooms of white families.

When racial discrimination was applied in consumer venues the result was racial segregation. Racial segregation was most pervasive in southern states where Jim Crow practices were often supported by both custom and law. Yet there were few sections of the country where the African-American traveler could be assured of service when requesting a meal at a restaurant, a drink in a tavern, or a room at a motel. Although few African Americans encountered trouble in Las Vegas, Boston, or Philadelphia, the story was altogether different in Salt Lake City, Baltimore, and St. Louis, where policies on admission varied widely from one establishment to another. Moreover, commercial establishments that admitted both white and black customers did not necessarily treat them with equal respect. Ushers directed black patrons to segregated balconies in movie theaters. Downtown department stores refused to let black shoppers use dressing rooms to try on outfits. In both northern and southern cities, clerks made black customers wait longer for service than white customers and were quick to accuse black children of pilfering merchandise. The bowling alleys that refused to host black leagues, the diners that forced African Americans to place their orders from back doors, and the trailer parks that refused admittance to black families were all symptomatic of a consumer culture that limited the access of nonwhites.

African Americans who tested the waters of mainstream consumer culture did so at their own peril. As Roy Wilkins, executive director of the NAACP explained to a Senate Committee in 1962, "From the time they leave their homes in the morning, en route to school or to work, to shopping, or to visiting, until they return home at night, humiliation stalks them." It could hardly have come as a surprise to civil rights leaders such as Wilkins to learn that according to a study conducted by the Wharton School of Business in 1956, African-American households spent far less on admissions to theaters and recreational outlets, restaurants and diners, and motel and hotel accommodations than white households at equivalent income levels. With each refusal to provide service and with each instance of rude treatment, postwar merchants circumscribed the boundaries of the culture of consumer abundance. Given these conditions, blacks could not fully participate in the middle majority culture of consumption, regardless of their incomes. Even if racial segregation did not become more pervasive with the emergence of a somewhat more inclusive middle majority consumer culture in the 1950s, it became more conspicuous, at least as far as African Americans were concerned. By seeming to unite previously separate, unequal, and fractious white populations, the continued disenfranchisement of African Americans was rendered even more stark.

The issue of consumer privileges resonated sharply with the aspirations and convictions of the college students who joined the ranks of the civil rights crusade by the tens of thousands in the early 1960s. The sit-ins and their variants were organized and conducted by young men and women raised in the era of postwar prosperity. They had grown up in an America that was defined by the middle-class suburban lifestyles depicted on television programs and advertised in popular magazines. They had listened to political and business leaders alike extol the virtues of democratic capitalism and hold up widespread consumer abundance as the embodiment of the American way of life. To be rejected as a paying customer was a supreme insult in a society that equated success and social mobility with the amenities that could only be purchased through commercial transactions. They knew that, but for the color of their skin, the American Dream was theirs to be had. The sit-in protesters, however, were motivated less by the attractions of the good life than by the humiliating manner in which it was denied them, a subtle but important distinction. It was, at root, about equality and respect. From where they stood, the inability to buy so much as a cup of coffee at a downtown lunch counter cut to the heart of racial oppression, constituting a manifestation of injustice on par with limited voting rights and inferior schools.

The scattershot approach of the sit-ins produced mixed results. By the end of 1961, almost 200 cities had begun the process of opening public facilities to people of all races and colors. But in many parts of the Deep South, white resistance did not crack. A more comprehensive resolution would not occur until 1964 when Congress passed the Civil Rights Act, which, in addition to authorizing the federal government to withhold public funds from programs that practiced discrimination and establishing an Equal Opportunity Employment Commission, outlawed racial segregation in public accommodations, a broad category that included stores, restaurants, taverns, movie theaters, and hotels.

For many historians and participants alike, the passage of the Civil Rights Act of 1964 marked the pinnacle of the civil rights movement. Certainly it was the most far-reaching civil rights law ever enacted in the United States. Much of what the sit-in movements achieved and the Civil Rights Act promised, however, was undermined by the persistence of housing segregation. Many of the massive subdivisions laid out just after World War II enforced racial segregation through use of restrictive covenants, deed clauses that prohibited owners from selling or renting their property to nonwhites. William Levitt employed the standard excuse to justify the use of restrictive covenants in his first Levittown. "As a Jew," he said, "I have no room in my mind or heart for racial prejudice." He quickly added, "But I have come to know that if we sell one house to a Negro family, then 90 or 95 percent of our white customers will not buy into the community."

This widely held perception within the housing industry supported a vast array of both formal and informal mechanisms for preserving racial segregation. Neighborhood associations continued to employ restrictive covenants well into the 1950s even though the U.S. Supreme Court outlawed the practice in 1948. To compensate for the questionable legality of discriminatory deed restrictions, the real estate industry eventually resorted to more subtle methods; usually realtors simply refused to sell racial minorities homes situated in white neighborhoods. In cases where the resolve of realtors and developers broke down, whites were not above using violence and intimidation to preserve their exclusive bastions. By the time Levitt built his second development outside of Philadelphia, he had done away with restrictive covenants, so residents took matters into their own hands. When African-American families tried to move into the community in 1957, they were pelted with rocks. The Levittowners, however, were mild-mannered in comparison to the white thugs of Chicago and Detroit who resorted to house bombings and violent assaults to achieve similar segregationist ends.

As a measure of last resort whites could always move when African Americans or other racial minorities managed to cross the residential color line. And flee they did, in droves, during the 1960s, pushing the borders of suburbia ever outward. The statistics on racial segregation in metropolitan areas are stupefying. According to one set of calculations, blacks were twice as likely to live in racially homogeneous neighborhoods in 1970 as they were in 1930. By the latter date, equalizing the racial demographics of American cities would have required the relocation of 70 percent of all African-American households. Thus, even as African Americans found it easier to exert their political rights, find factory jobs previously reserved for whites, buy hamburgers at downtown lunch counters, and even move into homes located in the innermost transitional suburbs, they found themselves more isolated than ever in essentially segregated urban neighborhoods with self-contained shopping and entertainment districts.

Keep Moving:
The Metropolitan Geography of
Postwar Consumer Culture

The racial geography of the postwar metropolis highlighted the distinctive landscape created by America's middle majority consumer culture. During the postwar era, the logic of consumption surpassed the logic of production as the most important factor governing the organization of urban space. Where and how households spent their money determined the flow of capital investment and jobs. While industrial areas, warehouse districts, and port facilities decayed in many parts of the country, billions

Suburban development, St. Louis, 1959. By the 1950s, retail firms were directing new investments to the metropolitan periphery. (Note the drive-in movie theater located at the top of this photograph.)

of dollars and millions of jobs poured into the suburban communities that hosted modern supermarkets, fast-food outlets, branch department stores, and eventually, enclosed shopping malls. Although there had been a significant movement of industrial jobs to outlying areas during the war years and their immediate aftermath, the more dramatic increase in service-sector jobs thereafter was a direct outgrowth of the burgeoning consumer economy that blossomed in the rapidly expanding suburbs. The fastest growing cities, on the other hand, tended to be those with economies that revolved around consumer spending. Meccas of entertainment and leisure like Las Vegas, Miami, and Anaheim witnessed some of the largest increases in population in the postwar years, although in each these specific case, the source of consumer spending was quite different: gamblers in Las Vegas, retirees in Miami, and vacationing families in Anaheim, the home of Disneyland.

Within metropolitan areas, the outward thrust of the consumer economy channeled new investment and, hence, the latest innovations in selling technique and commercial architecture to territories further and further removed from the urban core. Unlike the shopping districts that began appearing in upper-class

St. Louis, 1953. Closer to the urban core, the matrix of retail establishments was more likely to include pawnshops and dealers in surplus apparel.

residential neighborhoods in the 1920s, those that served the broad middle majority in the postwar suburbs did not try to replicate the look and feel of downtown. Keeping in line with modest budgets of their customers, suburban retailers adopted a high-volume, low-price formula that more closely resembled the merchandising techniques of Woolworth's and Sears than the prestigious stores along Fifth Avenue in New York City, Michigan Avenue in Chicago, and Broadway in Los Angeles. Indeed, even the large department stores that opened branch outlets in the 1950s abandoned their formal downtown sales techniques in favor of a no-frills, self-service approach more convenient and less intimidating to affluent blue-collar customers. The relationship between the buildings and the street also changed as shoppers increasingly arrived by automobile rather than public transportation; over the course of the 1950s and 1960s, stores were set back further and further from the road to accommodate ever larger anterior parking lots. Even the buildings themselves looked different in suburban locations where lower land values encouraged stores to spread out horizontally over the span of many blocks in one- or two-story structures rather than in vertical nucleations clustering at strategic inner-city intersections. Finally, and perhaps most importantly, an abundance of vacant land allowed developers to plan and design large integrated shopping centers in which chain and independently owned stores were selected on the basis of how well they complemented one another. Where these complexes were organized around a small outdoor promenade or plaza, they became forerunners of the enclosed mall.

The growing disparity between investments in inner-city and in suburban commercial districts gave rise to a new and well-defined geographic hierarchy. The social boundaries of postwar consumer culture were clearly etched in the city's physical space with distinct gradations of status marked by the mix of commercial establishments and the proliferation of certain architectural styles. Variations in the consumer landscape allowed families to measure their success by their surroundings. Shopping in the most up-to-date facilities—the drive-ins, the Miracle Mile shopping strips, and self-service supermarkets that catered most explicitly to families—validated attainment of the good life. Here customers could be assured that diners would have ample booth and table seating, that bowling alleys would rely on automatic pinsetters, and that trailer parks, if they existed at all, would be filled with respectable retirees.

Claims of social success were harder to support in neighborhoods closer to the urban core, where customers had less money and businesses operated according to more antiquated formulas. In older industrial areas, for example, diner proprietors still left their cooking grills behind the counter, eight-lane bowling alleys were still likely to be tucked away in basements, and trailer parks were more likely to house working families than affluent senior citizens. Approaching the railroad station on the edge of the central business district, one invariably encountered the stubborn relics of single-sex commercial networks, the pool rooms, tattoo parlors, saloons, and burlesque halls that catered exclusively to men, many of whom lived outside the context of broader family networks in rooming houses and single-occupancy hotels. Here, shops were usually set flush against littered streets and adorned with simple hand-painted signs or marquees with missing letters. These dark, dreary storefronts, often intermingled with warehouses and small manufacturing plants, offered a stark contrast to the sleek, futuristic chain stores with brightly lit displays behind plate-glass windows further out along the commercial thoroughfares that pierced the metropolitan periphery.

Because the consumer landscape was ever in flux, families who sought the prestige as well as the convenience that came with proximity to the most modern shopping facilities faced constant pressure to keep moving. Shifting patterns of commercial investment could easily transform yesterday's Miracle Mile into tomorrow's Skid Row, thus jeopardizing the long-term status of any given neighborhood. The pace of change quickened as businesses became more adventurous in selecting sites. Initially, retailers followed the outward movement of affluent consumers, locating their facilities where large concentrations of suburban households provided a ready market. Already by the 1950s, however, some savvy merchants began to base their locational decisions on population projections. In what became a self-fulfilling prophecy, developers and retailers channeled entrepreneurial capital to areas where they anticipated an eventual influx of young, affluent, white families. In the green fields of remote suburbia, new shopping centers sprouted, enticing residential developers to follow suit.

With fresh capital pumped into the fastest-growing areas on the metropolitan fringe, neighborhoods closer to the urban core suffered the consequences of systematic disinvestment. Corporations engaged in a process of creative destruction as they used the demographic characteristics of neighborhoods and population projections to guide decisions about where to allocate resources. Investing in green-field facilities came at the expense of updating and remodeling older facilities, which were eventually sold or abandoned. Once lending agencies withdrew loan privileges, the future of the neighborhood was sealed. Sudden changes in the matrix of consumer establishments—the closing of a branch department store, the conversion of a first-run cinema into one showing second-run films, the arrival of a pawn shop—signaled to nearby residents that it was time to move. Staying put could only be interpreted as a sure sign of downward social mobility. Thus, even when the postwar housing shortage was solved, the pace of urban residential migration within metropolitan areas continued unabated. Relocating was not necessarily a bargain, however. Leaving an area in the throes of decline, especially if abandonment had advanced far enough, often required homeowners to sell their property at a loss. Those who were already in a financially precarious state might then have little choice but to resettle in an area on the verge of a similar downward spiral.

Nowhere was the pressure to relocate more intense or the financial consequences so dire as in neighborhoods where commercial landscapes were driven into obsolescence by changing racial demographics. The discriminatory behavior that was fundamental to the construction of the postwar middle majority market trapped racial minorities behind a moving boundary. The mere presence of racial minorities immediately consigned a neighborhood to a permanent position on the low end of the urban geographic hierarchy. As whites fled en masse, commercial disinvestment reached

epidemic proportions, and neighborhoods fell into disrepair. Asso-
ciating people of color with poverty and crime, large commercial
operations and chain stores that could afford to divert investments
to more lucrative locations did so. Those that tried to stick it out,
often the most marginal enterprises to begin with, discovered
mounting obstacles to maintaining the viability of their businesses.
Insurance companies invariably hiked rates on their fire and theft
policies, while banks refused to grant loans for remodeling. Many
owners of commercial property felt they had no choice but to defer maintenance and wait for the arsonist. In this fashion, urban de-
cay followed even economically successful blacks as they integrated white working-class neighborhoods in transitional zones.
The systematic withdrawal of resources that proceeded in tandem
with neighborhood resegregation was visible in discrete stages of
dereliction. John Edgar Wideman recalled the demise of the
neighborhood A&P in the Homewood area of Pittsburgh: "Nobody mopped the filth from the floors. Nobody bothered to re-
stock the empty shelves. Fewer and fewer white faces among the
shoppers. A plate-glass display window gets broken and stays broken. When they finally close the store, they paste the going-out-
of-business notice over the jagged, taped crack." In hundreds of
similar neighborhoods across the country, wherever racial transitions occurred, residents watched corporations dismantle the vestiges of mass consumer culture, store by store, block by block.

Abandoned City:
The Consumer Culture of Neglect
in America's "Dark Ghettos"

Critics of urban sprawl frequently cite downtown areas as the major casualty of consumer-driven suburban development. There is
no question that the flight of retailing to the suburbs had negative

repercussions for downtown business districts. But the real losers were inner-city residential neighborhoods inhabited by racial minorities and the poor. Supermarkets, fast-food chains, and other pillars of mainstream consumer culture steered clear of neighborhoods where African Americans were concentrated, even those that supported a large segment of middle-income residents. Filling the vacuum were undercapitalized shops that stocked shoddy merchandise and off-brand products geared toward a low-end market. As businesses were sold and resold, buildings designed for one purpose were converted for quite different uses. Movie theaters became flea markets, bowling alleys became discount appliance stores, and restaurants became storefront churches. Properties that could find no buyers were simply boarded up. Although with the transfer of commercial properties the percentage of minority business owners tended to rise somewhat, many of the small mom-and-pop stores continued to be operated by white families who had since moved out of the neighborhood.

Higher proportions of female-headed households and greater numbers of single men with irregular employment schedules discouraged merchants from adopting the same family-oriented marketing strategies that predominated in the suburbs. Instead, consumer venues were more likely to support the sort of single-sex fraternization more common in the prewar era. In a depressed section of Washington, D.C., a dozen or so men made the New Deal Carry Out shop their regular point of congregation on a daily basis. Elsewhere, liquor stores, barbershops, pool halls, and record stores performed a similar function. While men monopolized the streets, women intersected with the commercial world from within the confines of their homes. Faced with the dual burden of earning a living and keeping house, women who headed single-parent households appreciated the convenience afforded by the omnipresent door-to-door peddler. Day after day, an army of salesmen roamed tenement stairwells and hallways, hawking linoleum, decorative mirrors, sheets, blankets, electric appliances, lamps, and clothing—everything but the proverbial kitchen sink (although they came close enough to that—one of the most popular items purchased from peddlers was a cabinet that fit beneath the bathroom sink).

The dynamics of inner-city retailing made the American Dream ever more elusive for consumers who lived and shopped in the nation's "dark ghettos." Because so many inner-city merchants operated on the margins, they engaged in a wide variety of detested practices that ranged from unscrupulous to fraudulent. Exploiting a captive market, they felt no need to offer competitive prices. Markups of 100 percent were not uncommon. Preying on the gullibility of inexperienced consumers, vendors sold reconditioned furniture and secondhand television sets as new. Through the use of bait-and-switch tactics and high-pressure sales pitches, they coaxed customers into buying more expensive products than they could afford. Frequently, the wrong goods were delivered to homes; repair warranties were worthless. Even when customers knew they were being swindled, they felt they had little recourse. The Los Angeles grocer who sold spoiled meat could get away with the deplorable practice because, as one of his customers explained, "Lots of folks don't have cars to go to other stores, so they have to buy from him."

Adding insult to injury, the marginal enterprises that sold furniture, clothes, and appliances tendered outrageous terms of credit. Neon signs flashing "easy credit" masked the fact that repayment of the loan was not always so easy, especially at above-market interest rates. The consequences of defaulting on a loan could be devastating: a ruined credit rating, the garnishment of wages, and the repossession of goods. As one exasperated inner-city resident complained, "You pay double the price and high carrying charges. When you miss a payment they are ready to pick your furniture up." As this comment so vividly reveals, impoverished minority consumers were perched on the precipice of consumer culture. Never secure in the knowledge that their possessions were permanent or that their credit rating would endure, their ability to function as consumers was always precarious.

It was not for these practices alone that inner-city merchants were viewed as parasites. In the eyes of local residents, the stores that lined the avenues of America's ghettos were not just consumer venues; they were potential sources of employment. Yet the white merchants who continued to do business in these communities, even after moving their own residences to newly minted suburbs, rarely hired local workers. Managing shoestring operations, they were more likely to staff their shops with family members than people who lived nearby. Thus the sting of discrimination was doubly felt. The overwhelming sentiment was that people who did business in the ghetto took whatever they could in the way of profits and gave nothing back to the community. According to the director of a community organization that operated in a distressed section of Chicago, the image that stuck in most people's minds was that of the "Brinks truck pulling up at the doors of all these merchants and carting the money out to the suburbs."

Alienated from white mainstream consumer culture, African Americans of all income levels had little choice but to fall back upon a subordinate consumer economy that thrived within the confines of black residential districts. On the streets of Chicago's South Side, Houston's Fifth Ward, Cleveland's Hough neighborhood, New Orleans's Rampart District, Atlanta's Auburn Avenue area, and Harlem, a discrete consumer network crystallized around neighborhood shops, door-to-door peddlers, and credit associations. Self-contained in the sense that shoppers came almost exclusively from the immediate neighborhood, inner-city commercial districts were nonetheless dependent on the larger economy for insurance coverage, merchandise, and infusions of investment capital from white-owned storeowners and banks. Yet for those who were forced to live and shop in these areas, it was abundantly clear that these commercial networks were connected to the larger economy in ways that were injurious, forcing them to pay higher

prices for goods and denying them many of the consumer opportunities available in other parts of the city. Especially as middle-
income blacks moved into housing vacated by middle-income
whites, leaving behind the poorest of the poor, accelerated disinvestment betrayed the American Dream as a raw deal.

Burn Baby Burn:
Mass Consumer Culture in Flames

The section of south central Los Angeles known as Watts was typical of America's inner-city minority enclaves. In the 1920s and
1930s, Watts was a multiracial mosaic composed of working-class
whites, blacks, and Mexican Americans. Subsequently, the percentage of African Americans increased steadily. As one of the few
neighborhoods close to downtown that did not employ restrictive
covenants to bar racial minorities, it became a magnet for African-
American job seekers who migrated to the city during and after
World War II. By 1965, nearly nine out of every ten residents of
Watts were African American, a demographic development that
resulted, in part, from the now-familiar white flight and corporate
withdrawal. Its narrow streets, lined with small one-story framed
houses, showed the signs of wear that characterized inner-city
neighborhoods across the country; dilapidated storefronts on the
major business thoroughfares revealed the telltale signs of disinvestment. When Watts exploded in six straight days of looting,
shooting, and burning, the inequities of mass consumer culture
were exposed to the nation in dramatic fashion.

The incident that precipitated the Watts uprising, however, had
nothing to do with consumption. Following the arrest of a young
black man on a charge of drunk driving, a scuffle ensued between
the police officers and a small group of onlookers. Police brutality
was a long-standing sore point in the community, and when word

Vermont Avenue shops, south central Los Angeles, 1950. These stores, once considered a prime example of modern suburban retailing, were looted and burned during the civil disturbances of 1965.

spread that the officers had roughed up a group of innocent by-standers, the lid blew off a wide range of frustrations that had been simmering for years. Watts residents expressed their anger in a variety of ways. Some pelted police cars with bottles and stones, some torched buildings, and a few assaulted white drivers passing through the neighborhood in their cars. The activity that engaged the largest number and broadest cross-section of people, however, was looting.

In what was surely the grandest fire sale Watts had ever seen, the streets filled each day with residents carrying sewing machines, mattresses, dresses, cameras, and groceries back to their homes. Within a matter of minutes, shoe stores, furniture stores, appliance stores, and liquor stores were stripped of their contents. Some people had the foresight to arrive on the scene with shopping carts; others simply grabbed whatever they could pile up in their arms. Pawnshops were a popular target; many residents were able to retrieve goods they had previously pledged. Eyewitnesses recall the spirit of liberation that attended the mass smorgasbord of commodities. After years of deprivation, this sudden acquisition of consumer commodities imbued the poor residents of Watts with a sense of freedom. As one participant put it, "Going into a store was uplifting yourself."

Ransacking shops represented justice to a community that had been shortchanged by a national consumer culture and knew it. Watts residents resented the shoddy merchandise that appeared on their shelves, the outrageous terms of credit they were forced to bear, and the rude treatment they received from white merchants. Plundering stores was not just about acquiring new consumer commodities, it was like sticking a knife in the belly of an oppressive beast. The pattern of looting reflected specific grievances. The first target in the department stores and clothing shops were the credit records, which were destroyed before the buildings were stripped and torched. Word spread that black shopkeepers would be spared if they placed "soul brother" signs in their window. For the most part, looters directed their wrath at shops owned by whites. Even if only a small percentage of Watts residents participated in the looting and burning, perhaps as little as 15 percent, post-riot surveys showed that most people in the neighborhood felt that the merchants who lost their stores and inventories got what they deserved.

Three characteristics of the Watts riot illuminated the specific nature of inner-city grievances. First, participants made no attempt to invade surrounding suburban communities. All looting and burning took place within the confines of ghetto boundaries. Second, most of the 700 buildings torched were owned and operated by whites who lived elsewhere (although it is important to note that those black merchants with a reputation for price gouging and deceptive sales practices tended to receive the same treatment as their white counterparts, while some white merchants who enjoyed honest reputations in the community were spared). The vast majority of homes and churches were left untouched. Clearly, anger was directed at outsiders who had established an exploitive presence in the community. The uprising may have unleashed latent hostility toward an exclusionary consumer culture, but it was no longer simply the segregation of consumer facilities that cut to the heart of the problem. Residents of Watts were not requesting access to suburban retail outlets, only to justice within their own neighborhoods and equal access to the consumer experience taken for granted by white America.

A third characteristic of the riots, often overlooked amid the sharp expressions of black rage, was the participation of hundreds of poor whites in the looting spree. Although by 1965, south central Los Angeles was predominantly black, whites represented about 13 percent of the population. The percentage was even higher in the surrounding neighborhoods, many of which also suffered heavy damage during the rioting. Many were longtime residents who were too poor to move elsewhere. Some of them lived in trailers. At least half a dozen ragtag trailer parks, most of them small and cramped, lay scattered through what became known as the "curfew area." It is not known how many trailer park residents, if any, took part in the looting and burning festivities. If they did, it was not out of "black rage" but as a protest against the same exploitative treatment faced by everyone else in the community. Through the lens of the mass media, the Watts uprising became a race riot. The active participation of whites, however, suggested that it was more than that. Unfortunately, Americans whose attitudes about race were formed in concert with the rise of the middle majority mass market could hardly comprehend the presence of whites wreaking havoc along with their black neighbors, so the media ignored their participation in the riots. The invisibility of trailer park dwellers everywhere applied equally to the impoverished white looters and burners of Watts.

The message telecast from Watts in August 1965 differed dramatically from the one relayed from Greensboro five years earlier. The sit-in demonstrators sought to lower the racial barriers that denied them equal access to the consumer manifestations of full citizenship. In looting shops, destroying credit records, and burning commercial buildings, residents of Watts displayed contempt for the local institutions that supported the larger consumer economy. However confrontational the sit-ins were, they reflected a fundamental faith in the American creed of equal opportunity and the promise of consumer abundance. However monumental the Civil Rights Act was, it conformed to a vision in which all groups in society could at least buy into a common vision of the American Dream. By the late 1960s, more and more Americans had abandoned the notion that the dominant values of consumer capitalism could bind a diverse people together. Along with the counterculture and women's movement, the urban riots of the 1960s shattered the illusory cultural consensus that manufacturers, retailers, and advertisers had both constructed and weakened during the two decades following World War II.

Over the next three years, the Watts scenario was repeated in hundreds of cities across the country. In 1966, disturbances flared in Chicago, Cleveland, Milwaukee, Dayton, and San Francisco. The next year brought exceptionally violent eruptions to Newark and Detroit. In Detroit alone, more than 2,500 buildings were looted or burned. By the end of 1968, some 50,000 people had been arrested and 8,000 had been injured in nearly 300 separate sprees of pillaging and burning. Nearly all occurred in places like Watts, inner-city neighborhoods or transitional suburbs inhabited primarily by African Americans where economic opportunities were shrinking. Nearly all were ignited by a police action perceived as abusive. Nearly everywhere the pattern of violence was identical: Stores were cleared of their inventories and then arsonists moved in to set the buildings ablaze. As in Watts, poor whites often joined in the free-for-all commodity giveaway. Whites comprised about 10 percent of the total number of people arrested in urban riots in nineteen cities in 1967. As in Watts, the participation of poor whites was largely ignored by the society at large, which associated ghetto living with people designated as nonwhites. In their cumulative impact, the urban disturbances of the late 1960s exposed the boundaries of the new postwar consumer culture, starkly demarcating its insiders and outsiders. In this way they gave evidence to a new hierarchy of social stratification in which skin color and relative purchasing power were conflated.

In the aftermath of the urban riots, impoverished inner-city residents expressed hope that some sort of phoenix would rise from the ashes. Perhaps the flames, the shootings, and the smashed storefronts would serve as a wake-up call to the rest of the nation. Perhaps the scope of the disturbances would elicit a response of equivalent breadth, one that would inject economic resources into inner-city neighborhoods and allow residents to control their own destiny without interference from exploitative interlopers. Nothing of the sort occurred, however. If anything, the riots only sped the flight of capital. Moreover, the loss of jobs that attended deindustrialization in the 1970s further undermined the resilience of inner-city minority enclaves, making any internally generated recovery even less likely. Caught in the spiral of continuing decline, America's urban core was thrust further toward its exile on the cultural periphery.

Luxor Lanes was one of the businesses that survived the Watts riot, if barely. Through the 1940s, the working-class districts of south central Los Angeles supported nearly a dozen bowling alleys—most of them small establishments with no more than fourteen lanes. The Luxor, a ten-lane alley that dated to 1929, was the premier spot in the neighborhood. Known as a high-scoring house, it hosted the most competitive leagues and drew the best bowlers, all of whom were white. During the 1950s and 1960s, white flight from south central Los Angeles, combined with the opening of lavish bowling houses featuring automatic pinsetters in more remote suburban communities, deprived most of the area's bowling houses of their regular clientele. Minimal patronage among African-American bowlers hardly compensated for the loss of white bowlers. By the early 1960s, many proprietors had given up on the area and closed down their businesses.

At the Luxor, however, business from its still predominantly white clientele remained strong enough to prompt the owner, Sock Hill, to defend it when the neighborhood was under siege in the summer of 1965. "It was touch and go for a while," recounted Hill a week after the disturbances. On either side of the bowling alley, vandals were breaking into stores and arsonists were setting them aflame. To ward them off, Hill armed several of his employees with guns and had them stake positions in the second-story billiard room. As the rioters approached, Hill gave the order for his workers to fire a series of warning shots. They did, and the rioters dispersed. The Luxor was spared. Within a year, however, Hill's commitment to the Luxor and the neighborhood had waned considerably. On August 20, 1966, only days after the first anniversary of the riot, the Luxor closed its doors for good, another casualty of a consumer culture that had proven itself to be far less inclusive than it proclaimed.

EPILOGUE

ACROSS THE BACK RIVER, just beyond Baltimore's city limit, the American Dream was bleeding to death on Eastern Avenue. Already by the 1970s, the once bustling thoroughfare bore the telltale markers of sustained disinvestment: deserted sidewalks, empty storefronts, and "For Lease" signs posted in windows. Vestiges of the great postwar boom were hard to find; most had either disappeared or been transformed beyond recognition. Decline came in incremental steps as merchants closed their doors one by one, forced out of business by decreasing profit margins or lured to areas where business was more lucrative. The departure of national chain stores—Woolworth's, the A&P, Read's Drugs—left local shoppers with no place to procure basic provisions, no place to buy groceries, no place to get a shirt pressed or a dress cleaned. Save for peddlers of pornographic material and vendors of cheap novelty items, few businesses expressed an interest in leasing commercial property.

The diners, bowling alleys, and trailer parks along Eastern Avenue did not fare particularly well in the depressed environment of

Eastern Avenue, Essex,. Md., 2000

the 1970s and 1980s. When the New Essex Bowling Alley burned
to the ground in the 1960s, the owners cut their losses and abandoned the venture. The owner of the Essex Diner tried to revive
business by covering his stainless steel exterior with a red brick
façade and a brown mansard roof. In 1977, he sold the business,
and the diner underwent a series of reincarnations as a Greek
restaurant, a catering establishment, and finally an office for a firm
selling security systems. Most of the area's trailer courts had disappeared after the housing shortage eased and defense workers
moved into newly constructed single-family homes during the
1960s. Those mobile-home parks that remained no longer catered
to families looking for starter housing. Rather, they were filled
with blue-collar retirees on fixed incomes who sought the security
of home ownership in their golden years.

The rapid gutting of Eastern Avenue in the 1970s, much like its equally precipitous development thirty years earlier, was a product of broad structural shifts in the American economy. Massive layoffs in manufacturing and the stagnation of industrial wages cut deeply into the earnings and purchasing power of blue-collar families. On the eastern edge of Baltimore, defense plants that had once employed thousands of workers now employed only hundreds. A population that had long thrived on high-paying union jobs came to rely increasingly on low-wage employment in the service sector. An area that boasted above-average incomes in the 1950s and 1960s suffered from soaring rates of poverty and unemployment into the 1980s and 1990s. As blue-collar families fell further behind their white-collar counterparts, the concept of a middle majority became less viable. With little incentive to go after a shrinking middle-income cluster, many manufacturers and retailers abandoned the mass market for the luxury market. Places like Eastern Avenue were among the first to suffer the consequences. The flight of chain stores and the disappearance of diners and bowling alleys from inner-suburban commercial strips made it difficult for people who lived and shopped there to maintain the illusion that they were still connected to the mainstream of American life. The influx of poor people of color from inner-city neighborhoods only magnified their sense of dislocation and dispossession.

Those who fared exceptionally well during the postwar boom, especially the children of blue-collar workers who had used their education to jump the collar line, followed their fortunes and spent them further afield form the urban core in the direction of enclosed shopping malls. In 1975, developers built Golden Ring Mall, two miles north of the Eastern Avenue shopping district. In 1981, the White Marsh Mall appeared another four miles out, beyond the I–695 beltway that ringed the metropolis. These multi-storied, climate-controlled, automobile-friendly meccas of con-

The Avenue at White Marsh, White Marsh, Md., 2000

sumption functioned as hubs for the new suburban boomtowns radiating outwards from the old urban centers and as incubators for the most cutting-edge merchandising techniques. Like so many other enclosed malls built after 1970, the ones in suburban Baltimore attempted the reinvention of Main Street by placing a mix of large and small stores along a pedestrian promenade. Yet, unlike the Main Street it sought to replace, the indoor version was thoroughly sanitized. Dress codes and rigid proscriptions on political behavior, enforced through the use of high-tech surveillance and private security patrols, kept away rabble-rousers, vagrants, and the unkempt, thereby providing a safe and tranquil environment for leisurely shopping. This pedestrian-friendly retailing arrangement, however sterile in the eyes of some critics, proved to be a fertile breeding ground for the proliferation of specialty stores employing historical and exotic motifs in gearing their product to a high-end market. The shopping mall of the 1970s and 1980s was largely responsible for the success of Victorian lingerie boutiques, barnlike country stores, jungle safari outfitters, futuristic gadget and gizmo bazaars, and other retail chains that adopted themed formulas.

It is precisely in these sorts of places, beyond the beltways of metropolitan America, in the nation's "edge cities," that a new version of the good life has crystallized in recent years. And it bears little resemblance to the one that flourished at mid-century when the middle majority mass market held sway. The most recent retailing extravaganza to make its appearance on the eastern fringe of Baltimore County is the $45 million development called The Avenue at White Marsh. Here, shoppers stroll along a re-created outdoor Main Street, sampling gourmet coffee, micro-brewed beer, and premium cigars while they peruse items on display at megabookstores, specialty craft boutiques, and golf equipment emporiums. Among the commercial attractions of the White Marsh area is a replica of a 1950s diner in which waiters and waitresses donned in bow-ties and vests serve halibut sautéed in lime pesto, steak diane, penne siciliano, and other nontraditional diner fare.

On the cusp of the twenty-first century, the middle majority, family-oriented consumer culture of the 1950s has enduring relevance only insofar as it can be milked for its nostalgic cachet. In the contemporary consumer landscape dominated by mega-bookstores, cybercafés, body-piercing parlors, New Age boutiques, and ethnic markets, the relics of an older era—diners, bowling alleys, and trailers—have remained viable by turning their backs on the masses and catering to specialized niche markets. The bowling centers that host "Rock 'n' Glow" parties after midnight, the vintage trailers purchased by movie stars, and the retro diners serving fancy cuisine have been repackaged once again, this time as themed entertainment and vehicles for projecting a hip attitude. The gleaming diners along San Francisco's Embarcadero and Connecticut Avenue in Chevy Chase, Maryland, as well as those

Empire Diner, New York City, 1999. The Empire was one of the first diners to cater to upscale consumers by combining a 1940s diner decor with haute cuisine and live piano performances.

exported abroad to places like Canary Wharf in London, are no longer places to grab a simple meal, but living museums designed to evoke the mood of a carefree America in a golden age of consumer abundance, the 1950s. Likewise, the Airstream and Spartan trailers displayed at collector shows draw their luster from their association with a less complicated era. Their buyers have no intention of living in them year round, however. The bowling industry, on the other hand, has chosen not to use 1950s nostalgia as a marketing hook, opting instead for a theme that might be described as futuristic-disco, complete with fog machines, glowing pins, laser lights, closed-circuit televisions, and loud, 1970s vintage music.

If the consumer culture of the 1950s was built around the fiction of a middle majority mainstream composed of happy suburban families, today's version makes no such pretense. Contemporary advertisers and retailers pitch their products, not to middle-class families, but to individuals as cultural free agents. Commodities once promoted as instruments of family cohesion and cultural amalgamation are presented as mediums of self-expression and personal transformation. Through the selection of the prerequisite clothes, accessories, food, magazines, and music, the commercial smorgasbord of the 1990s invites individuals to adopt the lifestyle of their choosing and move effortlessly from one consumer subculture to another. Once conventional wisdom led manufacturers and retailers to believe that they could sell to everyone if they finessed social tensions with sufficient care. After the 1960s, that was no longer possible. Clearly, America's unwillingness to incorporate racial minorities into the middle majority in the 1950s and 1960s, and the fragmentation of the family into separate market segments based on gender and generation in the 1960s and 1970s, were merely a prelude to more thorough atomization of the mass market in the 1980s and 1990s. Today's marketing consultants urge their clients to divide and subdivide the population into highly specialized buying clusters and to target them with the accuracy of a laser surgeon. Nowhere is this advice deemed more pertinent than for businesses that hope to tap the bulging bank accounts of the highly paid professionals, corporate executives, and savvy stock market investors who have watched their incomes soar in the 1990s. To facilitate a more sophisticated understanding of buying tendencies within this rather large group, market researchers have suggested breaking down high-income shoppers into distinct personality types—discriminating, trendy, sophisticated, conservative, adventurous—each requiring a different sales approach. Not that manufacturers and retailers have entirely abandoned the low-end market, as the success of the

Home Shopping Network and Wal-Mart makes quite clear. Yet, in recent years, most of the action has been on the high end, where purveyors of expensive goods and services can count on the patronage of, not only the rich and famous, but those who aspire to that lifestyle. And therein lies the rub.

More than ever before, class cuts a deep ravine through the mottled landscape of niche markets. In stark contrast to the 1950s, when the locus of innovation for products and services straddled the border between blue-collar and white-collar worlds, today's patterns of consumer emulation emanate from the upper reaches of the social spectrum. It is the sports utility vehicles, designer clothes, cellular phones, and exotic coffee drinks consumed by corporate executives and upwardly mobile professionals that shape the fashion consciousness and consumer objectives of those with more meager financial resources. Everyone has come down with a bad case of what one economist has called "luxury fever," even those who can hardly afford it.

For people who are not fortunate enough to enjoy incomes that fall within the top 20 or 30 percent, luxury fever can be fatal. To the detriment of the vast majority of Americans, the point of reference for consumer fashion has moved higher up the social ladder at the same time that the gap between rich and poor has widened. Rather than diminishing the lure of car phones, celebrity-sponsored athletic shoes, home entertainment centers, and gourmet chocolate, falling levels of median family income have only pressured households to put in more working hours and take out more personal debt to keep pace in the purchasing of these goods. Even the low-budget versions of high-end products—Wal-Mart manicures, convenience store cappuccinos—exact a steep toll when the impulse to splurge becomes a manic obsession. At best, the treadmill of upscale spending produces widespread frustration, at worst, it pushes millions of Americans to the brink of financial insolvency. By the late 1990s, a staggering 18 percent of all household income

went toward servicing personal debt, and Americans paid an average of $1,000 annually to cover fees and interest on their credit
card accounts alone. The allure of freedom that compels participation in the consumer whirligig has never been so deceptive. The
drive to keep pace with fashion has never been so fraught with financial and emotional risk.

No wonder the 1950s never looked so good. No wonder the
racism, sexism, and domestic strife that accompanied consumer
abundance so easily fades from the mental snapshot of the era.
And no wonder a romanticized version of postwar America res-
onates so powerfully with patrons at the Star Light Diner. When
you cross the Back River into Baltimore County along Eastern Avenue, the Star Light is the first landmark that catches your attention. It was imported to the neighborhood in 1993, and, like the
one eight miles away in White Marsh, it is a cookie-cutter replica
of a 1950s diner. Although nostalgia is part of the appeal—the
walls are covered with images of Elvis, Brando, Ike, and tail-finned
Chevys—there is nothing fancy about the place. The food is basic
and the prices are reasonable. Most of the customers are old-timers
who have spent the better part of their lives in the area—men who
toiled for years in the nearby steel mills and shipyards; women
who once joined bowling leagues, performed household chores
with appliances their mothers never dreamed of, and weaved their
shopping carts through the bustling sidewalk traffic on Eastern Avenue. It is not unusual to find them inspecting the clutter of memorabilia on the walls and drawing connections between the artifacts
and their own lives—the music they listened to, the cars they
drove, the movies they watched. Perhaps when they close their
eyes and lose themselves in the chatter of neighbors and the clatter of dishes, and the aroma of brewing coffee and griddle-fried
eggs, they can transport themselves back to a time when consumer
abundance went hand in hand with steady work, modern living,
and the promise of an even better future, a time not so long ago

Star Light Diner, Eastern Avenue, Essex, Md., 2000

when the flashing neon letters "D-I-N-E-R" promised that the American Dream was theirs to be had. And even if Eastern Avenue looks a little bedraggled these days, the shiny chrome and brilliant neon of the Star Light Diner reflects the belief, perhaps even more so among the younger folks who come in after a night of Cosmic bowling, that by chasing the consumer trends set by the wealthy they can still find some semblance of the good life, even if its content is a far cry from the family-oriented middle majority mainstream that reigned in the wake of World War II.

NOTES

1–2   Eastern Avenue: George J. Martinak, "A Short History of Essex and Middle River," term paper, English 102, Essex Community College, May 1963, 32–37, Essex Community College Library, Baltimore County, Maryland. R. L. Polk & Company, *Polk's Baltimore Suburban Directory, 1955* (Richmond: R. L. Polk & Company, 1955), 66. *Woodall's Trailer Park Directory* (Chicago: Trailer Travel Magazine, 1949), 107–109. *Woodall's 1956 Official Mobile Home Park Directory* (Chicago: Trailer Travel Magazine, 1955), 342–343. Ernest Imhoff, "Two War Babies That Grew into 'The Rising Suburb of the East,'" *Baltimore Evening Sun,* March 11, 1964, Essex folder, press clipping vertical file, Enoch Pratt Free Library, Baltimore, Maryland.

5   Data on consumer expenditures: Stanley Lebergott, *Pursuing Happiness: American Consumers in the Twentieth Century* (Princeton: Princeton

University Press, 1993), 113, 130, 152–155. Also see: Elaine Tyler May, *Homeward Bound: American Families in the Cold War Era* (New York: Basic Books, 1988), 166. George Katona, *The Powerful Consumer: Psychological Studies of the American Economy* (New York: McGraw-Hill, 1960), 19. U.S. Department of Labor, *How American Buying Habits Change* (Washington, D.C.: U.S. Government Printing Office, 1959), 3, 89–98.

7   Average weekly earnings: Gary Gerstle, "The Working Class Goes to War," *The War in American Culture: Society and Consciousness During World War II*, eds. Lewis A. Erenberg and Susan E. Hirsch (Chicago: University of Chicago Press, 1996), 115.

8   Wartime advertising: Frank W. Fox, *Madison Avenue Goes to War: The Strange Military Career of American Advertising, 1941–45*, Charles E. Merrill Monograph Series in the Humanities and Social Sciences (Provo, Utah: Brigham Young University, 1975). John Morton Blum, *V Was for Victory: Politics and American Culture During World War II* (New York: Harcourt Brace Jovanovich, 1976), 100–105.

8   Nash-Kelvinator advertisement: *Newsweek* 23 (January 24, 1944), inside front cover.

9   Wartime propaganda: Benjamin L. Alpers, "Imagining a Democratic Military," *Journal of American History* 85 (June 1988), 129–163. Lary May, "Making the American Consensus: The Narrative of Conversion and Subversion in World War II Films," *The War in American Culture: Society and Consciousness During World War II*, ed. Lewis A. Erenberg and Susan E. Hirsch (Chicago: University of Chicago Press, 1996), 71–102.

11   Postwar economic trends: "The Boom," *Fortune* 33 (June 1946), 97–103. David M. Gordon, "Chickens Come Home to Roost: From Prosperity to Stagnation in the Postwar U.S. Economy," *Understanding American Economic Decline*, ed. Michael A. Bernstein and David E. Adler (Cambridge: Cambridge University Press, 1994), 34–76. Bennett Harrison and Barry Bluestone, *The Great U-Turn: Corporate Restructuring and the Polarizing of America* (New York: Basic Books, 1988), 6.

12   Income redistribution: Jeffrey G. Williamson and Peter H. Lindert, *American Inequality: A Macroeconomic History*. Institute for Research on Poverty Monograph Series (New York: Academic Press, 1980), 92. Richard Polenberg, *War and Society: The United States, 1941–1945* (New York: J.B. Lippincott, 1972), 94.

13   Middle majority: The editors of *Fortune*, *The Changing American Market* (Garden City, N.Y.: Hanover House, 1953), 52–61.

19   Critiques of postwar suburbia: Peter Blake, *God's Own Junkyard: The Planned Deterioration of America's Landscape* (New York: Holt, Rinehart, and Winston: 1964). David Riesman, *Abundance for What?* (New Brunswick: Transaction Publishers, 1993), 266. Lewis Mumford, *The City in History: Its Origins, Its Transformation, and Its Prospects* (New York: Harcourt Brace & World, 1961), 486, 502–511.

Chapter 1: Diners

21–23   Chuck Wagon Diner: Telephone interview with George Yonko, Macon, Mississippi, May 23, 1994.

26–28   Early history of the diner: Richard J.S. Gutman, *American Diner: Then and Now* (New York: Harper Perennial, 1993), 12–38. Blake Ehrlich, "The Diner Puts on Airs," *Saturday Evening Post* (June 19, 1948), 130–131. Jerry O'Mahony Company, "35% to 40% Net Profit from the Operation of Lunch Cars" (sales brochure), circa 1922, files of Peter Lepera, Georgia-Pacific Corporation, Jarratt, Virginia.

28   Railroad car design: Jerry O'Mahony Company, "35% to 40% Net Profit from the Operation of Lunch Cars." P. J. Tierney Sons, Inc., "Just Picture Yourself—as the Owner!" (sales brochure), circa 1927, Diner archives, Kullman Industries, Lebanon, New Jersey (henceforth cited as Kullman archives.)

29   7,000 diners: Donald Dale Jackson, "The American Diner Is in Decline, Yet More Chic Than Ever," *Smithsonian* 17 (November 1986), 102.

29   Kullman estimate: "The Standard of Comparison," *The Diner* 2 (February 1941), 9.

29   Geographic distribution of diners prior to World War II: Gutman, *American Diner*, 59, 263. Brian A. Butko, "Seen Any Good Diners Lately?," *Pittsburgh History* 73 (Fall 1990), 111. *Cleveland and Suburban Telephone Directory* (Cleveland: Ohio Bell Telephone Company, 1939). John Hunter, "The Diner in Worcester, 1890–1976," unpublished paper, School of Geography, Clark University, 1978, Diner Collection, Worcester Historical Museum, Worcester, Massachusetts.

29   Preponderance of diners in New York, Philadelphia, and Boston: This information was gleaned primarily from the monthly listings of diner openings in the trade journal *The Diner* for the years 1946 to 1949. I have used these monthly listings to create a database comprising over 800 diners that opened for business between 1946 and 1959. Additional information was provided by Pat Fodero, formerly of the Fodero Dining Car Company, and Daniel Zilka, director of the American Diner Museum in Providence, Rhode Island. Most of the entries include the diner's name, owner, location, size, and manufacturer. In subsequent notes I will refer to this list as "Diner Master List."

29–30   Mary Townsend: Telephone interview with Mary Etta Cook (formerly Mary Townsend), June 30, 1994, Akron, Ohio. *The Wingfoot Clan*, November 15, 1979, 4.

30   "a good bet for stable business": *The Diner* 8 (February 1949), 15–16.

30   Bendix Diner: Interview with Bob DiLorenzo, Hasbrouck Heights, N.J., July 21, 2000.

31   Diner construction: *New York Times*, September 23, 1951, Section 3, 9.

31   Arthur Holst: "New Owners," *The Diner* 6 (July 1947), 15.

31–32   Late night clientele: "Alas, the Poor Night Worker There's No Place to Eat," *Worcester Sunday Telegram*, September, 17, 1967, Worcester pamphlet collection, Worcester Public Library, Worcester, Massachusetts.

32   Class divisions and consumption: Frank Stricker, "Affluence for Whom?—Another Look at Prosperity and the Working Class in the 1920s," *Labor History* 24 (Winter 1983), 5–33. Warren Belasco,

Americans on the Road: From Autocamp to Motel, 1910–1914 (Cambridge, Mass.: MIT Press, 1979).

33   Early twentieth-century restaurants: Harvey Levenstein, *Paradox of Plenty: A Social History of Eating in Modern America* (New York: Oxford University Press, 1993), 28, 45–47. American Restaurant Magazine, *Market Analysis of the Restaurant Industry* (Chicago: Patterson Publishing Company, 1952), 1–2. Philip Langdon, *Orange Roofs, Golden Arches: The Architecture of American Chain Restaurants* (New York: Alfred A. Knopf, 1986), 5–25. "Layouts for Locations," *Fountain & Fast Food Service* (October 1951), 33–35, 74. David Gerard Hogan, *Selling 'em by the Sack: White Castle and the Creation of American Food* (New York: New York University Press, 1997), 8–12, 24–82.

34–35   Background of diner builders: Gutman, *American Diner*, 42–47, 66, 228, 230, 232, 241–242.

35   Ethnic affiliations of diner owners: Telephone interview with Pat Fodero, Camarillo, California, September 17, 1993. Diner Master List.

36–37   Ethnic foods: Interview with Don Bailey (owner of Summitt Diner, Somerset, Pa.), Somerset, Pennsylvania, July 2, 1993. Interview with Mike Zappone (owner of Mr. Z's, Cleveland), Cleveland, Ohio, July 24, 1995. Interview with Ernest Iannone (owner of Prairie Diner, Providence, R.I.), Providence, Rhode Island, August 11, 1995. Interview with Harold Kullman, Avenel, New Jersey, June 1, 1994. Johnny Rogers, "State Diner Sets New Concept in City Diner-Restaurant Operation," *Fountain, Luncheonette and Diner* 1 (June 1954), 16.

36   Working-class homogenization: Nelson Lichtenstein, "The Making of the Postwar Working Class: Cultural Pluralism and Social Structure in World War II," *Historian* 51 (November 1988), 42–55. On antecedents see, Lizabeth Cohen, *Making a New Deal: Industrial Workers in Chicago, 1919–1939* (Cambridge: Cambridge University Press, 1990), 324–357, and Roy Rosenzweig, *Eight Hours for What We Will: Workers and Leisure in an Industrial City, 1870–1920* (Cambridge: Cambridge University Press), 171–221.

36   Chuck Wagon Diner: Yonko interview.

37   Diner menus: Interview with Marvin Zelin (owner Market Diner, New York, N.Y.), New York City, December 29, 1982. Interview with Alfred Welte (owner of Miss America Diner, Jersey City, N.J.), Jersey City, New Jersey, January 7, 1983. Lester Bammesberger (former owner of Lester's Diner, Cortland, N.Y.), Scottsdale, Arizona, May 30, 1994. Yonko interview.

37   Poor reputation of diners: "Editorial: Correction, Please," *The Diner* 7 (August 1948), 5.

37   Steffie's Diner: Press clipping from *Gary Post-Tribune*, circa 1949, scrapbook, Philip Rosenbloom Collection, Calumet Regional Archives, Gary, Indiana.

38   Poor hygiene: According to a 1949 survey, 19 percent of diners and lunch-counter restaurants lacked rest rooms. "An Objective Study of the Diner-Counter Service Restaurant Market," *The Diner* 8 (special supplement, 1949), 5.

38   Women and diners: Ehrlich, "The Diner Puts on Airs," 133. George H. Waltz Jr., "The Roadside Diners Are Rolling," *Coronet* 34 (September 1953), 133. Letter to the editor from A. D. Wayne, *The Diner* 5 (August 1946), 4.

38   "a comfortable home": P. J. Tierney Sons, Inc., "Just Picture Yourself—as the Owner!"

38   "to cast aside": Kullman Dining Car Company, "Is this your opportunity" (sales brochure), circa early 1930s, Kullman archives.

39   Diner financing and technical expertise: Silk City Diners, "Quality Diners That Make Excellent Profits" (sales brochure), 1958, file folder 2, series III, box 1, Grinwis collection, Paterson Vehicle Company (Silk City Diners), Records and Memorabilia Collection (henceforth cited as Grinwis collection), Passaic County Historical Society, Paterson, New Jersey. Mahony Diners, "A Design for Success" (sales brochure), circa 1956, Kullman archives. Jerry O' Mahony, Inc., "Over Forty Years Experience" (sales brochure), circa 1951, private collection of Richard J. S. Gutman, Roxbury, Massachusetts. Interview with Herb Enyart, PMC, Inc., Oakland, New Jersey, January 7, 1983.

39   ". . . sold the American Dream": Interview with Jerry Manno (Manno Dining Car Company), Montclair, New Jersey, January 7, 1983.

39–40   Reduction of entrepreneurial opportunities and redefinition of the
        American Dream: Ely Chinoy, *Automobile Workers and the American
        Dream* (New York: Doubleday & Co., 1955). C. Wright Mills, *White
        Collar: The American Middle Classes* (London: Oxford University Press,
        1951).

41   Joseph Hughes: "Alas the Poor Night Worker There's No Place to
        Eat."

41   Industrial dining: American Restaurant Magazine, *Market Analysis of
        the Restaurant Industry*, 1.

42   Fodero recollections: Fodero interview.

42   Trends reported in trade journals: "Nutrition . . . A Public De-
        mand," *The Diner* 5 (July 1946), 6. American Restaurant Magazine,
        Market Analysis of the Restaurant Industry, 1–4.

42   Diners reporting increased patronage: Letter from A. J. Brady, *The
        Diner* 6 (February 1947), 4.

43   Diversified clientele: Mike Flynn, "I Just Got Back from Lunch,"
        The Diner 5 (September 1946), 22. Ernie Gisin, "A La Carte," *The
        Diner* 5 (August 1946), 20. "Nutrition . . . A Public Demand," 6.

43   "host to everyone": Mountain View Diners, "A Modern Tribute to
        Good Taste," (sales brochure), circa 1949, 2, Kullman archives.

43   Diner production levels: Interview with Harold Kullman, Avenel,
        New Jersey, January 5, 1983. Manno interview. "The Diner Busi-
        ness," *Fortune* 46 (July 1952), 167. Ehrlich, "The Diner Puts on
        Airs," 133.

45   O'Mahony move to St. Louis: "Over the Counter," *Diner and Restau-
        rant* 11 (December 1952), 35. Jerry O'Mahony, Inc., fact sheet,
        October 1952, p. 2, American Diner Museum, Providence, R.I.
        New York Times, August 31, 1952, Section 3, 4.

45   Mountain View expansion: Mountain View Diners, Inc., "Offering
        Circular," June 20, 1956, 3, Kullman archives. Mountain View Din-
        ers, "A Modern Tribute to Good Taste," 14.

45   Bammesburger interview.

46   Drive-ins: Langdon, *Orange Roofs, Golden Arches*, 59–77. Chester
        Liebs, *From Main Street to Miracle Mile: American Roadside Architecture*
        (Boston: Bullfinch Press, 1985), 208. Spencer Crump, "Southern
        California Offers Good Prospects for Diners," *The Diner* 9 (March
        1950), 32, 45.

46   "irritating waits": *Gary Post-Tribune*, July 29, 1956, Panorama section, 4–5.

46   "stopping in": "Capsule Comments," *Diner, Drive-In* 18 (January 1959), 13.

47   Drive-in statistics: "News Roundup," *Diner, Drive-In* 18 (September 1959), 38. "A Roundup Report on Franchising," *Diner, Drive-In* 18 (October 1959), 18–19. Langdon, *Orange Roofs, Golden Arches*, 67.

48   Scarsdale diner: *New York Times*, April 23, 1934, 18.

48   Los Angeles zoning: "Los Angeles," *The Diner*, 5 (September 1946), 8.

48   Atlantic City restrictions: Ehrlich, "The Diner Puts on Airs," 19.

48–49   Kullman recollections: Kullman interview, June 1, 1994.

49   Fodero: Fodero interview.

49   advice column: "Pick Your Spot Scientifically," *The Diner*, 8 (February 1949), 15–16.

49   Manno recollections: Manno interview. Another diner builder, Harold Kullman, confirmed that diners were most successful in these neighborhoods. Kullman interview, June 1, 1994.

50   Godfrey Diner: "Godfrey Diner, A Showcase of Modern Food Service," *Diner, Drive-In and Restaurant* 14 (January 1955), 12.

50   Socio-economic profile of neighborhoods: U.S. Bureau of the Census, *U.S. Census of Population: 1950*. Vol. III: *Census Tracts Statistics*, ch. 42 (Washington, 1952), 20–29, 75–98. U.S. Bureau of the Censuses, *U.S. Censuses of Population and Housing: 1960. Census Tracts, Final Report, PHC (1)–115* (Washington, D.C., 1962), 30–48, 252–270.

50–51   DeRaffele recollections: Telephone interview with Phil DeRaffele, New Rochelle, New York, June 30, 1994.

51   Manhattan locations: Restaurant Listings, *Manhattan Telephone Directory*, Spring/Summer 1945. The far West Side of Manhattan is defined here as the area between the Hudson River and 10th Avenue above 14th Street, and the Hudson River and Hudson Street below 14th Street.

51   New York City demographic data: Bureau of the Census, *U.S. Census of Population: 1950. Vol. II, Characteristics of the Population, Part 32, New York, Chapter B* (Washington, D.C., 1952), 168. Bureau of the Census, *U.S. Census of Population: 1960. Vol. II, Characteristics of the Pop-*

ulation, Part 34, New York (Washington, D.C., 1963), 13, 207. U.S. Bureau of the Census, *U.S. Censuses of Population and Housing: 1960. Census Tracts. Final Report PHC (1)–104, Part 1* (Washington, D.C., 1962), 752. Note: The borough of Richmond (Staten Island) had slightly higher rates of home ownership than Queens but the population was roughly one-tenth the size.

51   Queens locations: Diner Master List. Of the forty-eight New York City openings announced in industry trade journals, thirty were located in Queens, six in the Bronx, five in Manhattan, four in Brooklyn, and three in Staten Island.

51   Queens neighborhoods: U.S. Bureau of the Census, *U.S. Censuses of Population and Housing: 1960. Census Tracts. Final Report PHC (1)–104, Part 1* (Washington, D.C., 1962), 23, 133–181, 973–997.

51–52 Pulaski Highway: U.S. Bureau of the Census, *U.S. Census of Population. 1950. Vol. III: Census Tract Statistics,* ch. 4 (Washington, D.C., 1952), 16–21, 35–39, 46–47. U.S. Bureau of the Census, *U.S. Census of Population and Housing: 1960. Census Tracts, Final Report PHC (1)–13* (Washington, D.C., 1962), 26–28, 40–41, 101, 113–114, 126–127, 151, 165–166, 174, 181–182.

52:    Irvington: U.S. Bureau of the Census, *U.S. Census of Population: 1950. Vol. II: Characteristics of the Population,* pt. 30, *New Jersey* (Washington, D.C., 1952), 36, 80. U.S. Bureau of the Census, *U.S. Census of Population: 1960. Vol. I: Characteristics of the Population,* pt. 32, *New Jersey* (Washington, D.C., 1963), 93, 198, 226, 254, 284.

52   Claremont Diner: U.S. Bureau of the Census, *U.S. Census of Population: 1960. Vol. I: Characteristics of the Population,* pt. 32, *New Jersey.* 232, 280. "They're Standing in Line for Hours at New Jersey's New Claremont Diner!" *Fountain, Luncheonette and Diner* 1 (November 1954), 15.

52   Hilltop Diner: U.S. Bureau of the Census, *U.S. Censuses of Population and Housing: 1960. Census Tracts. Final Report PHC (1)–13.* 26–28, 40–41, 101, 113–114, 126–127, 151, 165–166, 174, 181–182.

52   Rainbow Diner: U.S. Bureau of the Census, *U.S. Censuses of Population and Housing: 1960. Census Tracts. Final Report PHC (1)–104,* Pt. Two (Washington, D.C., 1962), 26, 31, 160, 165.

53   Florida: Rebecca Martin, "Once Around Florida," *The Diner* 7 (October 1948), 12–13. Lena Lencek and Gideon Bosker, *The Beach: A*

History of Paradise on Earth (New York: Viking Press, 1998), 241–245.

54   Godfrey Diner: "Godfrey Diner, A Showcase of Modern Food Service," 12.

54   "delicious meal": "Wednesday and Thursday. Michel's Cape Ann Diner Will Donate 10% to the G.H.S. football team for their Florida trip," press clipping, circa 1955, American Diner Museum.

54   Swingle: Albert S. Keshen, "A Diner Man's Diner," *Diner, Drive-In and Restaurant* 13 (January 1954), 11.

56   Diner signs: Gutman, *American Diner: Then and Now*, 173. The original "Eat Heavy" sign remains on display above the Tick Tock Diner, although the original building has long since been replaced.

56   "Space Age diner": Kullman Dining Car Company, "New Space Age Design" (brochure), circa 1960, Kullman archives.

56   Diner names: Diner Master List.

58   Nuclear families: *How Buying Habits Change*, 22. U.S. Bureau of the Census, *U.S. Census of Population: 1960. Subject Reports. Sources and Structure of Family Income*, Final Report PC(2)–4C (Washington, D.C.: Government Printing Office, 1964), 23–24.

60   Family dinners: "Make Your Meals a Family Affair," *Diner Drive-In*, 18 (February 1959), 17. "Diner Operators Meeting," *Diner Drive-In*, 15 (June 1956), 27.

61   "we had kiddie menus": Interview with Bill Noller, Beach Haven, New Jersey, August 11, 1982.

61   Herman Dight: "Diner Host of Western Pennsylvania," *Diner and Restaurant* 11 (November 1952), 18.

61   Peter Pan Diner: "Martindale's Peter Pan Diner," *Diner, Drive-In*, 16 (April 1957), 26–29.

61   Marketing family dining: Johnny Rogers, "Lido Diner Incorporates Latest in Design, Equipment and Food Service Methods," *Fountain, Luncheonette and Diner* 1 (April 1954), 13. "Enjoy Life! Eat Out More Often," *American Restaurant Magazine* 34 (July 1950), 43.

61   Little Chef Diner: "Enjoy Life! Eat Out More Often," *American Restaurant Magazine* 34 (July 1950), 43.

63   Working women: Mirra Komarovsky, "Working Wives and Mothers," *Modern Marriages and Family Living*, eds. Morris Fishbein and Ruby Jo Reeves Kennedy (New York: Oxford University Press,

1957), 275–276. U.S. Bureau of the Census, *U.S. Census of Population. 1950.* Vol. III: *Census Tract Statistics,* ch. 4, 16–21, 35–39, 46–47. U.S. Bureau of the Census, *U.S. Census of Population: 1950.* Vol. III: *Census Tracts Statistics,* ch. 42, 20–29, 75–98. U.S. Bureau of the Census, *U.S. Census of Population: 1950.* Vol. II: *Characteristics of the Population,* Pt. 30, *New Jersey,* 36, 80. U.S. Bureau of the Census, *U.S. Census of Population and Housing: 1960. Census Tracts, Final Report PHC (1)–13.* 26–28, 40–41, 101, 113–114, 126–127, 151, 165–166, 174, 181–182. U.S. Bureau of the Censuses, *U.S. Censuses of Population and Housing: 1960. Census Tracts, Final Report, PHC (1)–115.* 30–48, 252–270. U.S. Bureau of the Census, *U.S. Census of Population: 1960.* Vol. I: *Characteristics of the Population,* Pt. 32, *New Jersey,* 93, 198, 226, 254, 284.

64   Survey: "Why Do They Eat Out?" *American Restaurant Magazine* 43 (May 1959), 212.

64   Interview with Kathy Corbett, St. Louis, Missouri, June 21, 1995.

64   "special Sunday dinners": "Enjoy Life!—Eat Out More Often," *American Restaurant Magazine* 35 (July 1951), 49.

64   "Wives who cook": "Business Is Up 35% After Anniversary Promotion," *Diner, Drive-In* 18 (February 1959), 34.

65   Taxin's Diner: "How Taxins Raised Prices," *Diner, Drive-In* 17 (February 1958), 42–43.

65   Mari-Nay Diner: Johnny Rogers, "The Magic of the Mari-Nay Diner," *Fountain, Luncheonette and Diner* 1 (October 1954), 10.

65   Lido Diner: Rogers, "Lido Diner Incorporates Latest in Design, Equipment and Food Service Methods," 13.

65   "high hat": "How Taxins Raised Prices," 42–43.

66   Yaskell's Suburban Diner: "Dining Room and Delicatessen, A New Trend in Diner Operation," *Diner and Restaurant,* September 1952, 20–39.

67   Aldom's Diner: Interview with Earle Hersman, Lisbon, Ohio, July 24, 1995.

67   Hilltop Diner. Chip Silverman, *Diner Guys* (New York: Birch Lane Press, 1989), 29–30, 39.

68   Kullman diners: Kullman interview, January 5, 1983. "New Trends in Diners," *The Diner* 7 (August 1949), 14. Kullman Dining Car Company, "The Complete Story of the Dining Car" (sales

brochure), circa 1957, 5–14, Kullman archives. Kullman Dining Car Company, "New Space Age Design."

68   O'Mahony designs: "Needs of Operators Dictate Changes in Diner Design," *Diner and Counter Restaurant*, 9 (August 1950), 25.

69   Trends in house designs: Gwendolyn Wright, *Building the Dream: A Social History of Housing in America* (New York: Pantheon, 1981), 249–254. Clark, *The American Family Home*, 210–12. Gail Cooper, *Air Conditioning America: Engineering the Controlled Environment, 1900–1960* (Baltimore: Johns Hopkins University Press, 1998), 140–164.

69   "when the war ended": Zelin interview.

70   Waitresses in restaurants: Dorothy Sue Cobble, *Dishing It Out: Waitresses and Their Unions in the Twentieth Century* (Urbana: University of Illinois Press, 1991), 17–33.

70   "Women belong": "Completely Deluxe," *The Diner*, 6 (January 1947), 11.

70   Employers' assumptions: Cobble, *Dishing It Out*, 29–43.

71   Eunice Ramsey: Interview with Eunice Ramsey, Tastee Diner, Silver Spring, Maryland, August 5, 1993.

71   Surrogate mothers: Ramsey interview.

71   Jenny Bryant: Interview with Jenny Bryant, Tastee Diner, Bethesda, Maryland, August 5, 1993.

71   Testimonials: Paterson Vehicle Company, "Am I Happy!"(sales brochure), circa 1955, 5, American Diner Museum.

71   "better class": Valentine Manufacturing Inc., *Golden Opportunity for Your Golden Future* (sales brochure), circa late 1950s, 5, American Diner Museum.

73   Colonial and Western motifs: Gutman, *American Diner*, 176–182.

74   "we have a fight": "The Diner Goes to a Party," *The Diner* 5 (November 1946), 11.

74   "attractive salads": "Nutrition . . . A Public Demand," *The Diner*, July 1946, p. 6.

74   another article: "Now Is the Time for Promotion of Salads," *Diner and Counter Restaurant*, June 1950, p. 15.

74   Salad history: T. Sarah Peterson, *Acquired Taste: The French Origins of Modern Cooking* (Ithaca, N.Y.: Cornell University Press, 1994), 140–143.

75 New Ideal Diner: Telephone interview with George Englesson (owner of New Ideal Diner), Aberdeen, Maryland, May 20, 1994.

75 Mary-O Grill: "The Mary-O Grill: Showcase of Modern Equipment and Service," *Fountain, Luncheonette and Diner*, 2 (May 1955), 11.

75 Roland Michel: "Michel's Cape Ann Diner," press clipping, August 3, 1959, American Diner Museum.

75 Claremont Diner: "They're Standing in Line for Hours," 15.

75 Bailey interview.

75 Fanny Blentsen: Interview with Fanny Blentsen, Newport News, Virginia, August 6, 1993.

76–77 Hamburgers and hot dogs: David Gerard Hogan, *Selling 'em by the Sack: White Castle and the Creation of American Food* (New York: New York University Press, 1997), 32–33. John A. Jakle and Keith A. Sculle, *Fast Food: Roadside Restaurants in the Automobile Age* (Baltimore: Johns Hopkins University, 1999), 98–99, 163–165. The ethnic roots of the hamburger are less clear than those of the frankfurter. One theory among many holds that the "hamburg steak" was introduced to America by the steamers carrying German immigrants to the United States in the early nineteenth century. See Jakle and Sculle, *Fast Food*, 98–99.

77 Ethnic menu items: "Menu Exchange," *Diner, Drive-In*, 14 (September 1955), 26; 15 (May 1956), 44; 16 (March 1957), 29. Postcard, Meadowbrook Diner, 1954, photocopy displayed on wall of Connie's Soul Food Kitchen, Indianapolis, Ind.

77 On postwar pluralism: Olivier Zunz, *The American Century* (Chicago: University of Chicago Press, 1998).

78 Statistics on dining: Wharton School of Finance and Commerce, *Study of Consumer Expenditures, Incomes, and Savings*, Vol. III, Summary of Family Expenditures for Food, Beverages, and Tobacco (Philadelphia: University of Pennsylvania, 1956), 10–11, 48–54, 150–221. Wharton School of Finance and Commerce, *Study of Consumer Expenditures, Incomes, and Savings*, Vol. XII, Detailed Family Expenditures for Food, Beverages, and Tobacco (Philadelphia: University of Pennsylvania, 1957), 2–15. Bureau of Labor Statistics, *Consumer Expenditures and Income*, Report 237–93 (Washington, D.C.: U.S. Government Publication Office, 1966), supplement 2, 42–46. "Why Do They Eat Out?" 212.

79   White-collar diners: e.g, Town and Country Diner in Midland Park, New Jersey, and the White Diner in Greenwich, Connecticut.

79   Yonko: Yonko interview.

79   Zappone: Interview with Tony Zappone (owner Tony's Diner), Cleveland, Ohio, June 15, 1987.

79   New Ideal Diner: Waltz, "The Roadside Diners Are Rolling," 133.

69   Danza: Interview with Lenny Danza (owner Eat-Rite Diner), Maspeth, New York, January 3, 1983.

80   Cartoon: Robert Serbicki (artist), untitled cartoon, *Diner Drive-In*, 14 (October 1955), 46.

80   Ehrlich: Ehrlich, "The Diner Puts on Airs," 130.

81   Coffee: *The Diner* magazine, "An Objective Study of the Diner-Counter Service Restaurant Market," 7, Kullman archives. "Coffee Controversy," *The Diner*, 7 (October 1948), 25.

82   Market Diner: "'Truck Stop' in Manhattan," *Diner, Drive-In* 17 (March 1958), 37.

82   "wants no liquor": Paterson Vehicle Company, "Quality Diners That Make Excellent Profits."

82   Phil and Joe Roy: "Jet Diner with Rocket Service," *Fountain, Luncheonette and Diner* 1 (November 1954), 24–25.

82   Counter space: "Trends in Diner Construction," *Diner and Counter Restaurant*, 10 (August 1951), 28–30. DeRaffele interview.

82–83   Corbett: Corbett interview, p. 1.

83–84   Teenage trade: Albert S. Keshen, "Capturing the School Lunch Trade," *Diner, Drive-In and Restaurant* 13 (October 1954), 20. C. Thomas, "The Little Chickadees," *The Diner* 6 (August 1947), 8. "How the Triangle House Diner Quadrupled Sales," *Diner, Drive-In* 15 (September 1955), 22–23.

84   Levinson: Henry Scarupa, "Director by Default," *Baltimore Sun Magazine*, August 9, 1981, 15.

84   Doyle's Diner: "Two Peak Periods Pull 1,500 Checks at Doyle's Diner, Lodi, N.J.," *Fountain, Luncheonette and Diner* 1 (July-August 1954), 20–21.

84   Fischer: Interview with Eunice Fischer, Beach Haven, New Jersey, August 11, 1982.

85   Vonetes: U.S. Senate, *Hearings Before the Committee on Commerce, United States Senate, Eighty-Eighth Congress, First Session on S. 1732, A Bill to Eliminate Discrimination in Public Accommodations Affecting Interstate Commerce,* Serial 26 (Washington, D.C.: U.S. Government Printing Office, 1963), 1060–1063, 1081.

85–86   African-American market: Robert E. Weems, Jr., *Desegregating the Dollar: African American Consumerism in the Twentieth Century* (New York: New York University Press, 1998), 34, 72. Canadian market comparison: Raymond A. Bauer and Scott M. Cunningham, *Studies in the Negro Market* (Cambridge, Mass.: Market Sciences Institute, 1970), 2.

86   Sociological research: Joseph Greenblum and Leonard I. Pearlin, "Vertical Mobility and Prejudice: A Socio-Psychological Analysis," *Class, Status, and Power,* eds., Reinhard Bendix and Seymour Martin Lipset (New York, 1953), 480–491.

86   Shifting definitions of whiteness: David Roediger, *Towards the Abolition of Whiteness: Essays on Race, Politics, and Working Class History* (London: Verso Press, 1994), 181–198. Matthew Frye Jacobson, *Whiteness of a Different Color: European Immigrants and the Alchemy of Race* (Cambridge, Mass.: Harvard University Press, 1998), 91–135.

87   Vonetes: U.S. Senate, *Hearings Before the Committee on Commerce,* 1065–1066.

87   "pack a box lunch": "The Anger That Inflamed Route 40: Big Step Ahead," *Life* 51 (December 8, 1961), 37.

88   Blue Star Diner: Blentsen interview.

88   Johns-Mansville Diner: Interview with Margaret Hogarth (former manager of Johns-Manville Diner), Jarratt, Virginia, August 6, 1993.

89   Ramsey interview.

89   Meadowbrook Diner: Interview with Connie Smith (owner of Connie's Soul Food Kitchen, formerly Meadowbrook Diner), Indianapolis, August 20, 1993.

89   Discriminatory service in other cities: Catherine Raymond and George M. Houser, "CORE Techniques and Restaurant Discrimination," circa 1949, pp. 2–4, CORE Literature and Releases folder, Congress of Racial Equality, 1943–1971 box, Congress of Racial

Equality Collection, Document Group A, Swarthmore College Peace Collection, Swarthmore College, Swarthmore, Pennsylvania. On racial segregation in Pittsburgh diners see Butko, "Seen Any Good Diners Lately," 105.

89 Of the twenty-four diners that opened in Queens, New York, for which precise locations could be ascertained, only two were located in neighborhoods where the African-American population represented more than 1 percent of the total. In these two exceptional neighborhoods, African Americans constituted 6 and 7 percent of the total. Master Diner List. U.S. Bureau of the Census, *U.S. Census of Population: 1950, Volume III, Census Tract Statistics, Chapter 37* (Washington, D.C., 1952), 101–140.

89 "blacks would have been": Bailey interview.

89–90 Chuck Wagon Diner: Yonko interview. Telephone interview with Henry Bennett, former president of the NAACP, Gary branch, Gary, Indiana, May 25, 1994.

90 CORE accomplishments: August Meier and Elliot Rudwick, *CORE: A Study in the Civil Rights Movement, 1942–1968* (New York: Oxford University Press, 1973), 48–57, 92–93.

91 Highway 40: *Baltimore Afro-American*, December 19, 1961, 1, 8.

92 Restaurants in African-American neighborhoods: Victor H. Green, *The Negro Motorist Green Book* (Leonia, New Jersey: Victor H. Green Publishers, 1950). Allan Pred, "Business Thoroughfares as Expressions of Urban Negro Culture," *Economic Geography* 39 (July 1963), 217–233.

92 Competition from chains: Joan Oleck, "A Diner Odyssey," *Worcester Sunday Telegram*, June 27, 1976, 9.

93 Harvey House: Langdon, *Orange Roofs, Golden Arches*, 6–8. "Harvey Company Will Operate Illinois Tollway Restaurants," *Diner, Drive-In* 17 (February 1958), 76.

93–94 Howard Johnson's: Warren Belasco, "Toward a Culinary Common Denominator: The Rise of Howard Johnson's, 1925–1940," *Journal of American Culture* 2 (Fall 1979), 503–518. Langdon, *Orange Roofs, Golden Arches*, 46–55. "Howard D. Johnson," *American Restaurant Magazine* 42 (June 1958), 100. John A. Jakle and Keith A. Sculle, *Fast Food: Roadside Restaurants in the Automobile Age* (Baltimore: Johns Hopkins University Press, 1999), 73–75.

94–95   California coffee shops: Langdon, *Orange Roofs, Golden Arches*, 113–129. Alan Hess, *Googie: Fifties Coffee Shop Architecture* (San Francisco: Chronicle Books, 1985). Charles Bernstein, *Sambo's: Only a Fraction of the Action, The Inside Story of a Restaurant Empire's Rise and Fall* (Burbank, Calif.: National Literary Guild, 1984), 9, 16–17, 194.

95   Drive-In Diner: Advertisement, *Fountain, Luncheonette and Diner* 2 (January 1955), 23.

95   Wall paneling: "Across the Counter," *Diner, Drive-In and Restaurant*, 12 (May 1953), 22; 13 (April 1954), 34; *Diner, Drive-In*, 15 (June 1956), 60; 16 (May 1957), 72.

95   Fodero: Fodero interview.

95–97   McDonald's: John F. Love, *McDonald's: Behind the Arches* (Toronto: Bantam Books, 1986), 12–20, 163–166, 188–203, 216–224. Ray Kroc, with Robert Anderson, *Grinding It Out: The Making of McDonald's* (Chicago: Contemporary Books, 1977), 6–13. Hogan, *Selling 'em by the Sack*, 147. Max Boas and Steve Chain, *Big Mac: The Unauthorized Story of McDonald's* (New York: E.P. Dutton, 1976), 115–116. Jakle and Sculle, *Fast Food*, 139–162.

98   Burger King: James W. McLamore, *The Burger King: Jim McLamore and the Building of an Empire* (New York: McGraw-Hill, 1998), 15–18, 59–62.

99   Fast-food statistics: Robert L. Emerson, *Fast Food: The Endless Shakeout* (New York: Chain Store Publishing, 1979), 166. Mark C. Sawtelle, "Diner," *Historic Preservation* 31 (September/October 1979), 35.

99   Advertising budgets: Love, *McDonald's: Behind the Arches*, 311. McLamore, *The Burger King*, 183.

100   McDonald's training: Boas and Chain, *Big Mac*, 65–80.

101   Tastee Diner: Interview with May Keeney (waitress, Tastee Diner), Laurel, Maryland, August 1982.

101   Dean's Diner: Interview with Darrell Dean (proprietor of Dean's Diner), Blairsville, Pennsylvania, September 10, 1987.

101   Komondorea: Interview with Bill Komondorea (owner, Calli and Bill's Diner), Newburgh, New York, December 28, 1984.

101   Jim Aldom: Hersman interview.

101–102   Flamboyant diners and declining business: Gutman, *American Diner*, 182–183. Mark C. Sawtelle, "Diner," *Historic Preservation* 31 (September/October 1979), 31–35. Rick Van Warner, "Diners: Still Going Strong," *Metro Foodservice* 23 (August 15, 1986), 21–29. "Colonials and Statues: Diner-Maker Ends Era," *New York Times*, October 29, 1990, p. B1.

104   Sambo's: Bernstein, *Sambo's: Only a Fraction of the Action*, 94–95.

104   Denny's: Howard Kohn, "Service with a Sneer," *New York Times Magazine* (November 6, 1994), 42–47, 58, 78, 81.

Chapter 2: Bowling Alleys

108   Slocum: Bill Slocum, "Togetherness Hits the Bowling Alleys," February 10, 1961, press clipping, Sam Tarlowe scrapbook, International Bowling Museum and Hall of Fame, St. Louis, Missouri (henceforth cited as IBM/HF).

108   1946 study: Paul Gold, "Bowling Is No. 2," *Bowling* 15 (October 1948), 14.

108   1960s statistics: AMF Corporation, *Editor's Bowling Guide, 1964–1965* (Westbury, N.Y., 1964), 2–5, AMF Public Relations box, IBM/HF. Cunningham & Walsh, "The Size and Character of the Market for Bowling," July 1960, 25, AMF Collection, IBM/HF.

110   European antecedents: Ulrich Troubetzkoy, "Bowls and Skittles," *Virginia Cavalcade* 9 (Spring 1960), 11–12.

111   German-American bowling: Herman Weiskopf, *The Perfect Game: The World of Bowling* (Englewood Cliffs, N.J.: Rutledge Books, 1978), 37–38. Mort Luby, Jr., "The History of Bowling," *Bowlers Journal* 70 (November 1983), 114.

111   Elite bowling: Foster Rhea Dulles, *A History of Recreation: America Learns to Play* (New York: Appleton-Century Crofts, 1960), 150. Dale A. Somers, *The Rise of Sports in New Orleans, 1850–1900* (Baton Rouge: Louisiana State University Press, 1972), 62–65. Luby, "History of Bowling," 104–106.

112   Brunswick: Rick Kogan, *Brunswick: The Story of an American Company from 1845 to 1985* (Skokie: Brunswick Corporation, 1985), 22–23.

112–113   Tavern bowling: Weiskopf, *Perfect Game*, 50. Pat McDonough, "Honored," *Bowling* 12 (September 1945), 7.

113   Toledo survey: John J. Phelan, *Pool, Billiards, and Bowling Alleys as a Phase of Commercialized Amusements in Toledo, Ohio* (Toledo: Little Book Press, 1919), 32–39, 152–163.

113   Thumm: Luby, "History of Bowling," 108.

114   Alley construction: Jim Dressel, "Evolution of the Industry," *Bowlers Journal* 70 (November 1983), 107.

115–116   Gambling: Weiskopf, *Perfect Game*, 50.

115   Regulations: Phelan, *Pool, Billiards, and Bowling Alleys*, 119–133.

115   New immigrants: Steven A. Riess, *City Games: The Evolution of American Society and the Rise of Sports* (Urbana: University of Illinois Press, 1989), 81.

115–116   Toledo survey: Phelan, *Pool, Billiards, and Bowling Alleys*, 12, 22–23.

116   Prohibition: John L. Smith, "New Season Underway," *Bowling Magazine* 19 (September 1952), 9.

116   Chicago statistic: Riess, *City Games*, 77.

117   "followers of this game": Brunswick Balke Collender Company, "Bowling—America's Passport to Health," (booklet), circa 1923, 8, Instruction; Brunswick; "Learn How to Bowl Better" folder, Brunswick Miscellaneous Items box, IBM/HF.

117   recreation centers: Brunswick Balke Collender Company, "The Bowling Catalog," circa 1920, 20–21, Catalog: Brunswick c.1920 folder, Brunswick Catalogs box, IBM/HF.

117   Early women bowlers: "Montana Bowler for 33 Years," *Woman Bowler* 24 (December 1959), 10. "The Ladies Hit the Lanes," *Woman Bowler* 23 (November 1959), 10.

117–118   Aesthetic modifications: Brunswick Balke Collender Company, "The Bowling Catalog," 27. Ernest Reiss, "Modernization Is Keynote of Tenpin Palace Decoration," *National Bowlers Journal and Billiard Revue* 28 (July-August 1941), 21.

118   Whelanite: Brunswick Balke Collender Company, "Brunswick Billiard and Bowling Supply Catalog," (1929), 138, Catalog: Brunswick 1928 folder, Brunswick Catalogs box, IBM/HF.

118   "no place for a woman": Bowling Proprietors' Association of America, Inc., "Free Lessons in Bowling," circa 1935, no page numbers, Instruction; Brunswick; "Learn How to Bowl Better" folder, Brunswick Miscellaneous Items box, IBM/HF.

118   WIBC statistics: Alma Noel Spring, *History of the Women's International Bowling Congress, Inc.* (1947), 42. Weiskopf, *Perfect Game*, 57. "Women's Classic Expects 1500 Teams," *National Bowlers Journal and Billiard Revue* 27 (January 1940), 22. Ben Hochstadter, "At Home with the W.I.B.C.," *Woman Bowler* 24 (November 1960), 6.

118   predominance of men: Harold Johnson, "Bowling Accelerates Expansion Rate," *National Bowlers Journal and Billiard Revue* 29 (April 1942), 25.

119   Marino: Weiskopf, *Perfect Game*, 218–221. Luby, "History of Bowling," 116.

120   Varipapa: Pat Rorre, "Amazing Andy Varipapa," *National Bowlers Journal and Recreation Age* 23 (March 1937), 20–21. "Andy Varipapa," *Bowling Magazine* 17 (June 1951), 6–7, 26. Weiskopf, *Perfect Game*, 64. "Bowling: Handy Andy," *Newsweek* 28 (December 23, 1946), 78.

121   Bowling costs: "Hitting the Headpin," *Detroit Free Press*, January 11, 1942, press clipping, Detroit scrapbook, Bowling Hall of Fame. National Billiard Supply Company advertisement, *The National Bowlers Journal and Billiard Revue* 28 (November 1941), 1.

122   Ward: Bill Franklin, "Walter Ward," *Bowling Magazine* 19 (February 1952), 10–11.

122   Ostroski: "Swoyerville Socker," *Bowling Magazine* 18 (July 1952), 8–9.

122   Benkovic: Eli Whitney, "Benny the Blaster," *Bowling Magazine* 18 (November 1951), 8.

122–123   Industrial leagues: The Brunswick Balke Collender Company, "Promoting, Operating and Managing Your Bowling Business" (1940), 33–34, Brunswick Miscellaneous Materials box, IBM/HF. Duke Hutchinson, "Declares Bowling Bigger Than Ever," *National Bowlers Journal and Billiard Review* 28 (October 1941), 17. "266 Quintets Compete in Douglas Aircraft League," *National Bowlers Journal and Billiard Revue* 29 (April 1942), 38. "Sport Center," *Cleveland Kegler*, April 22, 1941, 10. "Sport Center," *Cleveland Kegler*, April 29, 1941, 16. "St. Clair-Ontario," *Cleveland Kegler*, November 25, 1941, 21. M.G.M., "St. Clair-Ontario," *Cleveland Kegler*, December 2, 1941, 14.

123   Curtiss-Wright: Marie J. Wigginton, "The Curtiss-Wright Colum-
        bus, O., Bomber Plant, Largest Women's Commercial League in
        the U.S.," *Woman Bowler* 8 (November 1943), 10–11.

123   60 percent: Minutes of National Bowling Council Meeting, July
        18–19, 1944, National Bowling Council Minutes, vol. 2, 40,
        IBM/HF.

124   "once the game": "From the Editor's Desk," *Woman Bowler* 8 (No-
        vember 1943), 1.

124   "damned": "From the Editor's Desk," *Woman Bowler* 9 (November
        1944), 1.

124   labor shortage: "Boys in Demand," *Business Week*, December 25,
        1943, 44–48.

124   Chester House: *Bowling News*, February 10, 1945, 1.

124   "with all the money": Joe Petroski, "Joe Petroski, Speaking for Al-
        ley Owners Says Tenpin Business All Not 'Bed of Roses'; Have
        Tried Very Best," *Dorp Sporting News*, August 14, 1946, 6.

124–125 military bowling: Smith, "New Season Underway," 9. Kogan,
        Brunswick, 57. John Walter, "4,000,000 New Bowlers," *Detroit News*,
        September 7, 1943, press clipping, Detroit scrapbook, Bowling
        Hall of Fame. Paul Gardner, "Queens of the Kingpins," *Woman
        Bowler* 10 (April 1946), 21.

126   Corporate bowling programs: Brunswick Balke Collender, *Promot-
        ing, Operating, and Managing Your Bowling Business*, 34. Val Deisenroth,
        "Fashion—Stein Bloch: A Case History of Successful Industrial
        Bowling," *Bowling* 13 (September 1946), 15. "America Bowls," *Bowl-
        ing Magazine* 16 (September 1949), 15.

126   "no bowlers ever turn": "Communism vs. Bowling," *Bowling News*, 10
        (September 15, 1947), 4.

126   Industrial league statistic: Minutes of National Bowling Council
        Meeting, November 9, 1954, National Bowling Council Minutes,
        vol 2, 433.

127   Cash prizes: Advertisement, *Classic Bowling League of Chicago, Official
        Schedule, Souvenir Program, 1946–1947* (1946), 60, Program: Schedule
        1946–47 Classic Bowling League of Chicago folder, Classic Bowl-
        ing Association Miscellaneous Items box, IBM/HF. Advertisement,
        *Classic Bowling League of Chicago, Official Schedule, Souvenir Program,
        1950–1951* (1950), 15, Program; Classic Bowling League;

195–1951; Chicago folder, Chicago Bowling Association, Miscellaneous Items box, IBM/HF.

127   State Farm: "State Farm Insurance League," *Woman Bowler* 14 (March 1950), 21.

129   Schenectady: "Sch'dy Bowling Association Keglers Protest Price Increase; League, Open Bowling Banned," *Dorp Sporting News*, August 28, 1946, 1, 6.

129   "Bowling in this town": Pin Spotter, "Bowling Headlines," *Dorp Sporting News*, September 25, 1946, 8.

129   "I can also realize": Pinspotter, "What Price Bowling?" *Dorp Sporting News*, August 14, 1946, 7.

129   labor and material shortages: "Bowling, How to Score It," *Dorp Sporting News*, January 16, 1946, 2.

129–130   business conditions: Joe Petroski, "Joe Petroski, Speaking for Alley Owners Says Tenpin Business All Not 'Bed of Roses'; Have Tried Very Best," *Dorp Sporting News*, August 14, 1946, 6. "Bowling, How to Score It," *Dorp Sporting News*, January 30, 1946, 7. "Cleveland Bowling Association Sees Record-Breaking Year," *Cleveland Kegler*, September 17, 1946, 1. Minutes of National Bowling Council meeting, July 8, 9, 1947, National Bowling Council Minutes, vol. 1, 78.

130   open play: "New BPAA Officers," *Bowling Magazine* 18 (August 1951), 12. Minutes of National Bowling Council meeting, November 13, 14, 1952, National Bowling Council Minutes, vol. 2, 310.

131   pinboy earnings: American Bowling Congress, Research Department, report on pinsetter wages and bowling fees, circa 1951, AMF Public Relations box, IBM/HF. Minutes of National Bowling Council Meeting, September 27, 1950, National Bowling Council Minutes, vol. 2, 252. Minutes of National Bowling Council Meeting, November 14, 15, 1950, National Bowling Council Minutes, vol. 2, 262. Minutes of National Bowling Council Meeting, July 14, 1953, National Bowling Council Minutes, vol. 2, 378. U.S. Department of Labor, Bureau of Labor Standards, *The Boy Behind the Pins: A Report on Pinsetters in Bowling Alleys*, Bulletin 170 (Washington, D.C.: U.S. Government Printing Office, 1953), 7.

131   gratuities: Minutes of National Bowling Council meeting, November 14, 1944, National Bowling Council Minutes, vol. 1, 20–21.

131   picket: Ed G. Lawler, vice-president, Eastern Bowling Proprietors Association (New York) to Proprietors, January 29, 1948, Letter: Eastern Bowling Proprietors Association, Inc., 1948, About Strike by Building Service Employees folder, Bowling Proprietors of America, Miscellaneous Items Box, IBM/HF.

132   pinboy earnings: U.S. Department of Labor, Bureau of Labor Standards, *The Boy Behind the Pins: A Report on Pinsetters in Bowling Alleys*, Bulletin 170 (Washington, D.C.: U.S. Government Printing Office, 1953), 17.

132   pinsetter tasks: Brunswick Balke Collender Company, "The Catalog," 18.

133   injuries: Kate Clugston, "When Pin-Setters Are Children" (abbreviated version) *Journal of Home Economics* 37 (March 1945), 170. U.S. Department of Labor, Bureau of Labor Standards, *The Boy Behind the Pins*, 9.

133   additional duties: John Walter, "Proprietor with Ideas," *National Bowlers Journal and Billiard Revue* 37 (December 1950), 92. Brunswick Balke Collender Company, "Promoting, Operating, and Managing Your Bowling Business," 77–78.

133–134   labor conditions and pinboy recruitment: U.S. Department of Labor, Bureau of Labor Standards, *The Boy Behind the Pins*, 8, 18.

134   child labor laws: Minutes of National Bowling Council Meeting, July 14, 1953, National Bowling Council Minutes, vol. 2, 388.

134–135   underage pinsetters: Minutes of National Bowling Council meeting, November 11, 12, 1947, National Bowling Council Minutes, vol. 1, 84. U.S. Department of Labor, Bureau of Labor Standards, *Boy Behind the Pins*, 20–22, 40–45. Minutes of National Bowling Council meeting, February 11, 12, 1947, National Bowling Council Minutes, vol. 1, 73.

135   Subterfuge: U.S. Department of Labor, Bureau of Labor Standards, *Boy Behind the Pins*, 14.

135   1953 report: U.S. Department of Labor, Bureau of Labor Standards, *Boy Behind the Pins*, 17.

135   Corralling idle bodies: U.S. Department of Labor, Bureau of Labor
        Standards, *Boy Behind the Pins*, 7.

136   deliberately hitting pinboys: Telephone interview with Frank
        Keats (former pinsetter and past president of the Bowling Writers
        Association of America), Los Angeles, California, May 18, 1998.

136   "Bowlers fiddle": Robert B. Mohr, "Arizona Proprietor Expresses
        His Views on the Pin-Boy Situation," *Woman Bowler* 9 (July-August
        1945), 6.

136   pinboy harassment: Luby, "History of Bowling," 122.

137   unfavorable publicity: U.S. Department of Labor, Bureau of Labor
        Standards, *Boy Behind the Pins*, 3–4. Dickson Hartwell, "America's
        Bruised and Beaten Children," *Liberty Magazine*, July 5, 1947, 71.

138   "older men": U.S. Department of Labor, Bureau of Labor Stan-
        dards, *Boy Behind the Pins*, 35.

138   Canelli: Minutes of National Bowling Council Meeting, July 14,
        1953, National Bowling Council Minutes, vol. 2, 388.

138   BPAA: Minutes of National Bowling Council Meeting, November
        10, 1953, National Bowling Council Minutes, vol. 2, 399.

138   Progressive proprietors: "Baird Recreation Pin-Setter Scholarship
        to John Schuck," *National Bowlers Journal and Billiard Revue* 40 (August
        1953), 2. Luby, "History of Bowling," 123. Bruce Pluckhahn, "Ten-
        pin Upstart," *Bowling Magazine* 24 (April 1958), 20–21, 42–43.

139   "It makes no difference": Brunswick Balke Collender Company,
        "The Bowling Catalog," circa 1920, 17, Catalog: Brunswick c.1920
        folder, Brunswick Catalogs box, IBM/HF.

139   masking devices: U.S. Department of Labor, Bureau of Labor Stan-
        dards, *Boy Behind the Pins*, 9. Advertisement, *National Bowlers Journal
        and Billiard Revue* 37 (February 1950), 41.

140   "it can be operated": Brunswick Balke Collender Company, "Bowl-
        ing Catalog," 22. Brunswick Balke Collender Company, "Brunswick
        Billiard and Bowling Supply Catalog," (1929), 170–72, Catalog:
        Brunswick 1928 folder, Brunswick Catalogs box, IBM/HF.

140   automatic ball lift: Advertisement, *National Bowlers Journal and Bil-
        liard Revue* 37 (February 1950), back cover. Advertisement, *National
        Bowlers Journal and Billiard Revue* 39 (June 1952), back cover.

141   AMF Pinspotter: "Pin Boy's Poison," *Life*, 32 (January 14, 1952), 50.

142   Brunswick Pinsetter: Luby, "History of Bowling," 122. Kogan, *Brunswick*, 60–67. "What Mama Wants," *New Yorker*, 35 (September 5, 1959), 23–24.

142   Foul detector: Advertisement, *Woman Bowler* 20 (February 1956), back cover.

142   AMF Pindicator: Advertisement, *Woman Bowler* 21 (December 1956), back cover.

143   Hand dryer: Advertisement, *Woman Bowler* 20 (January 1956), inside front cover.

143   Underlane ball return: AMF Corporation, Promotional flyer, 1956, Non-Catalog material folder 91–15, AMF Pinspotter Box, IBM/HF. Advertisement, *Cleveland Kegler*, October 28, 1958, 3.

143   Adoption of electronic and mechanical devices: "'Round the Clock Bowling," *Industrial Sports and Recreation* 17 (April 1956), 15–16. Arthur W. Baum, "Bowling Is Booming," *Saturday Evening Post* 232 (January 16, 1960), 76.

143   Industry leaders on effects of automated pinsetting: Minutes of National Bowling Council Meeting, November 10, 1953, National Bowling Council Minutes, vol. 2, 398, 402. "Trade Talk," *National Bowlers Journal and Billiard Revue* 42 (December 1955), 93. Minutes of National Bowling Council meeting, February 3, 1959, National Bowling Council Minutes, Vol. 3, Part 2, 6.

145   Jack Garay: Jack Garay to the editor, *Cleveland Kegler*, April 7, 1959, 2.

145   "high scores": Don Snyder, "West Coast Pin Pointer," *National Bowlers Journal and Billiard Revue* 41 (April 1954), 21.

145   "to bowl more games": Advertisement, *National Bowlers Journal and Billiard Revue* 39 (December 1952), inside cover.

146   "More and more enthusiastic bowlers": Advertisement, *National Bowlers Journal and Billiard Revue* 39 (March 1953), inside front cover.

146   "I don't care": Advertisement, *Cleveland Kegler*, October 28, 1958, 3.

146   Initial reactions to automated pinsetters: Pat McDonough, "Metropolitan Merry-Go-Round," *National Bowlers Journal and Billiard Revue* 43 (October 1956), 35.

147   Pinsetter financing: Minutes of National Bowling Council Meeting, November 10, 1953, National Bowling Council Minutes, vol.

2, 398. Seymour Freedgood, "Brunswick's Automatic Money-Maker," *Fortune* 60 (November 1959), 157.

147 "Pin-boy ulcers": Advertisement for AMF Pinspotters, *National Bowlers Journal and Billiard Revue* 44 (January 1957), inside front cover.

147 Jewel City: "Automatic Pin Boy," *Time*, 62 (November 16, 1953), 98.

147 Airport Bowl: "Trade Talk," *National Bowlers Journal and Billiard Revue* 43 (November 1956), 30–31.

147 "The AMF machine": Advertisement, *Cleveland Kegler*, August 10, 1954, 74.

148 Les Miller: AMF Pinspotters, Inc., "101 Bowling Promotion Ideas," circa 1958, 36.

149 "At 2 a.m.": "2 More Houses Become 'Automatic,'" *Chicago Bowler*, October 31, 1953, 1.

149 Amherst Recreation: "Pinboys Eliminated As Robots Move in on Bowling Alleys," *Buffalo Evening News*, September 17, 1952, press clipping in AMF Company brochure, "How Buffalo acclaimed the Hometown Machine that made good!" (circa 1952), Negative, paper: 1952 Brochure, AMF Automatic Pinspotter, 91–15–4 folder, American Machine Foundry 1st Automatic Pinspotter box, IBM/HF.

149 Bowl-O-Drome: "Round the Clock Bowling," *Industrial Sports and Recreation*, 17 (April 1956), 15.

150 pinboy "apprenticeship": Editorial, *National Bowlers Journal and Billiard Revue* 43 (June-July 1956), 3, 16.

151 Television: Steve Cruchon, "TV Bowling Comes of Age," *Bowling Magazine* 23 (September 1956), 20–22. "The Surging Urge to Bowl . . . And Why," *Newsweek* 52 (September 15, 1958), 96. Luby, "The History of Bowling," 129.

151 Bowling accessories for women and children: Brunswick Corporation, "Balls, Bags, Shoes and Accessories" (catalog), 1961, Catalog; Brunswick; 1961–1962; "Balls, Bags, Shoes, and Accessories," folder, Brunswick Catalogs box, IBM/HF. Brunswick-Balke-Collender Company, *Brunswick Catalog*, circa 1950, n.p., Catalog: Brunswick c. 1950 folder, Brunswick Catalogs box, IBM/HF. "Trade Talk," *National Bowlers Journal and Billiard Revue* 44 (November 1957), 30.

151   "Bowl Close to Home": Advertisement, *Cleveland Kegler*, April 28, 1959, 7.

151   Ben Mason: AMF Pinspotters, Inc., "101 Bowling Promotion Ideas," 14.

152   Frank Caprise: Bruce Pluckhahn, "Headquarters for the Younger Set," *Bowling Magazine* 22 (November 1955), 26–27.

153   New bowling centers: Arthur W. Baum, "Bowling Is Booming," *Saturday Evening Post* 232 (January 16, 1960), 76. "And There's a New Look, Too!" *Bowling Magazine* 23 (September 1956), 23–25. "A New Luxury World of Bowling," *Life* 44 (March 17, 1958), 128–135.

154   Powers, Daly, and DeRosa: Mort Luby, Jr. "Powers, Daly & DeRosa," *National Bowlers Journal and Billiard Review* (September 1962), 32–50. Telephone interview with Pat DeRosa, Long Beach, California, May 26, 1998. Luby, "History of Bowling," 124.

156   Mages Sporting Goods Company: "Mages Opens First of Pin Centers," *Chicago Bowler*, August 22, 1959, 7.

156   "Isn't it a lot nicer": "I'd Like to Know," *Woman Bowler* 23 (September 1959), 9.

157   "the people's country clubs": "The Social Whirl of Ladies' Bowling," *Life* 49 (December 12, 1960), 101.

157   "country club for the public": Evan Jones, "Bowling Makes a Social Strike," *New York Times Magazine*, March 30, 1958, 36.

157   Holiday Bowl: "Holiday Bowl Heralds New Era in Super Recreation Centers," *Chicago Bowler*, August 8, 1959. Advertisement, *Chicago Bowler*, August 15, 1959, 4.

157   Kansas City establishment: William Barry Furlong, "Big Strike— From 'Alley' to 'Supermarket,' *New York Times Magazine*, November 29, 1959, 42.

158   Fred Magee: Joseph P. Blank, "The Big Boom in Bowling," *Rotarian* 96 (March 1960), 33–34.

158   Northfield Lanes: Advertisement, *Cleveland Kegler*, August 5, 1958, 9.

158   Ranch Bowl: "Modern Living," *Time* 74 (September 28, 1959), 86.

159   Family togetherness: "A Man's Place Is in the Home," *McCall's* 81 (May 1954), 29–34. Barbara M. Kelly, *Expanding the American Dream: Building and Rebuilding Levittown* (Albany: State University of New

York Press, 1993), 70–72. Betty Friedan, *The Feminine Mystique* (New York: W. W. Norton, 1963), 48.

159 "welding family life": Don Snyder, "West Coast Pin Pointer," *National Bowlers Journal and Billiard Revue* 53 (February 1959), 53.

160 "The number one reason": "The Surging Urge to Bowl . . . and Why," *Newsweek*, 52 (September 15, 1958), 96.

160 Mr. Pinspotter: Advertisement, *Chicago Bowler*, March 9, 1957, 10.

161 AMF brochure: AMF Corporation, "Bowling Tips to Improve Your Score," 1958, 4–5, Instruction; Brunswick; "Learn How to Bowl Better," folder, Brunswick , Miscellaneous Items box, IBM/HF.

161 Alcohol consumption: Margaret "Mac" Salley, "Woes of Alley Manager As They Sound to Wife," *Bowling News*, November 10, 1943, 3.

162 Separate bar areas: Brunswick Balke Collender Company, "Promoting, Operating, and Managing Your Bowling Business," (1940), 31, Brunswick miscellaneous materials box, IBM/HF.

162 "revenue from a bar": "Business or Pleasure, Bowling Is the Greatest to Max Newman," *Chicago Bowler*, February 2, 1957, 10.

162 "We didn't want that type": William Barry Furlong, "Big Strike— From 'Alley' to 'Supermarket,'" 47.

162 All Star Bowl: Arthur W. Baum, "Bowling Is Booming," *Saturday Evening Post* 232 (January 16, 1960), 76.

164 Cloverleaf Lanes: AMF Pinspotters, Inc., "101 Bowling Promotion Ideas," 12.

164–165 Milton Raymer: "Teen-Age Keglers," *National Bowlers Journal and Billiard Revue* 34 (August 1947), 22–23. Minutes of National Bowling Council meeting, November 13–14, 1945, National Bowling Council Minutes, vol. 1, 41–42. Milton Raymer, "American Junior Bowling Congress Periodical Report for Months of November, December, and January, 1947–48," February 10–11, 1948, 1–2; Milton Raymer, "American Junior Bowling Congress Periodical Report for Months of February, March, April, May, and June, 1949," July 12–13, 1949, 1–2, American Junior Bowling Congress, Miscellaneous Items box, IBM/HF. "Raymer to Organize in Four States," *Prep Pin Patter*, 6 (October 1951), 2. "Raymer's Illinois Trip—The Best Ever!" *Prep Pin Patter*, 6 (November 1951), 1.

165   Walnut Bowl: AMF Pinspotters, Inc., "101 Bowling Promotion Ideas," 57.

165   Lloyd Bloom: AMF Pinspotters, Inc., "101 Bowling Promotion Ideas," circa 1958, 15.

165   Pike Lanes: The establishment, strategically situated in the Pike Plaza Shopping Center on Scenic Drive in north Little Rock, promised both fully automated bowling and "wholesome surroundings." Advertisement, *Arkansas Bowler*, April 22, 1961, 3, American Junior Bowling Congress, Miscellaneous Items box, IBM/HF.

166   Fairview Lanes: AMF Pinspotters, Inc., "101 Bowling Promotion Ideas," 6.

166   "Something for the Girls Program": "Trade Talk," *National Bowlers Journal and Billiard Revue* 46 (August 1959), 59.

166   Phil's Recreation: Helen Ochs, "What's New—That You Can Do," *Woman Bowler* 23 (December 1958), 11.

167   Modifications for youth: National Bowling Council, Minutes of Meeting, November 8, 1957, 12, vol. 3, part 1, IBM/HF.

167–168 Alternative leagues: AMF Pinspotters, Inc., "101 Bowling Promotion Ideas," 7. John E. Waters, "Grannies League," *Woman Bowler* 24 (March 1960), 19. Sue Hefflinger, "Nun's Tournament in Omaha," *Woman Bowler* 23 (November 1959), 3.

168   Housewives League: Francis Hile, "Don't Call Us Dishpan Girls," *Woman Bowler* 12 (January 1948), 16.

168   "I used to sit around": John E. Waters, "Grannies League," *Woman Bowler* 24 (March 1960), 19.

169   "bowlerette": "Introducing 'Table Talk,'" *Woman Bowler* 12 (December 1947), 9.

169   "When housework": Hile, "Don't Call Us Dishpan Girls," 16.

170   Women's Greater Houston League: "Houston Husbands Revolt," *Bowling* 13 (November 1946), 16.

170   LaVerne Haverly "Blonde Pin Bombshell Hits Town," *Chicago Bowler*, September 8, 1951, 1. "Bombshell Ends Busy Week Here," *Chicago Bowler*, September 22, 1951, 3.

170–171 Nurseries: Minutes of National Bowling Council meeting, July 11, 1958, National Bowling Council Minutes, vol. 3, 271. Sam Levine, "Sportshots," *Cleveland Kegler*, April 28, 1959, 2.

172   Closed-circuit televisions: Sam Levine, "Sportshots," *Cleveland Kegler*, March 3, 1959, 2. Joseph P. Blank, "The Big Boom in Bowling," *Rotarian* 96 (March 1960), 33. Arthur Baum, "Bowling Is Booming," *Saturday Evening Post* 232 (January 16, 1960), 76–77.

172   Shopping service: AMF Pinspotters, Inc., "101 Bowling Promotion Ideas," 23.

172   Laundry facilities: William Barry Furlong, "Big Strike—From 'Alley' to 'Supermarket,' " 42.

172   "it gives the housekeeper": Judge Madge Taggart, "Woman Judge Recommends Bowling," *Woman Bowler* 18 (December 1953), 24.

173   "hubby and wife": Byron Schoeman, "Ah, Women," *National Bowlers Journal and Billiard Revue* 43 (April 1957), 9.

173   Laverne Carter: "Blond Bombshell of Bowling," *Woman Bowler* 23 (November 1959), 26.

174   Dempsey: Gladys Dempsey, "'I Remember Mama,'" *Woman Bowler* 24 (December 1959), 15.

174   Paul Prescott: Advertisement, *Woman Bowler* 11 (July-August 1947), 9.

174–175   "Any outfit": Jane Moran, "A-B-C's of Good Bowling," *Woman Bowler* 24 (December 1959), 25.

176   "graceful movement": Advertisement, *Woman Bowler* 10 (September 1946), 11.

176   "Big League Bowler": Advertisement, *Woman Bowler* 19 (November 1955), 4–5.

176   "Ken-Master": Advertisement, *Woman Bowler* 13 (September 1949), 7.

176–177   Green Lantern banquet: Pin Spotter, "Bowling Headlines," *Dorp Sporting News*, March 6, 1946, 10.

177   "stag": "Around Town," *Dorp Sporting News*, March 27, 1946, 2.

177   Cascade Bowling Center: "Stars and Strikes," *Woman Bowler* 11 (November 1947), 19.

177   Little Rock proprietor: "Stars and Strikes," *Woman Bowler* 12 (November 1948), 23.

177   Mixed-doubles tournaments: Woodlawn Bowling Center: "Capitol District Mixed Doubles Handicap Tourney Prelude to Close of 1945–46 Kegling Campaign," *Dorp Sporting News*, March 20, 1946, 1. "Mixed Doubles Keglers to Split Lush Prize Melon," *Dorp Sport-*

ing News, April 24, 1946, 1, 10. Pat McDonough, "Metropolitan Merry-Go-Round," *National Bowlers Journal and Billiard Revue* 40 (October 1953), 23.

177–178   Cartoon: *National Bowlers Journal and Billiard Revue* 46 (February 1959), 44.

178   "Bowling with women": Jack Brown, Chicago, Illinois, "Opinion," *Bowling Magazine* 20 (June 1954), 30.

178   proper decorum: Irene Stuber, "Keglerette Kapers," *Cleveland Kegler*, December 30, 1958, 11. Don Snyder, "Mixed Bowling: For Better or for Worse," *National Bowlers Journal and Billiard Revue* 46 (October 1959), 36.

178   "she might find a new caddy": Don Snyder, "Mixed Bowling: For Better or for Worse?" 35–36.

178   All-Star Lanes: Arthur Baum, "Bowling Is Booming," 76–77.

178–179   1958 statistics: "House, Mixed Loops 65% of Membership," *Bowling Magazine* 24 (May 1958), 13.

179   "almost all wives": Don Snyder, "Mixed Bowling: For Better or for Worse?" 35.

180   laws prohibiting children from bowling alleys: New York City, for instance, had a law on its books until 1956 that prohibited any person under sixteen years of age from entering a public bowling alley. In 1948, Manistique, Michigan, passed similar legislation, and in 1950, Seattle debated doing the same. Minutes of National Bowling Council meeting, February 11, 12, 1947, National Bowling Council Minutes, vol. 1, 79. Minutes of National Bowling Council Meeting, July 12, 13, 1949, National Bowling Council Minutes, vol. 2, 206. Minutes of National Bowling Council Meeting, December 9, 1949, National Bowling Council Minutes, vol. 2, 220. Minutes of National Bowling Council Meeting, June 16, 1950, National Bowling Council Minutes, vol. 2, 240.

180   "a boundless offering": Georgia E. Veatch, "Bowlers Can Help," *Woman Bowler* 10 (November–December 1945), 7, 22.

180   Detroit and St. Louis: "Just Boys," *Bowling Magazine* 14 (June 1948), 9. Robert A Hereford, "Ex-Cop Bowls Over Boy Crime," *Bowling Magazine* 15 (March 1949), 19.

180   Raymer and Hoover: Minutes of the National Bowling Council Meeting, February 15, 1946, vol. 1, 48, IBM/HF. "Teen-Age

Keglers," *National Bowlers Journal and Billiard Review* 34 (August 1947), 23.

181   Modifications made on behalf of children: AMF Pinspotters, Inc., "101 Bowling Promotion Ideas," circa 1958, 22, 23. "A.J.B.C. Code," (c. 1950), American Junior Bowling Congress, Official Manual for Certified Instructors n.d., American Junior Bowling Congress Miscellaneous Items box, IBM/HF. Minutes of National Bowling Council Meeting, February 14, 15, 1951, National Bowling Council Minutes, vol. 2, 282–83.

181   J. Henry Aronson: "'Uncle Henry' to Thousands of 'Good' Youngsters . . . That's Henry J. Aronson," *Chicago Bowler*, March 2, 1957, 12.

181   Pepsi Cola program: Steve Cruchon, "Detroit Looks Ahead," *National Bowlers Journal and Billiard Revue* 41 (April 1954), 20.

181   "spend their time": Sally Tinner to Miss Kirkendall, "We Get Letters," *Woman Bowler* 24 (April 1960), 27.

182   Paul Harvey: "Harvey Praises Junior Bowling Over Radio Network," *Woman Bowler* 21 (November 1957), 24.

182   Youth bowling statistics: Minutes of National Bowling Council meeting, February 8, 1955, National Bowling Council Minutes, Vol. 3, 10. Minutes of National Bowling Council meeting, July 20, 1956, National Bowling Council Minutes, Vol. 3, 119. Minutes of National Bowling Council meeting, November 13, 1959, National Bowling Council Minutes, Vol. 3, part 2, 80. American Junior Bowling Congress, "American Junior Bowling Congress Official Manual for Certified Instructors," circa 1962, n.p., American Junior Bowling Congress Miscellaneous Items box, IBM/HF.

183   Family tournaments: "Jay-Cees Sponsor Father-Son Night," *Prep Pin Patter*, 5 (August 1951), 13. "400 In Kiwanis Nat'l Kid's Day Bowling School," *Prep Pin Patter*, 6 (November 1951), 13. Milton Rayner, "American Junior Bowling Congress Periodical Report for February, March, April, May, and June, 1956," July 20, 1956, 5, American Junior Bowling Congress Miscellaneous Items box, IBM/HF. "Win in Family Affair," *Prep Pin Patter*, 8 (April 1954), 9. "Bantam Wins in Father and Son Contest," *Prep Pin Patter*, 5 (October 1950), 10.

184   Brunswick estimates: Brunswick Company, "Junior's Insure America's Bowling Future" (press release), circa 1961, Press kit:
Brunswick 1961–1962 National Bowling Month, Learn to Bowl
folder, Brunswick Miscellaneous Items box, IBM/HF.

184   1960 Market Survey: Cunningham & Walsh, "The Size and Character of the Market for Bowling," 8–9.

184   Industry experts: "To His Majesty—The Proprietor," *Prep Pin Patter*,
5 (October 1950), 1.

185   Terry Moore's Bowling Alley: *St. Louis Argus*, June 8, 1962, 1.

185   Toledo survey: Phelan, *Pool, Billiards, and Bowling Alleys*, 22–23.

186–187   Segregated alleys: Minutes of National Bowling Council Meeting,
May 25, 1949, National Bowling Council Minutes, Vol. 2, 180.
"Big Boom in Bowling," *Ebony* 17 (September 1962), 36–38. J.
Elmer Reed, "The NBA History," circa 1973, Negro Bowling Asso-
ciation Collection, IBM/HF.

187   Organized labor: Minutes of National Bowling Council meeting,
February 11, 1947, National Bowling Council Minutes, vol. 1,
73–74. Minutes of National Bowling Council meeting, September
9, 10, 1948, National Bowling Council Minutes, Vol. 1, 125.

187   ABC resistance: Minutes of National Bowling Council meeting,
November 11, 12, 1947, National Bowling Council Minutes, vol.
1, 96. Minutes of National Bowling Council meeting, July 8, 9,
1947, National Bowling Council Minutes, Vol. 1, 71.

188   Legal assault: "Report on the ABC," *National Bowlers Journal and Billiard Revue* 37 (May 1950), 13. Minutes of National Bowling Congress meeting, February 10, 1949, National Bowling Congress
Minutes, vol. 1, 130. "ABC Banned From State Properties," press
clipping, circa 1949, Detroit scrapbook, IBM/HF.

188   Allen Supermarkets: Lafayette Allen, Jr. to editor, *The National
Bowlers Journal and Billiard Revue* 41 (June-July 1954), 48.

189   Interview with Margaret Lee (executive secretary/treasurer, National Bowling Association), New York City, New York, July 18
1996.

189   Terry Moore's Bowling Alley: *St. Louis Argus*, June 15, 1962, p. 1.

189   Orangeburg Massacre: Jack Bass and Jack Nelson, *The Orangeburg
Massacre* (Macon: Mercer University press, 1984).

191   Saturated markets: Minutes of National Bowling Council Meeting,
       April 2, 1959, vol. 3, part II, 32. Minutes of National Bowling
       Council Meeting, November 13, 1959, vol. 3, pt. II, 80.

191   Revival of business: John R. Kelly, *Leisure* (Englewood Cliffs, N.J.:
       Prentice-Hall, 1982), 323. "Success Story Looks for Sequel," *Busi-
       ness Week*, January 12, 1963, 57–58.

191   Demographic profile: Market Facts, "A National Study of the Mar-
       ket for Bowling," July 1964, 36, AMF Collection, IBM/HF. Cun-
       ningham and Walsh, Inc., "The Size and Character of the Market
       for Bowling," 25–27. AMF, *Editor's Bowling Guide, 1964–1965*, (West-
       bury, New York: 1964), 4, AMF Public Relations box, IBM/HF.

192   Nixon: Minutes of the National Bowling Council meeting, No-
       vember 14, 1958, National Bowling Council minutes, vol. 3, 293.

Chapter 3: Trailer Parks

196   Bucks County: E. Digby Baltzell, "Urbanization and Governmental
       Administration in Lower Bucks County," *Social Problems* 2 (July
       1954), 38–46. Don Hager, "Trailer Towns and Community Con-
       flict in Lower Bucks County," *Social Problems* 2 (July 1954), 33–38.
       Don Hager, "The Construction Worker and Trailer-Living in Bucks
       County, Pa., *Housing Research* (April 1954), 47–60. Barry Norman
       Checkoway, "Suburbanization and Community: Growth and Plan-
       ning in Postwar Lower Bucks County, Pennsylvania," (Ph.D. dis-
       sertation, University of Pennsylvania, 1977), 153–161. "Mor-
       risville Trailer Ban Under Study," *Trenton Sunday Times Advertiser*,
       Morrisville Area Study News Releases, vol. 3, MSC–612, box 1,
       Bucks County Historical Society, Bucks County, Pennsylvania.

197   Trailer ownership statistics: "Trailers: More and More Americans
       Call Them Home," *Newsweek* 40 (August 25, 1952), 70. Frank Foga-
       rty, "Trailer Parks: The Wheeled Suburbs," *Architectural Forum* 111
       (July 1959), 127.

199   Auto-camping: Warren James Belasco, *Americans on the Road: From
       Autocamp to Motel, 1910–1945* (Baltimore: Johns Hopkins University
       Press, 1997), 7–17.

200   Prefabricated units: Allan D. Wallis, *Wheel Estate: The Rise and Decline of Mobile Homes* (New York: Oxford University Press, 1991), 31–39, 50–57. David A. Thornburg, *Galloping Bungalows: The Rise and Demise of the American House Trailer* (Hamden, Conn.: Archon Books, 1991), 5–18.

200   Parking nuisance: Belasco, *Americans on the Road*, 74–75.

200   Campgrounds: Wallis, *Wheel Estate*, 39–41. Belasco, *Americans on the Road*, 75–79.

201   Sarasota: Jeff LaHurd, "The First Snowbirds Arrive," *Sarasota* 16 (April 1994), 98–99. "Sarasota Tourist Park" (brochure), circa 1937, personal collection of Pete Esthus, Sarasota Lock and Key, Sarasota, Florida. "Where Needles Flash in the Sun," *Christian Science Monitor*, February 13, 1943, magazine section, 14. Joseph Lawren, "Service Makes This Trailer Park Profitable for Sarasota, Fla." *American City* 60 (November 1945), 133.

201–202   Privately owned courts: Wallis, *Wheel Estate*, 40–45.

202   1930s trailer courts: American Municipal Association, *The House Trailer: Its Effect on State and Local Government*, Report No. 114 (Chicago: American Municipal Association, 1937), 18–19.

203   Bell Trailer City: Interview with George Simmons (former owner, Bell Trailer City), Huntington Beach, California, February 9, 1998.

203   Wartime boomtowns: Carl Abbott, *The New Urban America: Growth and Politics in Sunbelt Cities* (Chapel Hill: University of North Carolina Press, 1981), 98–119. Richard Polenberg, *War and Society: The United States, 1941–1945* (Philadelphia: J. B. Lippincott, 1972), 139–143.

203–204   Trailers as emergency housing: "Trailers: More and More Americans Call Them Home," *Newsweek* 40 (August 25, 1952), 70. Taylor W. Meloan, *Mobile Homes: The Growth and Business Practices of the Industry* (Homewood, Ill.: Richard D. Irwin, 1954), 13–16. Wallis, *Wheel Estate*, 83–93.

205   Restrictive legislation: American Municipal Association, *The House Trailer*, 2, 7, 19. William H. Ludlow, "Trailers and Cities," *American City* 51 (October 1936), 61–62. Wallis, *Wheel Estate*, 71–76.

205   Poor quality of wartime trailers and courts: Wallis, *Wheel Estate*, 85–93.

205–206   Schult Luxury Liner: Advertisement, *Trailer Topics* 9 (March 1945), back cover.

207–208   Huntington Beach: *Huntington Beach News*, February 24, 1949, p. 1. "Renters Object to Raise," *Trail-R-News* 7 (May 1949), 81.

209–210   Postwar housing shortage: Richard O. Davies, *Housing Reform During the Truman Administration* (Columbia, Missouri: University of Missouri Press, 1966), 40–41. "The Great Housing Shortage," *Life* 19 (December 17, 1945), 29. Kenneth Jackson, *Crabgrass Frontier: The Suburbanization of the United States* (New York: Oxford University Press, 1985), 232. U.S. Congress, *Hearings Before a Subcommittee of the Committee on Banking and Currency*, 79th Congress, 2nd session, on H.R. 4761, Veterans Emergency Housing Act of 1946 (Washington, D.C.: U.S. Government Printing Office, 1946), 9–10.

209–210   American preference for home ownership: Witold Rybczynski, *City Life* (New York: Simon & Schuster, 1995), 72–73, 82–83. John P. Dean, "The Ghosts of Home Ownership," *Journal of Social Issues* 7 (1951), 59–68. Margaret Marsh, *Suburban Lives* (New Brunswick: Rutgers University Press, 1990). Robert Fishman, *Bourgeois Utopias: The Rise and Fall of Suburbia* (New York: Basic Books, 1987), 126–133, 146–147. Kenneth T. Jackson, *Crabgrass Frontier* 76–81, 94–97.

210   Political commentary: Ronald Tobey, Charles Wetherell, and Jay Brigham, "Moving Out and Settling In: Residential Mobility, Home Owning, and the Public Enframing of Citizenship, 1921–1950," *American Historical Review* 95 (December 1990), 1416–1420.

211   Expert predictions of housing shortage duration: "The Great Housing Shortage," *Life* 19 (December 17, 1945), 27.

211   Stufts: Forrest H. Stufft, "A Trailer Can Really Be Home," *Trailer Topics Magazine* 13 (April 1949), 22–23.

212   Postwar trailer demand: Wallis, *Wheel Estate*, 94.

212   Veteran and student housing: Janice Fleming, "Ex-GI's Solve 'Where to-Live' Problem with Homey Trailers," *Trailer Topics* 10 (July 1946), 14. "Milwaukee Housing Lauds Trailers; Buy 400, Plan Parks," *Trailer Topics*, 11 (February 1947), 31. L. T. Bruhnke, "A Trailer Camp for Veterans," *Public Works* 79 (December 1948), 37, 41. Lyle E. Ashelford, "A New Kind of Joe," *Trailer Topics* 11 (August

1947), 8–9. Malcolm Hyatt, "Trailers Solve Rutgers Housing Problem," *Trailer Topics*, 10 (March 1946), 15.

213   1948 survey: Cecil L. Dunn and Company, Inc., *The Trailer Coach Industry and the Trailer Coach Residents of Southern California* (Los Angeles, 1948), 8–19.

214   Prefabricated housing: Simon Breines, "Prefabricated Houses," *Consumer Reports* 11 (May 1946), 126–129. Wallis, *Wheel Estate*, 103–109.

214   Levittown: Barbara M. Kelly, *Expanding the American Dream: Building and Rebuilding Levittown* (Albany: State University of New York Press, 1993), 21–33.

215   The Levitt formula applied elsewhere: Marc A. Weiss, *The Rise of the Community Builders: The American Real Estate Industry and Urban Land Planning* (New York: Columbia University Press, 1987), 147–158. Ned Eichler, *The Merchant Builders* (Cambridge, Mass.: MIT Press, 1982), 3–130. Greg Hise, "Home Building and Industrial Decentralization in Los Angeles: The Roots of the Postwar Urban Region," *Journal of Urban History* 19 (February 1993), 95–125. Cornelia F. Sexauer, "The Development of a St. Louis County Suburb: St. Ann, Missouri, 1942–1953," paper presented at the Organization of American Historians meeting, April 5, 1998, Indianapolis. U.S. Department of Commerce, Bureau of the Census, *Historical Statistics of the United States, Colonial Times to 1957* (Washington, D.C.: U.S. Government Printing Office, 1960), 393.

215   "indefinitely": Trailer Coach Association, *The West's 3rd Largest City . . . Is on Wheels* [1956], np.

216   Housing policies: Sylvie Murray, "Suburban Citizens: Domesticity and Community Politics in Queens, New York, 1945–1960" (Ph.D. dissertation, Yale University, 1994), 195–196.

216   Trailer prices: Harold Nash, "Veterans Housing," *Western Trailer Life* 7 (May 1948), 39, 43), Faith and Pat Terry, "At Home on the Trail," *Trailer Park Progress* 2 (September 1948), 6. "The State of the Industry," *Trailer Topics Magazine* 18 (January 1954), 26, 106. Robert H. Nulsen, *All About Parks for Mobile Homes and Trailers: A Guide for Selecting the Park That Is Best for You* (Beverly Hills: Trail-R-Club of America, 1960), 9–13.

218   Construction workers: "Who Uses Trailer Coaches?" *Trailer Life* 10 (July 1950), 26. Meloan, *Mobile Homes*, 22–28. "A Report on Trailer Living," *Consumer Reports* 21 (March 1956), 115.

218   Transient workers: Meloan, *Mobile Homes*, 18–20. Interview with Jose Palacios, Sarasota, Florida, December 27, 1997. Telephone interview with Bob Bross, St. Charles, Missouri, November 9, 1999.

218   Hanasaki family: Interview with Swanel Berra (Hanasaki), St. Louis, Missouri, July 3, 1997.

220   Trailer manufacturing trends: U.S. Bureau of the Census, "Trailer Coaches (Housing Types Only)," *Facts for Industry*, Series M45A–85 (November 5, 1945), 1. Meloan, *Mobile Homes*, 40, 44. Harold H. Martin, "Don't Call Them Trailer Trash," *Saturday Evening Post* 225 (August 2, 1952), 85.

221   Washrooms and toilets: "A Report on Trailer Living," *Consumer Reports* 21 (March 1956), 113–114. "The State of the Industry," *Trailer Topics Magazine* 18 (January 1954), 106.

222   12,000 parks: Wallis, *Wheel Estate*, 114.

222   Varieties of residential trailer courts: Marion C. Oaks, *Fell's Guide to Mobile Home Living: A Complete Guide to the Trailer Way of Life* (New York: Frederick Fell, 1965), 69.

224   Industry campaigns: Wallis, *Wheel Estate*, 173–174. "Twenty-Nine States Covered by TCMA Scout in Park Inspections," *Trailer Park Progress* 1 (August 1947), 1.

224   Favorable publicity: Morris Horton, "There's No Crack in Our Picture Window," *Trailer Topics* 21 (May 1957), 7, 74–6." Leona A. Proctor, "The Trailer Coach from a Feminine Viewpoint," *Trailer Topics* 13 (June 1949), 10, 74–76. "This 'n' That," *Trailer Topics* 15 (December 1951), 22.

224   Virtues of trailer living: Virginia Weddington, "Nomads in Luxury," *Trailer Life* 10 (July 1950), 14. Frank J. O'Neill, "There's a Hitch to It!" *Trailer Life* 10 (October 1950), 21. "2-Bedroom Millstone," *Trailer Life* 10 (March 1951), 4. Leslie J. Reagan, "Mobilehomes vs. Fixed Homes," *Trailer Topics* 23 (October 1959), 12, 74–80.

225   "more apt to roll": D. Warwick Brown, "The 'A' Bomb . . . and Trailer Safety," *Trailer Topics* 15 (March 1951), 23, 74–75.

227–228   Sally Skyline: "Meet Sally Skyline," *Trailer Topics* 22 (August 1958), 7–9.

228   Levitt: Kelly, *Rebuilding the American Dream*, 12, 58–87.

228–229   Trailer floor plans: Nulsen, *All About Parks for Mobile Homes and Trailers*, 16. Oaks, *Fell's Guide to Mobile Home Living*, 34. Advertisement for Skyline Mobile Homes, *Trailer Topics* 22 (June 1958), 18–19. "Choice of 48 Different Interiors in American," *Trailer Topics* 16 (November 1952), 48.

229   Sleeping arrangements: Doris K. Brundage, "Solution: Half-Crib," *Trailer Topics* 15 (May 1951), 15. "This 'n' That," *Trailer Topics* 15 (April 1951), 23. Oaks, *Fell's Guide to Mobile Home Living*, 27.

230   Virtues of cramped space: Oaks, *Fell's Guide to Mobile Home Living*, 147, 197. Fran Freeman, "Baby Goes to College," *Trailer Topics* 11 (October 1947), 50.

230   Benefits for women: Oaks, *Fell's Guide to Mobile Home Living*, 122.

231   Standards of cleanliness: Friedan, *The Feminine Mystique*, 233–257. Oaks, *Fell's Guide to Mobile Home Living*, 123.

232–233   Consumer possessions: Oaks, *Fell's Guide to Mobile Home Living*, 15–17. Announcement for *Trailer Topics'* "Mobilehomecoming," *Trailer Topics* 23 (November 1959), 46–47. "RCA Offers New Phonograph As Boon to Nation's Trailerites," *Trailer Topics* 13 (August 1949), 34. R. E. Conlee, "Aluminum Unlimited," *Trailer Topics* 15 (June 1951), 8–9. Howard E. Jackson, "Hi-Fi in the Mobilehome," *Trailer Topics* 23 (October 1959), 10. Robert Yaller, "In a Trailer with TV," *Trailer Topics* 14 (August 1950), 20, 65.

233   "Jimmy would love": Alexander C. Wellington, "Trailer Camp Slums," *Survey* 87 (October 1951), 420.

233   Kitchen appliances: "New 'Buy' Products," *Trailer Topics* 18 (April 1954), 24.

233   Space-saving techniques: "This 'n' That," *Trailer Topics* 19 (December 1955), 28. Charlotte Foster, "Baby in a House Trailer," *Trailer Topics* 10 (January 1946), 23. Oaks, *Fell's Guide to Mobile Home Living*, 26.

234   Patios, cabanas, and awnings: "Alum-O-Room Available for Trailers," *Trailer Topics* 13 (May 1949), 39. Nulsen, *All About Parks for Mobile Homes and Trailers*, 65–67.

235–236   Lawns: Marvin Mack, "Does Your Trailer Reflect Your Personality by Outside Appearance?" *Trailer Topics* 11 (July 1947), 9, 64. Bernice McMahon, "Buy for Perfection: Trailer Tree," *Trailer Life* 10 (December 1950), 11.

236   "couldn't dress up": Fran Freeman, "Baby Goes to College," *Trailer Topics* 11 (October 1947), 49.

236   "everybody is on exhibition": Alexander C. Wellington, "Trailer Camp Slums," *Survey* 87 (October 1951), 420.

237   Bross family: Telephone interview with Robert Bross, St. Charles, Missouri, June 9, 1997.

237   "I posted a set of rules": Don L. Weber, "Dogs, Trailers—and Park Operators," *Trailer Topics* 14 (February 1950), 22.

237–238   Pets: Marge Strickler, "Adults Only!" *Trailer Topics* 16 (May 1952), 87. Wanda MacKinnon, "Parks and Dogs," *Trailer Life* 10 (June 1951), 41–2, 50. Nulsen, *All About Parks for Mobile Homes and Trailers*, 79.

238   "If a park": Arthur S. Green, "Family Section—Or Not?" *Mobile Home Park Management* 9 (February 1961), 8.

239   Wiggins Trailer Court: "'Children Welcome' Sign Makes Trailer Court Popular," *Western Trailer Life* 6 (August 1946), 19.

239   "Our retired residents": Green, "Family Section—Or Not?" 8.

239   "mischief": "Greenlee Doesn't Like Trailers," *Trail-R-News* 12 (October 1953), 6–7.

240   "They break up everything": "Should You Take Children?" *Mobile Home Park Management* 8 (October 1959), 12.

240   "They think it is smart": "A Custodian Talks Back," *Trail-R-News* 8 (May 1950), 2.

240   "They give the children": Marge Strickler, "Adults Only!" *Trailer Topics* 16 (May 1952), 87.

240   Play areas and children's activities: Dorothy Orchard, "Trailer Children Are 'All-American' Kids," *Trailer Topics* 14 (January 1950), 60. Green, "Family Section—Or Not?" 8–9.

240   "It doesn't take long": "Should You Take Children?" 12.

240   Happy Hollow Trailer Park: Vollie Tripp, "'Lick the Problem—Not the Kids,' Says Olsen," *Trailer Park Management* 6 (June 1957), 20.

241   Adult-only parks: Robert Yaller, "Children Love Trailer Life," *Trailer Topics* 12 (October 1948), 56.

242   "It's a great comfort": Oaks, *Fell's Guide to Mobile Home Living*, 18.

242–243   Park regulations: Nulsen, *All About Parks for Mobile Homes and Trailers*, 73, 80, 82. April Mari Miles, "Women Look at Trailercoach Parks," *Trail-R-News* 7 (January 1949), 114.

243–244   Trailer park names: *Woodall's Trailer Park Directory* (Chicago: Trailer Travel Magazine, 1949).

244   Hurricane Donna: Memorandum from Martin O'Neill, Mobile Home Park Manager, to Kenneth Thompson, City Manager (Sarasota), September 13, 1960, historical materials file folder, Sarasota City Mobile Home Park.

244–245   Tornadoes and hurricanes: *New York Times*, May 14, 1947, p. 21. *New York Times*, October 19, 1950, p. 26. Elizabeth A. Taylor, "Hurricane!" *Trailer Topics* 11 (March 1947), 13, 64.

246   Babysitting and day care: Interview with Ray Millard, Bradenton, Florida, November 24, 1997. Interview with Doris Garvey, Van Nuys, California, March 30, 1998. Eugene A. Conklin, "Play Rooms for Trailer Children," *Trailer Topics* 14 (April 1950), 20. Oaks, *Fell's Guide to Mobile Home Living*, 21–22.

246   Playtime rituals: Robert Yaller, "Children Love Trailer Life," *Trailer Topics* 12 (October 1948), 56.

246   Greater St. Louis Trailer Park: Berra interview.

247   Parents' concerns: Interview with Mary Messerly (former trailer park tenant), Port Charlotte, Florida, December 1, 1997. *Birmingham Bugle* (Birmingham Village Trailer Park), October 13, 1948, p. 6.

247   Berube: Allan Berube with Florence Berube, "Sunset Trailer Park," in eds. Matt Wray and Annalee Newitz, *White Trash: Race and Class in America* (New York: Routledge, 1997), 23.

247   "When I had kids": Interview with Carolyn Wilson (former trailer park resident), St. Peters, Missouri, June 27, 1997.

247   "when we were going to have": Interview with Thomas Crouthamel, Bradenton, Florida, November 21, 1997.

248   "Today nearly one couple": Cited in Berube, "Sunset Trailer Park," 19.

249   Pittsburgh trailer camp: Wellington, "Trailer Camp Slums," 418–20.

249–251   Attitudes about home ownership and doubts about trailer parks: Ronald Tobey, Charles Wetherell, and Jay Brigham, "Moving Out and Settling In: Residential Mobility, Home Owning, and the Public Enframing of Citizenship, 1921–1950," *American Historical Review* 95 (December 1990), 1416. Martin, "Don't Call Them Trailer

Trash," 86. I. W. Delp, "Is Mobile Living a Social Asset or Liability?" *Trailer Topics* 14 (August 1950), 27–28. Wellington, "Trailer Camp Slums," 420.

251   "trailer trash": Martin, "Don't Call Them Trailer Trash," 86.

251   "to have the rent raised": *Huntington Beach News*, February 24, 1949, 1.

252   Mexican and Chinese-American tenants: Palacios interview. Berube, "Sunset Trailer Park," 20.

252   Exclusion of African Americans: Vollie Tripp, "Must Parks Lose Their Right to Choose?" *Mobile Home Park Management* 10 (March 1962), 7–8, 20.

252–253   Berube: Berube, "Sunset Trailer Park," 32–33.

254   Rockford, Illinois: "A Sociologist Looks at an American Community," *Life* 27 (September 12, 1949), 108–119.

254   Opposition to trailer parks: Richard D. Duke, "Mobility—A New Aspect of Community Life," *Urban Land* 12 (July-August 1953), 6. William F. Cornett, "Increased Use of Trailer Coaches Recognized by Zoning Ordinances," *Western City* 34 (October 1958), 33. *Lawrenceville News-Herald* (Georgia), March 18, 1965. Wellington, "Trailer Camp Slums," 420. Ken Willert, "You and Your Community," *Trailer Topics* 17 (April 1953), 112.

255   Spending statistics: "Sarasota's Municipal Trailer Park," *American City* 73 (April 1958), 16, 241. Richard D. Duke, "Mobility—A New Aspect of Community Life," *Urban Land* 12 (July-August 1953), 5.

255   Ideal Trailer Park: "Brooklyn Arrests 13 in Trailers," *Trail-R-News* 13 (August 1954), 23.

255–256   Legal restrictions on trailer parks: William Jabine, "Legally Speaking . . . About Parks," *Trailer Park Management* 16 (May 1958), 28–29. Vollie Trip, "Parks Are Your Problem," *Trailer Topics* 22 (October 1958), 18. Richard D. Duke, "Mobility—A New Aspect of Community Life," *Urban Land* 12 (July-August 1953), 7. *Gwinnett Daily News*, October 31, 1963.

255–256   Bell, California: Simmons interview.

256   Zoning: William F. Cornett, "Increased Use of Trailer Coaches Recognized By Zoning Ordinances," *Western City* 34 (October 1958), 33, 53. *Gwinnett Daily News*, August 7, 1966.

257   Trailer park locations: Wellington, "Trailer Camp Slums," 418. Jabine, "Legally Speaking . . . About Parks," 29. D. Crane Taylor, "Improvements Needed for Trailer Living," *Trailer Topics* 14 (January 1950), 37. Duke, "Mobility—A New Aspect of Community Life," 4. J. Ross McKeever, "The Motionless Mobile Home," *Urban Land* 19 (April 1960), 4. Willert, "You and Your Community," 33.

258   Lending practices: "Report on Trailer Living," *Consumer Reports*, 116. McKeever, "Motionless Mobile Home," 3–4. Fogarty, "Trailer Parks: The Wheeled Suburbs," 130. Federal Housing Administration, *Minimum Property Requirements for Mobile Home Courts* (Washington, D.C.: U.S. Government Printing Office, 1957).

259   Retiree market: Tracy Webb, "Retire . . . to a Trailer Home," *Trailer Life* 10 (September 1950), 6–7. Carl Edwards, "Half a Million Retired," *Trailer Topics* 23 (August 1959), 30.

259   Bradenton Trailer Park: Glenn D. Kittler, "Florida's City on Wheels," *Coronet* 35 (February 1954), 23–26. "You Have to be Retired to Live in Florida's Bradenton Park," *Trailer Topics* 13 (March 1953), 23, 154. Meloan, *Mobile Homes*, 32.

260–261 Trailer Estates: Interview with Sydney Adler, Bradenton, Florida, December 22, 1997. "Trailer Park with Ideas," *Trailer Life* 15 (November 1955), 9–10. "New Look for Older Residents," *Trailer Park Management* 6 (June 1957), 12–14. Evelyn B. Findley, "Florida—Own Your Own Lot at Trailer Estates," *Trail-R-News* 18 (March 1960), 10–17. Claude and Pearl Mallory: Interview with William and Florence Mallory, Bradenton, Florida, December 9, 1997. Thomas G. Crouthamel, *A History of Trailer Estates* (Langeloth, Pa.: Keystone Press, 1987), 4, 15.

262   Subdivision parks: Manatee County Planning and Development Department, "Manatee County Mobile Home Study," June 1973, p. 7, Eaton Room, Bradenton Public Room, Bradenton, Florida. Nulsen, *All About Parks for Mobile Homes and Trailers*, 47–48. Evelyn Findley, "Are Subdivisions Setting a Trend," *Trailer Park Management*

8 (July 1959), 22–30. Evelyn Findley, "More About Those Subdivision Parks," *Mobile Home Park Management* 8 (August 1959), 24–27.

262   Racial restrictions: Nulsen, *All About Parks for Mobile Homes and Trailers*, 151. Crouthamel interview.

263   Limitations of subdivision parks: Adler interview, December 22, 1997. Findley, "Are Subdivisions Setting a Trend," 25.

263   Adler: Adler interview, December 22, 1997.

263–264 Costs of subdivision park living: "New Look for Older Residents," *Trailer Park Management* 6 (June 1957), 12.

264   1960 retiree market: Carl Edwards, "Half a Million Retired," *Trailer Topics* 23 (August 1959), 30.

264   Active retirement: Frances Fitzgerald, *Cities on a Hill: A Journey Through Contemporary American Culture* (New York: Touchstone Books, 1987), 203–245.

265–266 Surveys: "The Trailer Coach Industry and the Trailer Coach Residents of Southern California, 1948," 11, 13, 15. Trailer Coach Association, *The West's Third Largest City . . . Is on Wheels* (Los Angeles, circa 1956). "Trailer Topics Readership Survey, 1957" Reference material for F.P. #203 folder, Mobile Home/Recreational Vehicle Heritage Foundation, Elkhart, Indiana. Mobile Home Park Management Magazine, "A Study of the Mobile Home Park Market" (Chicago, 1965), Carl Edwards collection, Mobile Home/Recreational Vehicle Heritage Foundation, Elkhart, Indiana.

266   Trailers as poor investments: "Report on Trailer Living," 116–118. The Center for Auto Safety, *Mobile Homes: The Low Cost Housing Hoax* (New York: Grossman Publishers, 1975).

266–267 Miami: U.S. Bureau of the Census, *U.S. Census of Population and Housing: 1960. Census Tracts, Final Report PHC (1)–90* (Washington, D.C.: U.S. Government Printing Office, 1962), page 15. U.S. Bureau of the Census, *U.S. Census of Population and Housing: 1970. Census Tracts, Final Report PHC (1)–129, Miami, Fla. SMSA* (Washington, D.C.: U.S. Government Printing Office, 1972), pages P–5, P–27.

266–267 Los Angeles: U.S. Bureau of the Census, *U.S. Census of Population and Housing: 1960. Census Tracts, Final Report PHC (1)–82* (Washington, D.C.: U.S. Government Printing Office, 1962), pages 25–27. U.S. Bureau of the Census, *U.S. Census of Population and Housing: 1970. Cen-*

sus Tracts, *Final Report PHC (1)–117, Los Angeles-Long Beach, Calif.,* SMSA (Washington, D.C.: U.S. Government Printing Office, 1972), pages P–136 through P–139.

266–267 St. Louis: U.S. Bureau of the Census, *U.S. Census of Population and Housing: 1960. Census Tracts, Final Report PHC (1)–131* (Washington, D.C.: U.S. Government Printing Office, 1962), 16. U.S. Bureau of the Census, *U.S. Census of Population and Housing: 1970. Census Tracts, Final Report PHC (1)–181, St. Louis, Mo.-Ill., Fla. SMSA* (Washington, D.C.: U.S. Government Printing Office, 1972), page P–1.

267 "We'd tie up everything": Elaine Kendall, "The Invisible Suburbs," *Horizon* 13 (Winter 1971), 109.

267 Mobility rates: Kendall, "Invisible Suburbs," 106.

268 Racial discrimination: Kendall, "Invisible Suburbs," 107.

268 "See all those?": Tripp, "Must Parks Lose Their Right to Choose?" 8.

268 Justifications for excluding racial minorities: Tripp, "Must Parks Lose Their Right to Choose?" 7–8, 20.

269 Self-contained communities: Nulsen, *All About Parks for Mobile Homes and Trailers,* 77–78. Evalyn B. Findlay, "It's True What They Say About California," *Trailer Topics* 13 (March 1949), 64. Helen Gundlach, "Bell Trailer Tales," *Bell-Maywood Industrial Post,* August 30, 1962, scrapbook, recreation hall, Bell Mobile Home City, Bell, California.

270–271 Internal social hierarchies: Berube, "Sunset Trailer Park," 21. Interview with Carolyn Wilson, St. Peters, Missouri, June, 27, 1997.

271 "You wouldn't want": Kendall, "Invisible Suburbs," 110.

271 "a notch below": Kendall, "Invisible Suburbs," 105–111.

272 Cooperation and friendship: Billie Byers, "People in Our Park," *Trailer Topics* 22 (March 1958), 7, 136–140. Interview with William McAvera, date, Bell, California. "Rides Wanted," *Birmingham Bugle,* October 13, 1948, 6, personal collection of Doris Garvey, Birmingham Trailer Village, Van Nuys, California.

Conclusion: Giving Chase

274 Eisenhower's economic report: *New York Times,* January 21, 1960, 17.

274   Kitchen debate: May, *Homeward Bound*, 16–20, 162–164. "At the Fair, Fascinated Russians Flock to U.S. Exhibits," *Life* 47 (August 10, 1959), 28–35. *New York Times*, July 25, 1959, 1, 3.

278   Family-oriented marketing: Warren Susman, with the assistance of Edward Griffin, "Did Success Spoil the United States? Dual Representations in Postwar America," in Lary May, ed., *Recasting America: Culture and Politics in the Age of Cold War* (Chicago, 1989), 22.

278   Ivory Soap: Juliann Sivulka, *Soap, Sex, and Cigarettes: A Cultural History of American Advertising* (Belmont, Calif.: Wadsworth Publishing, 1998), 266. Squirt: *Life*, 41 (July 2, 1956), 26. Hammond Organ: Advertisement, *Saturday Evening Post* 231 (February 28, 1959), 7. ChapStick: Advertisement, *Saturday Evening Post* 229 (January 12, 1957), 60.

280   Suburban family arrangements: William Dobriner, *Class in Suburbia* (Englewood Cliffs, N.J.: Prentice-Hall, 1963), 19. Laura J. Miller, "Family Togetherness and the Suburban Ideal," *Sociological Forum* 10 (September 1995), 393–418.

281–282   Suburban consumer products: Karal Ann Marling, *As Seen on TV: The Visual Culture of Everyday Life in the 1950s* (Cambridge, Mass.: Harvard University Press, 1994), 232–236. "The Power Explosion," *House and Garden* (April 1967), 200. Landon Y. Jones, *Great Expectations: America and the Baby Boom Generation* (New York: Coward, McCann & Geoghegan, 1980), 41. "New Products: Prometheus Unbound," *Time* 76 (September 19, 1960), 94–101. Suellen Hoy, *Chasing Dirt: The American Pursuit of Cleanliness* (New York: Oxford University Press, 1995), 170–171. Virginia Scott Jenkins, *The Lawn: A History of an American Obsession* (Washington, D.C.: Smithsonian Institute Press, 1994), 110–112.

282   Schwinn bicycles: Judith Crown and Glenn Coleman, *No Hands: The Rise and Fall of the Schwinn Bicycle Company, An American Institution* (New York: Henry Holt & Company, 1996), 41.

282   Midas Muffler: Daniel Boorstin, *The Americans: The Democratic Experience* (New York: Vintage Books, 1974), 432.

282–283   Race tracks: John Willig, "Housewives at the $2 Window," *New York Times Magazine* April 1, 1962, 48–52.

282–283   Branch outlets: Lizabeth Cohen, "From Town Center to Shopping Center: The Reconfiguration of Community Marketplaces in Postwar America," *American Historical Review* 101 (October, 1996), 1072–1073.

284   Downward filtration of consumer goods: Thorstein Veblen, *The Theory of the Leisure Class: An Economic Study of Institutions* (New York: Modern Library, 1934), 84, 103–104. Kathy Peiss, *Hope in a Jar: The Making of America's Beauty Culture* (New York: Metropolitan Books, 1998), 22–23.

284–285   Walt Disney: David Koenig, *Mouse Tales: A Behind-the-Ears Look at Disneyland* (Irvine, 1994). Randy Bright, *Disneyland: An Inside Story* (New York, 1987). Al Griffin, *"Step Right Up Folks"* (Chicago, 1974), 214–222. John M. Findlay, *Magic Lands: Western Cityscapes and American Culture After 1940* (Berkeley, 1992), 52–116. Karal Ann Marling, *As Seen on TV*, 87–126.

285   Television: Lynn Spigel, *Make Room for TV: Television and the Family Ideal in Postwar America* (Chicago: University of Chicago Press, 1992), 137–159. George Lipsitz, *Time Passages: Collective Memory and American Popular Culture* (Minneapolis: University of Minnesota Press, 1990), 39–42.

286   McCarthy: Michael Sherry, *In the Shadow of War: The United States Since the 1930s* (New Haven: Yale University Press, 1995), 172. Richard Polenberg, *One Nation Divisible: Class, Race, and Ethnicity in the United States* (New York: Viking Press, 1980), 124–125.

286   Nixon: Garry Wills, *Nixon Agonistes: The Crisis of the Self-Made Man* (New York: Houghton Mifflin, 1969), 135–145.

287–288   Berger: Bennett Berger, *Working-Class Suburb: A Study of Auto Workers in Suburbia* (Berkeley: University of California Press, 1960). Into the 1980s, sociologists continued to find evidence that blue-collar workers had not fully integrated themselves into the middle class. See William Kornblum, *Blue Collar Community* (Chicago: University of Chicago Press, 1974) and David Halle, *America's Working Man: Work, Home and Politics Among Blue-Collar Property Owners* (Chicago: University of Chicago Press, 1984).

288   "Chicago . . . is full," Burleigh B. Gardner, "Social Status and Consumer Behavior," *Consumer Behavior, Vol. II, The Life Cycle and Consumer Behavior*, ed. Lincoln H. Clark (New York: New York University Press, 1955), 59.

288　　　"myth of the happy worker": Swados, "The Myth of the Happy Worker," *Nation* 185 (August 17, 1957), 65–68.

288–289　Working-class debt: Riesman, *Abundance for What?*, 152–155, 163–165. Faith M. Williams, "Standards and Levels of Living of City-Worker Families," *Monthly Labor Review* 79 (September 1956), 1015–1023. "1936–1956, Twenty Years in Review," *Consumer Reports* 21 (May 1956), 252–256. William H. Whyte Jr., "Budgetism: Opiate of the Middle Class," *Fortune* 53 (May 1956), 133–137, 164–172.

289　　　Working-class tastes: Packard, *The Status Seekers*, 72–73, 146. Marling, *As Seen of TV*, 40–41, 141–142, 220–222, 239. Research Division, *Chicago Tribune*, *The New Consumer* (Chicago: *Chicago Tribune*, 1957), 11–13, 60. Lee Rainwater, Richard P. Coleman, and Gerald Handel, *Workingman's Wife: Her Personality, World, and Life Style* (New York: Oceana Publications, 1959), 184–202.

290　　　New snobbery: Russell Lynes, "Highbrow, Lowbrow, Middlebrow," *Harper's Magazine* 198 (February 1949), 19–28. Packard, *The Status Seekers*, 61–73.

291　　　Eleven pairs of shoes: Research Division of the *Chicago Tribune*, *The New Consumer* (Chicago, 1957), 5.

292　　　Household spending decisions: "Who Decides: Man or Wife?" *Business Week* (September 14, 1957), 46–50. Beth L. Bailey, *From Front Porch to Back Seat: Courtship in Twentieth-Century America* (Baltimore: Johns Hopkins University Press, 1988), 84.

293　　　Balanced homemaker: Friedan, *The Feminine Mystique*, 209–211, 225.

293　　　Chevrolet: Advertisement, *Life* 40 (May 21, 1956).

294　　　Advertisements for tires, banks, and air conditioners: *Saturday Evening Post* (229) April 6, 1957, 12, 123; (229) April 13, 1957, 64; June 8, 1957, 12; (230) July 27, 1957, 60; *Popular Mechanics* 106 (September 1956), 236, 242; 106 (October 1956), 9.

294　　　*Playboy*: Jesse Isaac Berrett, "The Secret Lives of Consumer Culture: Masculinity and Consumption in Postwar America," (Ph.D. dissertation, University of California, Berkeley, 1996), 190–232. Barbara Ehrenreich, *The Hearts of Men: American Dreams and the Flight from Commitment* (New York: Anchor Books, 1983), 42–51.

296–297   Teenage markets: "Teenage Consumers," *Consumer Reports* 22 (March 1957), 140–141. Grace Palladino, *Teenagers: An American History* (New York: Basic Books, 1996), 131.

298   Hot-rods: Reuel Denney, *The Astonished Muse* (Chicago: University of Chicago Press, 1957), 145–153. Stephen S. Conroy, "Popular Technology and Youth Rebellion in America," *Journal of Popular Culture* 16 (Spring 1983), 123–133.

298   Rock 'n' roll: Steve Chapple and Reebee Garofalo, *Rock 'n' Roll Is Here to Pay: The History and Politics of the Music Industry* (Chicago, 1977), especially ch. 7. David Szatmary, *Rockin' in Time: A Social History of Rock-and-Roll* (Englewood Cliffs, 1991), 1–72. Charlie Gillett, *Sound of the City: The Rise of Rock and Roll* (New York, 1984), 3–65. Palladino, *Teenagers*, 125–135.

299   Drive-ins: Don Sanders and Susan Sanders, *The American Drive-In Movie Theatre* (Osceola: Motorbooks International, 1997), 48, 63–64, 86, 92–101, 118–120. James J. Flink, *The Automobile Age* (Cambridge, Mass.: MIT Press, 1988), 161–162. Michael Karl Witzel, *The American Drive-In: History and Folklore of the Drive-In Restaurant in American Car Culture* (Osceola: Motorbooks International, 1994), 144, 150–166.

301   Haight-Ashbury: Barney Hoskins, *Beneath the Diamond Sky: Haight-Ashbury, 1965–1970* (New York: Simon and Schuster, 1997), 37, 87. Charles Perry, *The Haight-Ashbury: A History* (New York: Random House, 1984), 75–81, 92–93, 106–107.

301–302   Women's movement: Friedan, *The Feminine Mystique*, 233–257. Rochelle Gatlin, *American Women Since 1945* (Jackson: University of Mississippi Press, 1987), 77–137. Rosalind Rosenberg, *Divided Lives: American Women in the Twentieth Century* (New York: Hill and Wang, 1992), 180–219.

302–303   Record companies: George Lipsitz, "Who'll Stop the Rain? Youth Culture, Rock 'n' Roll, and Social Crisis," *The Sixties: From Memory to History*, ed. David Farber (Chapel Hill: University of North Carolina Press, 1994), 211.

303   Marketing women's liberation: Gatlin, *American Women Since 1945*, 100–103. Ted Sanchagrin, "How Have Cigarette Advertisers Held the Line?" *Marketing/Communications* 296 (November 1968), 24–30.

303–304   Blue-collar families: Mirra Komarovsky, *Blue Collar Marriage* (New York: Random House, 1962), 63–72, 290–292. Lillian B. Rubin, *Worlds of Pain: Life in the Working-Class Family* (New York: Basic Books, 1992), 130–132, 194.

304   Greensboro sit-in: Milton Viorst, *Fire in the Streets: America in the 1960s* (New York: Simon and Schuster, 1979), 94. Harvard Sitkoff, *The Struggle for Black Equality, 1954–1980* (New York: Hill and Wang, 1981), 69–72.

305   Earlier civil rights protests: Weems, *Desegregating the Dollar*, 56–69.

305   Spread of sit-ins: August Meier and Elliot Rudwick, *CORE: A Study in the Civil Rights Movement, 1942–1968* (New York: Oxford University Press, 1973), 101–131, 159–162. Viorst, *Fire in the Streets*, 93–124. Taylor Branch, *Parting the Waters: America in the King Years, 1954–1963* (New York: Touchstone, 1988), 271–275.

306   African-American consumption levels: U.S. Bureau of the Census, *United States Census of Housing, 1960, Vol. I, States and Small Areas, Part 1: United States Summary* (Washington, D.C.: U.S. Government Printing Office, 1963), 44, 221.

307   Race in advertising copy: Kern-Foxworth, *Aunt Jemima, Uncle Ben, and Rastus*, 116–117. Henry Allen Bullock, "Consumer Motivations in Black and White—Part 1," in George Joyce and Norman A. P. Govoni, eds., *The Black Consumer: Dimensions of Behavior and Strategy* (New York: Random House, 1971), 173.

307   "From the time they leave": U.S. Senate, *Hearings Before the Committee on Commerce*, 656.

307–308   Wharton study: Wharton School of Finance and Commerce, *Study of Consumer Expenditures, Incomes, and Savings*, 11 vols., (Philadelphia: University of Pennsylvania, 1956). For a summary of the findings in this study regarding African-American consumption patterns see U.S. Senate, *Hearings Before the Senate Committee on Commerce*, 695–696.

308   Social background of sit-in protesters: Clayborne Carson, *In Struggle: SNCC and the Black Awakening of the 1960s* (Cambridge, Mass.: Harvard University Press, 1981), 12–17. Ruth Searles and J. Allen Williams, Jr., "Negro College Students' Participation in Sit-Ins," *Social Forces* 40 (March 1962), 215–220.

309   Effectiveness of sit-ins: Sitkoff, *The Struggle for Black Equality*, 82.

309 "As a Jew": Cited in Bruce Lambert, "Levittown Anniversary Stirs Memory of Bias," *New York Times*, December 28, 1997, 14.

309–310 Residential segregation: Douglas S. Massey and Nancy A. Denton, *American Apartheid: Segregation and the Making of the Underclass* (Cambridge Mass.: Harvard University Press, 1993), 37, 50. Yutaka Sasaki, "'But Not Next Door': Housing Discrimination and the Emergence of the 'Second Ghetto' in Newark, New Jersey, after World War II," *Japanese Journal of American Studies* 5 (March 1994), 113–135. Lambert, "Levittown Anniversary Stirs Memory of Bias," 14. Arnold R. Hirsch, *Making the Second Ghetto: Race and Housing in Chicago, 1940–1960* (Cambridge,: Cambridge University Press, 1983), 68–99. Thomas Sugrue, *The Origins of the Urban Crisis: Race and Inequality in Postwar Detroit* (Princeton: Princeton University Press, 1996), 231–258.

310 Black suburbanization: Dennis E. Gale, *Washington, D.C.: Inner-City Revitalization and Minority Suburbanization* (Philadelphia: Temple University Press, 1987), 111–128. Gunnar Myrdal, *An American Dilemma: The Negro Problem and Modern Democracy* (New York: Harper and Brothers, 1944), 606–627, 1011. St. Clair Drake and Horace R. Cayton, *Black Metropolis: A Study of Negro Life in a Northern City*, revised and enlarged edition (New York: Harcourt, Brace, & World, 1962), 174–213, 379–397. Massey and Denton, *American Apartheid*, 46. Joe T. Darden, "Black Residential Segregation Since the 1948 Shelley v. Kraemer Decision," *Journal of Black Studies* 25 (July 1995), 680–691.

311 Urban growth and service economy: Zukin, *Landscapes of Power*. Matthias Judt, "Reshaping Shopping Environments: The Competition Between the City of Boston and Its Suburbs," *Getting and Spending: European and American Consumer Societies in the Twentieth Century*, eds., Susan Strasser, Charles McGovern, Matthias Judt (Cambridge: Cambridge University Press, 1998), 317–337.

311–313 Shopping districts: Richard Longstreth, *City Center to Regional Mall: Architecture, the Automobile, and Retailing in Los Angeles, 1920–1950* (Cambridge, Mass.: MIT Press, 1997).

314 Inner-city commercial districts: Donald J. Bogue, *Skid Row in American Cities* (Chicago: University of Chicago Press, 1963).

316 Commercial dynamics in African American neighborhoods: Frederick D. Sturdivant, "Better Deal for Ghetto Shoppers," *Harvard Business Review* (March-April 1968), 130–139. Douglas S. Massey and Nancy A. Denton, *American Apartheid: Segregation and the Making of the Underclass* (Cambridge: Harvard University Press, 1993), 39.

316 "Nobody mopped": cited in Zukin, *The Culture of Cities*, 206.

317 Inner-city African-American commercial districts: Sharon Zukin, *The Culture of Cities* (Oxford: Blackwell Publishers, 1995), 207–212. David Caplovitz, *The Poor Pay More: Consumer Practices of Low-Income Families* (Glencoe, Ill.: Free Press, 1963), 18. Allan Pred, "Business Thoroughfares as Expressions of Urban Negro Culture," *Economic Geography* 39 (July 1963), 217–233. Elliot Liebow, *Tally's Corner: A Study of Negro Streetcorner Men* (Boston: Little, Brown and Company, 1967), 29–71.

318 Itinerant salesmen: Caplovitz, *The Poor Pay More*, 58–80.

318 "dark ghettos": the phrase was coined by Kenneth B. Clark, *Dark Ghetto* (New York: Harper and Row, 1965).

318 Fraudulent tactics: Caplovitz, *The Poor Pay More*, 16–28, 137–169. Raymond J. Murphy and James M. Watson, "The Structure of Discontent: The Relationship Between Social Structure, Grievance, and Support for the Los Angeles Riot," Los Angeles Riot Study, coordinator, Nathan E. Cohen (University of California, Institute of Government and Public Affairs, 1967), MR–92, 20, 21.

319 "Brinks truck": *Wall Street Journal*, August 16, 1966, p. 1.

320 Watts neighborhood: Nathan Cohen, "The Context of the Curfew Area," Los Angeles Riot Study (University of California, Los Angeles, Institute of Government and Public Affairs, 1967), coordinator, Nathan E. Cohen, MR–94, 4–5.

321–322 Watts riot: State of California, Governor's Commission on the Los Angeles Riots, *Violence in the City—An End or a Beginning* (Los Angeles, 1965), 23–24. Viorst, *Fire in the Streets*, 322, 330–334. Cite Horne for quote. "Chronology," in "California Governor's Commission of the Los Angeles Riots, Transcripts, Depositions, Consultants Reports, and Selected Documents," Vol. II, photocopy, University of California at Los Angeles, Law Library, Los Angeles, California, 103. Gerald Horne, *Fire This Time: The Watts Uprising and the 1960s* (Charlottesville: University of Virginia Press, 1995),

64–66, 99–100. Murphy and Watson, "The Structure of Discontent," 19.

322   Post-riot surveys: David O. Sears and John B. McConahay, "Riot Participation," Los Angeles Riot Study (University of California, Los Angeles, Institute of Government and Public Affairs, 1967), coordinator, Nathan E. Cohen, MR–99, 6. T. M. Tomlinson and David O. Sears, "Negro Attitudes Toward the Riot," Los Angeles Riot Study (University of California, Los Angeles, Institute of Government and Public Affairs, 1967), coordinator, Nathan E. Cohen, MR–97, 16–17.

323   Targets of arson attacks: Sturdivant, "Better Deal for Ghetto Shoppers." *Los Angeles Times*, August 14, 1965, 2.

323   White participation: Police records revealed 141 Caucasians arrested in the curfew area during the disturbances. Accepting the 6-to-1 ratio of arrestees to rioters determined by a UCLA-sponsored post-riot survey, the number of white participants may be estimated at 826. "Riot Arrests by Los Angeles Police Department," in "Chronology," in "California Governor's Commission of the Los Angeles Riots, Transcripts, Depositions, Consultants Reports, and Selected Documents," Vol. II, photocopy, University of California at Los Angeles, Law Library, Los Angeles, California, 243. Robert M. Fogelson, *Violence as Protest: A Study of Riots and Ghettos* (Garden City: Doubleday & Company, 1971), 38.

324–325 Riots elsewhere: Sitkoff, *The Struggle for Black Equality*, 200. Sidney Fine, *Violence in the Model City: The Cavanagh Administration, Race Relations, and the Detroit Riot of 1967* (Ann Arbor: University of Michigan Press, 1989), 155–367. Robert M. Fogelson and Robert B. Hill, *Who Riots? A Study of Participation in the 1967 Riots* (New York: Columbia University Bureau of Applied Social Research, 1968), 246. National Advisory Commission on Civil Disorders, *Report of the National Advisory Commission on Civil Disorders* (New York: Bantam Books, 1968).

325–326 Luxor Lanes: Telephone interview with Bob Ogden, (regular bowler at Luxor Lanes), Long Beach, California, June 1, 1962. Telephone interview with Frank DelConte, Mission Viejo, (former owner of Vermont Bowl), California, June 1, 1962. Telephone interview with Frank Keats (bowling journalist), Los Angeles, California, May 20, 1998. *California Bowling News*, 26 (August 20, 1965), 10. *California Bowling News*, 27 (August 19, 1966), 6.

Epilogue

327–329   Eastern Avenue: *Baltimore Sun*, July 31, 1973, C24. Maryland Department of Labor, Licensing, and Regulation, *Small Area labor Force Statistics, 1997 Annual Average by Census Tract* (Baltimore, 1998), 6–7. U.S. Bureau of the Census, *Census of Population and Housing: 1960. Census Tracts. Final Report PHC (1)–13* (Washington, D.C.: U.S. Government Printing Office, 1962), 15, 34, 119–120. U.S. Bureau of the Census, *Census of Population and Housing: 1980. Census Tracts. Final Report PHC80–2–82* (Washington, D.C.: U.S. Government Printing Office, 1983), 254, 545, 636. U.S. Bureau of the Census, *Census of Population and Housing: 1990. Population and Housing Characteristics for Census Tracts and Block Numbering Areas. Final Report 1990 CPH–3–80* (Washington, D.C.: U.S. Government Printing Office, 1993), 174, 634.

330–331   Shopping malls: Richard Keller Simon, "The Formal Garden in the Age of Consumer Culture: A Reading of the Twentieth-Century Shopping Mall," *Mapping American Culture*, eds., Wayne Franklin and Michael Steiner (Iowa City: University of Iowa Press, 1992), 231–250.

333–334   Market segmentation: Joseph Turow, *Breaking Up America: Advertisers and the New Media World* (Chicago: University of Chicago Press, 1997).

334   "luxury fever": Robert Frank, *Luxury Fever: Why Money Fails to Satisfy in an Era of Excess* (New York: Free Press, 1999), 14–48.

335   Upscale spending: Juliet B. Schorr, *The Overspent American: Upscaling, Downshifting, and the New Consumer* (New York: Basic Books, 1998), 4, 72.

INDEX

ABOUT THE AUTHOR

Andrew Hurley is Associate Professor of History at the University of Missouri–St. Louis and the author of *Environmental Inequalities: Class, Race, and Industrial Pollution in Gary, Indiana, 1945–1980.* He is also the editor of *Common Fields: An Environmental History of St. Louis.*

A NOTE ON THE TYPE

Rudolf Weiss designed this typeface in 1926 for the Bauer foundry of Frankfurt. Weiss is based on typefaces from the Italian Renaissance, and is one of the earliest contemporary serif types to have italics based on the chancery style of writing. The vertical strokes that are heavier at the top than at the bottom are unusual, and give Weiss a distinct beauty. Weiss is a legible text type and an elegant display face for headlines or titles. Weiss is a registered trademark of Bauer Types, S.A.